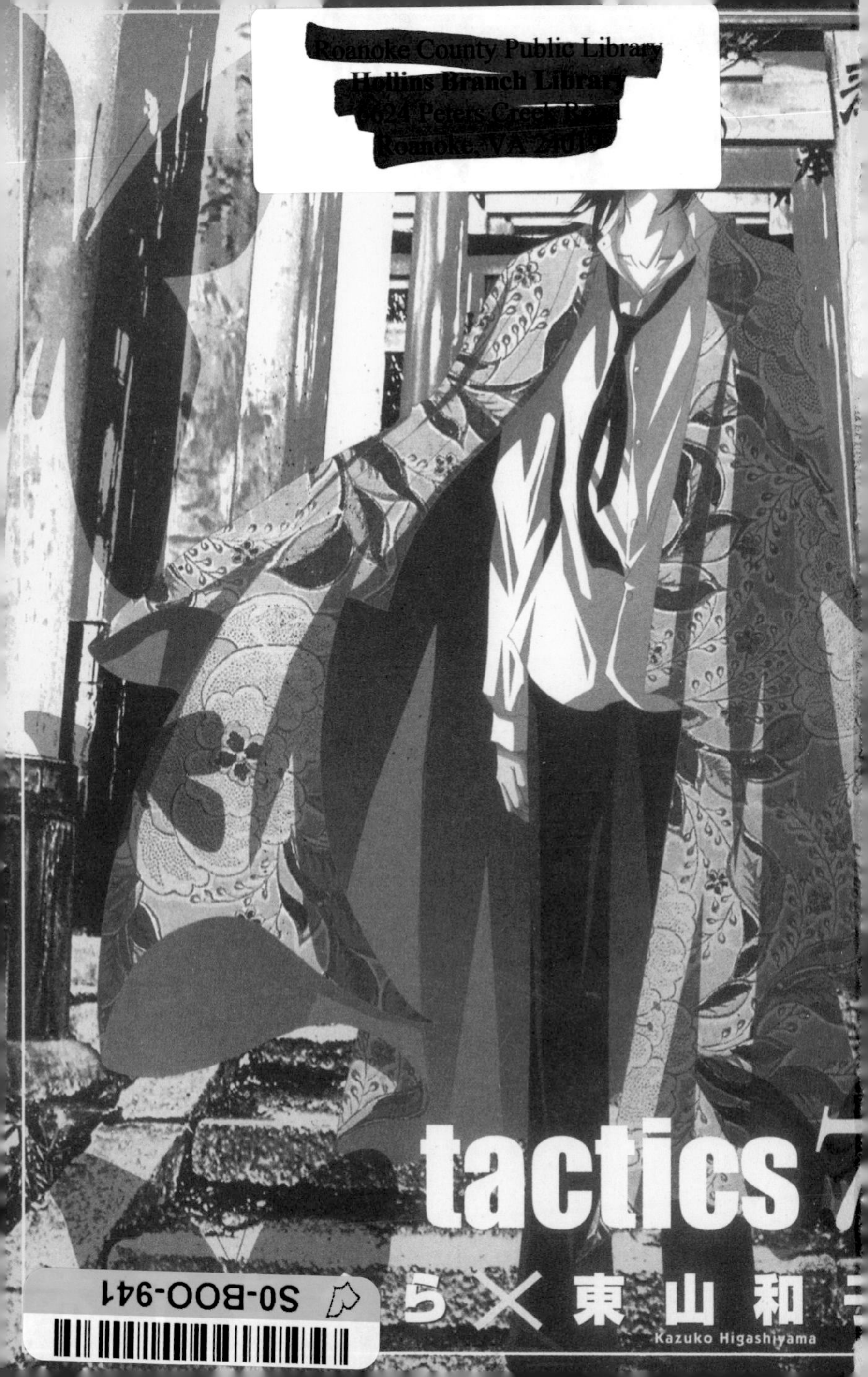
tactics
ら×東山和
Kazuko Higashiyama

tactics

Sakura Kinoshita × Kazuko Higashiyama

7

MEMOIRS OF A DEMON-EATING TENGU: THE FUJI TALES

CHIMERA STAGE

tactics

**Volume 7
by Sakura Kinoshita and
Kazuko Higashiyama**

HAMBURG // LONDON // LOS ANGELES // TOKYO

tactics Volume 7
Art & Story by Sakura Kinoshita x Kazuko Higashiyama

Translation - Christine Schilling
English Adaptation - Magda Erik-Soussi
Retouch and Lettering - Star Print Brokers
Associate Editor - Stephanie Duchin
Production Artist - Michael Paolilli
Cover Design - James Lee

Senior Editor - Bryce P. Coleman
Pre-Production Supervisor - Vicente Rivera, Jr.
Pre-Production Specialist - Lucas Rivera
Managing Editor - Vy Nguyen
Senior Designer - Louis Csontos
Senior Designer - James Lee
Senior Editor - Jenna Winterberg
Associate Publisher - Marco F. Pavia
President and C.O.O. - John Parker
C.E.O. and Chief Creative Officer - Stu Levy

A  Manga

TOKYOPOP and  are trademarks or registered trademarks of TOKYOPOP Inc.

TOKYOPOP Inc.
5900 Wilshire Blvd. Suite 2000
Los Angeles, CA 90036

E-mail: info@TOKYOPOP.com
Come visit us online at www.TOKYOPOP.com

ISBN: 978-1-59816-966-9

First TOKYOPOP printing: December 2008
10 9 8 7 6 5 4 3 2 1
Printed in the USA

...EVEN THOUGH I KNOW I WON'T GET AN ANSWER, I CAN'T HELP BUT WONDER EVERY TIME I COME HERE.

WHAT WERE YOU THINKING, WAY BACK WHEN?

HEY.

DID YOU LOVE ME?

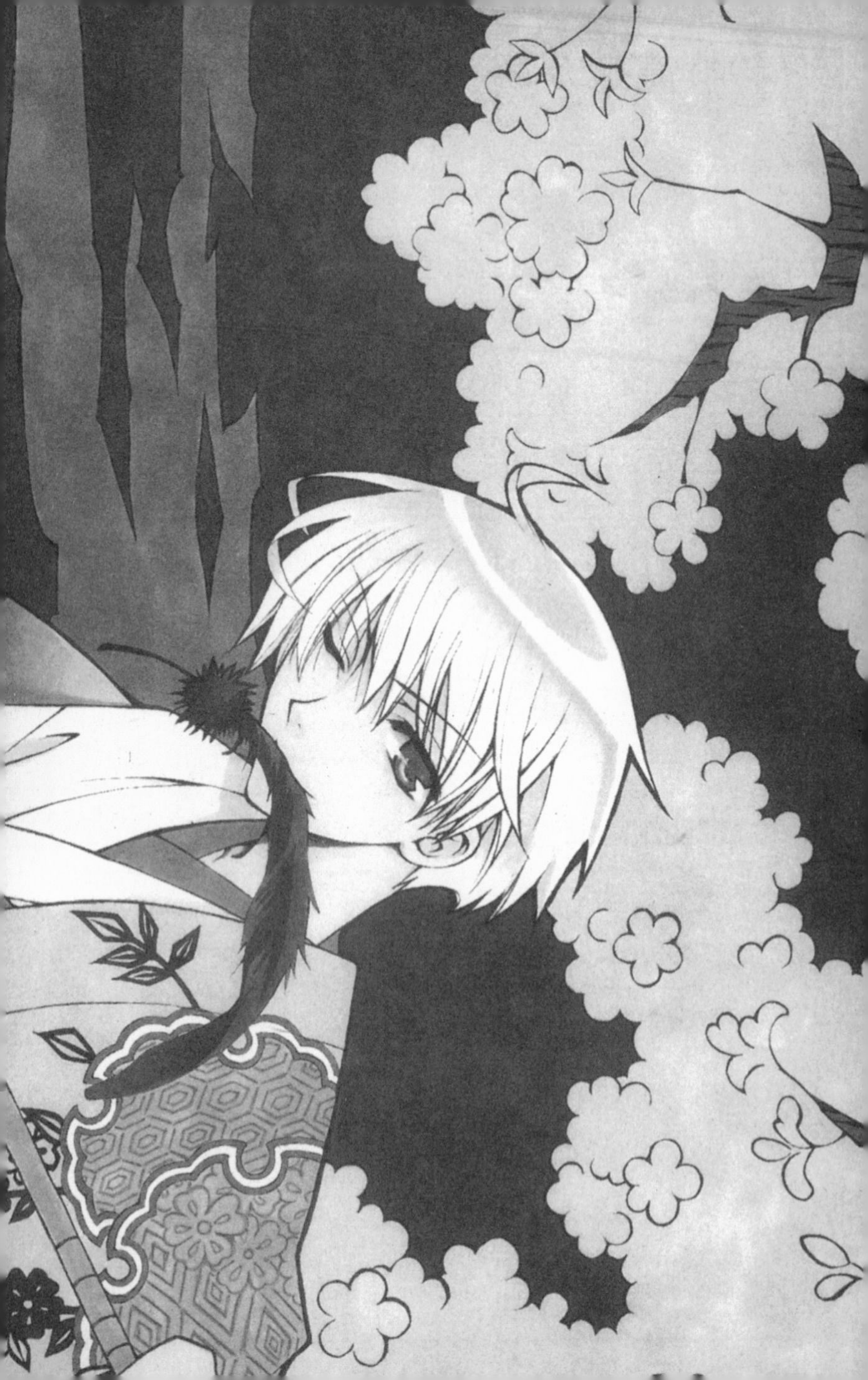

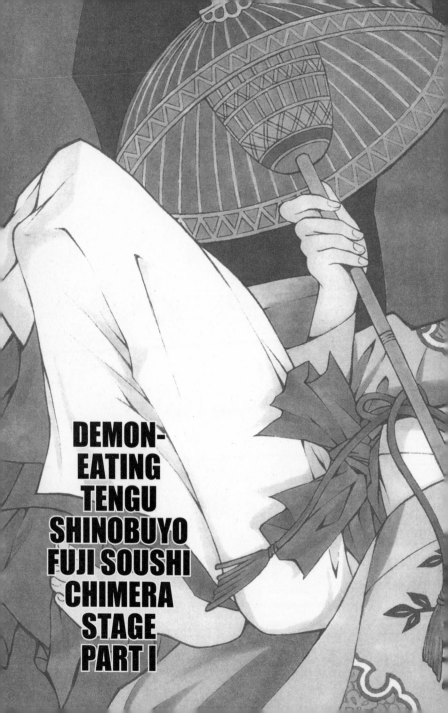

DEMON-EATING TENGU SHINOBUYO FUJI SOUSHI CHIMERA STAGE PART I

tactics

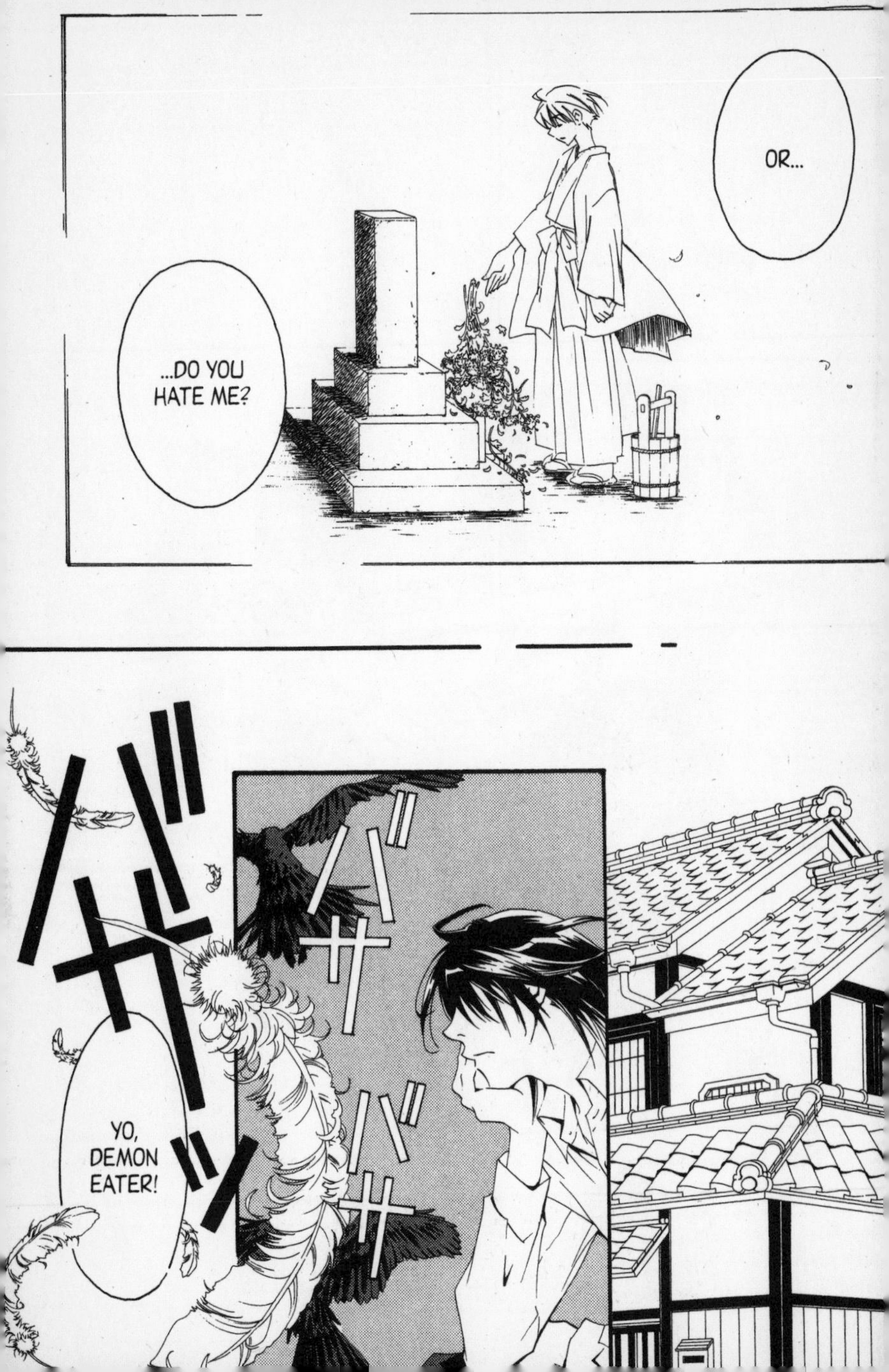
OR...
...DO YOU HATE ME?
YO, DEMON EATER!

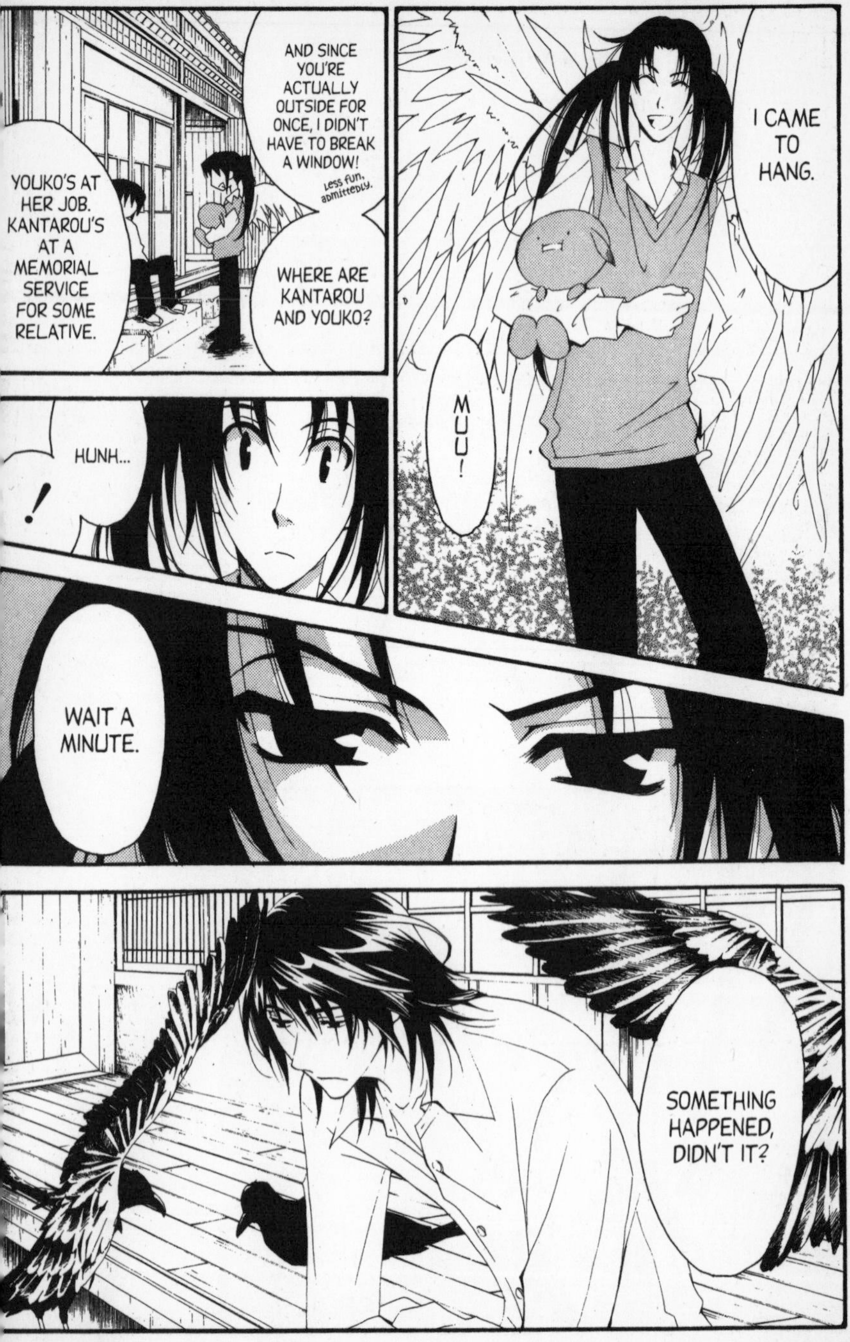
I CAME TO HANG.
MUU!
AND SINCE YOU'RE ACTUALLY OUTSIDE FOR ONCE, I DIDN'T HAVE TO BREAK A WINDOW!
Less fun, admittedly.
WHERE ARE KANTAROU AND YOUKO?
YOUKO'S AT HER JOB. KANTAROU'S AT A MEMORIAL SERVICE FOR SOME RELATIVE.
HUNH...
!
WAIT A MINUTE.
SOMETHING HAPPENED, DIDN'T IT?

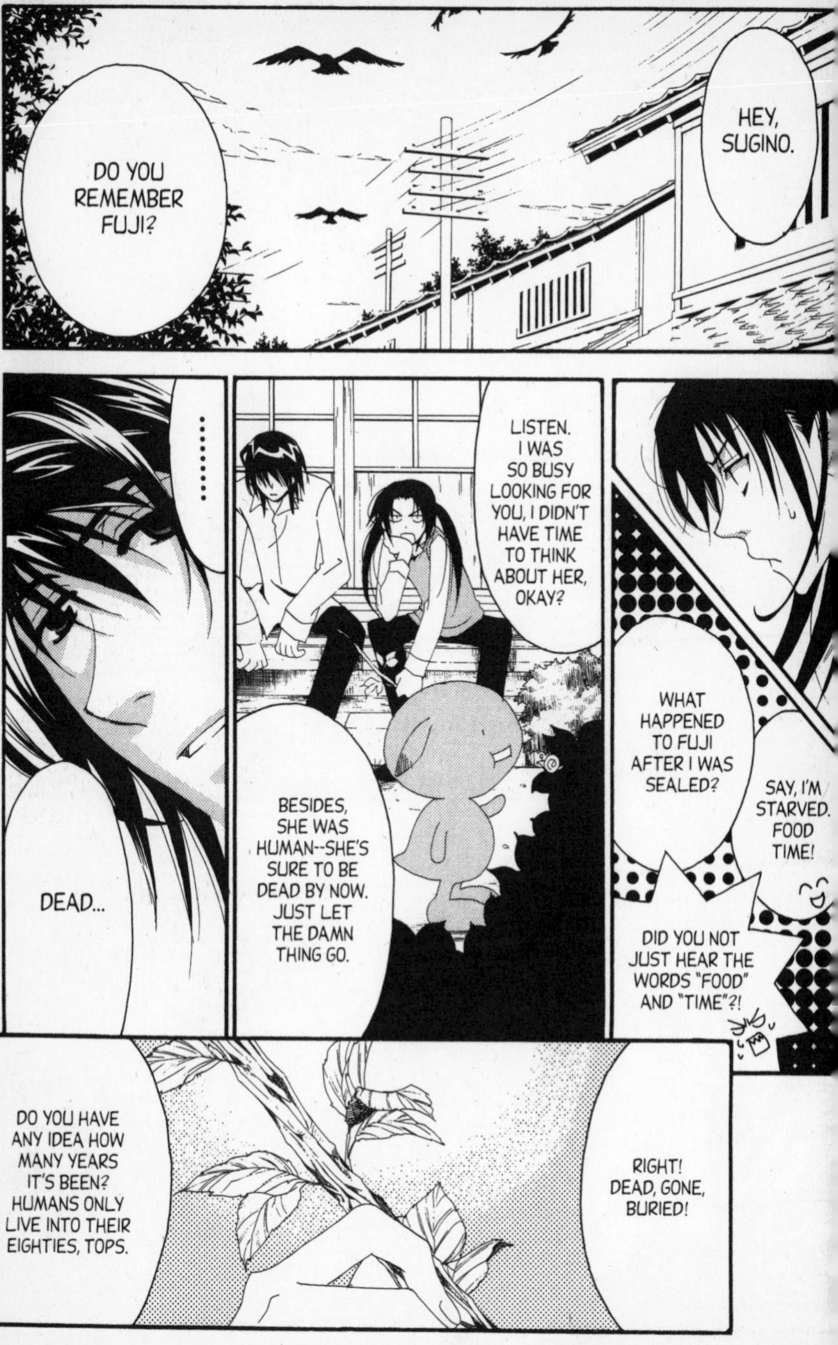
HEY, SUGINO.
DO YOU REMEMBER FUJI?
WHAT HAPPENED TO FUJI AFTER I WAS SEALED?
SAY, I'M STARVED. FOOD TIME!
DID YOU NOT JUST HEAR THE WORDS "FOOD" AND "TIME"?!
LISTEN. I WAS SO BUSY LOOKING FOR YOU, I DIDN'T HAVE TIME TO THINK ABOUT HER, OKAY?
BESIDES, SHE WAS HUMAN--SHE'S SURE TO BE DEAD BY NOW. JUST LET THE DAMN THING GO.
......
DEAD...
RIGHT! DEAD, GONE, BURIED!
DO YOU HAVE ANY IDEA HOW MANY YEARS IT'S BEEN? HUMANS ONLY LIVE INTO THEIR EIGHTIES, TOPS.

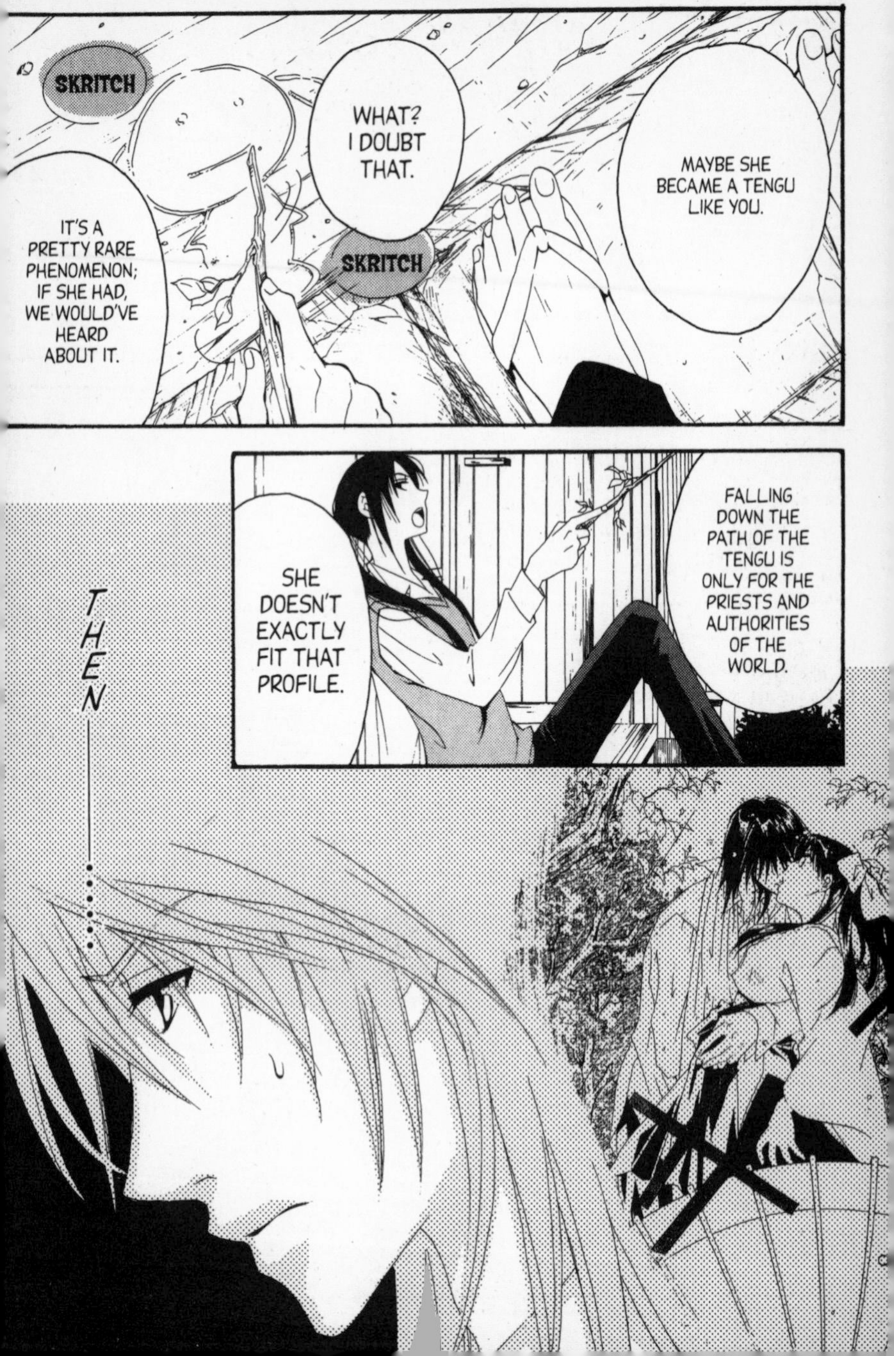
MAYBE SHE BECAME A TENGU LIKE YOU.
WHAT? I DOUBT THAT.
SKRITCH
SKRITCH
IT'S A PRETTY RARE PHENOMENON; IF SHE HAD, WE WOULD'VE HEARD ABOUT IT.
FALLING DOWN THE PATH OF THE TENGU IS ONLY FOR THE PRIESTS AND AUTHORITIES OF THE WORLD.
SHE DOESN'T EXACTLY FIT THAT PROFILE.
THEN——......

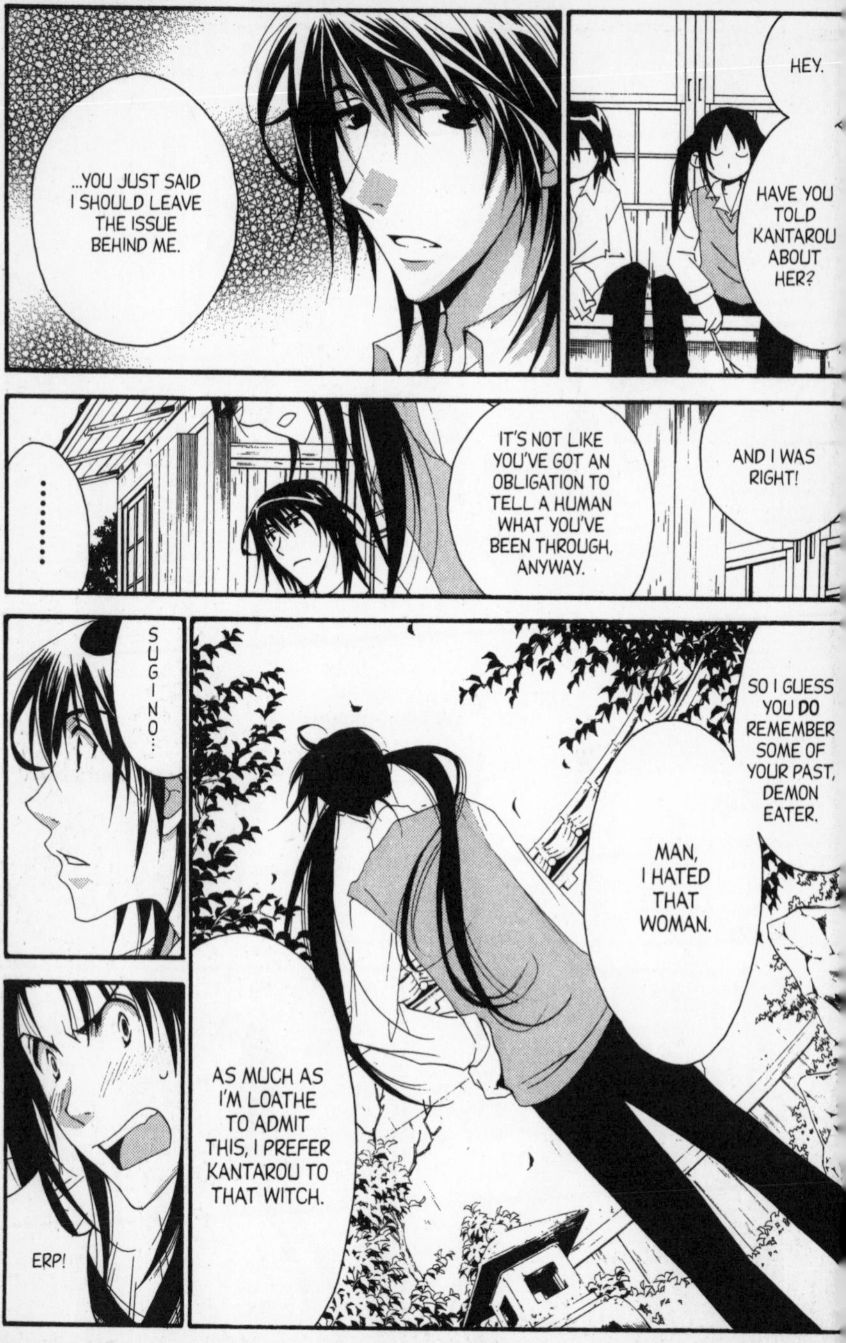
HEY.
HAVE YOU TOLD KANTAROU ABOUT HER?
...YOU JUST SAID I SHOULD LEAVE THE ISSUE BEHIND ME.
AND I WAS RIGHT!
IT'S NOT LIKE YOU'VE GOT AN OBLIGATION TO TELL A HUMAN WHAT YOU'VE BEEN THROUGH, ANYWAY.
......
SO I GUESS YOU DO REMEMBER SOME OF YOUR PAST, DEMON EATER.
MAN, I HATED THAT WOMAN.
AS MUCH AS I'M LOATHE TO ADMIT THIS, I PREFER KANTAROU TO THAT WITCH.
SUGINO...
ERP!

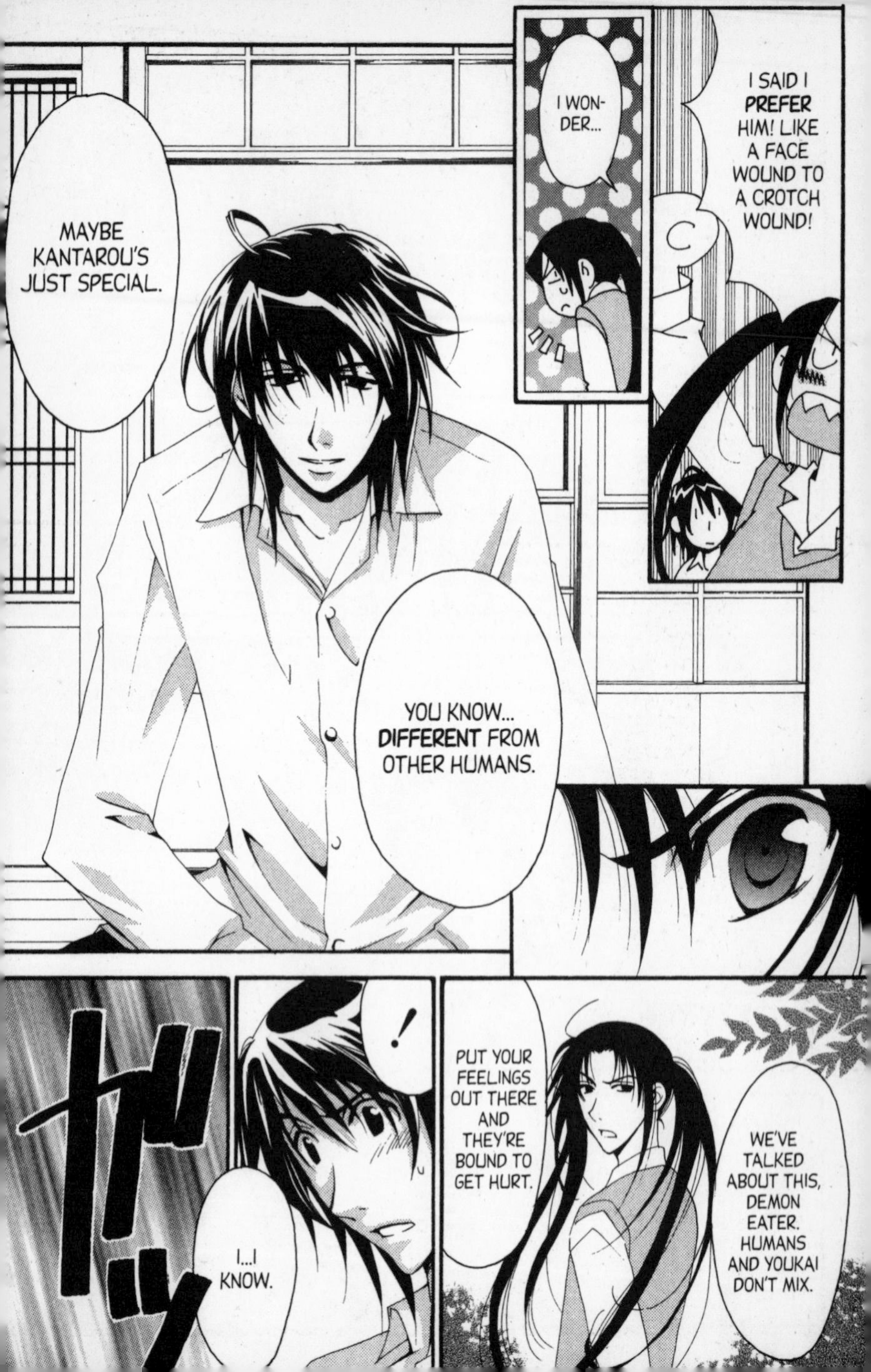
I SAID I PREFER HIM! LIKE A FACE WOUND TO A CROTCH WOUND!
I WONDER...
MAYBE KANTAROU'S JUST SPECIAL.
YOU KNOW... DIFFERENT FROM OTHER HUMANS.
WE'VE TALKED ABOUT THIS, DEMON EATER. HUMANS AND YOUKAI DON'T MIX.
PUT YOUR FEELINGS OUT THERE AND THEY'RE BOUND TO GET HURT.
!
I...I KNOW.

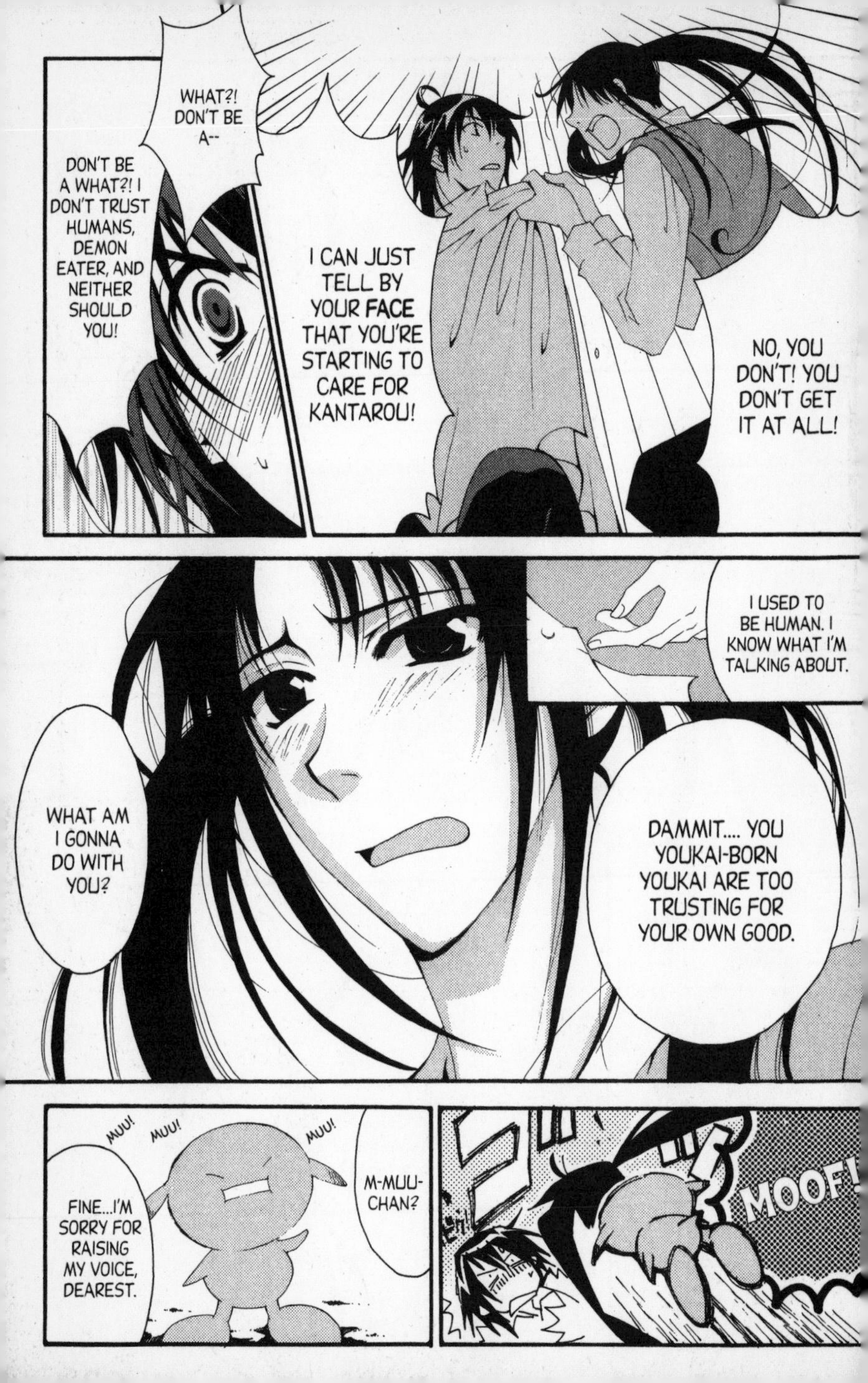
I CAN JUST TELL BY YOUR FACE THAT YOU'RE STARTING TO CARE FOR KANTAROU!
WHAT?! DON'T BE A--
DON'T BE A WHAT?! I DON'T TRUST HUMANS, DEMON EATER, AND NEITHER SHOULD YOU!
NO, YOU DON'T! YOU DON'T GET IT AT ALL!
I USED TO BE HUMAN. I KNOW WHAT I'M TALKING ABOUT.
DAMMIT.... YOU YOUKAI-BORN YOUKAI ARE TOO TRUSTING FOR YOUR OWN GOOD.
WHAT AM I GONNA DO WITH YOU?
MOOF!
MUU!
MUU!
MUU!
M-MUU-CHAN?
FINE...I'M SORRY FOR RAISING MY VOICE, DEAREST.

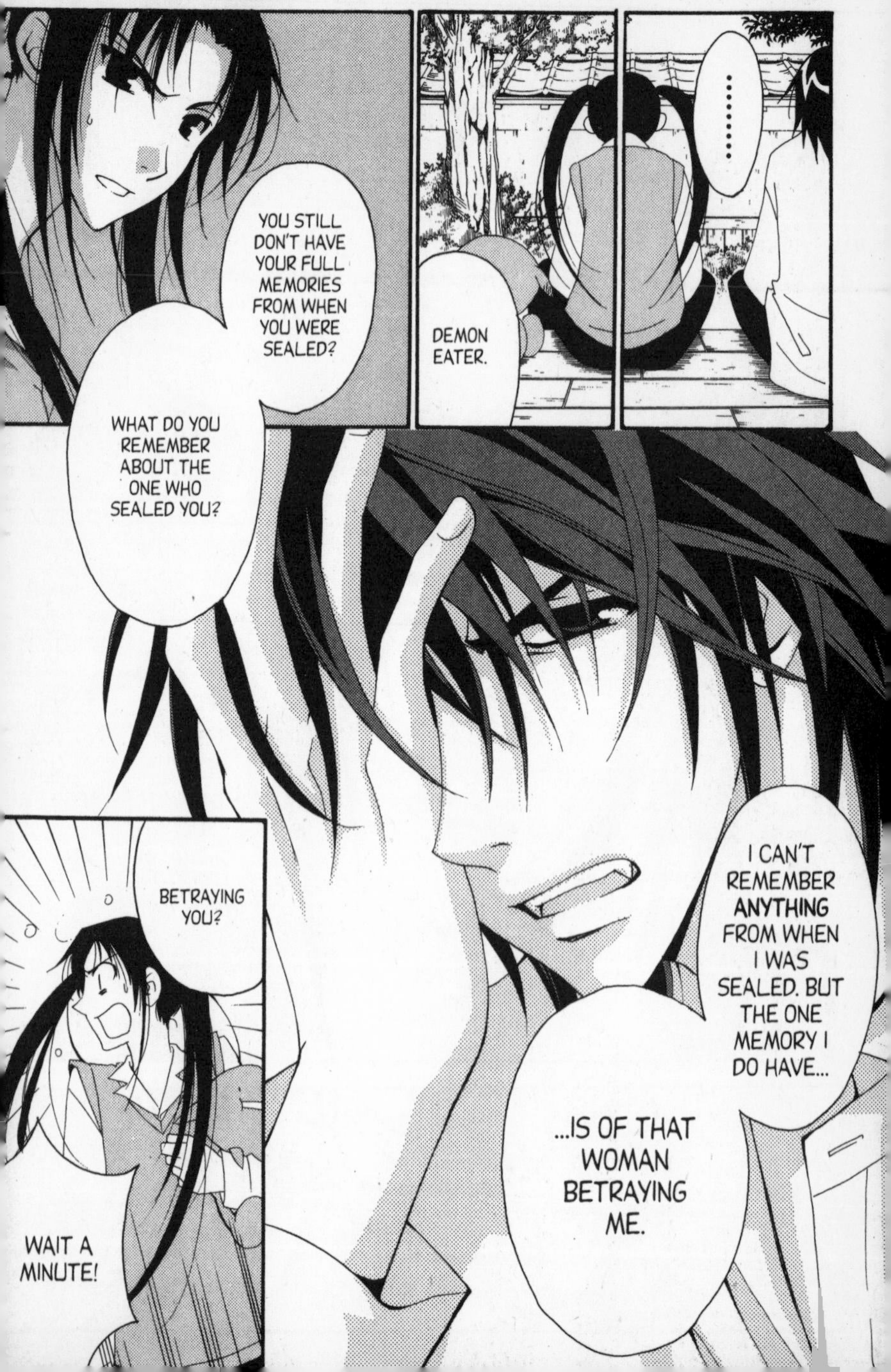
……
DEMON EATER.
YOU STILL DON'T HAVE YOUR FULL MEMORIES FROM WHEN YOU WERE SEALED?
WHAT DO YOU REMEMBER ABOUT THE ONE WHO SEALED YOU?
I CAN'T REMEMBER ANYTHING FROM WHEN I WAS SEALED. BUT THE ONE MEMORY I DO HAVE...
...IS OF THAT WOMAN BETRAYING ME.
BETRAYING YOU?
WAIT A MINUTE!

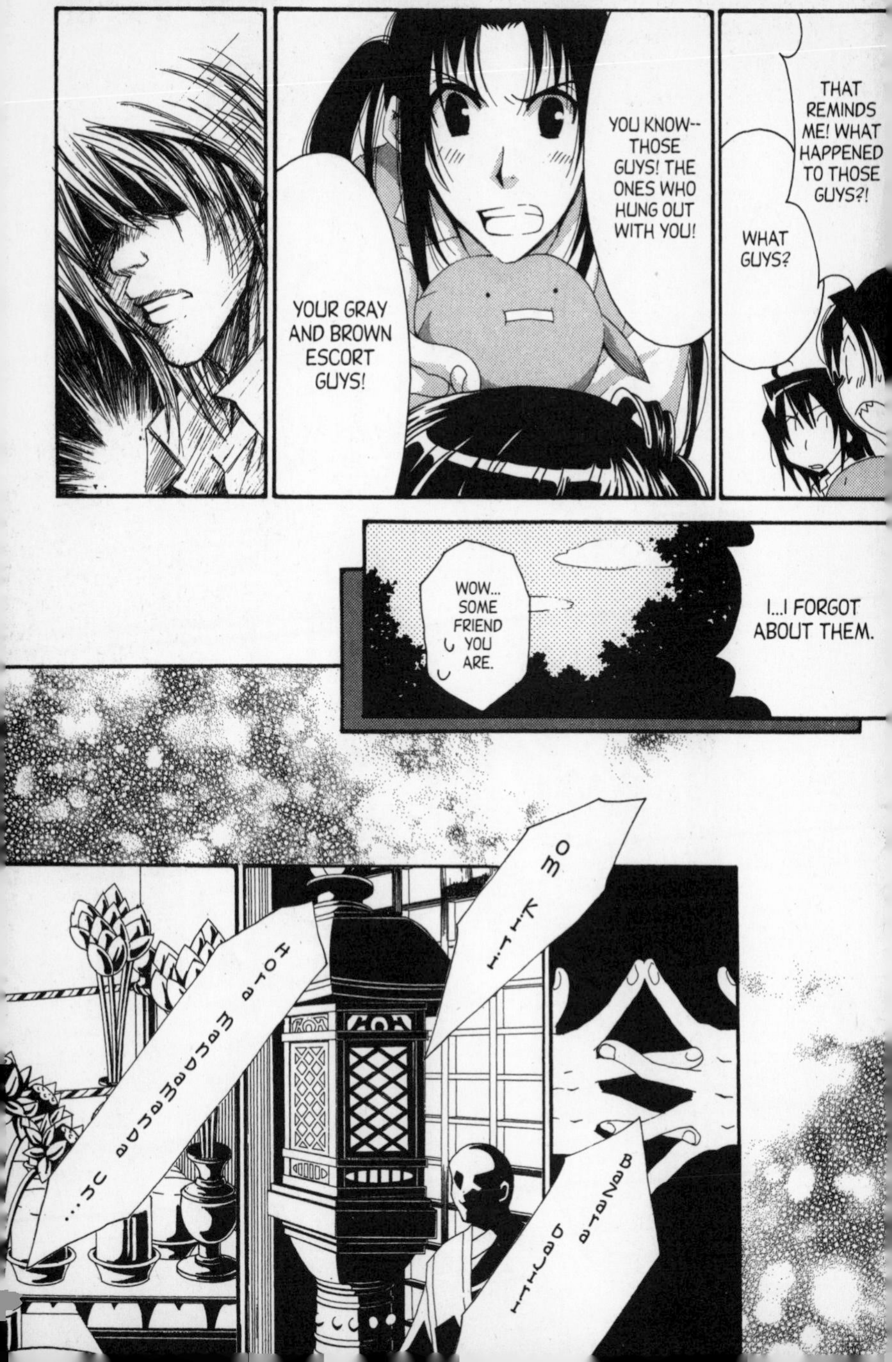
THAT REMINDS ME! WHAT HAPPENED TO THOSE GUYS?!
WHAT GUYS?
YOU KNOW-- THOSE GUYS! THE ONES WHO HUNG OUT WITH YOU!
YOUR GRAY AND BROWN ESCORT GUYS!
I...I FORGOT ABOUT THEM.
WOW... SOME FRIEND YOU ARE.

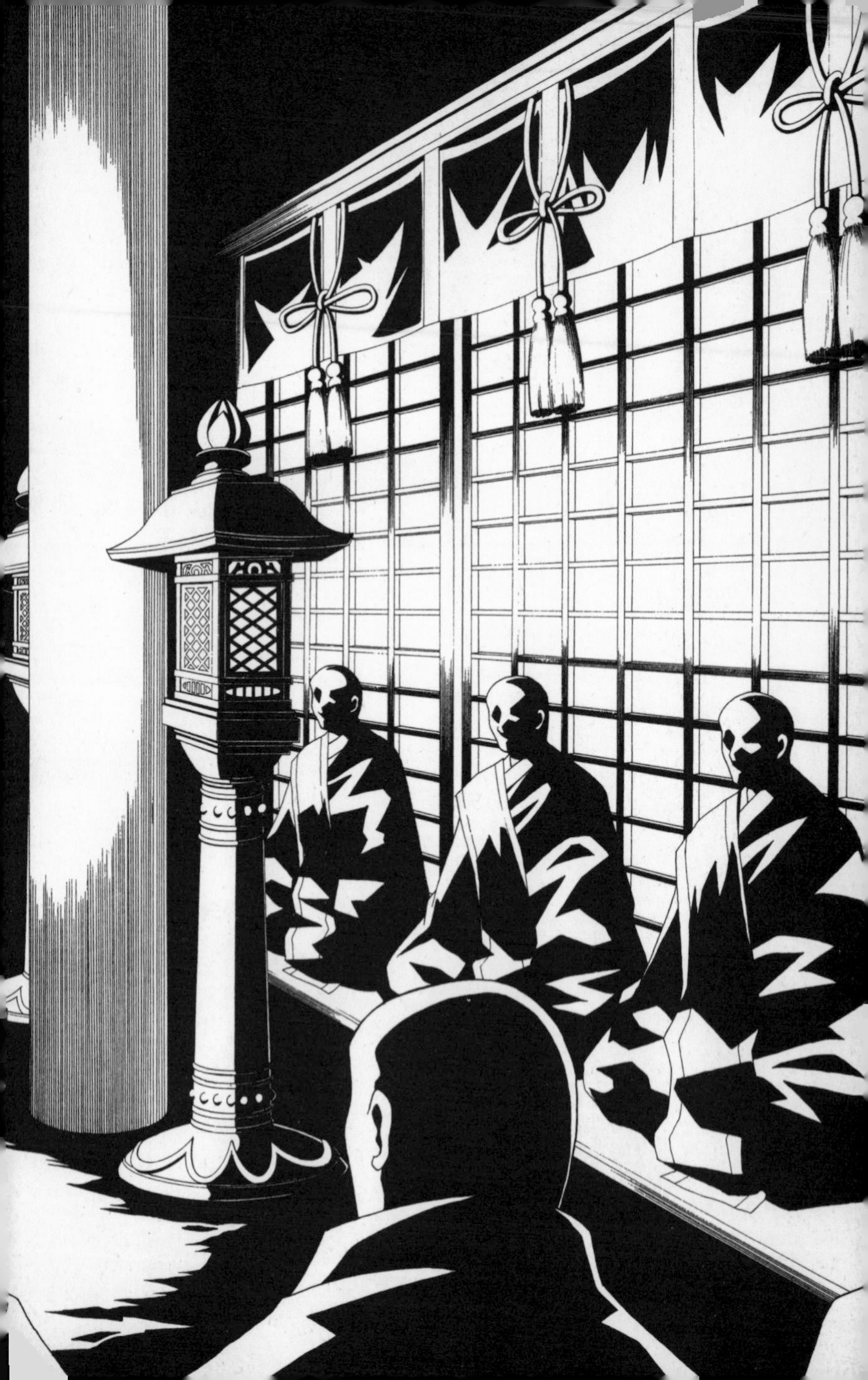

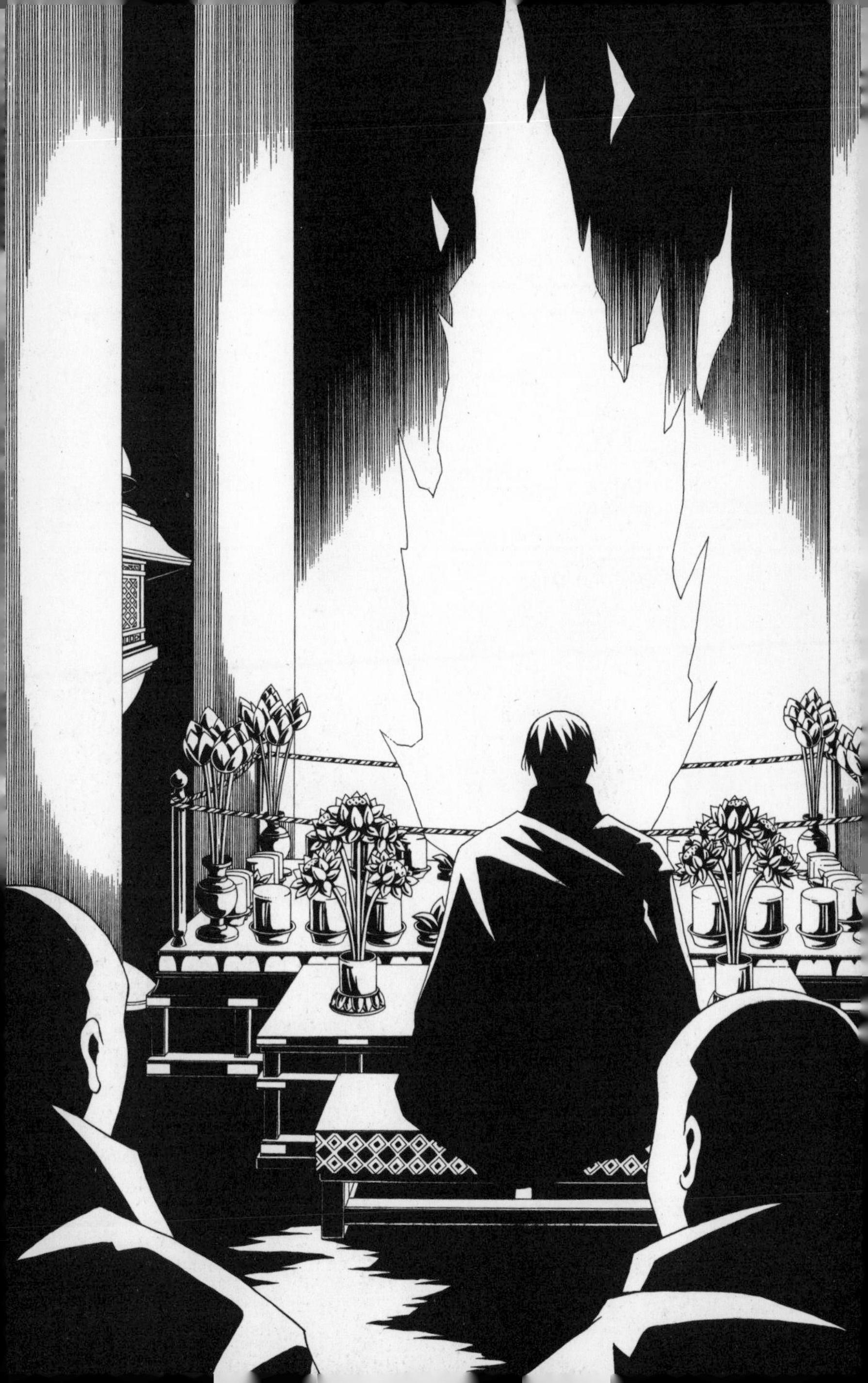

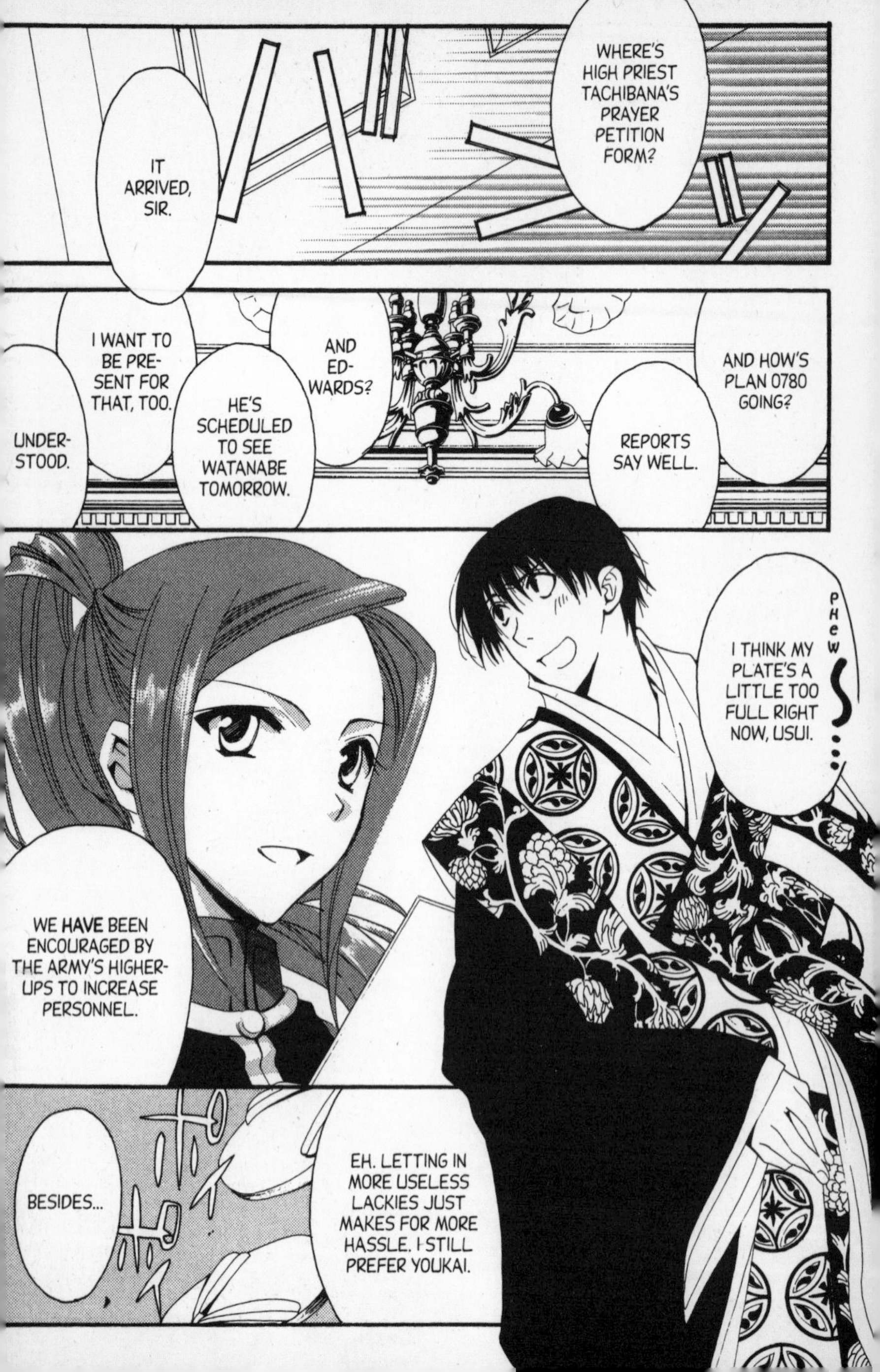
WHERE'S HIGH PRIEST TACHIBANA'S PRAYER PETITION FORM?
IT ARRIVED, SIR.
AND HOW'S PLAN 0780 GOING?
REPORTS SAY WELL.
AND ED-WARDS?
HE'S SCHEDULED TO SEE WATANABE TOMORROW.
I WANT TO BE PRE-SENT FOR THAT, TOO.
UNDER-STOOD.
PHEW...
I THINK MY PLATE'S A LITTLE TOO FULL RIGHT NOW, USUI.
WE **HAVE** BEEN ENCOURAGED BY THE ARMY'S HIGHER-UPS TO INCREASE PERSONNEL.
EH. LETTING IN MORE USELESS LACKIES JUST MAKES FOR MORE HASSLE. I STILL PREFER YOUKAI.
BESIDES...

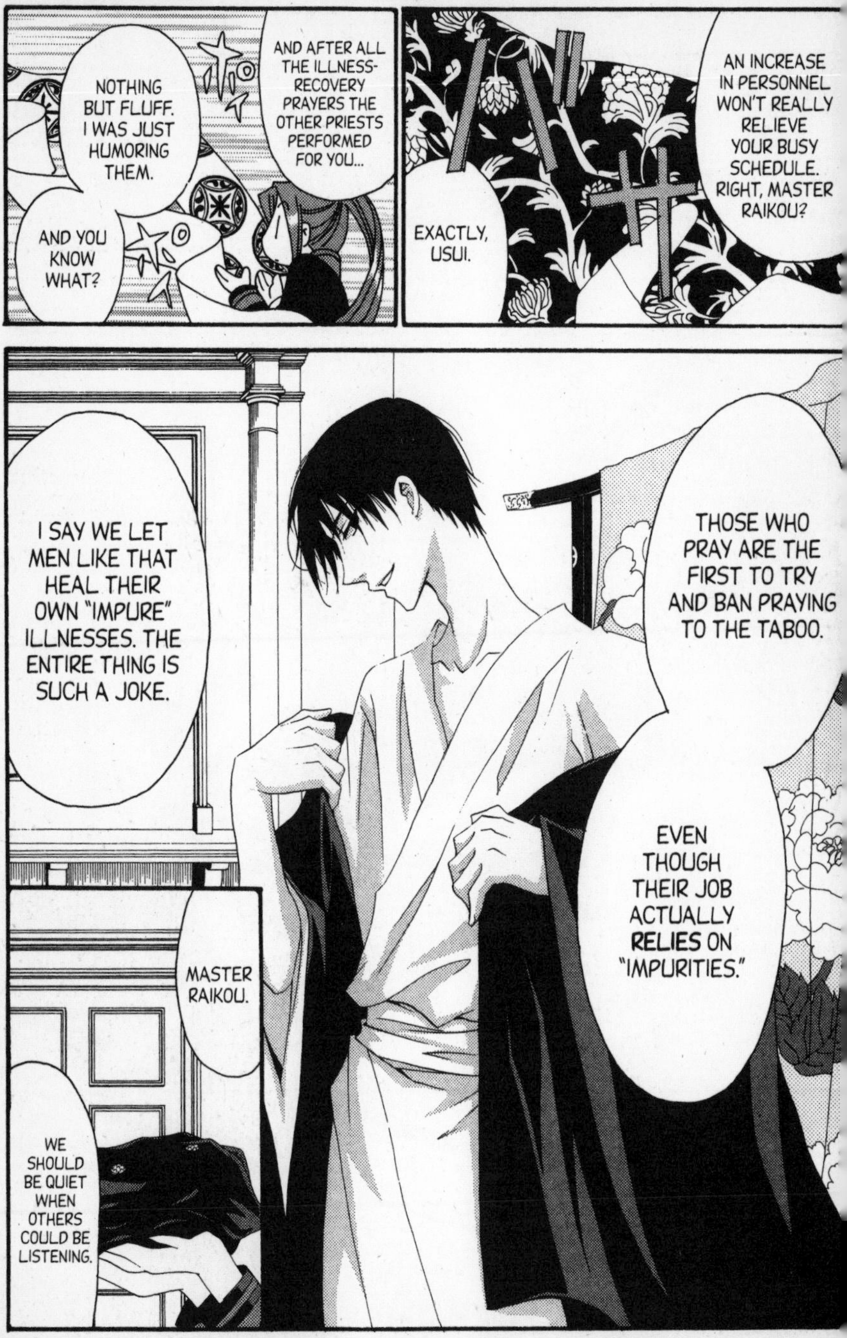
AN INCREASE IN PERSONNEL WON'T REALLY RELIEVE YOUR BUSY SCHEDULE. RIGHT, MASTER RAIKOU?
EXACTLY, USUI.
AND AFTER ALL THE ILLNESS-RECOVERY PRAYERS THE OTHER PRIESTS PERFORMED FOR YOU...
NOTHING BUT FLUFF. I WAS JUST HUMORING THEM.
AND YOU KNOW WHAT?
THOSE WHO PRAY ARE THE FIRST TO TRY AND BAN PRAYING TO THE TABOO.
EVEN THOUGH THEIR JOB ACTUALLY RELIES ON "IMPURITIES."
I SAY WE LET MEN LIKE THAT HEAL THEIR OWN "IMPURE" ILLNESSES. THE ENTIRE THING IS SUCH A JOKE.
MASTER RAIKOU.
WE SHOULD BE QUIET WHEN OTHERS COULD BE LISTENING.

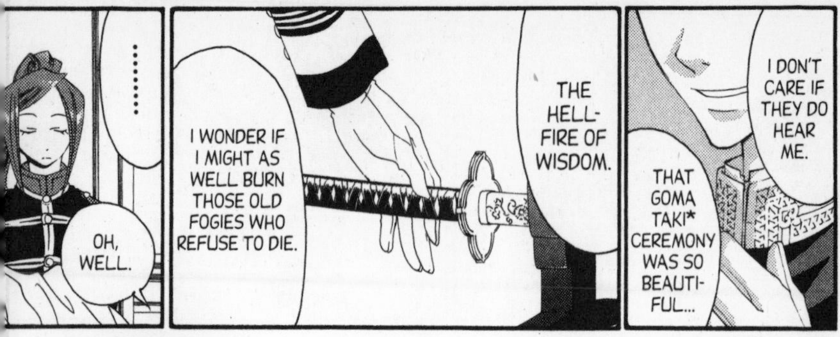
I DON'T CARE IF THEY DO HEAR ME.
THAT GOMA TAKI* CEREMONY WAS SO BEAUTIFUL...
THE HELL-FIRE OF WISDOM.
I WONDER IF I MIGHT AS WELL BURN THOSE OLD FOGIES WHO REFUSE TO DIE.
......
OH, WELL.

*A tantric fire ritual that takes place on New Year's Eve in Japan.

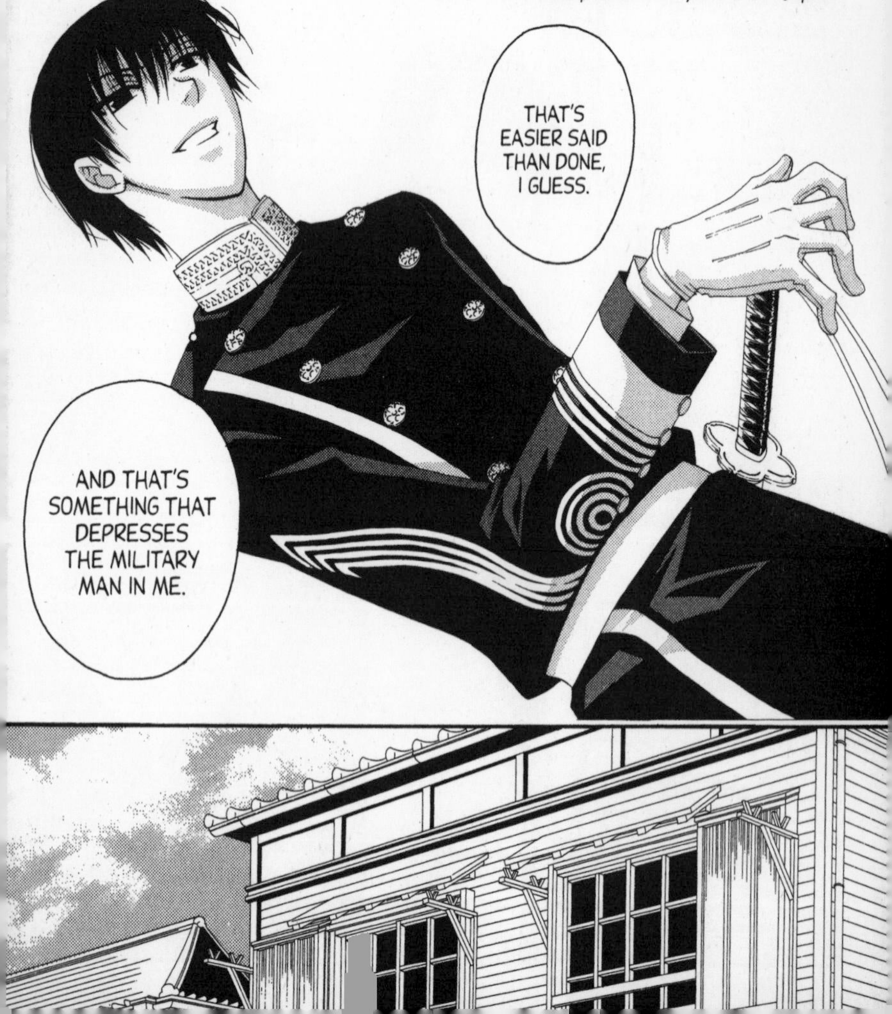
THAT'S EASIER SAID THAN DONE, I GUESS.
AND THAT'S SOMETHING THAT DEPRESSES THE MILITARY MAN IN ME.

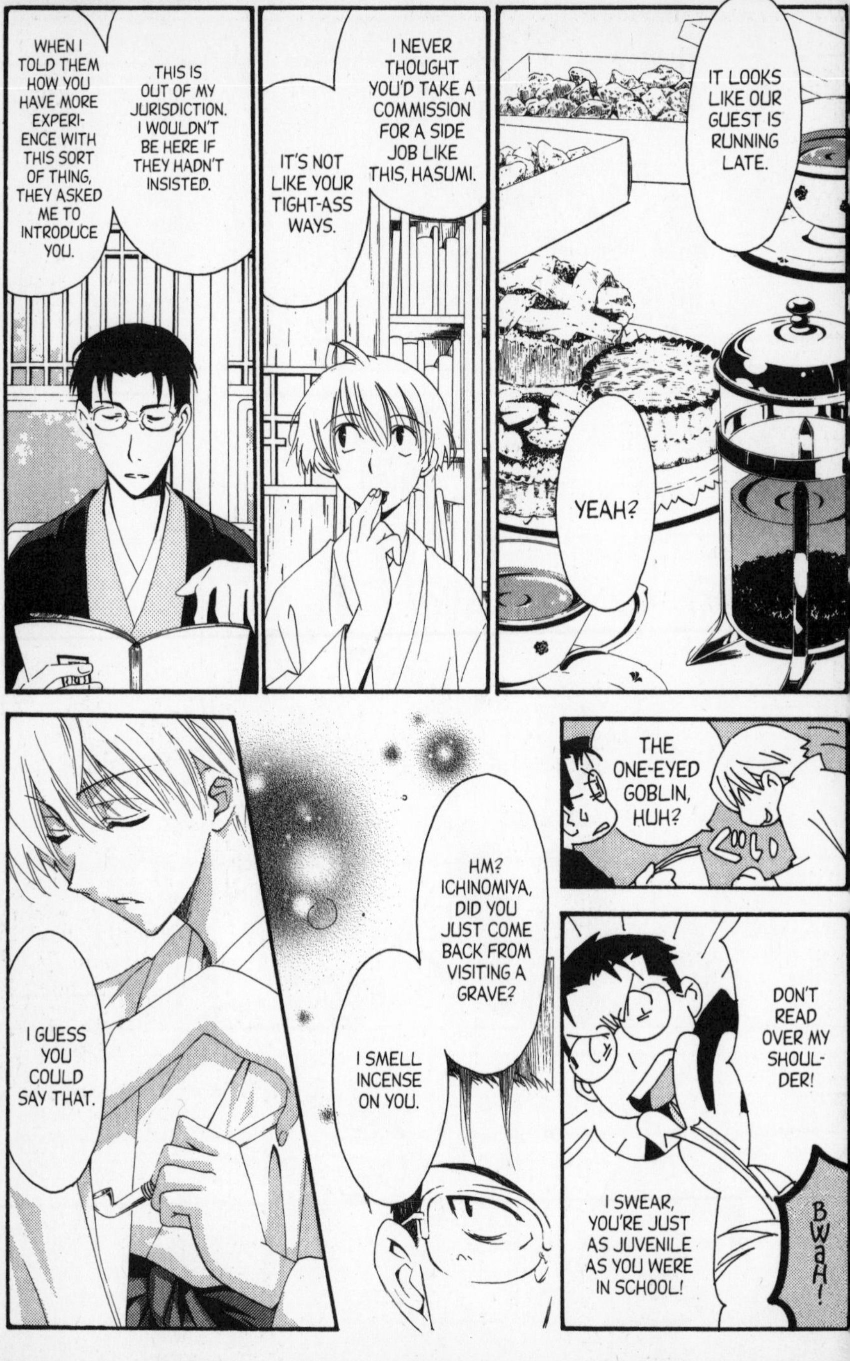
IT LOOKS LIKE OUR GUEST IS RUNNING LATE.
YEAH?
I NEVER THOUGHT YOU'D TAKE A COMMISSION FOR A SIDE JOB LIKE THIS, HASUMI.
IT'S NOT LIKE YOUR TIGHT-ASS WAYS.
THIS IS OUT OF MY JURISDICTION. I WOULDN'T BE HERE IF THEY HADN'T INSISTED.
WHEN I TOLD THEM HOW YOU HAVE MORE EXPERI-ENCE WITH THIS SORT OF THING, THEY ASKED ME TO INTRODUCE YOU.
THE ONE-EYED GOBLIN, HUH?
DON'T READ OVER MY SHOUL-DER!
BWAH!
I SWEAR, YOU'RE JUST AS JUVENILE AS YOU WERE IN SCHOOL!
HM? ICHINOMIYA, DID YOU JUST COME BACK FROM VISITING A GRAVE?
I SMELL INCENSE ON YOU.
I GUESS YOU COULD SAY THAT.

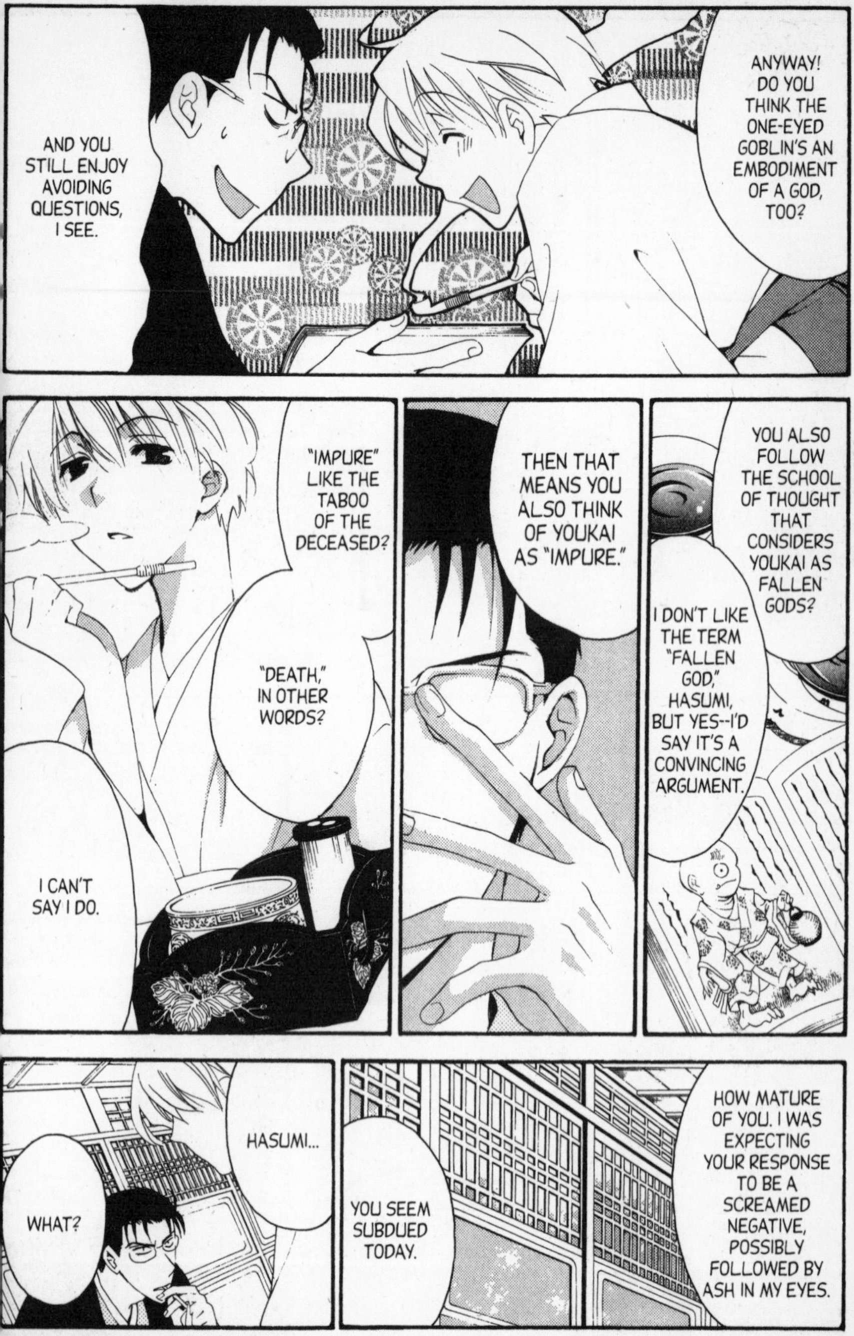
ANYWAY! DO YOU THINK THE ONE-EYED GOBLIN'S AN EMBODIMENT OF A GOD, TOO?
AND YOU STILL ENJOY AVOIDING QUESTIONS, I SEE.
YOU ALSO FOLLOW THE SCHOOL OF THOUGHT THAT CONSIDERS YOUKAI AS FALLEN GODS?
I DON'T LIKE THE TERM "FALLEN GOD," HASUMI, BUT YES--I'D SAY IT'S A CONVINCING ARGUMENT.
THEN THAT MEANS YOU ALSO THINK OF YOUKAI AS "IMPURE."
"IMPURE" LIKE THE TABOO OF THE DECEASED?
"DEATH," IN OTHER WORDS?
I CAN'T SAY I DO.
HOW MATURE OF YOU. I WAS EXPECTING YOUR RESPONSE TO BE A SCREAMED NEGATIVE, POSSIBLY FOLLOWED BY ASH IN MY EYES.
YOU SEEM SUBDUED TODAY.
HASUMI...
WHAT?

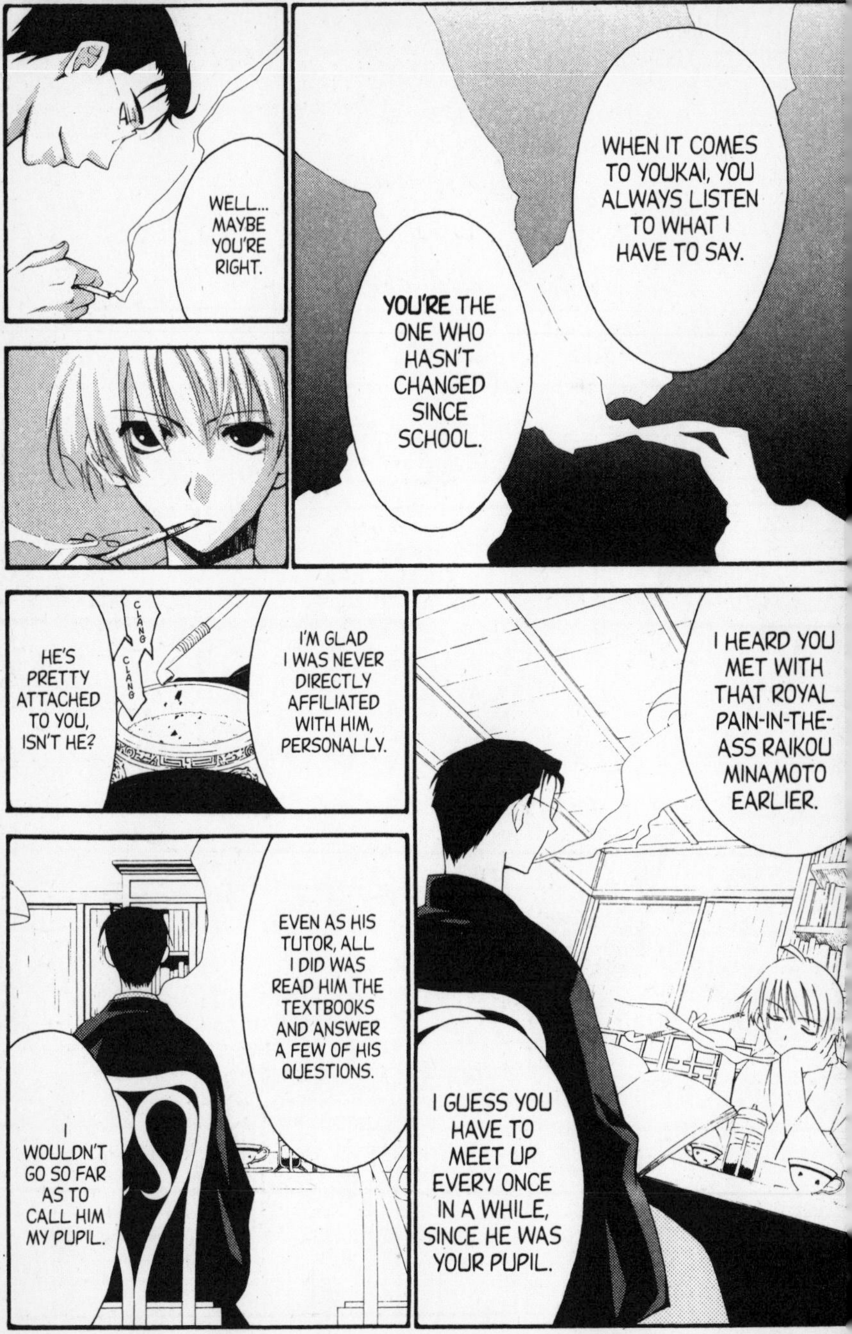
WHEN IT COMES TO YOUKAI, YOU ALWAYS LISTEN TO WHAT I HAVE TO SAY.
YOU'RE THE ONE WHO HASN'T CHANGED SINCE SCHOOL.
WELL... MAYBE YOU'RE RIGHT.
I HEARD YOU MET WITH THAT ROYAL PAIN-IN-THE-ASS RAIKOU MINAMOTO EARLIER.
I GUESS YOU HAVE TO MEET UP EVERY ONCE IN A WHILE, SINCE HE WAS YOUR PUPIL.
I'M GLAD I WAS NEVER DIRECTLY AFFILIATED WITH HIM, PERSONALLY.
CLANG
CLANG
HE'S PRETTY ATTACHED TO YOU, ISN'T HE?
EVEN AS HIS TUTOR, ALL I DID WAS READ HIM THE TEXTBOOKS AND ANSWER A FEW OF HIS QUESTIONS.
I WOULDN'T GO SO FAR AS TO CALL HIM MY PUPIL.

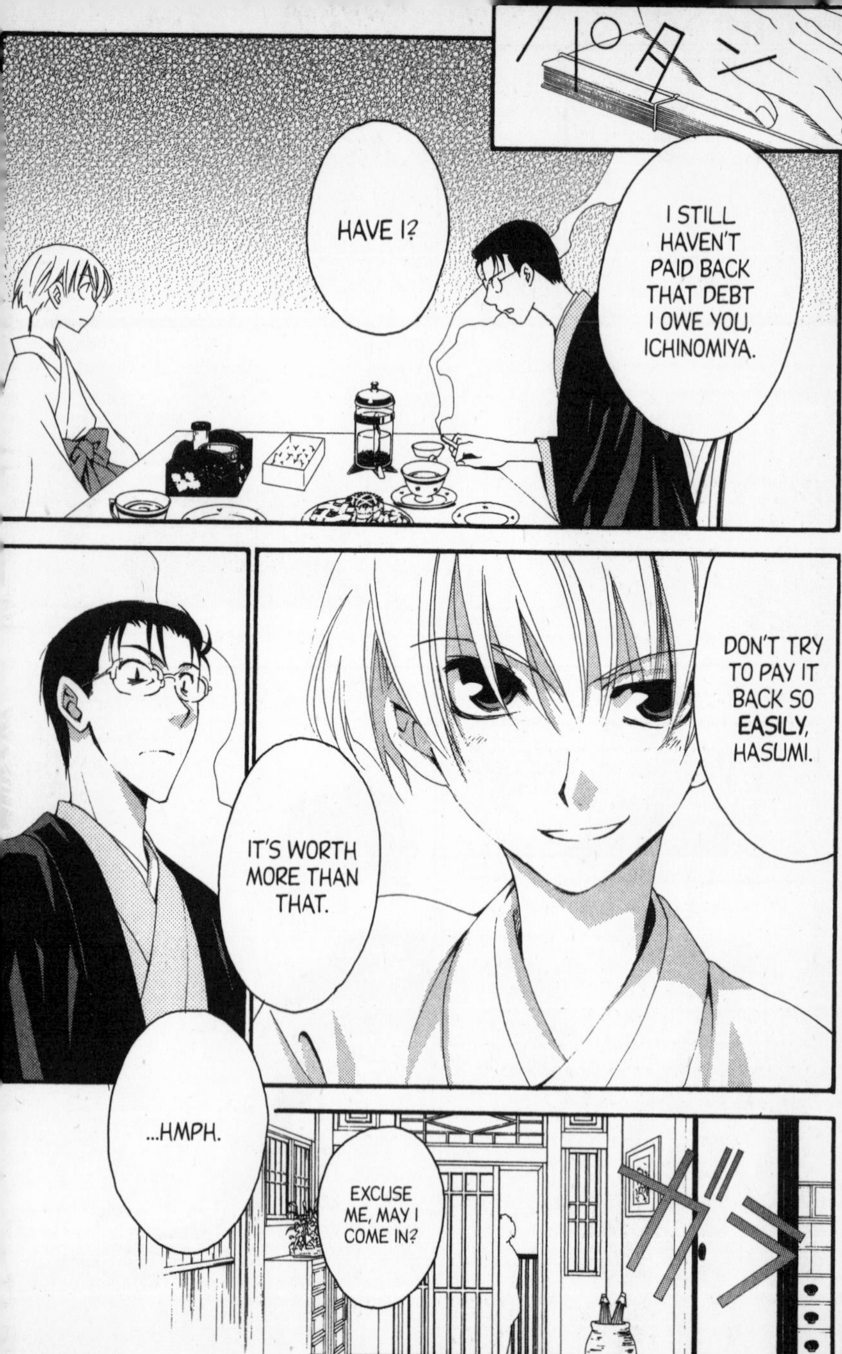

I STILL HAVEN'T PAID BACK THAT DEBT I OWE YOU, ICHINOMIYA.
HAVE I?
DON'T TRY TO PAY IT BACK SO **EASILY**, HASUMI.
IT'S WORTH MORE THAN THAT.
...HMPH.
EXCUSE ME, MAY I COME IN?

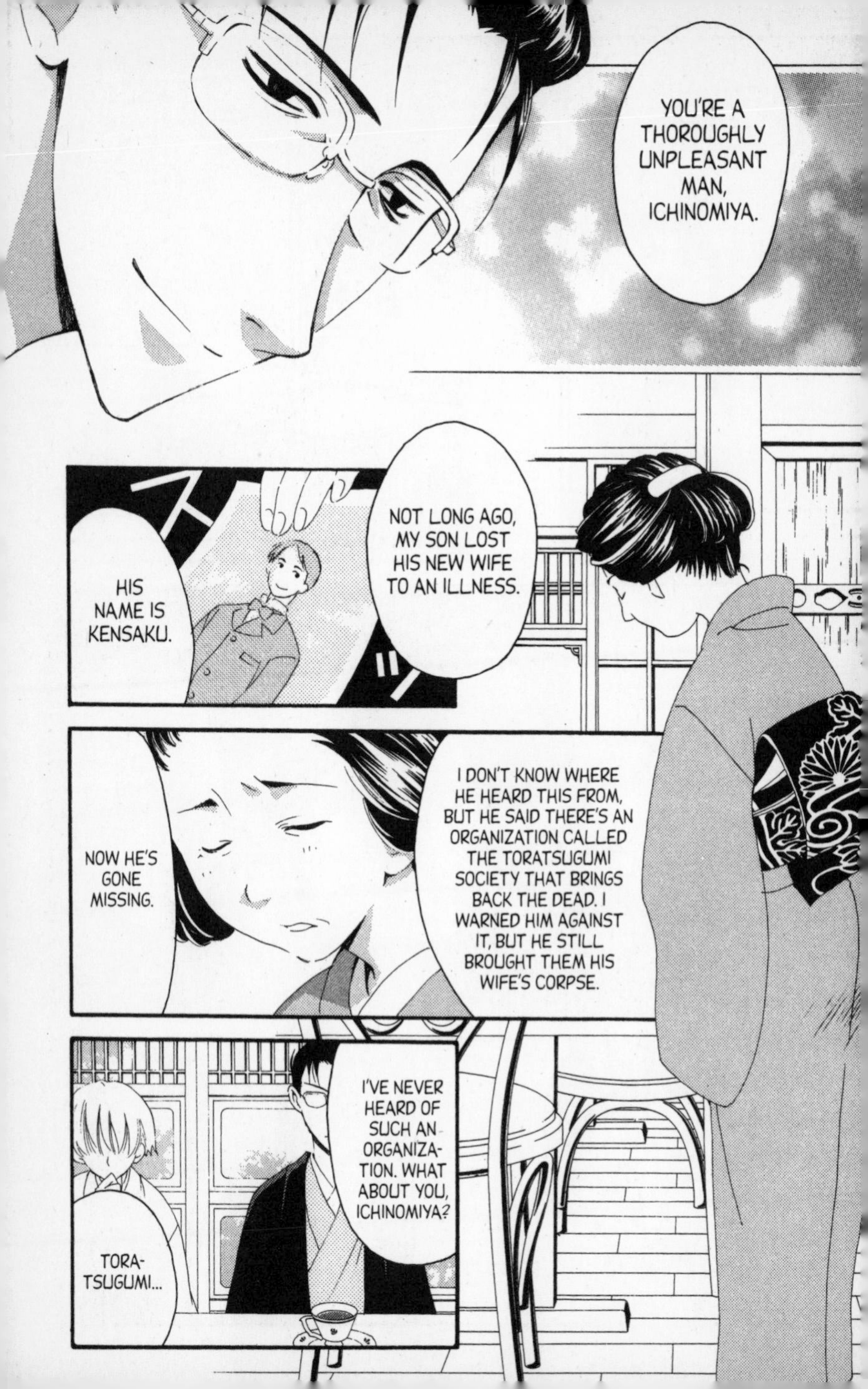
YOU'RE A THOROUGHLY UNPLEASANT MAN, ICHINOMIYA.
NOT LONG AGO, MY SON LOST HIS NEW WIFE TO AN ILLNESS.
HIS NAME IS KENSAKU.
I DON'T KNOW WHERE HE HEARD THIS FROM, BUT HE SAID THERE'S AN ORGANIZATION CALLED THE TORATSUGUMI SOCIETY THAT BRINGS BACK THE DEAD. I WARNED HIM AGAINST IT, BUT HE STILL BROUGHT THEM HIS WIFE'S CORPSE.
NOW HE'S GONE MISSING.
I'VE NEVER HEARD OF SUCH AN ORGANIZA-TION. WHAT ABOUT YOU, ICHINOMIYA?
TORA-TSUGUMI...

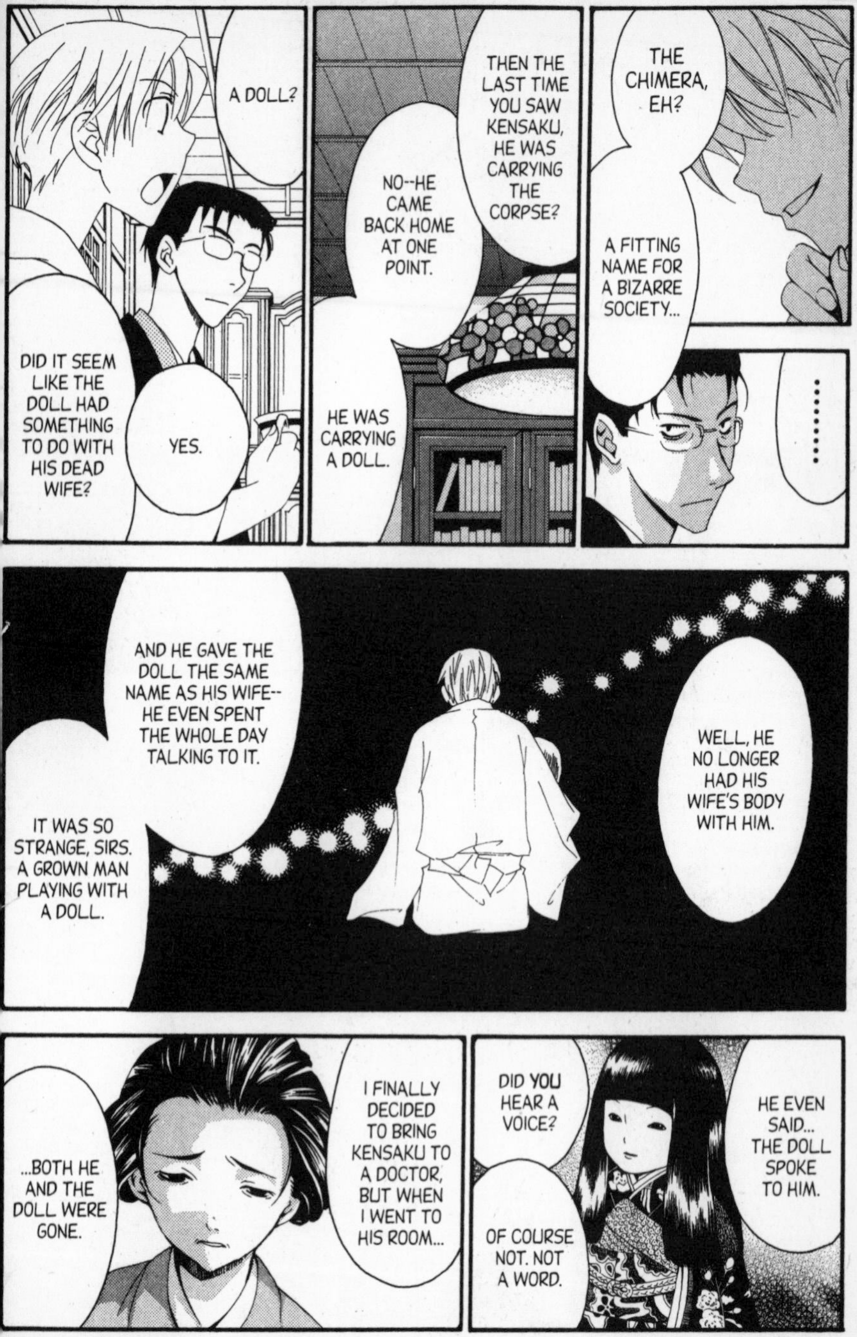
THE CHIMERA, EH?
A FITTING NAME FOR A BIZARRE SOCIETY...
....
THEN THE LAST TIME YOU SAW KENSAKU, HE WAS CARRYING THE CORPSE?
NO--HE CAME BACK HOME AT ONE POINT.
HE WAS CARRYING A DOLL.
A DOLL?
DID IT SEEM LIKE THE DOLL HAD SOMETHING TO DO WITH HIS DEAD WIFE?
YES.
WELL, HE NO LONGER HAD HIS WIFE'S BODY WITH HIM.
AND HE GAVE THE DOLL THE SAME NAME AS HIS WIFE-- HE EVEN SPENT THE WHOLE DAY TALKING TO IT.
IT WAS SO STRANGE, SIRS. A GROWN MAN PLAYING WITH A DOLL.
HE EVEN SAID... THE DOLL SPOKE TO HIM.
DID YOU HEAR A VOICE?
OF COURSE NOT. NOT A WORD.
I FINALLY DECIDED TO BRING KENSAKU TO A DOCTOR, BUT WHEN I WENT TO HIS ROOM...
...BOTH HE AND THE DOLL WERE GONE.

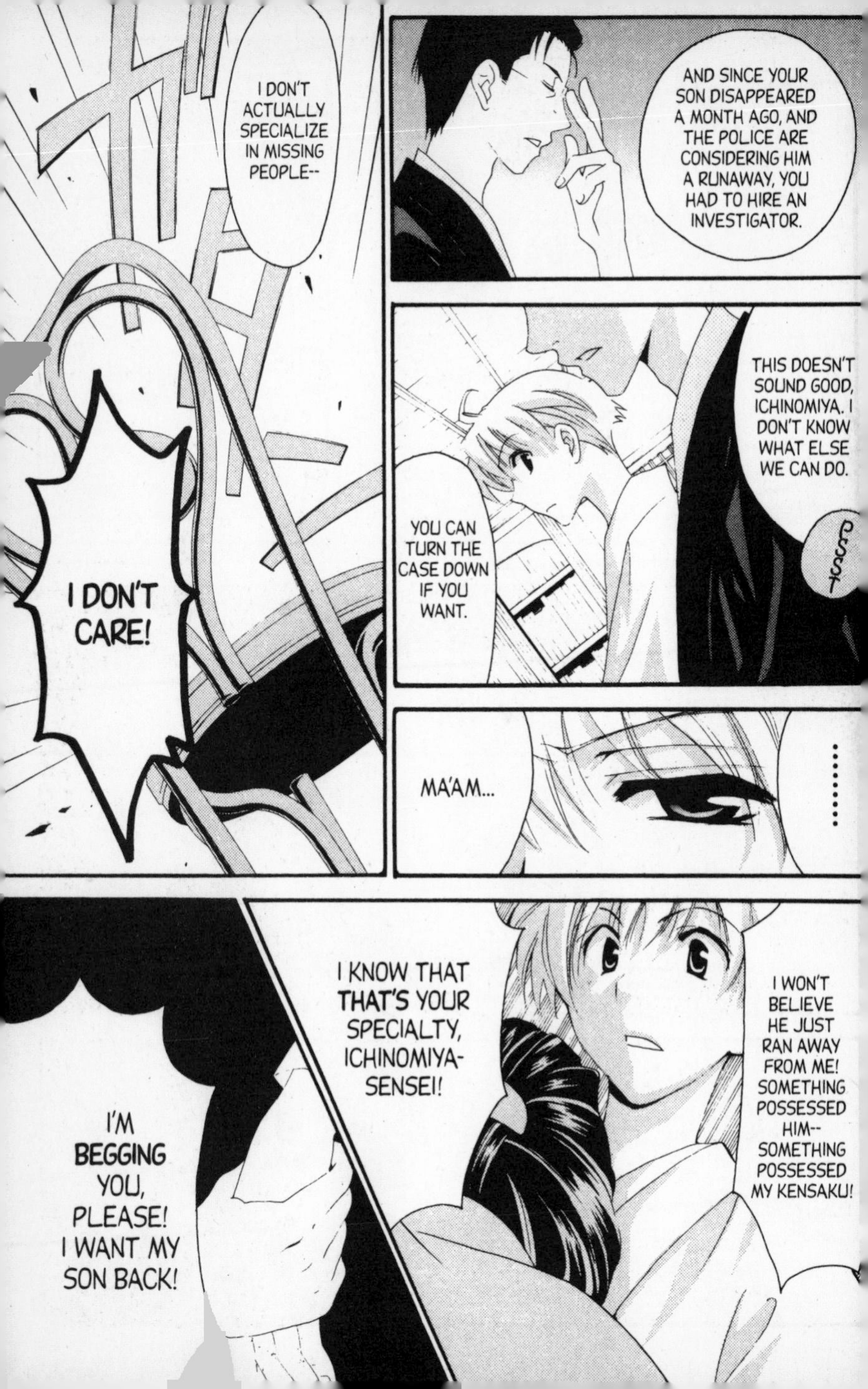
AND SINCE YOUR SON DISAPPEARED A MONTH AGO, AND THE POLICE ARE CONSIDERING HIM A RUNAWAY, YOU HAD TO HIRE AN INVESTIGATOR.
THIS DOESN'T SOUND GOOD, ICHINOMIYA. I DON'T KNOW WHAT ELSE WE CAN DO.
PSSST
YOU CAN TURN THE CASE DOWN IF YOU WANT.
....
MA'AM...
I DON'T ACTUALLY SPECIALIZE IN MISSING PEOPLE--
I DON'T CARE!
I WON'T BELIEVE HE JUST RAN AWAY FROM ME! SOMETHING POSSESSED HIM-- SOMETHING POSSESSED MY KENSAKU!
I KNOW THAT **THAT'S** YOUR SPECIALTY, ICHINOMIYA-SENSEI!
I'M **BEGGING** YOU, PLEASE! I WANT MY SON BACK!

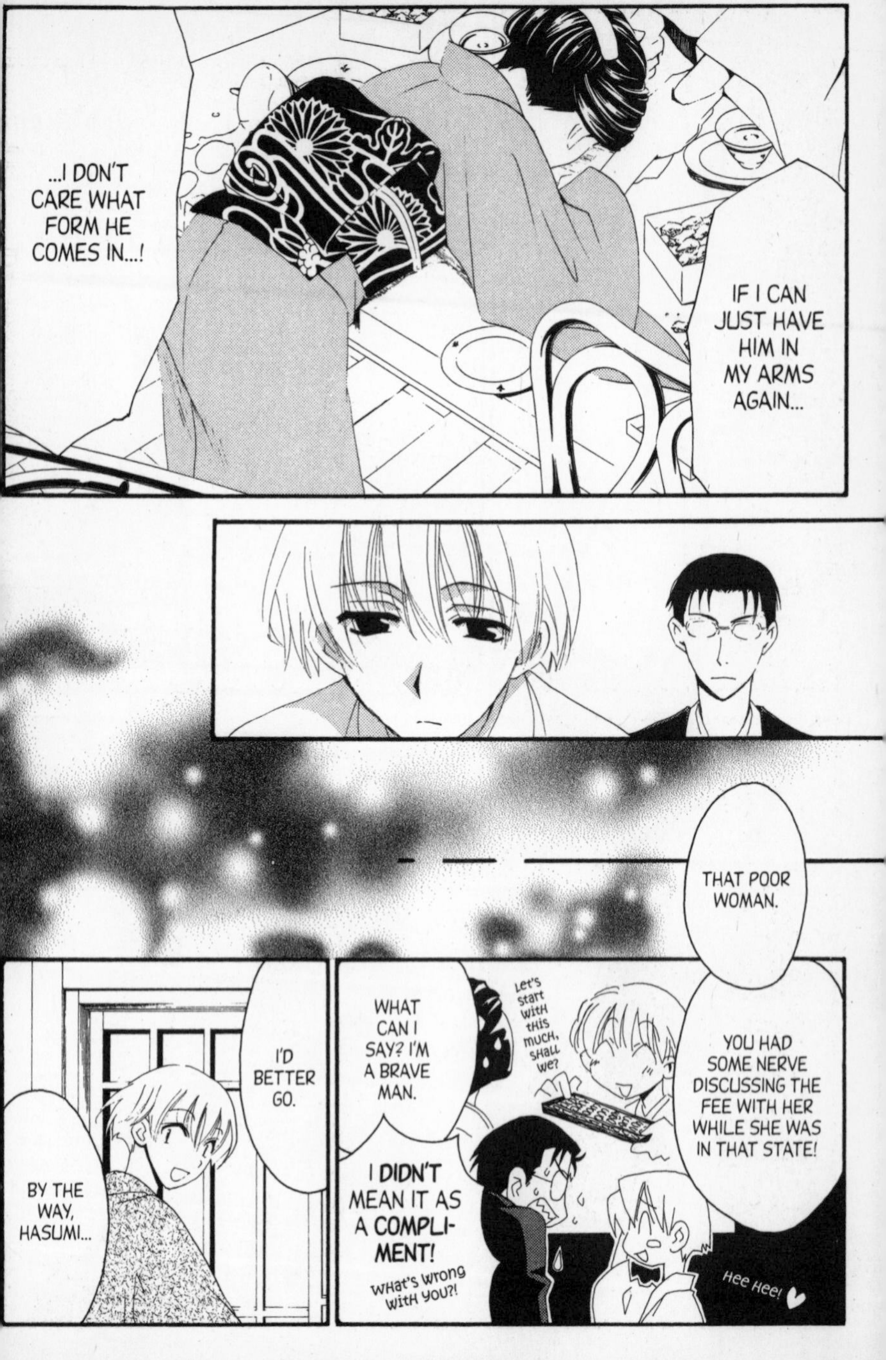
IF I CAN JUST HAVE HIM IN MY ARMS AGAIN...
...I DON'T CARE WHAT FORM HE COMES IN...!
THAT POOR WOMAN.
YOU HAD SOME NERVE DISCUSSING THE FEE WITH HER WHILE SHE WAS IN THAT STATE!
Let's start with this much, shall we?
WHAT CAN I SAY? I'M A BRAVE MAN.
Hee Hee!
I DIDN'T MEAN IT AS A COMPLIMENT!
What's wrong with you?!
I'D BETTER GO.
BY THE WAY, HASUMI...

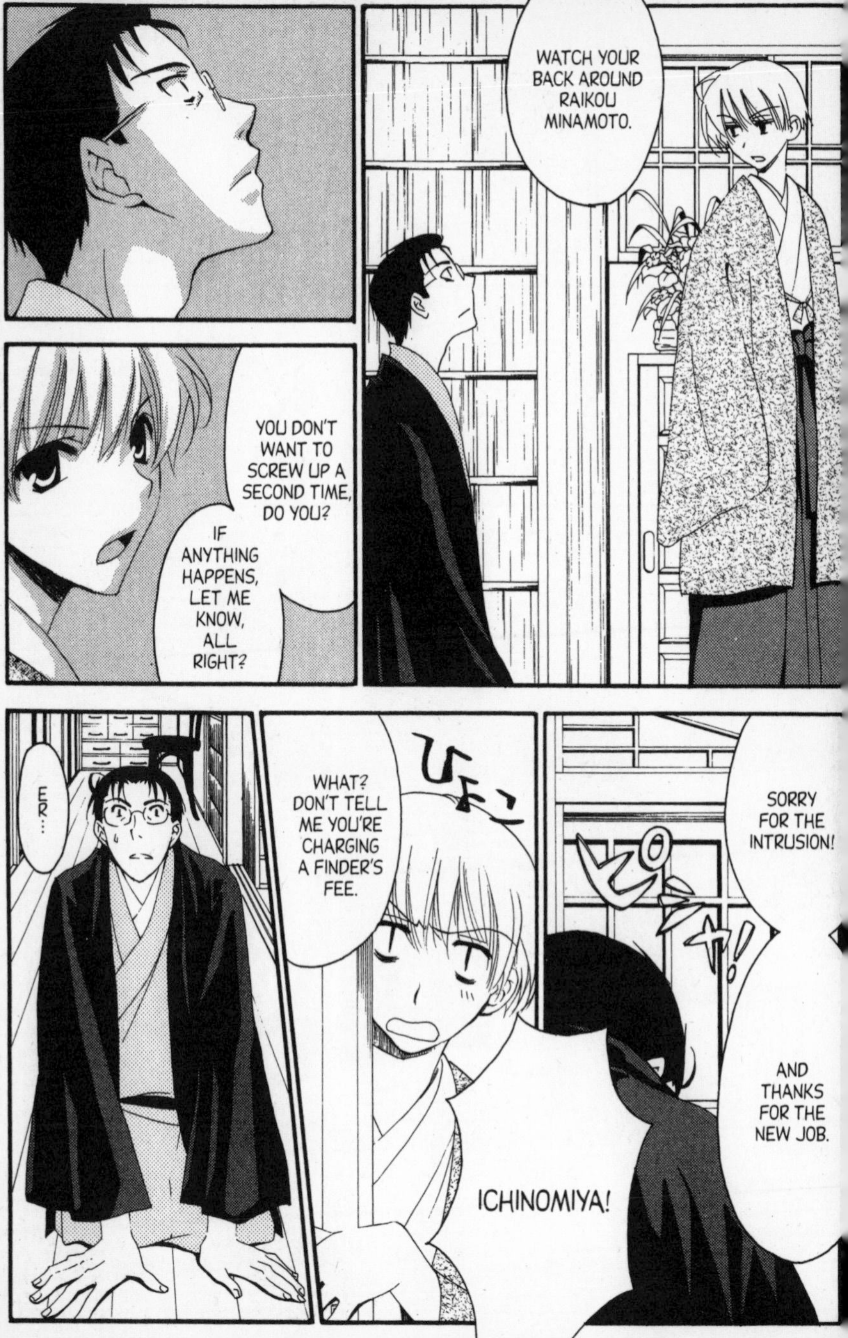
WATCH YOUR BACK AROUND RAIKOU MINAMOTO.
YOU DON'T WANT TO SCREW UP A SECOND TIME, DO YOU?
IF ANYTHING HAPPENS, LET ME KNOW, ALL RIGHT?
SORRY FOR THE INTRUSION!
AND THANKS FOR THE NEW JOB.
ひょこ
WHAT? DON'T TELL ME YOU'RE CHARGING A FINDER'S FEE.
ICHINOMIYA!
ER...

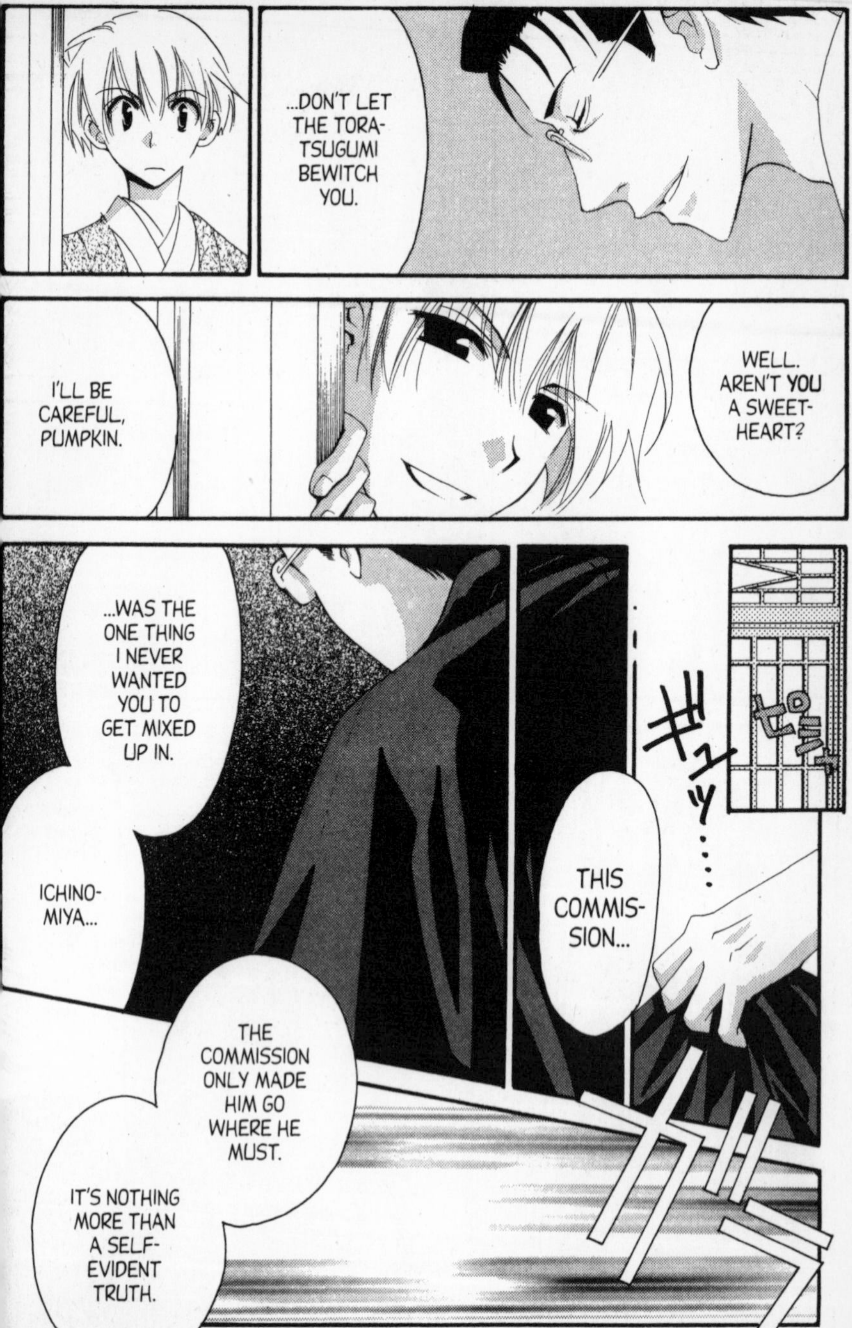

...DON'T LET THE TORA-TSUGUMI BEWITCH YOU.
WELL. AREN'T YOU A SWEET-HEART?
I'LL BE CAREFUL, PUMPKIN.
ピシャ
ギュッ...
THIS COMMIS-SION...
...WAS THE ONE THING I NEVER WANTED YOU TO GET MIXED UP IN.
ICHINO-MIYA...
THE COMMISSION ONLY MADE HIM GO WHERE HE MUST.
IT'S NOTHING MORE THAN A SELF-EVIDENT TRUTH.

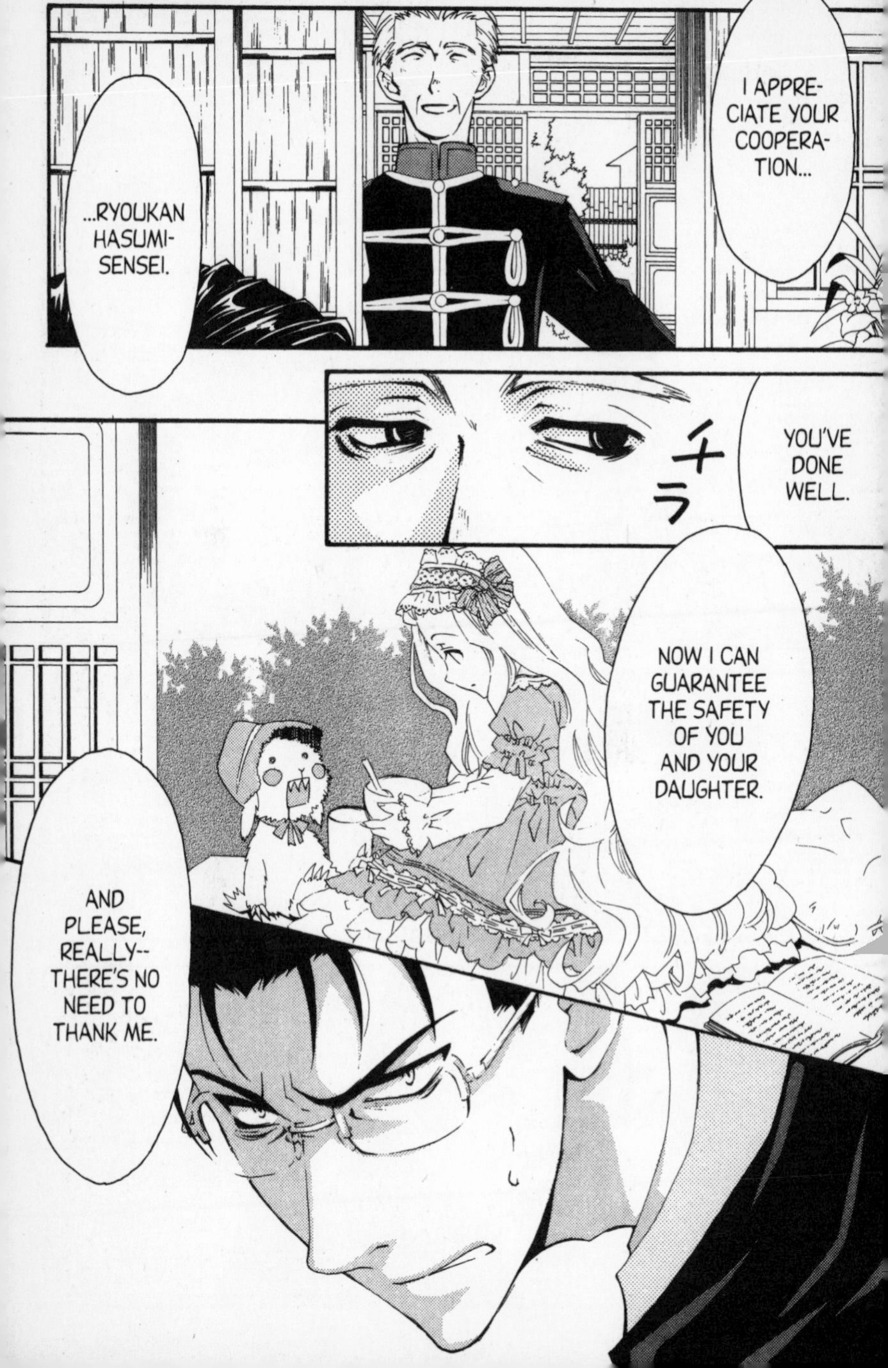
I APPRE-CIATE YOUR COOPERA-TION...
...RYOUKAN HASUMI-SENSEI.
YOU'VE DONE WELL.
チラ
NOW I CAN GUARANTEE THE SAFETY OF YOU AND YOUR DAUGHTER.
AND PLEASE, REALLY-- THERE'S NO NEED TO THANK ME.

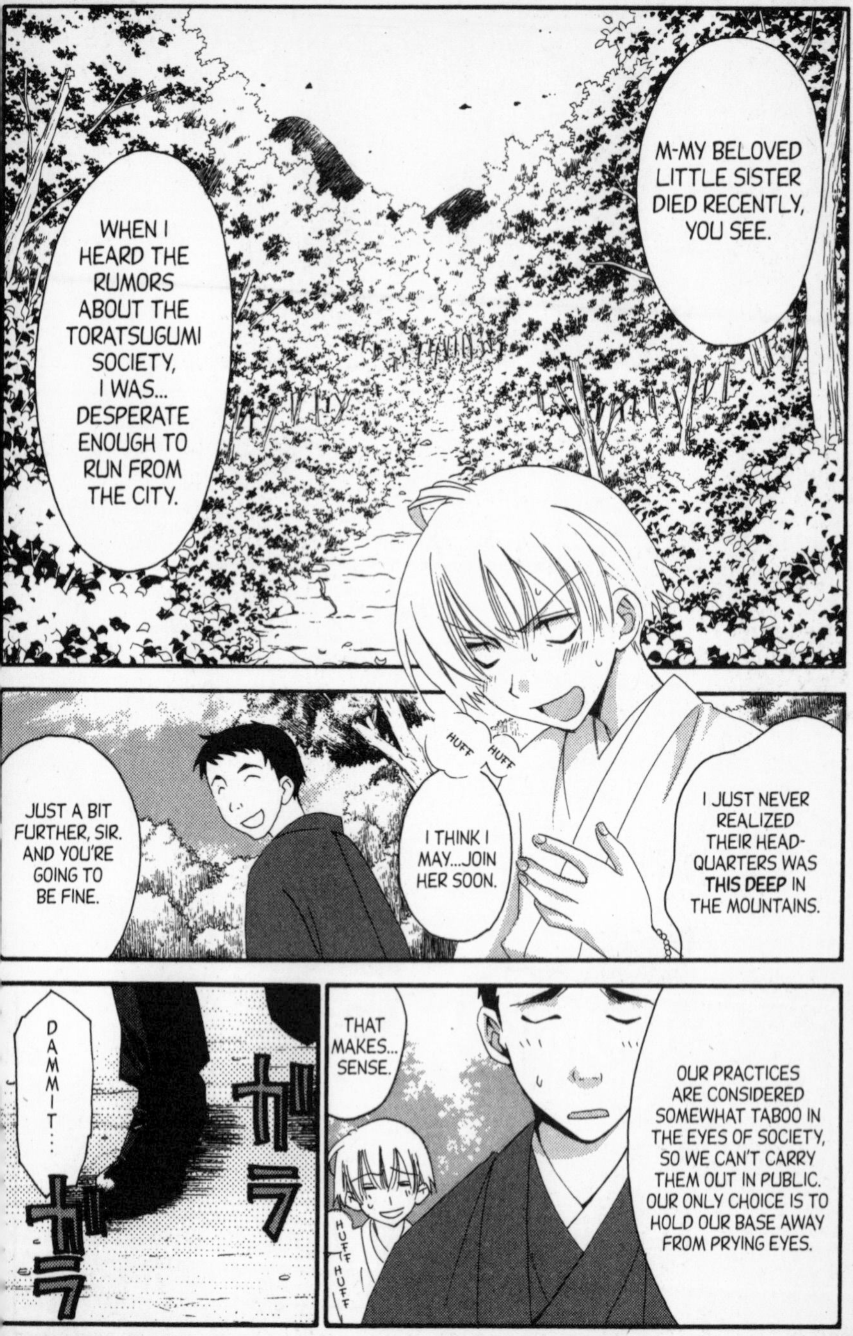
M-MY BELOVED LITTLE SISTER DIED RECENTLY, YOU SEE.
WHEN I HEARD THE RUMORS ABOUT THE TORATSUGUMI SOCIETY, I WAS... DESPERATE ENOUGH TO RUN FROM THE CITY.
I JUST NEVER REALIZED THEIR HEAD-QUARTERS WAS **THIS DEEP** IN THE MOUNTAINS.
HUFF HUFF
I THINK I MAY...JOIN HER SOON.
JUST A BIT FURTHER, SIR. AND YOU'RE GOING TO BE FINE.
OUR PRACTICES ARE CONSIDERED SOMEWHAT TABOO IN THE EYES OF SOCIETY, SO WE CAN'T CARRY THEM OUT IN PUBLIC. OUR ONLY CHOICE IS TO HOLD OUR BASE AWAY FROM PRYING EYES.
THAT MAKES... SENSE.
HUFF HUFF
DAMMIT...
カラ
カラ

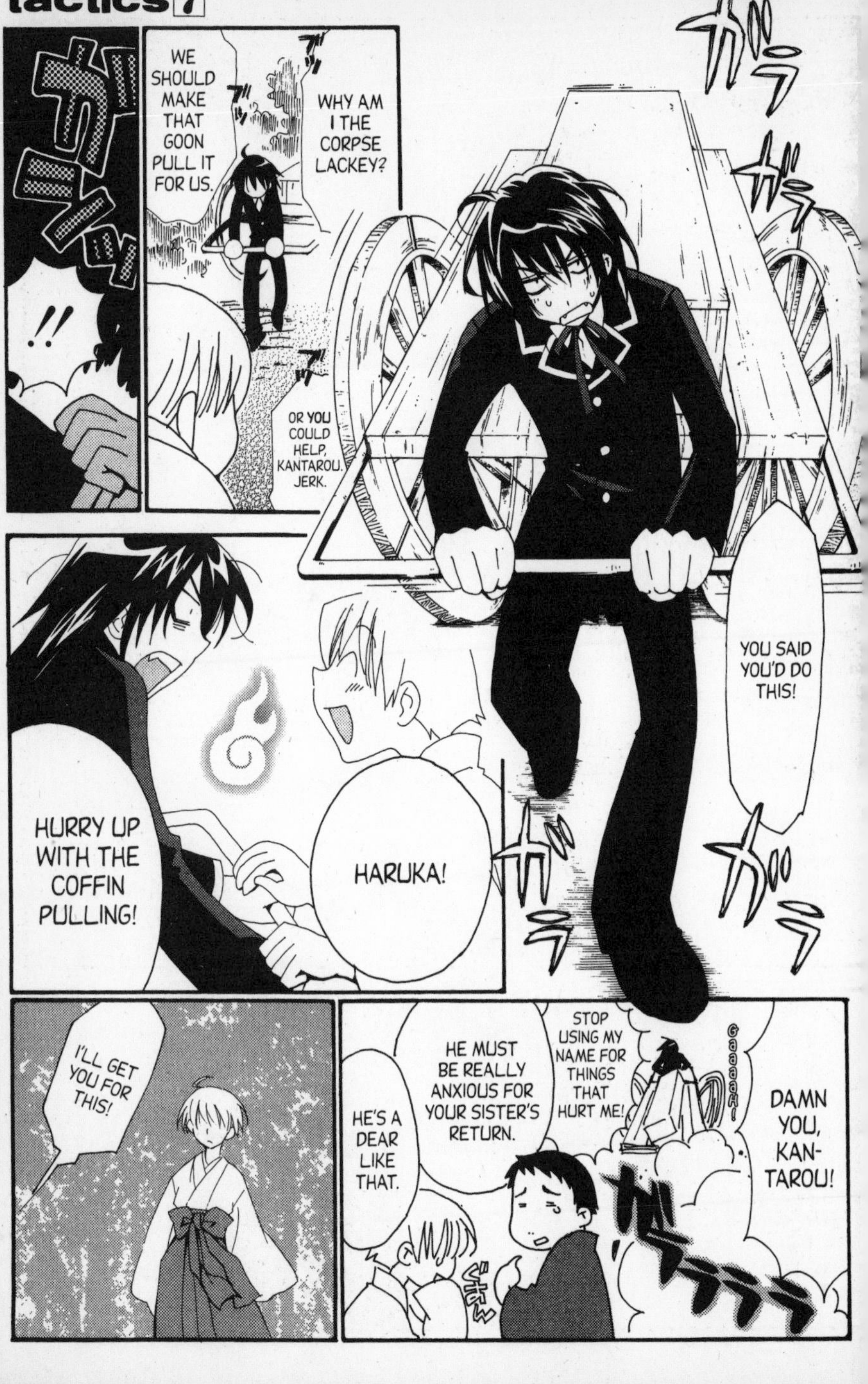
YOU SAID YOU'D DO THIS!
WHY AM I THE CORPSE LACKEY?
WE SHOULD MAKE THAT GOON PULL IT FOR US.
OR YOU COULD HELP, KANTAROU. JERK.
!!
HARUKA!
HURRY UP WITH THE COFFIN PULLING!
DAMN YOU, KAN-TAROU!
STOP USING MY NAME FOR THINGS THAT HURT ME!
HE MUST BE REALLY ANXIOUS FOR YOUR SISTER'S RETURN.
HE'S A DEAR LIKE THAT.
I'LL GET YOU FOR THIS!

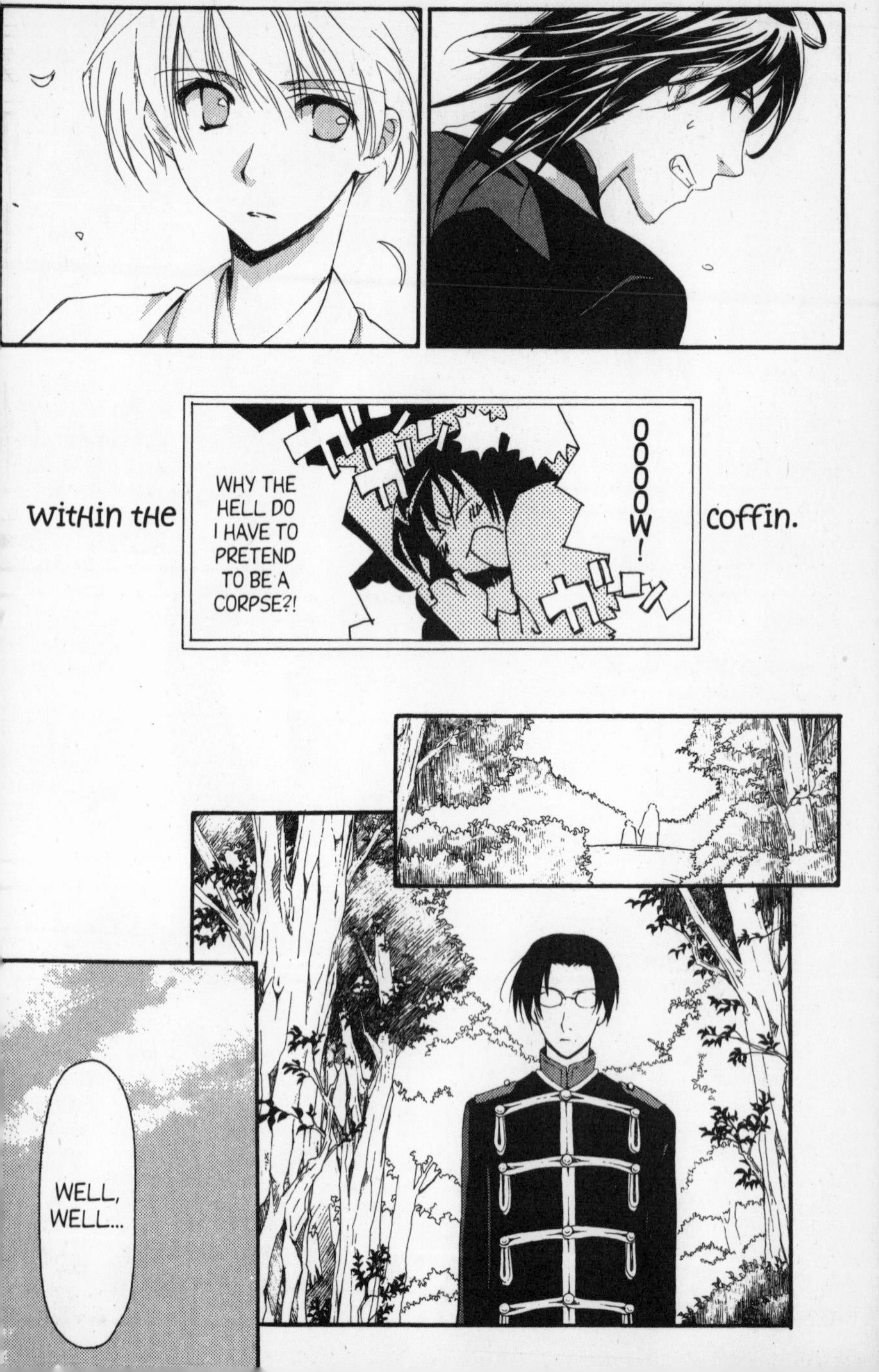
Within the coffin.
OOOOW!
WHY THE HELL DO I HAVE TO PRETEND TO BE A CORPSE?!
WELL, WELL...

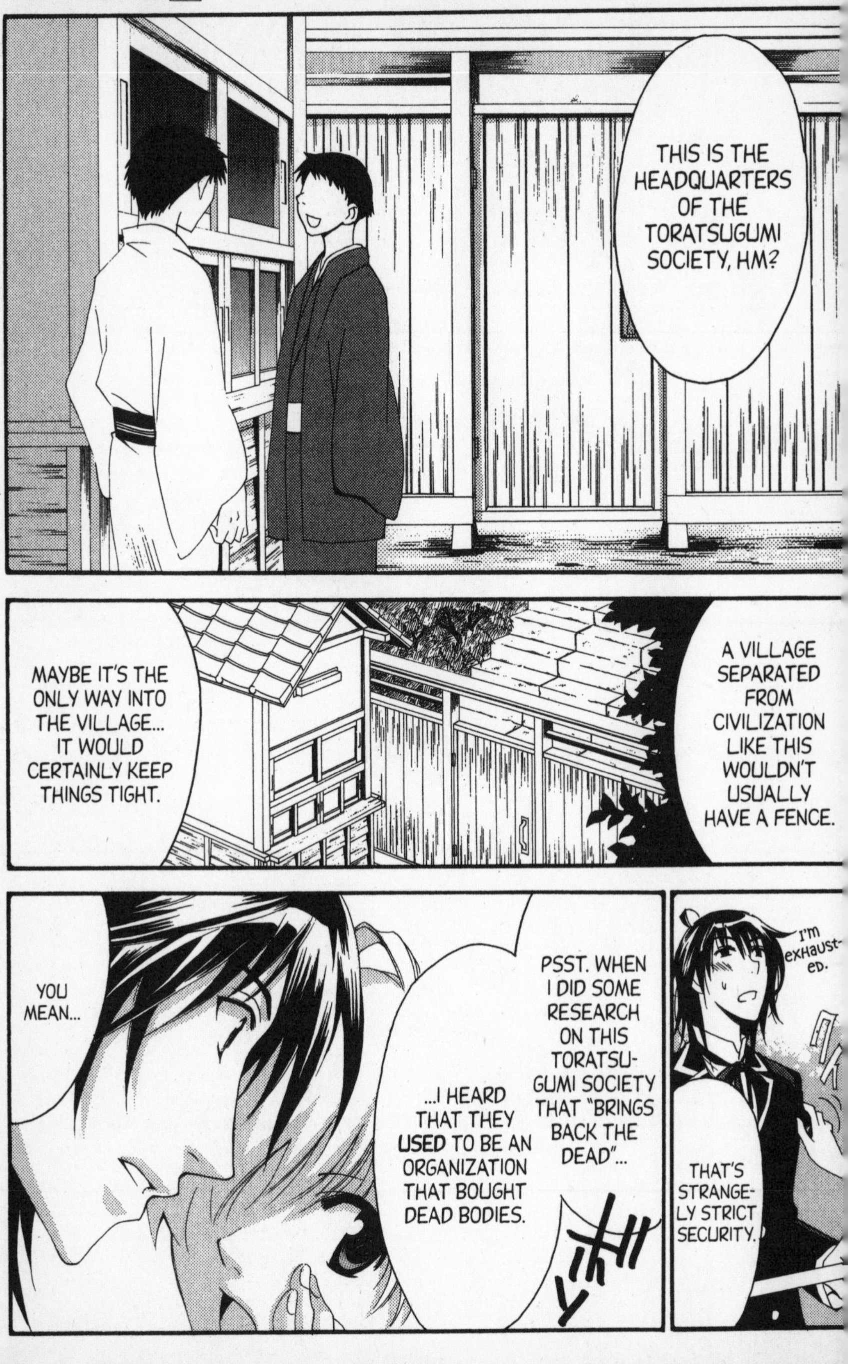
THIS IS THE HEADQUARTERS OF THE TORATSUGUMI SOCIETY, HM?
A VILLAGE SEPARATED FROM CIVILIZATION LIKE THIS WOULDN'T USUALLY HAVE A FENCE.
MAYBE IT'S THE ONLY WAY INTO THE VILLAGE... IT WOULD CERTAINLY KEEP THINGS TIGHT.
I'm exhaust-ed.
THAT'S STRANGE-LY STRICT SECURITY.
PSST. WHEN I DID SOME RESEARCH ON THIS TORATSU-GUMI SOCIETY THAT "BRINGS BACK THE DEAD"...
...I HEARD THAT THEY **USED** TO BE AN ORGANIZATION THAT BOUGHT DEAD BODIES.
YOU MEAN...

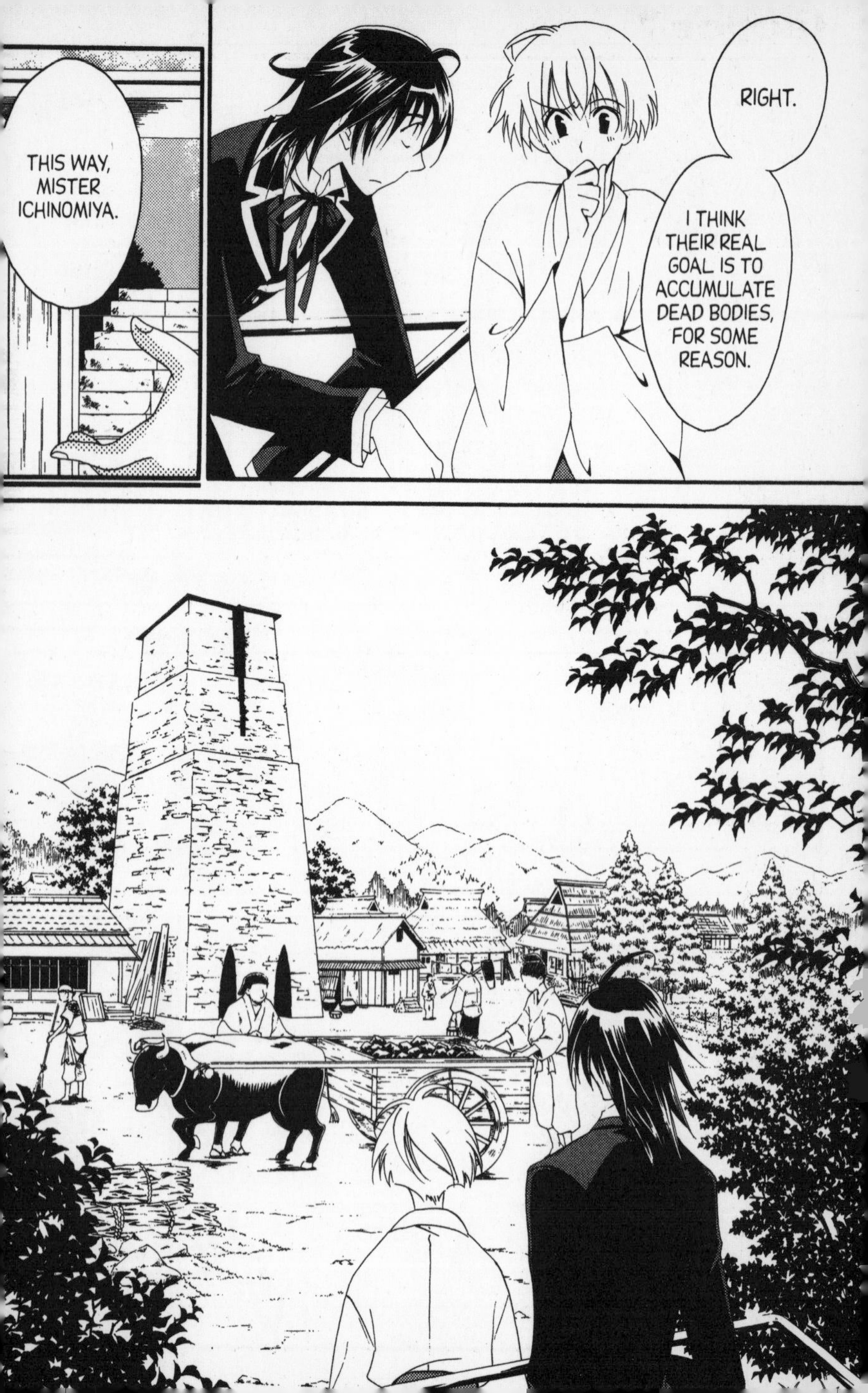
RIGHT.
I THINK THEIR REAL GOAL IS TO ACCUMULATE DEAD BODIES, FOR SOME REASON.
THIS WAY, MISTER ICHINOMIYA.

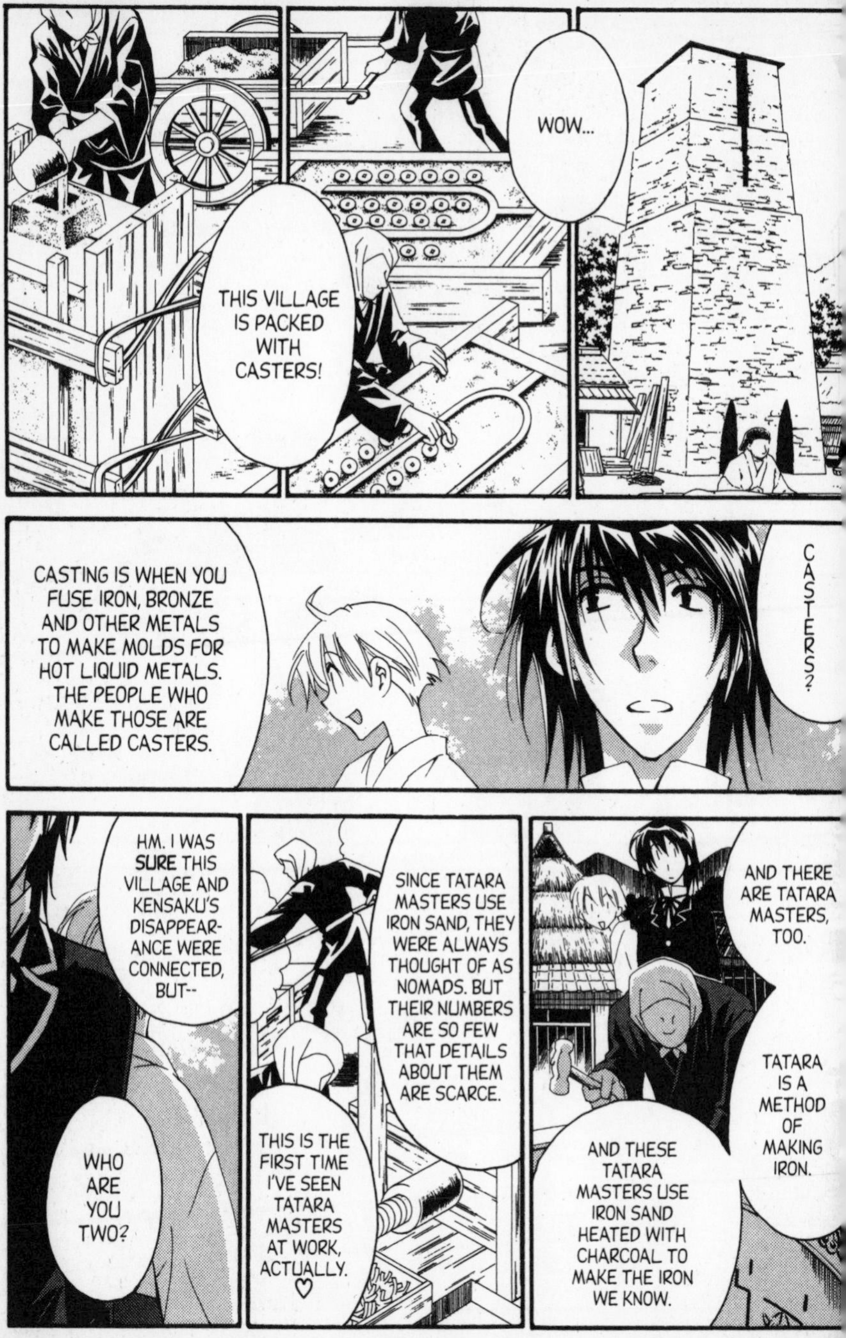
WOW...
THIS VILLAGE IS PACKED WITH CASTERS!
CASTERS?
CASTING IS WHEN YOU FUSE IRON, BRONZE AND OTHER METALS TO MAKE MOLDS FOR HOT LIQUID METALS. THE PEOPLE WHO MAKE THOSE ARE CALLED CASTERS.
AND THERE ARE TATARA MASTERS, TOO.
TATARA IS A METHOD OF MAKING IRON.
AND THESE TATARA MASTERS USE IRON SAND HEATED WITH CHARCOAL TO MAKE THE IRON WE KNOW.
SINCE TATARA MASTERS USE IRON SAND, THEY WERE ALWAYS THOUGHT OF AS NOMADS. BUT THEIR NUMBERS ARE SO FEW THAT DETAILS ABOUT THEM ARE SCARCE.
THIS IS THE FIRST TIME I'VE SEEN TATARA MASTERS AT WORK, ACTUALLY. ♡
HM. I WAS **SURE** THIS VILLAGE AND KENSAKU'S DISAPPEARANCE WERE CONNECTED, BUT--
WHO ARE YOU TWO?

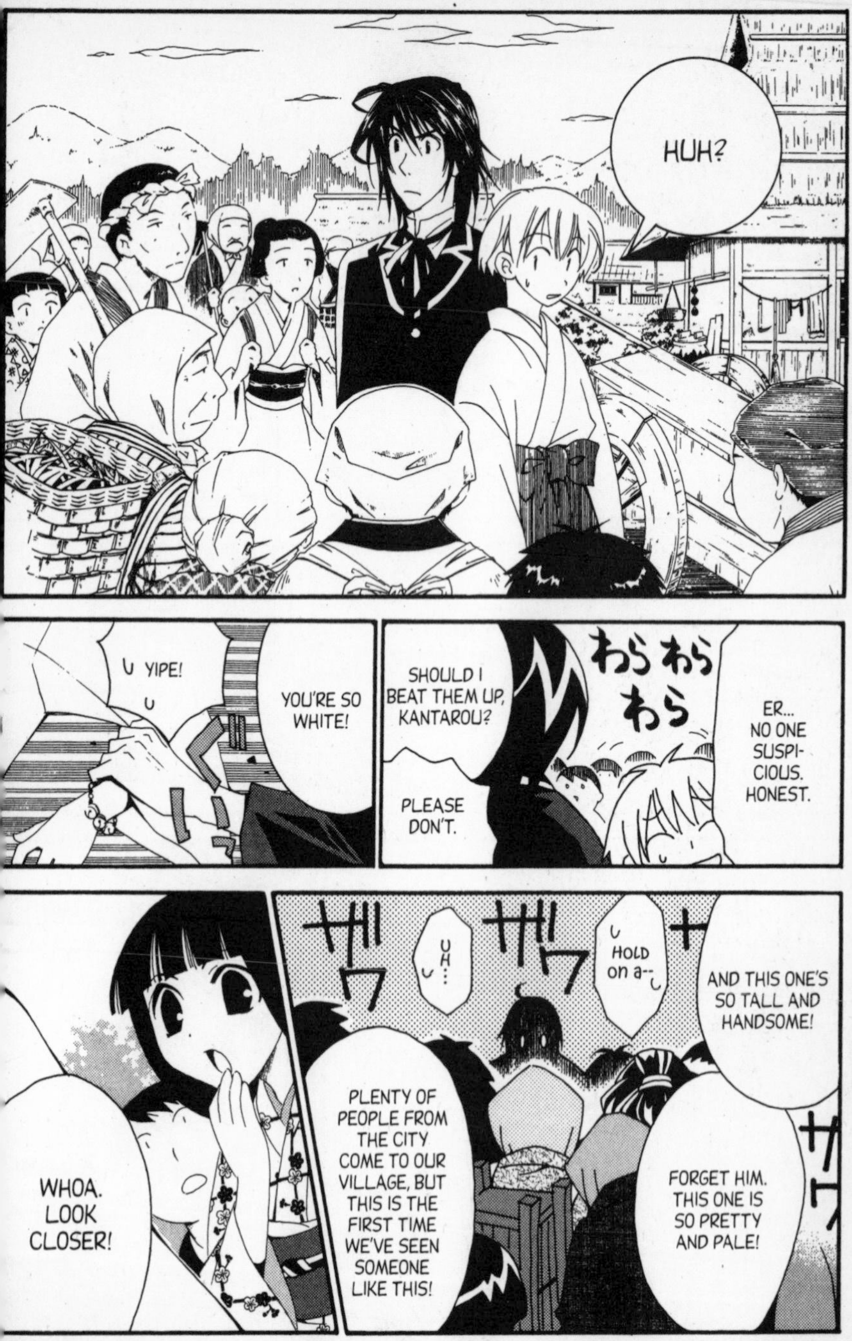
HUH?
わら わら わら
ER... NO ONE SUSPICIOUS. HONEST.
SHOULD I BEAT THEM UP, KANTAROU?
PLEASE DON'T.
YOU'RE SO WHITE!
YIPE!
AND THIS ONE'S SO TALL AND HANDSOME!
ザワ
HOLD ON A--
UH...
ザワ
ザワ
FORGET HIM. THIS ONE IS SO PRETTY AND PALE!
PLENTY OF PEOPLE FROM THE CITY COME TO OUR VILLAGE, BUT THIS IS THE FIRST TIME WE'VE SEEN SOMEONE LIKE THIS!
WHOA. LOOK CLOSER!

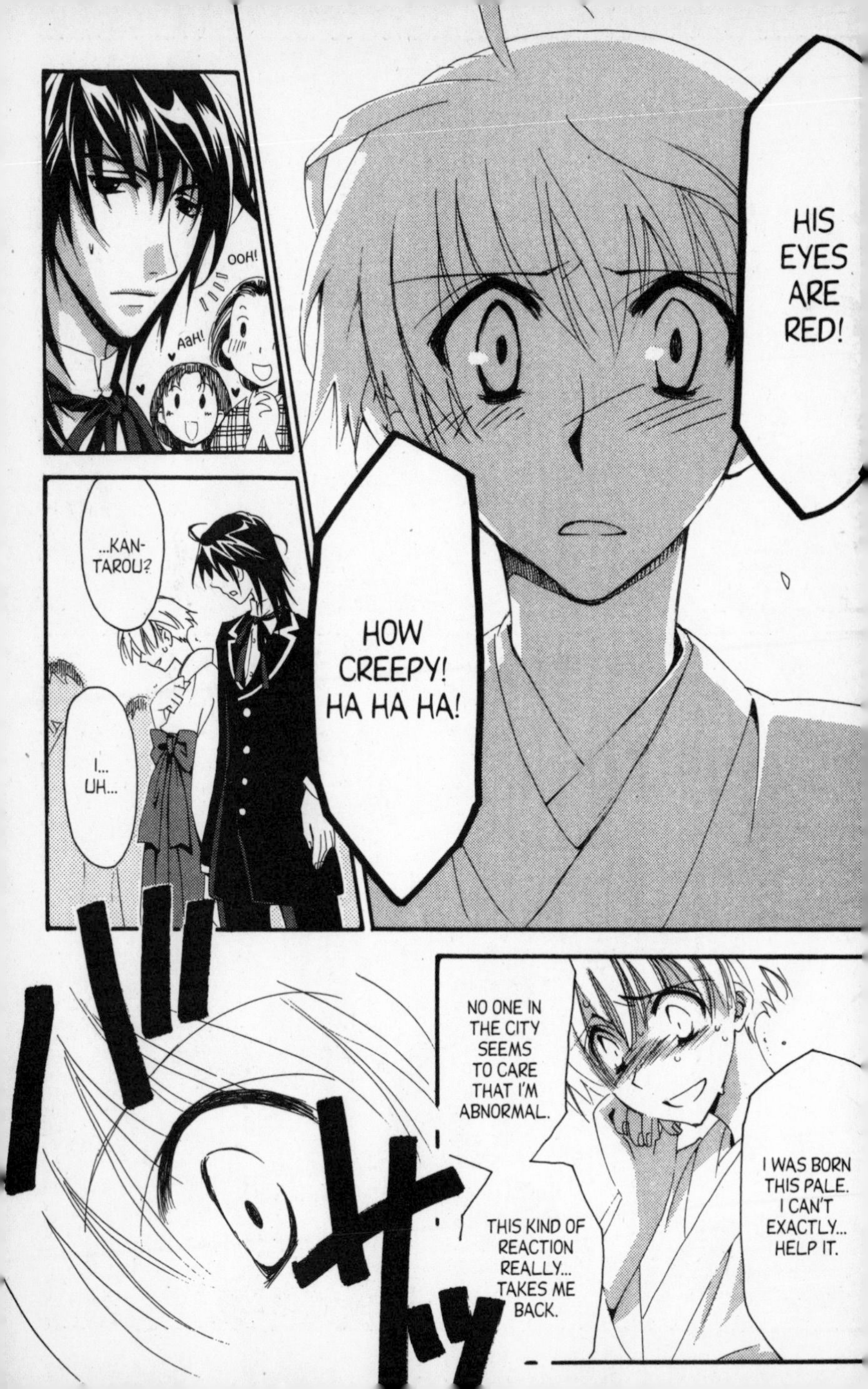
HIS EYES ARE RED!
HOW CREEPY! HA HA HA!
OOH!
AAH!
...KAN-TAROU?
I... UH...
I WAS BORN THIS PALE. I CAN'T EXACTLY... HELP IT.
NO ONE IN THE CITY SEEMS TO CARE THAT I'M ABNORMAL.
THIS KIND OF REACTION REALLY... TAKES ME BACK.

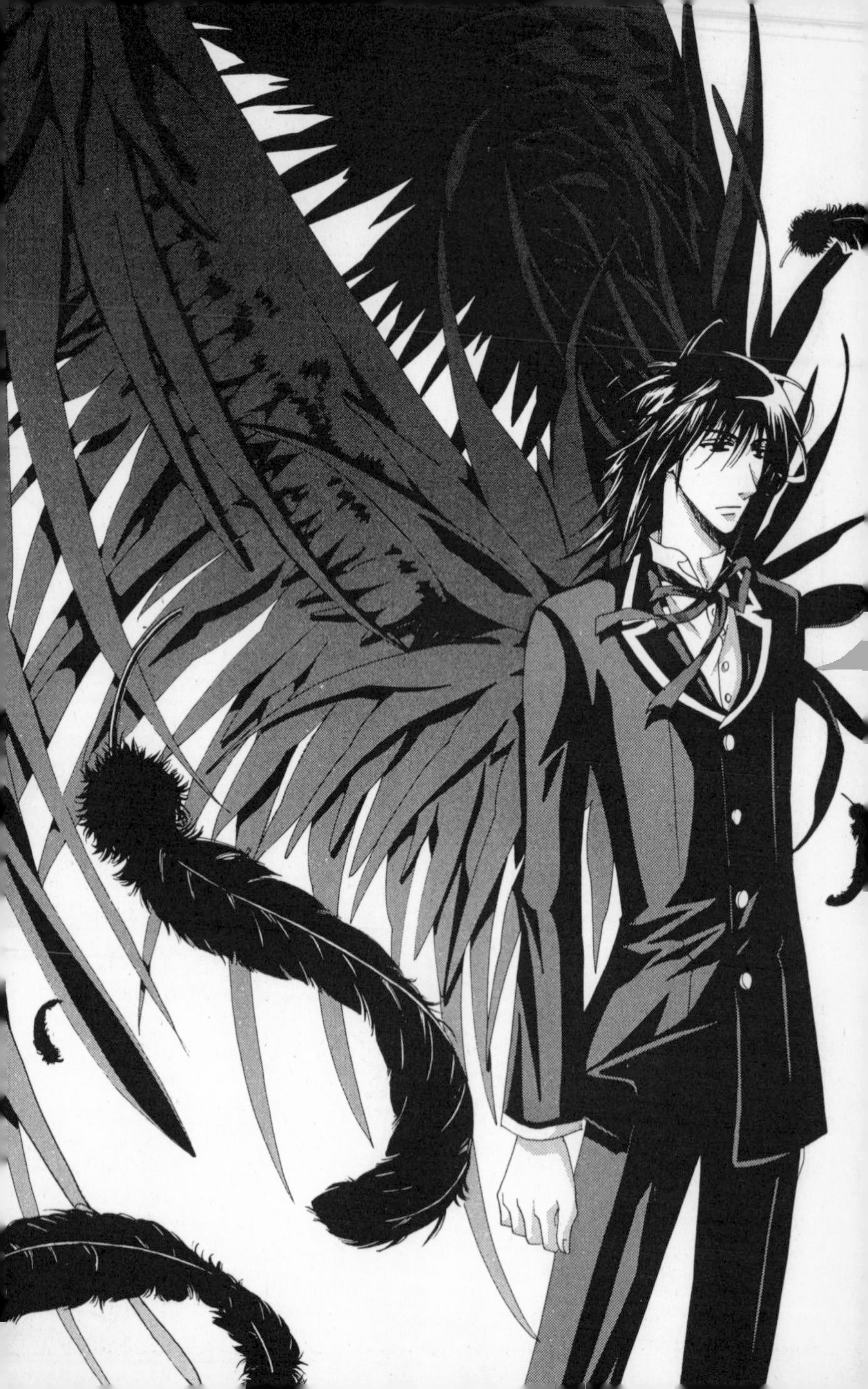

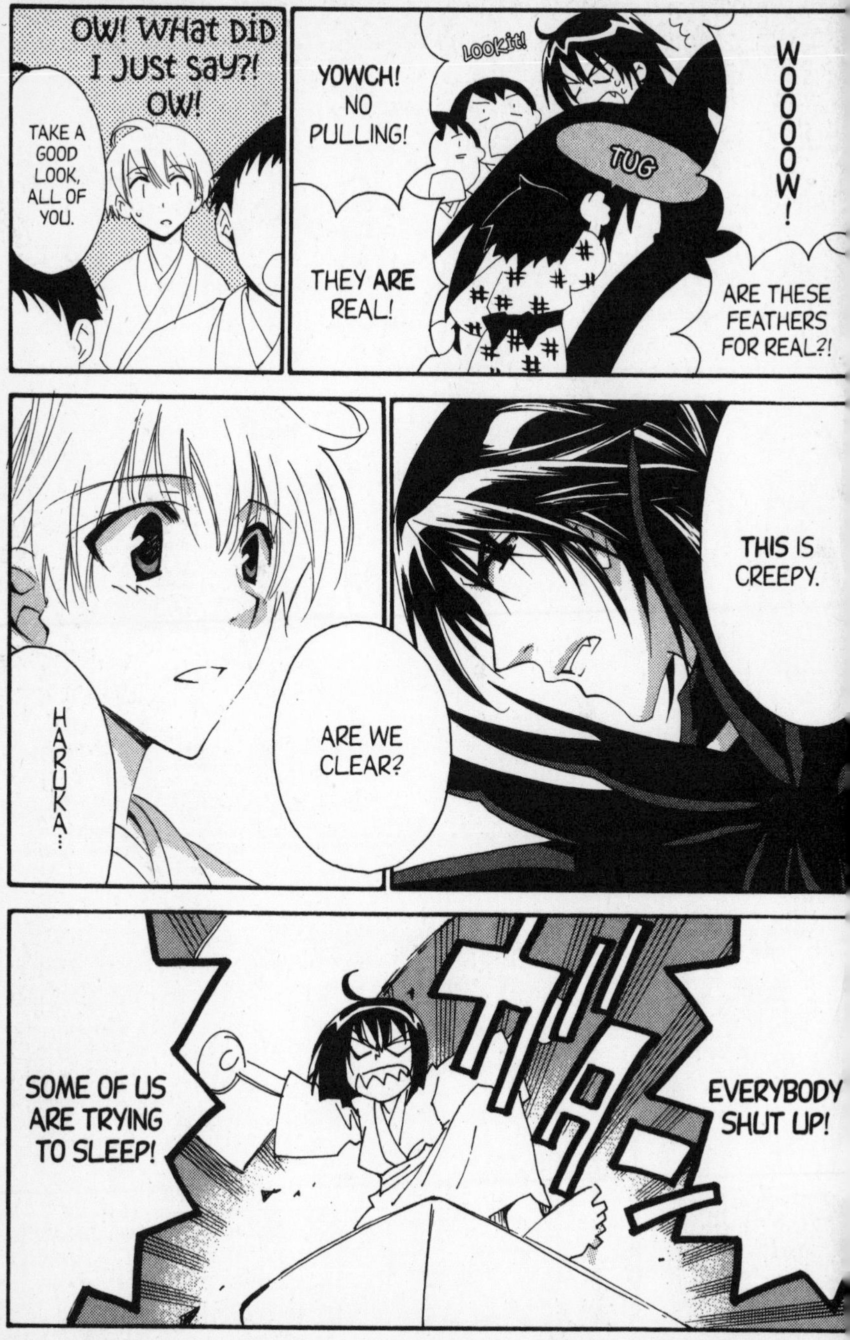
WOOOOW!
ARE THESE FEATHERS FOR REAL?!
TUG
LOOKIT!
YOWCH! NO PULLING!
THEY ARE REAL!
OW! WHAT DID I JUST SAY?! OW!
TAKE A GOOD LOOK, ALL OF YOU.
THIS IS CREEPY.
ARE WE CLEAR?
HARUKA...
EVERYBODY SHUT UP!
SOME OF US ARE TRYING TO SLEEP!

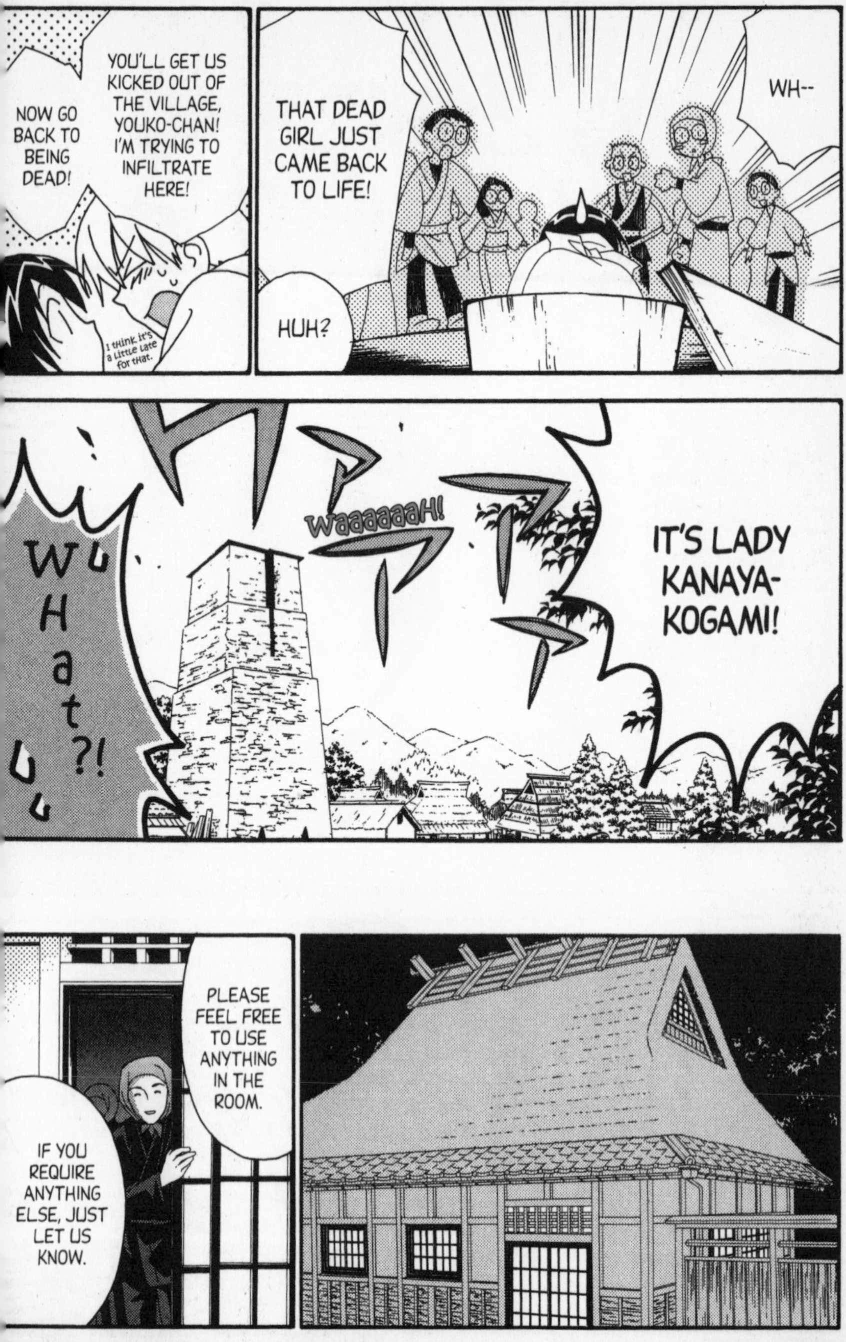
WH--
THAT DEAD GIRL JUST CAME BACK TO LIFE!
HUH?
YOU'LL GET US KICKED OUT OF THE VILLAGE, YOUKO-CHAN! I'M TRYING TO INFILTRATE HERE!
NOW GO BACK TO BEING DEAD!
I think it's a little late for that.
IT'S LADY KANAYA-KOGAMI!
WAAAAAAH!
WHAT?!
PLEASE FEEL FREE TO USE ANYTHING IN THE ROOM.
IF YOU REQUIRE ANYTHING ELSE, JUST LET US KNOW.

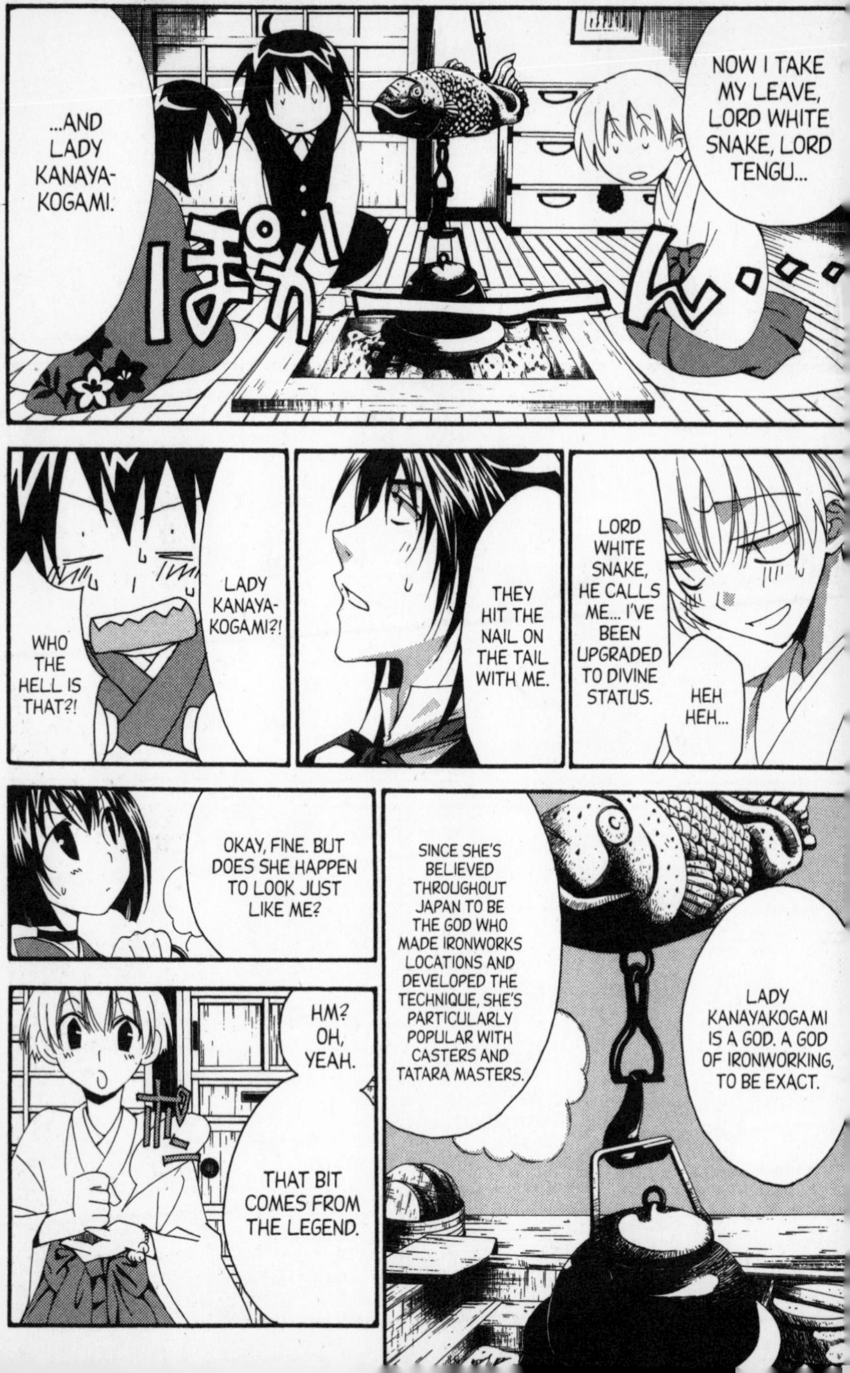
NOW I TAKE MY LEAVE, LORD WHITE SNAKE, LORD TENGU...
...AND LADY KANAYA-KOGAMI.
ぽわーん
LORD WHITE SNAKE, HE CALLS ME... I'VE BEEN UPGRADED TO DIVINE STATUS.
HEH HEH...
THEY HIT THE NAIL ON THE TAIL WITH ME.
LADY KANAYA-KOGAMI?!
WHO THE HELL IS THAT?!
LADY KANAYAKOGAMI IS A GOD. A GOD OF IRONWORKING, TO BE EXACT.
SINCE SHE'S BELIEVED THROUGHOUT JAPAN TO BE THE GOD WHO MADE IRONWORKS LOCATIONS AND DEVELOPED THE TECHNIQUE, SHE'S PARTICULARLY POPULAR WITH CASTERS AND TATARA MASTERS.
OKAY, FINE. BUT DOES SHE HAPPEN TO LOOK JUST LIKE ME?
HM? OH, YEAH.
THAT BIT COMES FROM THE LEGEND.

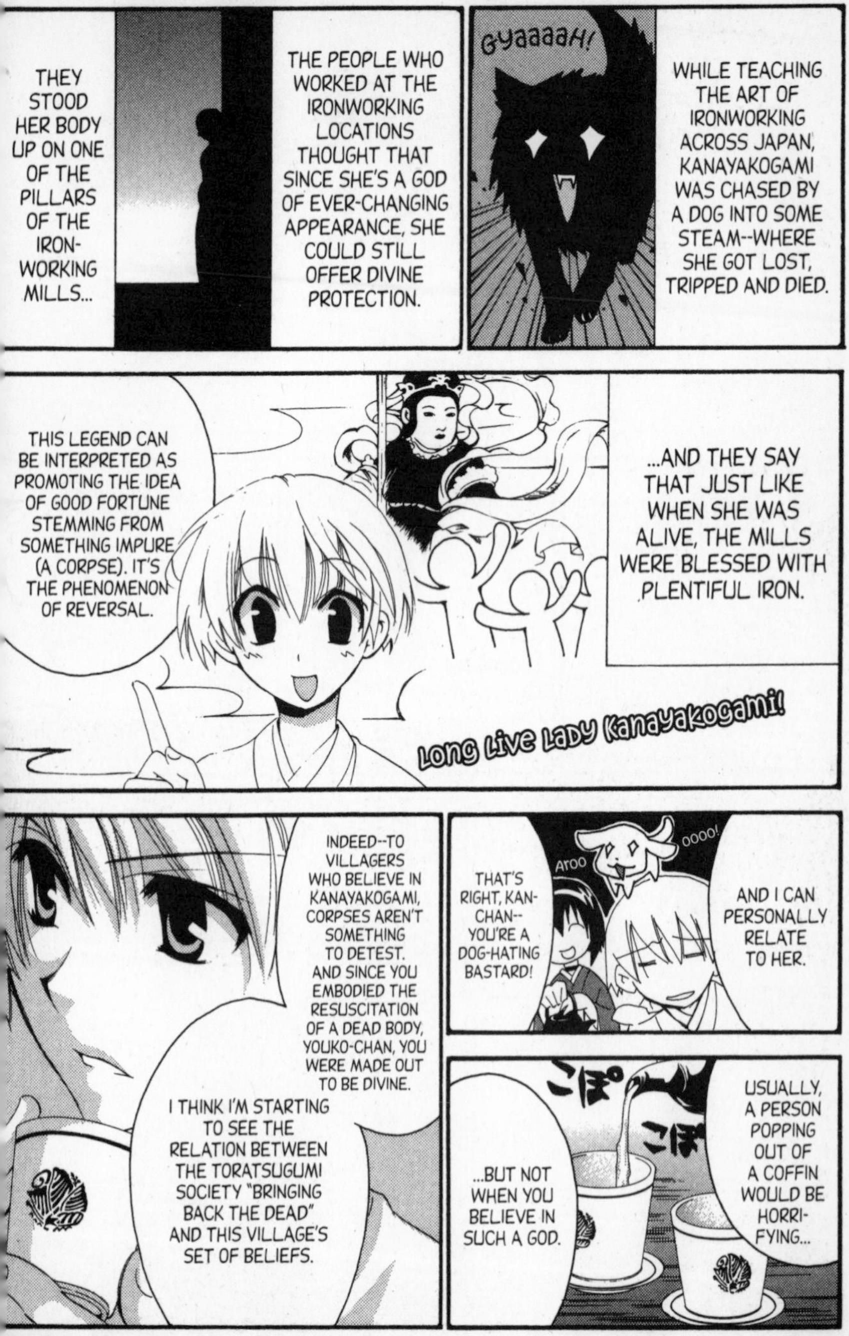
GYAAAAH!
WHILE TEACHING THE ART OF IRONWORKING ACROSS JAPAN, KANAYAKOGAMI WAS CHASED BY A DOG INTO SOME STEAM--WHERE SHE GOT LOST, TRIPPED AND DIED.
THE PEOPLE WHO WORKED AT THE IRONWORKING LOCATIONS THOUGHT THAT SINCE SHE'S A GOD OF EVER-CHANGING APPEARANCE, SHE COULD STILL OFFER DIVINE PROTECTION.
THEY STOOD HER BODY UP ON ONE OF THE PILLARS OF THE IRON-WORKING MILLS...
...AND THEY SAY THAT JUST LIKE WHEN SHE WAS ALIVE, THE MILLS WERE BLESSED WITH PLENTIFUL IRON.
Long Live Lady Kanayakogami!
THIS LEGEND CAN BE INTERPRETED AS PROMOTING THE IDEA OF GOOD FORTUNE STEMMING FROM SOMETHING IMPURE (A CORPSE). IT'S THE PHENOMENON OF REVERSAL.
AND I CAN PERSONALLY RELATE TO HER.
OOOO!
ATOO
THAT'S RIGHT, KAN-CHAN-- YOU'RE A DOG-HATING BASTARD!
USUALLY, A PERSON POPPING OUT OF A COFFIN WOULD BE HORRI-FYING...
こぽ
こぽ
...BUT NOT WHEN YOU BELIEVE IN SUCH A GOD.
INDEED--TO VILLAGERS WHO BELIEVE IN KANAYAKOGAMI, CORPSES AREN'T SOMETHING TO DETEST. AND SINCE YOU EMBODIED THE RESUSCITATION OF A DEAD BODY, YOUKO-CHAN, YOU WERE MADE OUT TO BE DIVINE.
I THINK I'M STARTING TO SEE THE RELATION BETWEEN THE TORATSUGUMI SOCIETY "BRINGING BACK THE DEAD" AND THIS VILLAGE'S SET OF BELIEFS.

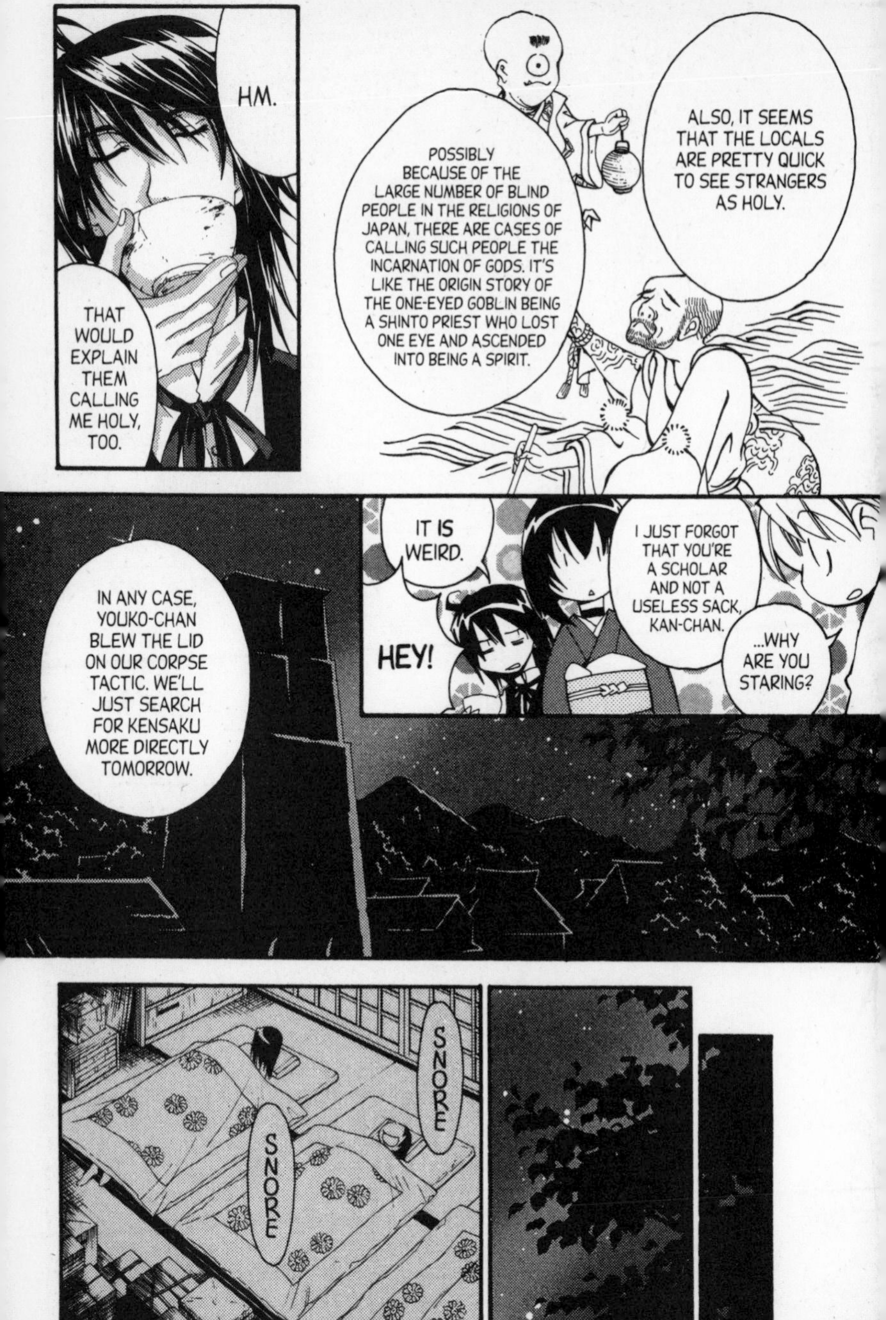
ALSO, IT SEEMS THAT THE LOCALS ARE PRETTY QUICK TO SEE STRANGERS AS HOLY.
POSSIBLY BECAUSE OF THE LARGE NUMBER OF BLIND PEOPLE IN THE RELIGIONS OF JAPAN, THERE ARE CASES OF CALLING SUCH PEOPLE THE INCARNATION OF GODS. IT'S LIKE THE ORIGIN STORY OF THE ONE-EYED GOBLIN BEING A SHINTO PRIEST WHO LOST ONE EYE AND ASCENDED INTO BEING A SPIRIT.
HM.
THAT WOULD EXPLAIN THEM CALLING ME HOLY, TOO.
IT IS WEIRD.
HEY!
I JUST FORGOT THAT YOU'RE A SCHOLAR AND NOT A USELESS SACK, KAN-CHAN.
...WHY ARE YOU STARING?
IN ANY CASE, YOUKO-CHAN BLEW THE LID ON OUR CORPSE TACTIC. WE'LL JUST SEARCH FOR KENSAKU MORE DIRECTLY TOMORROW.
SNORE
SNORE

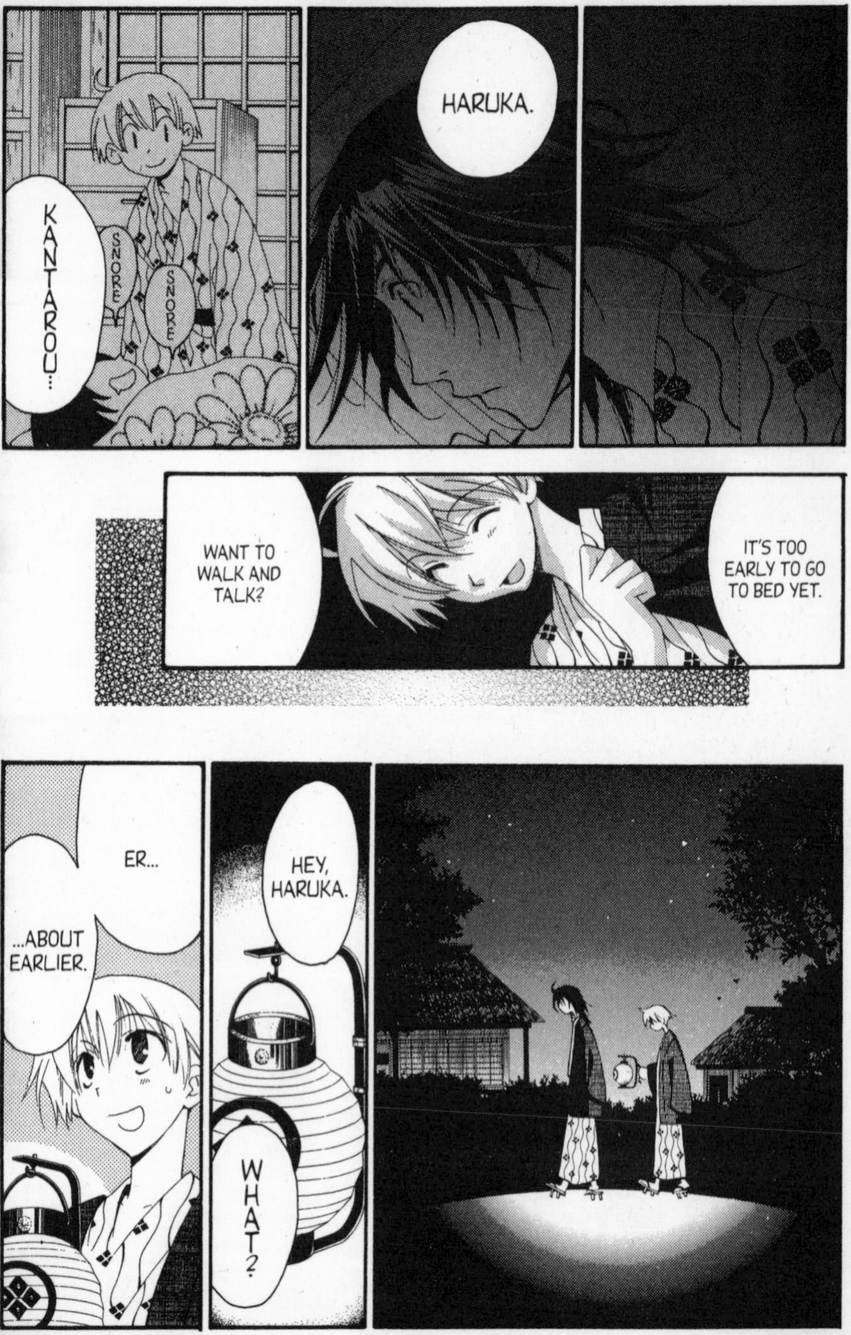
HARUKA.
SNORE
SNORE
KANTAROU...
IT'S TOO EARLY TO GO TO BED YET.
WANT TO WALK AND TALK?
HEY, HARUKA.
WHAT?
ER...
...ABOUT EARLIER.

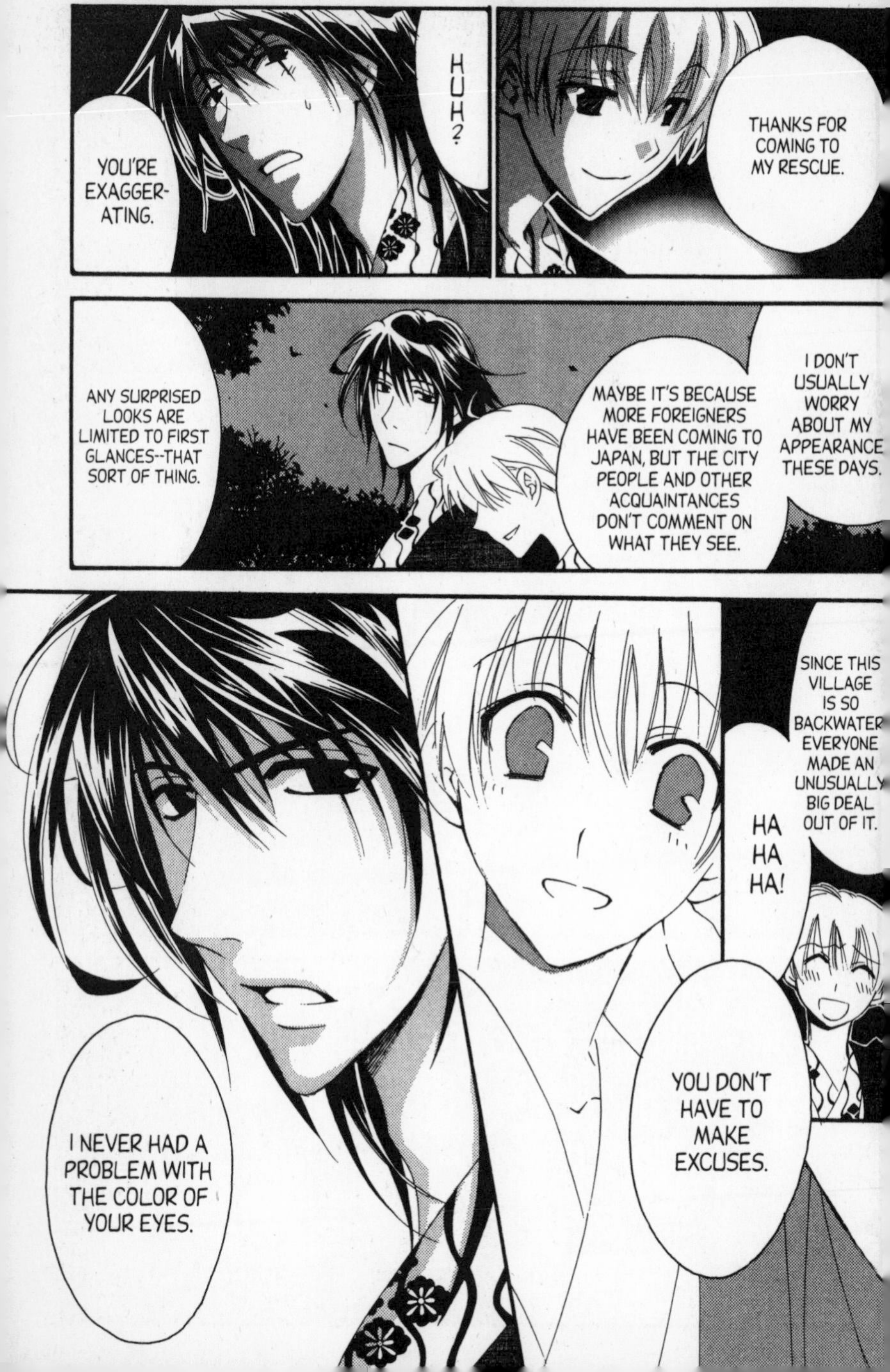
THANKS FOR COMING TO MY RESCUE.
HUH?
YOU'RE EXAGGER-ATING.
I DON'T USUALLY WORRY ABOUT MY APPEARANCE THESE DAYS.
MAYBE IT'S BECAUSE MORE FOREIGNERS HAVE BEEN COMING TO JAPAN, BUT THE CITY PEOPLE AND OTHER ACQUAINTANCES DON'T COMMENT ON WHAT THEY SEE.
ANY SURPRISED LOOKS ARE LIMITED TO FIRST GLANCES--THAT SORT OF THING.
SINCE THIS VILLAGE IS SO BACKWATER EVERYONE MADE AN UNUSUALLY BIG DEAL OUT OF IT.
HA HA HA!
YOU DON'T HAVE TO MAKE EXCUSES.
I NEVER HAD A PROBLEM WITH THE COLOR OF YOUR EYES.

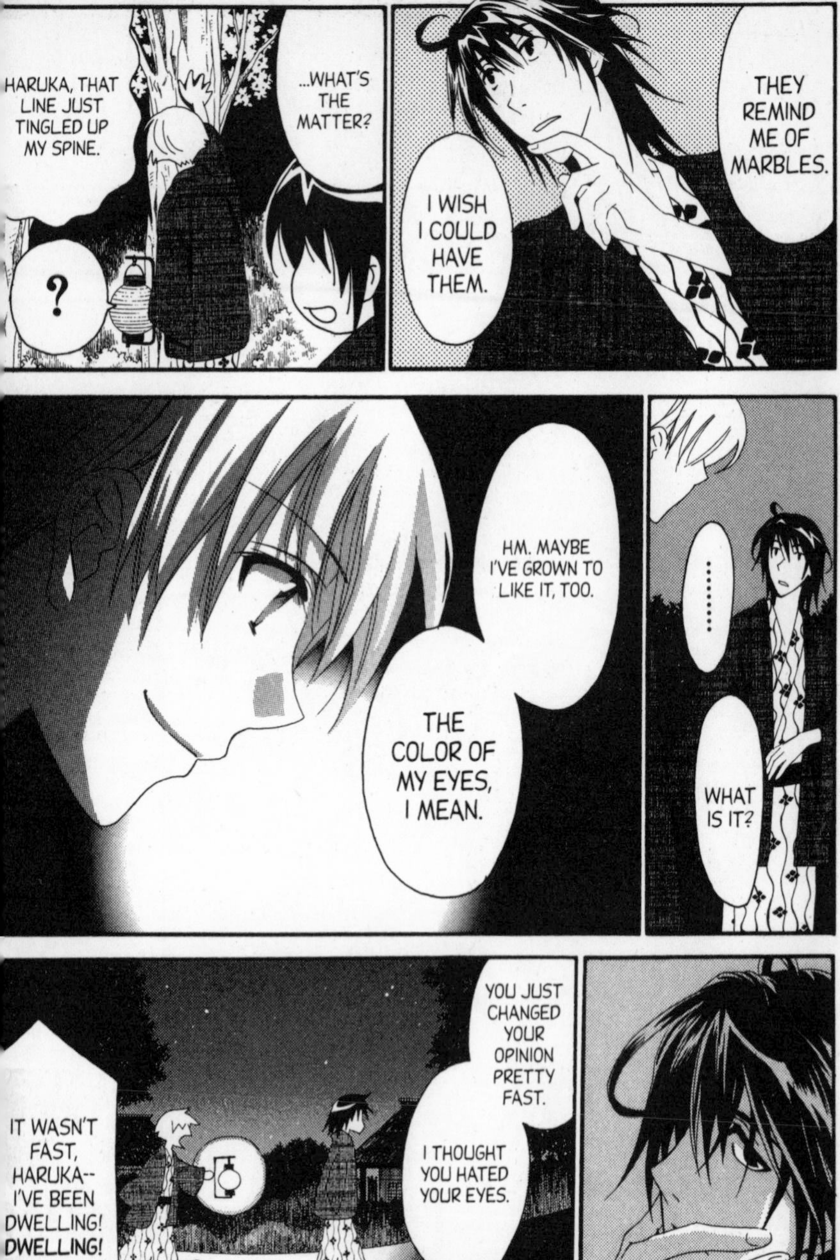
THEY REMIND ME OF MARBLES.
I WISH I COULD HAVE THEM.
...WHAT'S THE MATTER?
HARUKA, THAT LINE JUST TINGLED UP MY SPINE.
?
....
WHAT IS IT?
HM. MAYBE I'VE GROWN TO LIKE IT, TOO.
THE COLOR OF MY EYES, I MEAN.
YOU JUST CHANGED YOUR OPINION PRETTY FAST.
I THOUGHT YOU HATED YOUR EYES.
IT WASN'T FAST, HARUKA-- I'VE BEEN DWELLING! **DWELLING!**

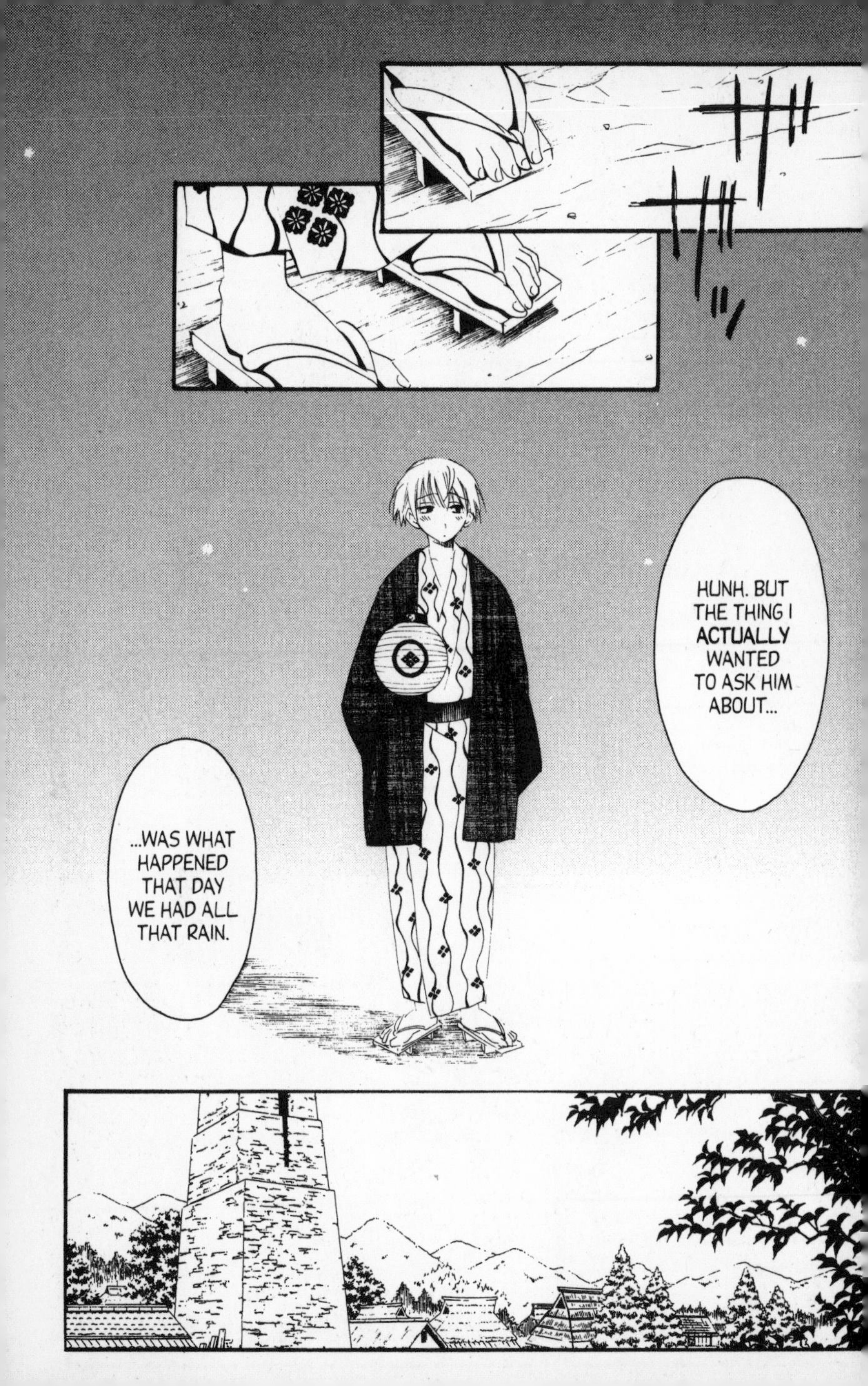
HUNH. BUT THE THING I ACTUALLY WANTED TO ASK HIM ABOUT...
...WAS WHAT HAPPENED THAT DAY WE HAD ALL THAT RAIN.

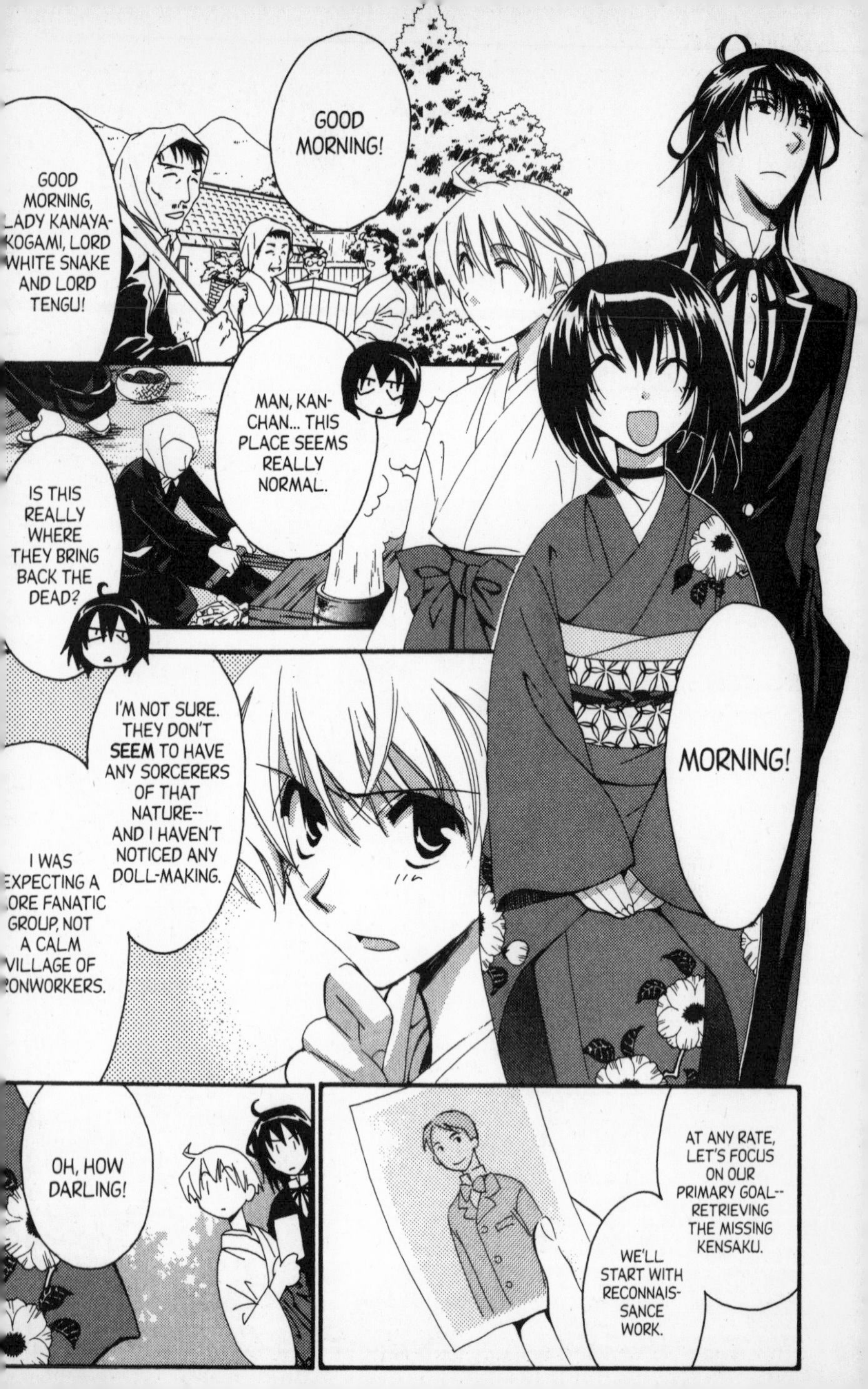
GOOD MORNING, LADY KANAYA-KOGAMI, LORD WHITE SNAKE AND LORD TENGU!
GOOD MORNING!
MORNING!
MAN, KAN-CHAN... THIS PLACE SEEMS REALLY NORMAL.
IS THIS REALLY WHERE THEY BRING BACK THE DEAD?
I'M NOT SURE. THEY DON'T **SEEM** TO HAVE ANY SORCERERS OF THAT NATURE-- AND I HAVEN'T NOTICED ANY DOLL-MAKING.
I WAS EXPECTING A ORE FANATIC GROUP, NOT A CALM VILLAGE OF ONWORKERS.
AT ANY RATE, LET'S FOCUS ON OUR PRIMARY GOAL-- RETRIEVING THE MISSING KENSAKU.
WE'LL START WITH RECONNAIS-SANCE WORK.
OH, HOW DARLING!

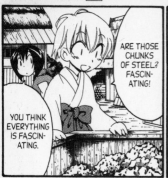

LOOK AT THAT LOVELY LITTLE KATANA! WHO LOVES YOU KATANA!
It looks so expensive! ♡
ARE THOSE CHUNKS OF STEEL? FASCINATING!
YOU THINK EVERYTHING IS FASCINATING.
HUSH, YOUKO-CHAN. STEEL CHUNKS LIKE THIS ARE THE BASE MATERIAL FOR JAPANESE SWORDS. THEY'RE VERY DIFFICULT TO MAKE.
IT'S WHY THEY'RE CURRENTLY BEING TRADED TO FOREIGN COUNTRIES IN EXCHANGE FOR WESTERN IRON.
YOU ARE VERY INFORMED MY LORD
WELL, I'M NO EXPERT.
HM? WHAT'S WRITTEN ON THESE KATANA?
Teigorou Sakatou
Kamematsu Suzuki
Tomonomatsu Okita
Kinu Takeda
DOES SOMETHING TROUBLE YOU?
WELL, WELL! SO YOU THREE ARE THE LIVING GODS!
......

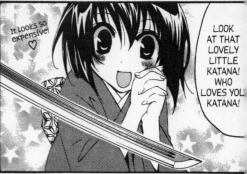

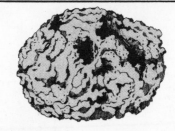

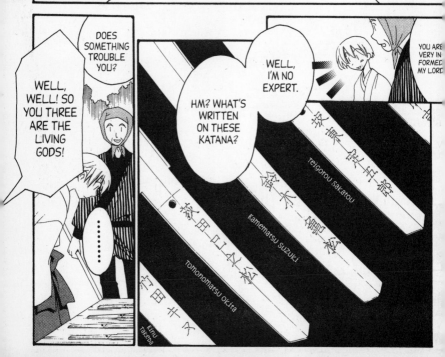

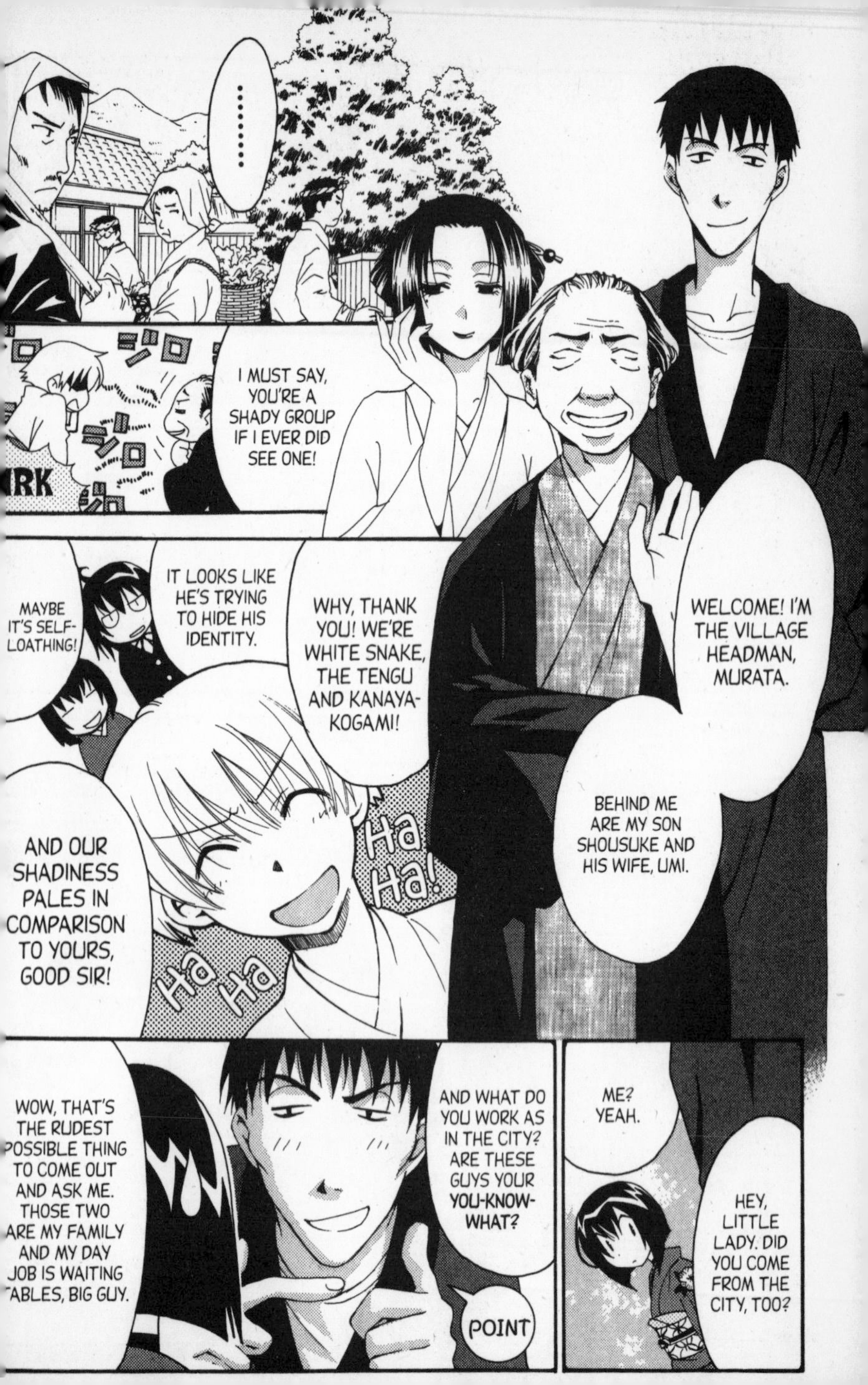
WELCOME! I'M THE VILLAGE HEADMAN, MURATA.
BEHIND ME ARE MY SON SHOUSUKE AND HIS WIFE, UMI.
......
I MUST SAY, YOU'RE A SHADY GROUP IF I EVER DID SEE ONE!
RK
WHY, THANK YOU! WE'RE WHITE SNAKE, THE TENGU AND KANAYA-KOGAMI!
IT LOOKS LIKE HE'S TRYING TO HIDE HIS IDENTITY.
MAYBE IT'S SELF-LOATHING!
Ha Ha!
AND OUR SHADINESS PALES IN COMPARISON TO YOURS, GOOD SIR!
Ha Ha
HEY, LITTLE LADY. DID YOU COME FROM THE CITY, TOO?
ME? YEAH.
AND WHAT DO YOU WORK AS IN THE CITY? ARE THESE GUYS YOUR YOU-KNOW-WHAT?
POINT
WOW, THAT'S THE RUDEST POSSIBLE THING TO COME OUT AND ASK ME. THOSE TWO ARE MY FAMILY AND MY DAY JOB IS WAITING TABLES, BIG GUY.

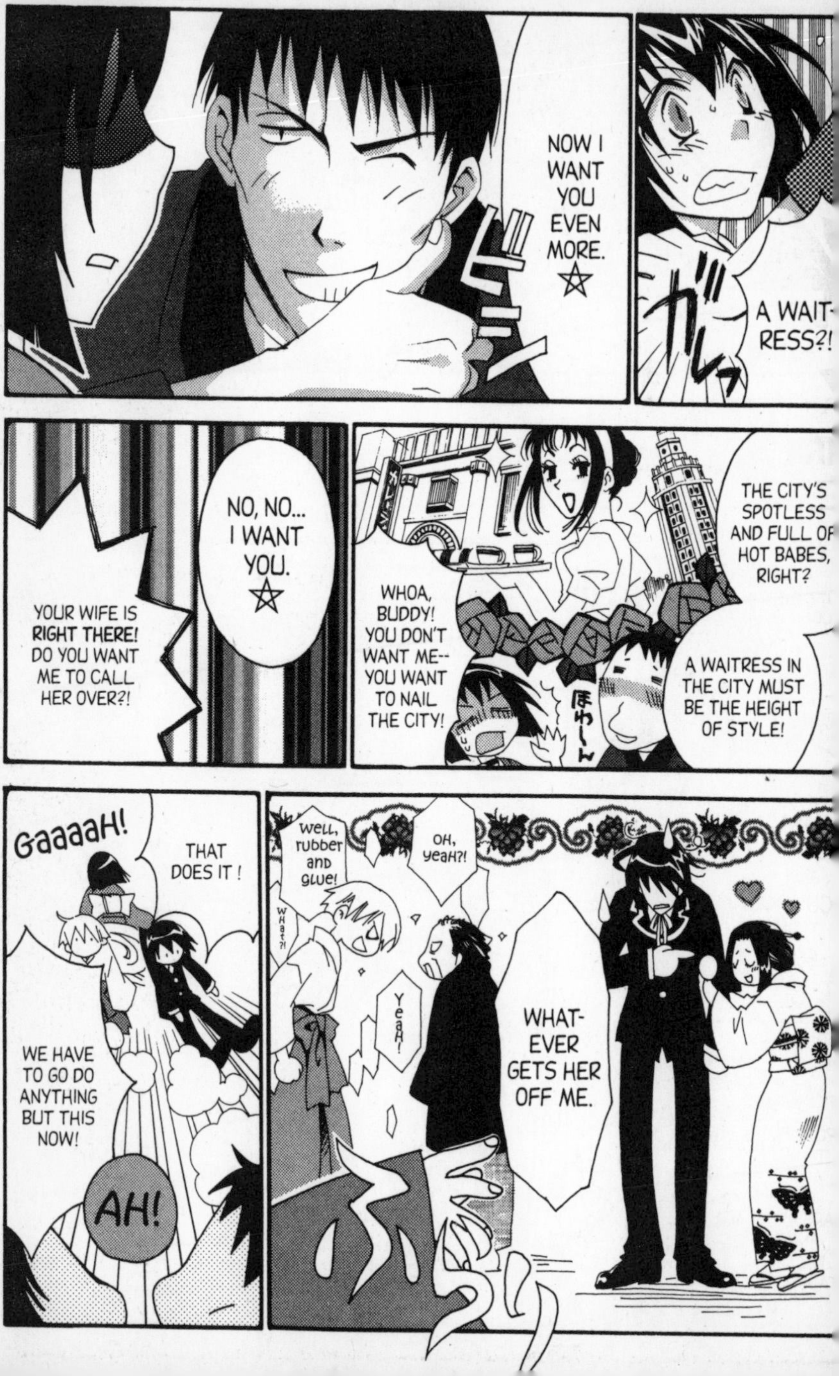
A WAIT-RESS?!
NOW I WANT YOU EVEN MORE. ☆
THE CITY'S SPOTLESS AND FULL OF HOT BABES, RIGHT?
A WAITRESS IN THE CITY MUST BE THE HEIGHT OF STYLE!
ほわ～ん
WHOA, BUDDY! YOU DON'T WANT ME-- YOU WANT TO NAIL THE CITY!
NO, NO... I WANT YOU. ☆
YOUR WIFE IS RIGHT THERE! DO YOU WANT ME TO CALL HER OVER?!
OH, yeah?!
Well, rubber and glue!
What?!
Yeah!
WHAT-EVER GETS HER OFF ME.
THAT DOES IT !
GaaaaH!
WE HAVE TO GO DO ANYTHING BUT THIS NOW!
AH!

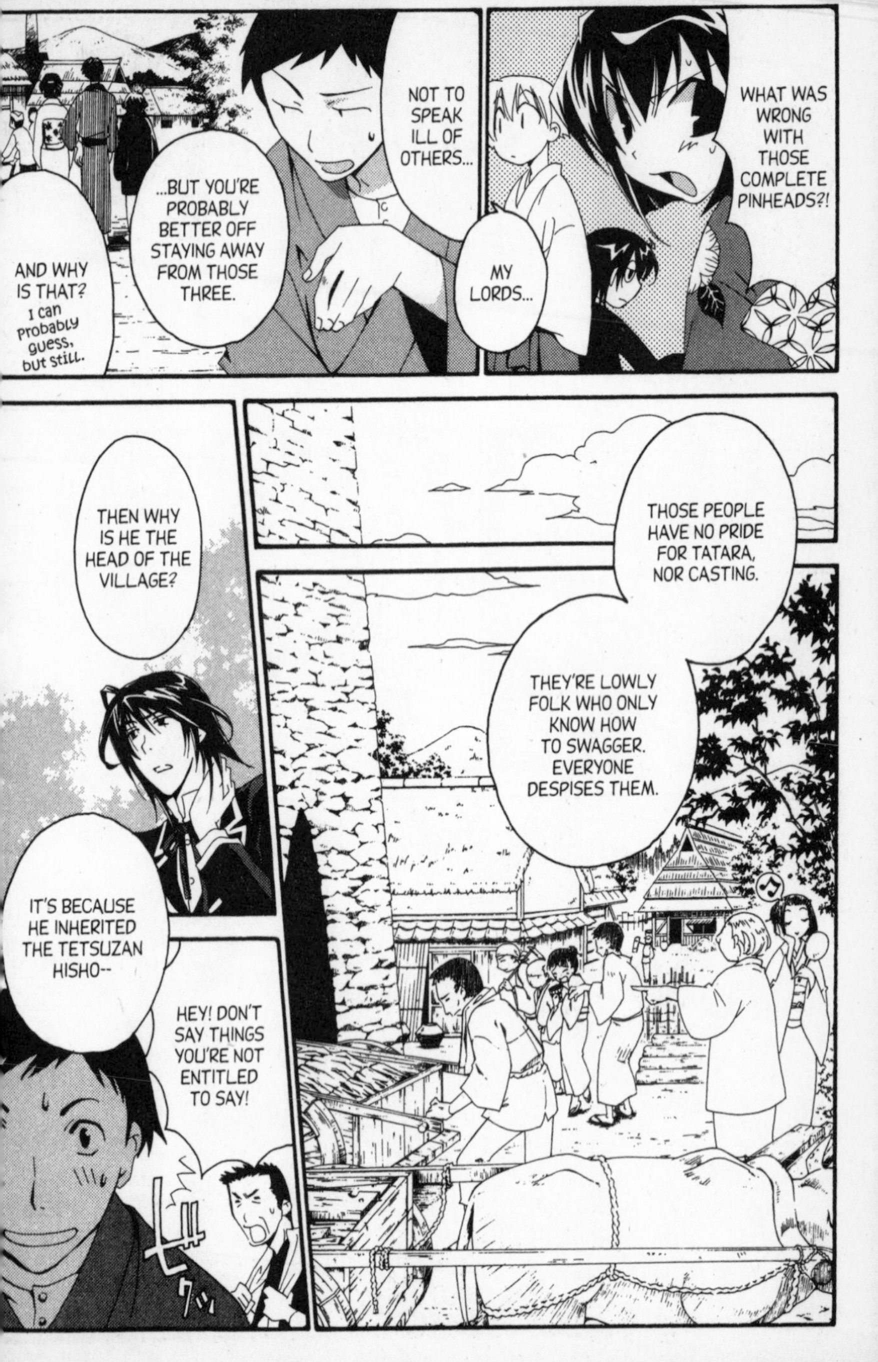
WHAT WAS WRONG WITH THOSE COMPLETE PINHEADS?!
MY LORDS...
NOT TO SPEAK ILL OF OTHERS...
...BUT YOU'RE PROBABLY BETTER OFF STAYING AWAY FROM THOSE THREE.
AND WHY IS THAT?
I can probably guess, but still.
THOSE PEOPLE HAVE NO PRIDE FOR TATARA, NOR CASTING.
THEY'RE LOWLY FOLK WHO ONLY KNOW HOW TO SWAGGER. EVERYONE DESPISES THEM.
THEN WHY IS HE THE HEAD OF THE VILLAGE?
IT'S BECAUSE HE INHERITED THE TETSUZAN HISHO--
HEY! DON'T SAY THINGS YOU'RE NOT ENTITLED TO SAY!

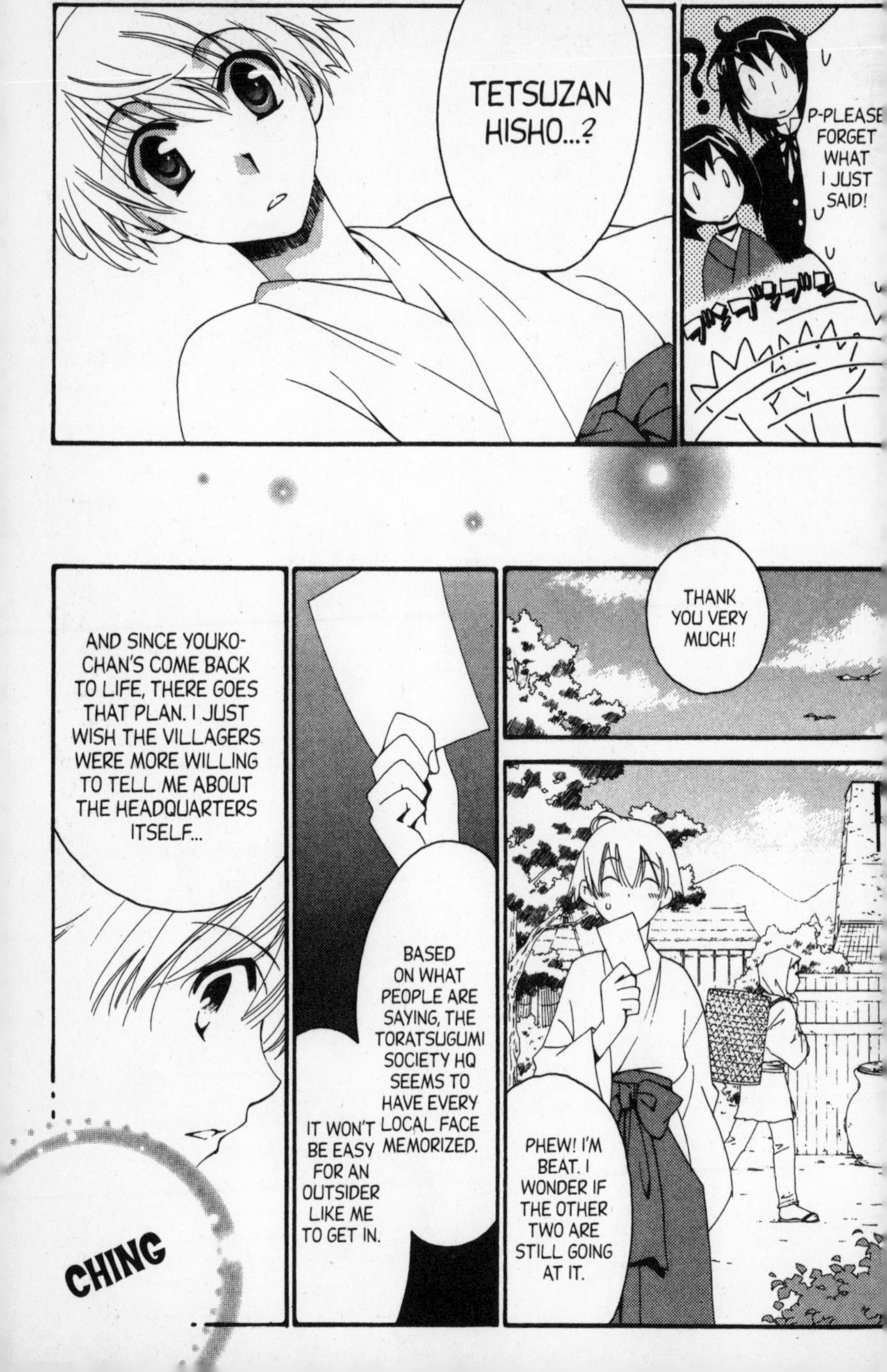
P-PLEASE FORGET WHAT I JUST SAID!
TETSUZAN HISHO...?
THANK YOU VERY MUCH!
PHEW! I'M BEAT. I WONDER IF THE OTHER TWO ARE STILL GOING AT IT.
BASED ON WHAT PEOPLE ARE SAYING, THE TORATSUGUMI SOCIETY HQ SEEMS TO HAVE EVERY LOCAL FACE MEMORIZED.
IT WON'T BE EASY FOR AN OUTSIDER LIKE ME TO GET IN.
AND SINCE YOUKO-CHAN'S COME BACK TO LIFE, THERE GOES THAT PLAN. I JUST WISH THE VILLAGERS WERE MORE WILLING TO TELL ME ABOUT THE HEADQUARTERS ITSELF...
CHING

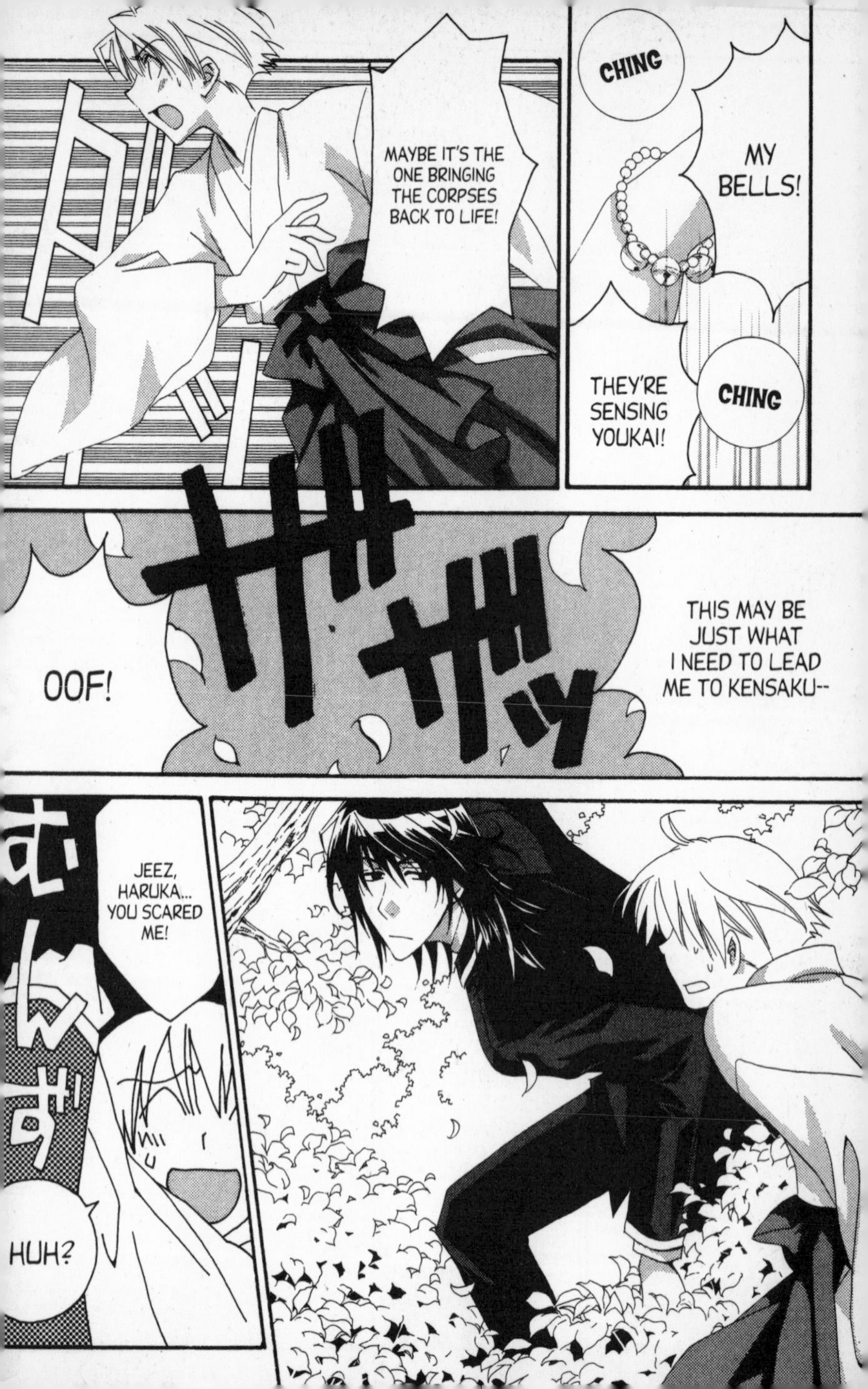
CHING
MY BELLS!
CHING
THEY'RE SENSING YOUKAI!
MAYBE IT'S THE ONE BRINGING THE CORPSES BACK TO LIFE!
THIS MAY BE JUST WHAT I NEED TO LEAD ME TO KENSAKU--
ザザッ
OOF!
むんず
JEEZ, HARUKA... YOU SCARED ME!
HUH?

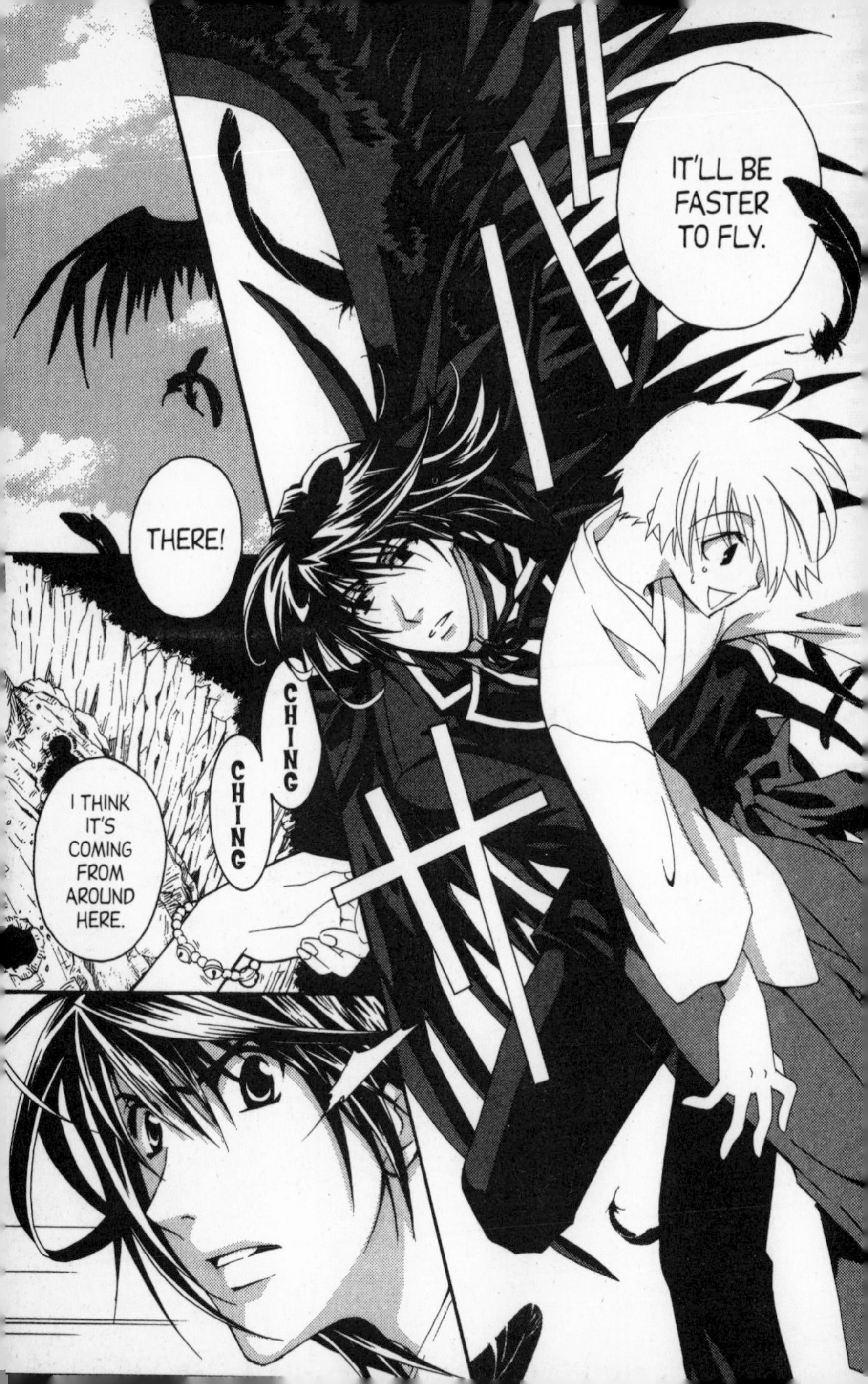
IT'LL BE FASTER TO FLY.
THERE!
CHING
CHING
I THINK IT'S COMING FROM AROUND HERE.

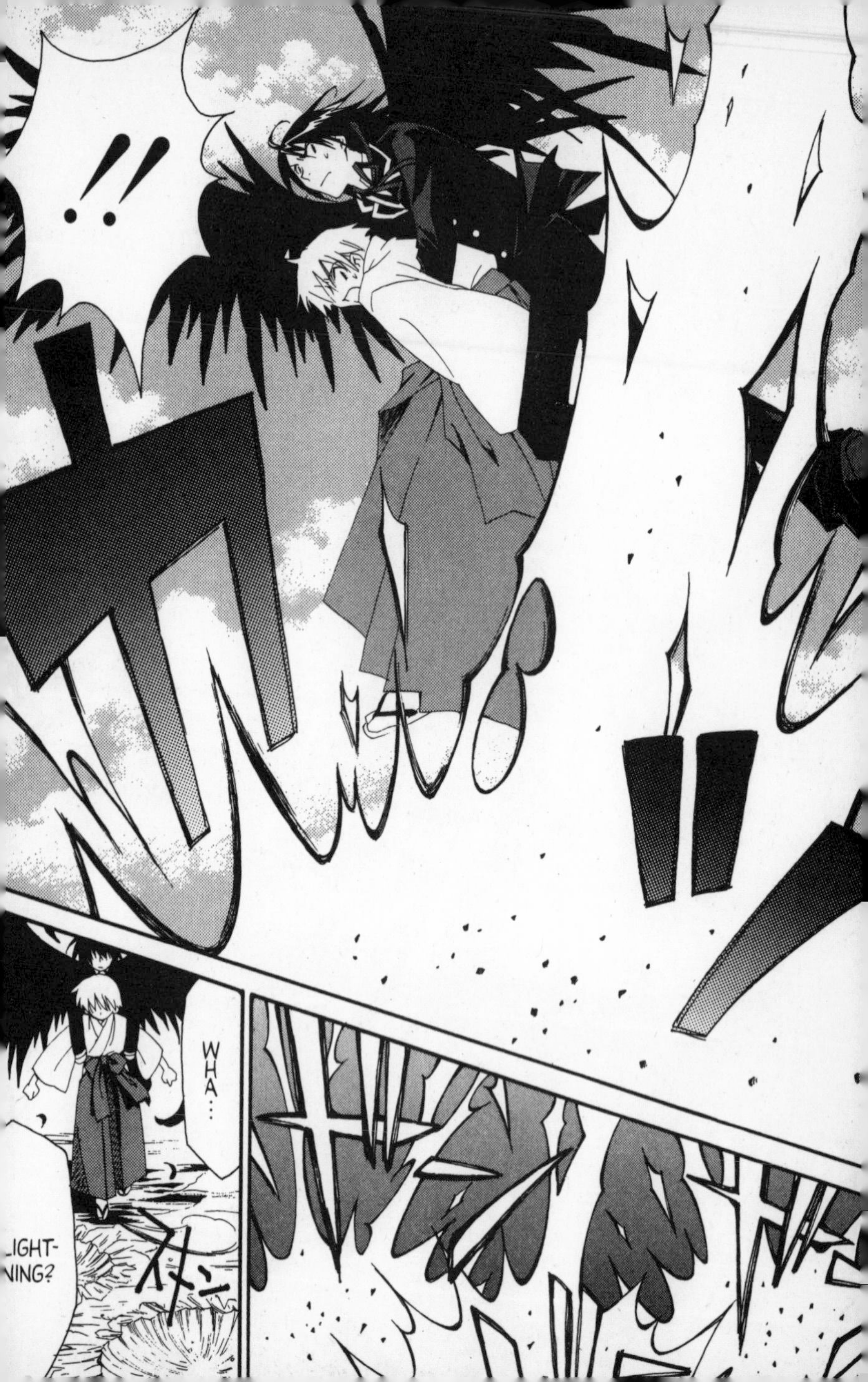
!!
WHA...
LIGHT-
NING?

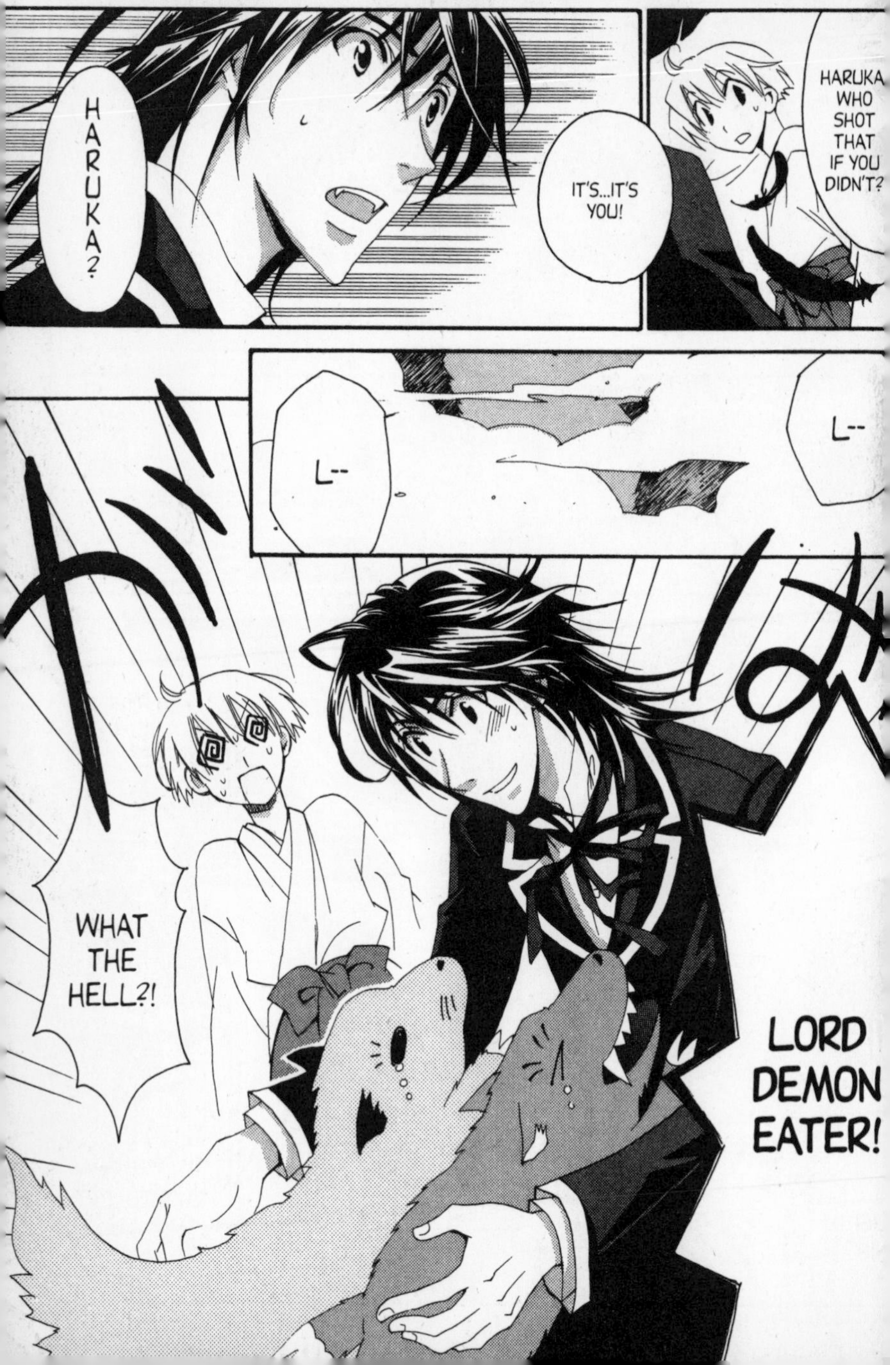
HARUKA WHO SHOT THAT IF YOU DIDN'T?
IT'S...IT'S YOU!
HARUKA?
L--
L--
LORD DEMON EATER!
WHAT THE HELL?!

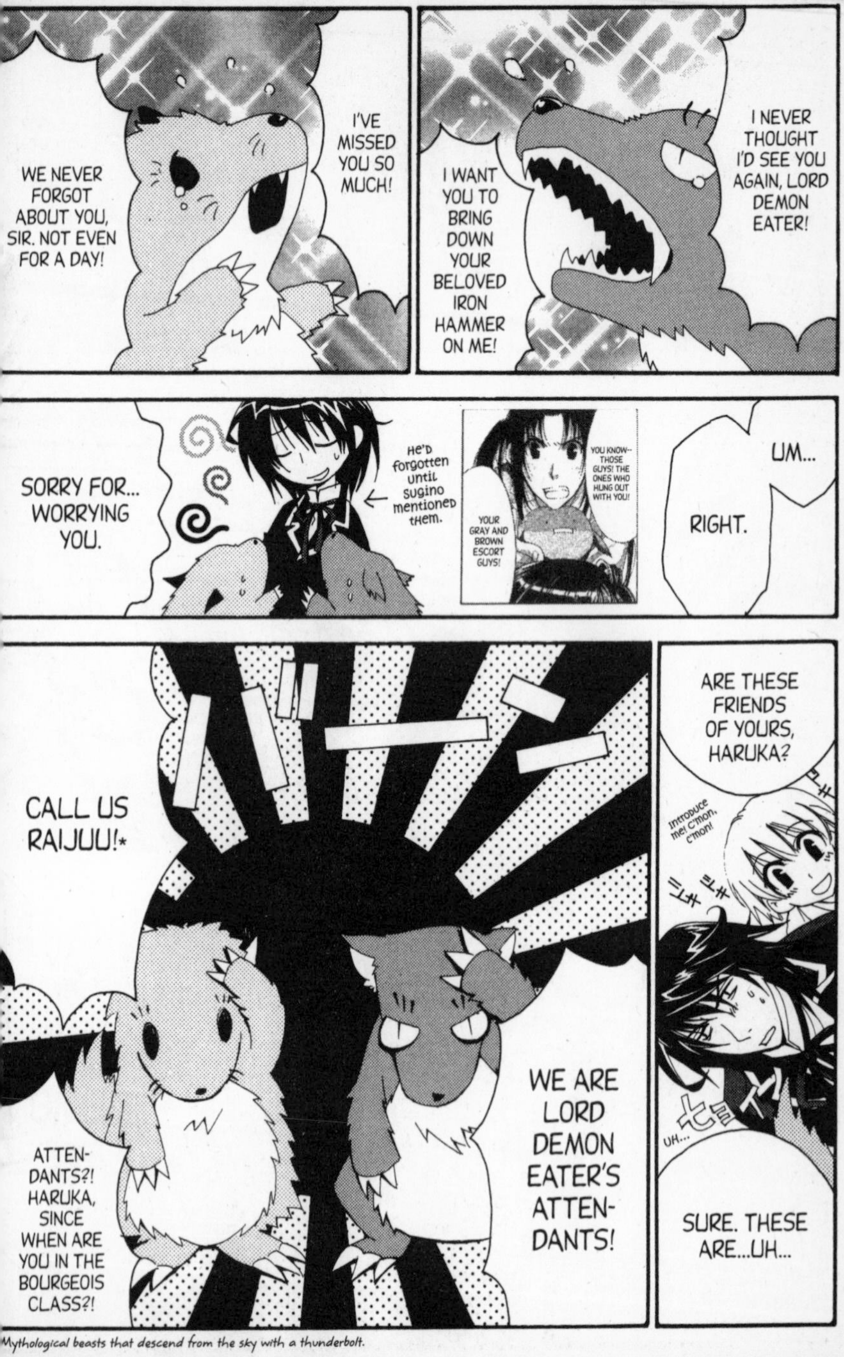
I NEVER THOUGHT I'D SEE YOU AGAIN, LORD DEMON EATER!
I WANT YOU TO BRING DOWN YOUR BELOVED IRON HAMMER ON ME!
I'VE MISSED YOU SO MUCH!
WE NEVER FORGOT ABOUT YOU, SIR. NOT EVEN FOR A DAY!
UM...
RIGHT.
YOU KNOW--THOSE GUYS! THE ONES WHO HUNG OUT WITH YOU!
YOUR GRAY AND BROWN ESCORT GUYS!
He'd forgotten until Sugino mentioned them.
SORRY FOR... WORRYING YOU.
ARE THESE FRIENDS OF YOURS, HARUKA?
Introduce me! C'mon, c'mon!
UH...
SURE. THESE ARE...UH...
CALL US RAIJUU!*
WE ARE LORD DEMON EATER'S ATTENDANTS!
ATTENDANTS?! HARUKA, SINCE WHEN ARE YOU IN THE BOURGEOIS CLASS?!

Mythological beasts that descend from the sky with a thunderbolt.

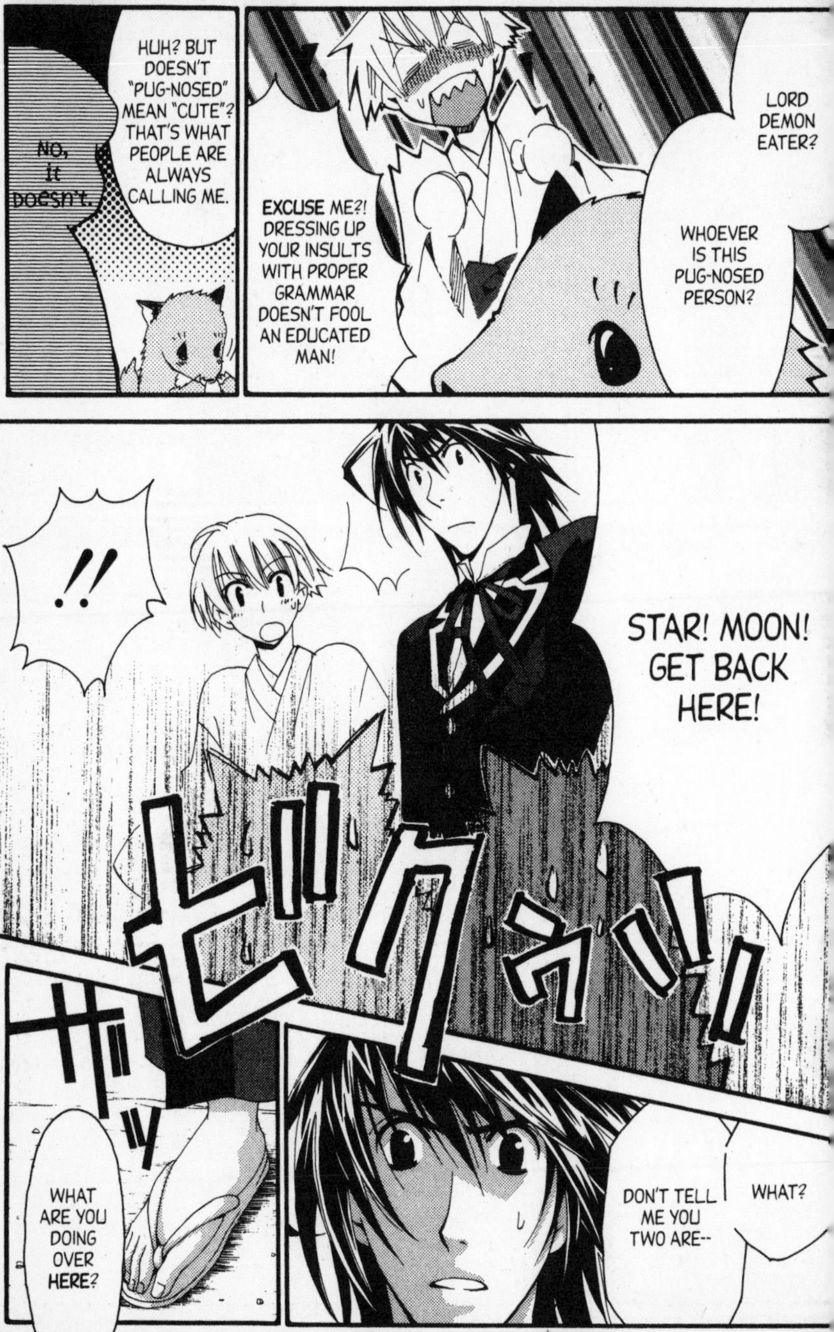
LORD DEMON EATER?
WHOEVER IS THIS PUG-NOSED PERSON?
EXCUSE ME?! DRESSING UP YOUR INSULTS WITH PROPER GRAMMAR DOESN'T FOOL AN EDUCATED MAN!
HUH? BUT DOESN'T "PUG-NOSED" MEAN "CUTE"? THAT'S WHAT PEOPLE ARE ALWAYS CALLING ME.
NO, it doesn't.
STAR! MOON! GET BACK HERE!
!!
ビクゥッ
WHAT?
DON'T TELL ME YOU TWO ARE--
ザッ
WHAT ARE YOU DOING OVER HERE?

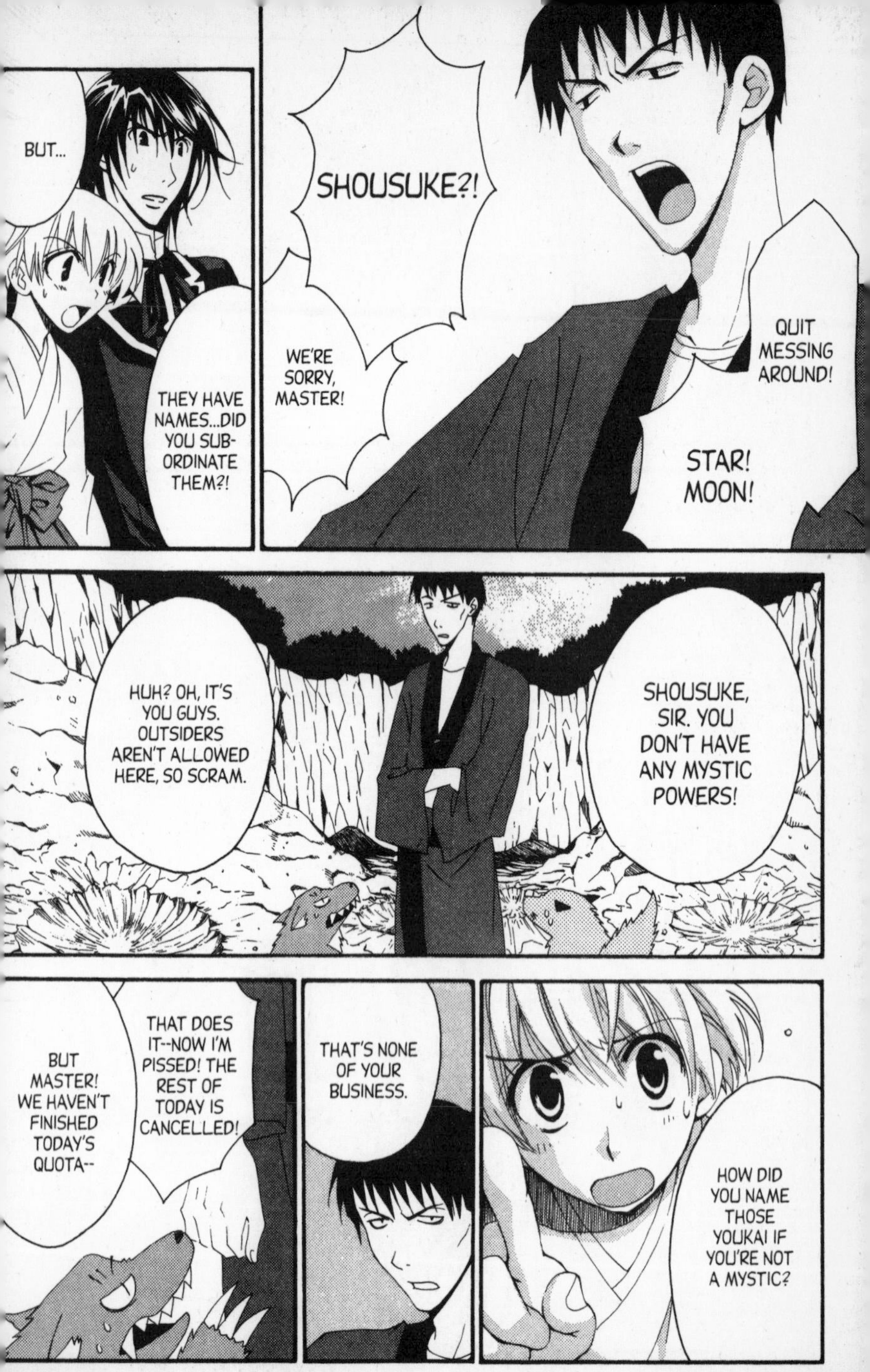
QUIT MESSING AROUND!
STAR! MOON!
SHOUSUKE?!
WE'RE SORRY, MASTER!
THEY HAVE NAMES...DID YOU SUB-ORDINATE THEM?!
BUT...
SHOUSUKE, SIR. YOU DON'T HAVE ANY MYSTIC POWERS!
HUH? OH, IT'S YOU GUYS. OUTSIDERS AREN'T ALLOWED HERE, SO SCRAM.
HOW DID YOU NAME THOSE YOUKAI IF YOU'RE NOT A MYSTIC?
THAT'S NONE OF YOUR BUSINESS.
THAT DOES IT--NOW I'M PISSED! THE REST OF TODAY IS CANCELLED!
BUT MASTER! WE HAVEN'T FINISHED TODAY'S QUOTA--

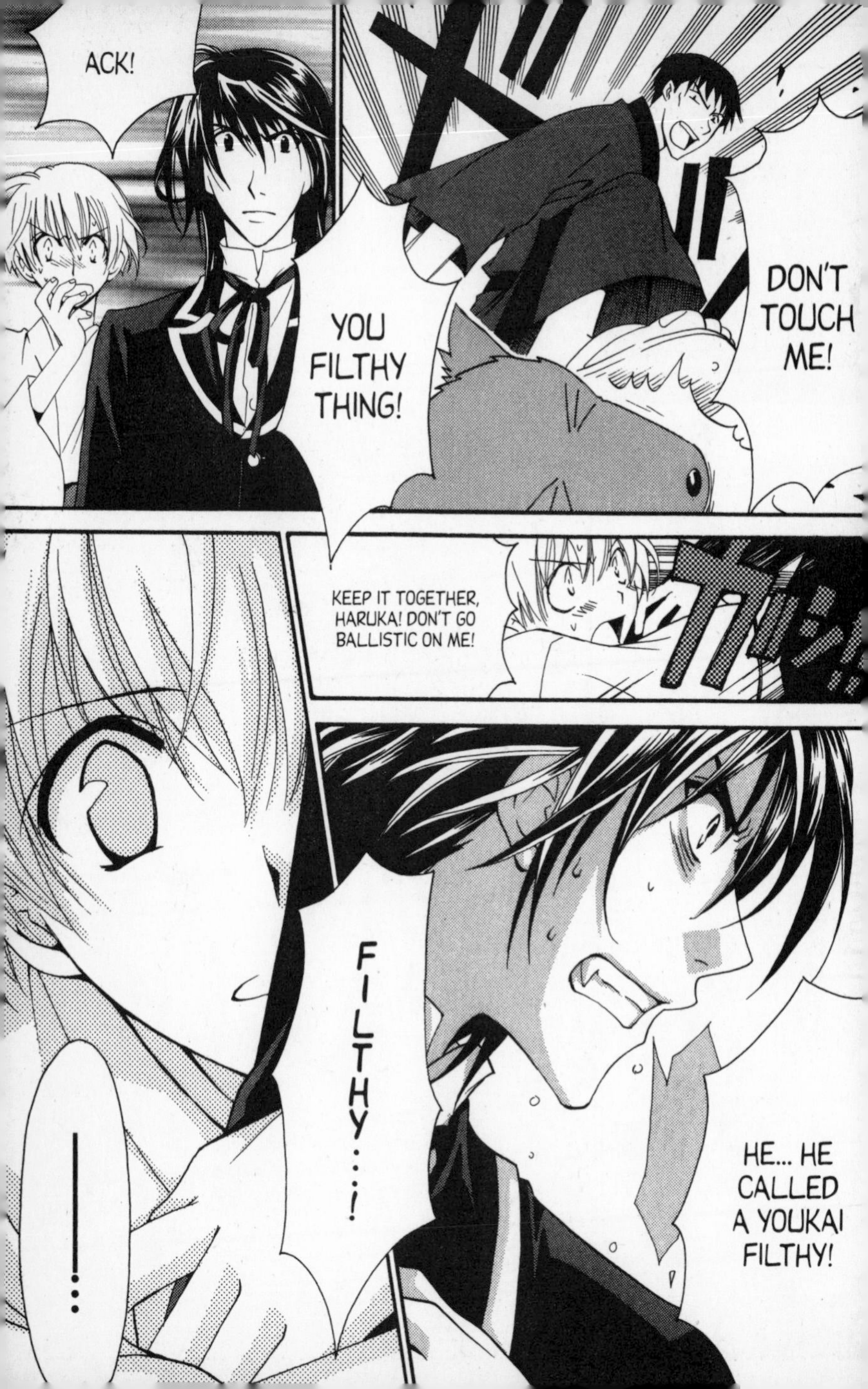
DON'T TOUCH ME!
YOU FILTHY THING!
ACK!
KEEP IT TOGETHER, HARUKA! DON'T GO BALLISTIC ON ME!
FILTHY...!
HE... HE CALLED A YOUKAI FILTHY!
......!

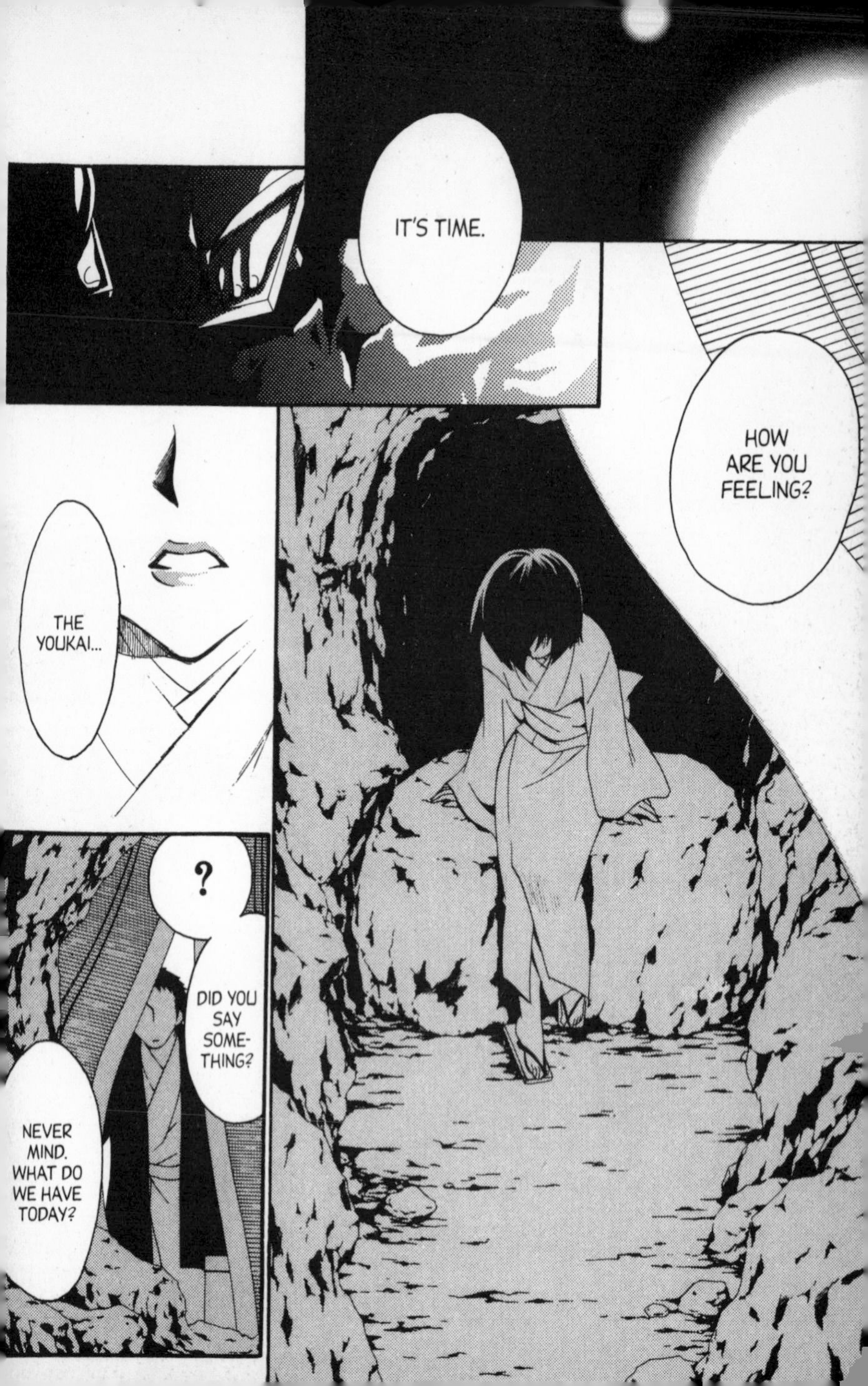
IT'S TIME.
HOW ARE YOU FEELING?
THE YOUKAI...
?
DID YOU SAY SOME-THING?
NEVER MIND. WHAT DO WE HAVE TODAY?

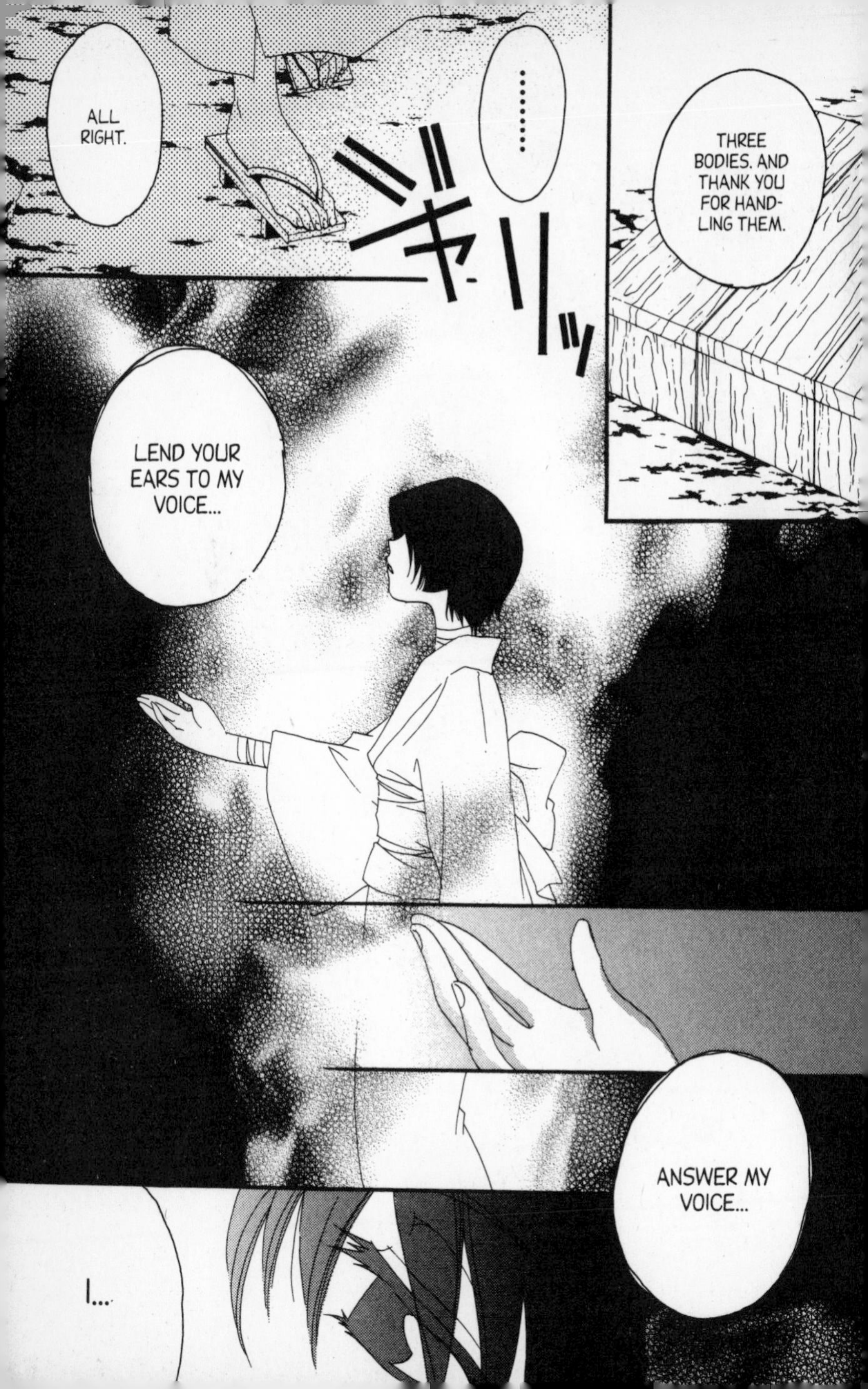
THREE BODIES. AND THANK YOU FOR HAND-LING THEM.
……
ジャリッ
ALL RIGHT.
LEND YOUR EARS TO MY VOICE...
ANSWER MY VOICE...
I...

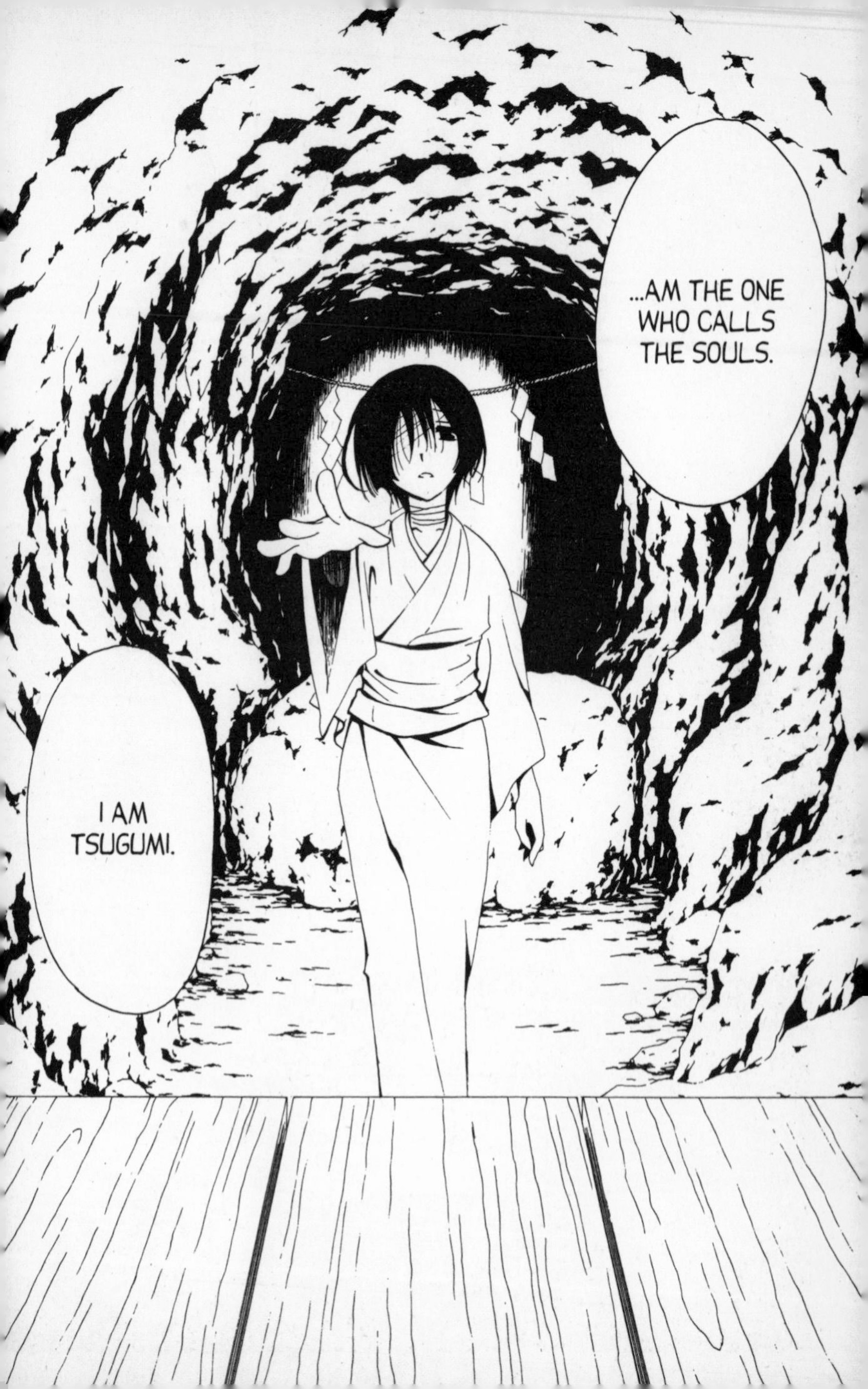
...AM THE ONE WHO CALLS THE SOULS.
I AM TSUGUMI.

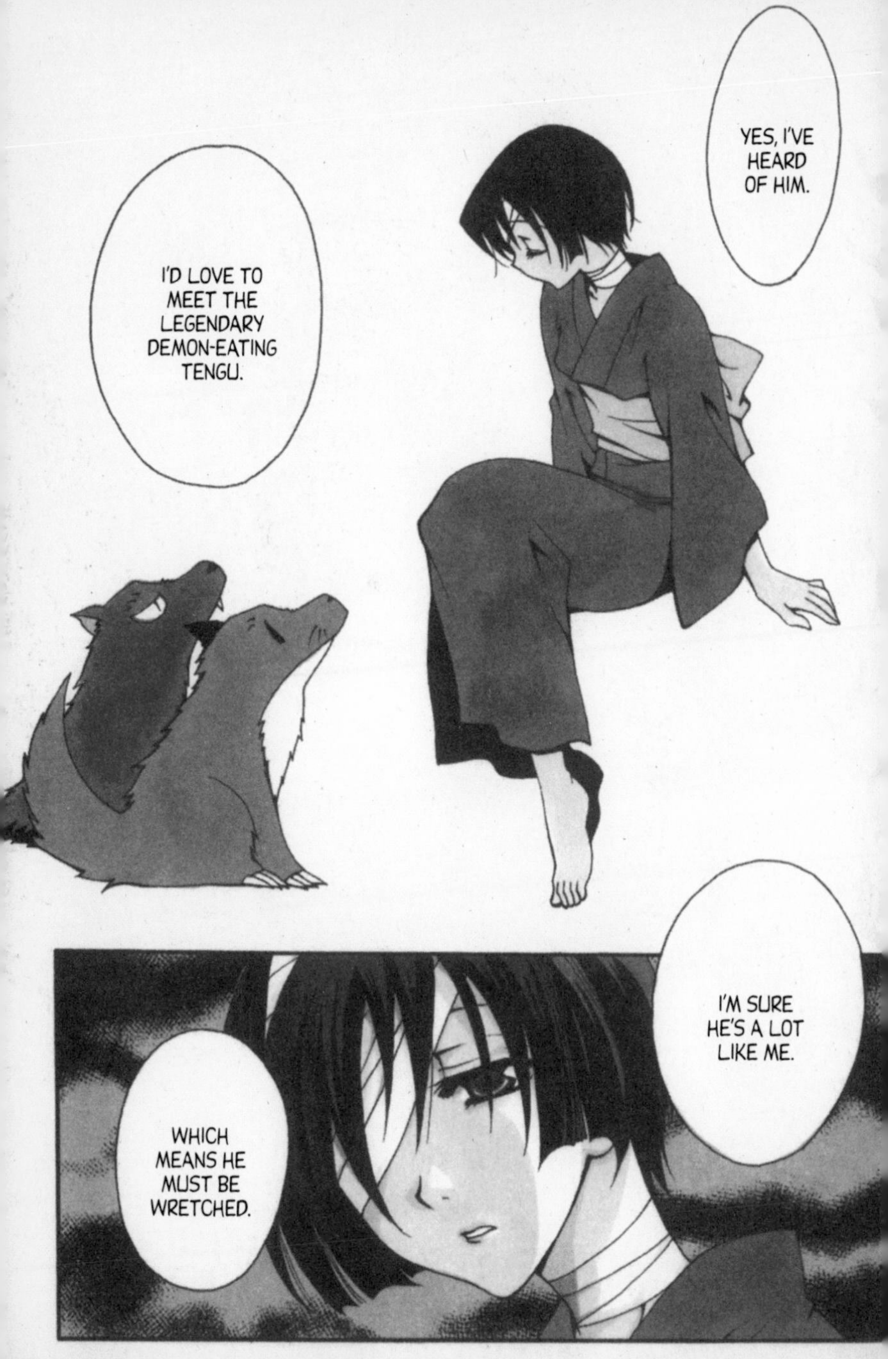
YES, I'VE HEARD OF HIM.
I'D LOVE TO MEET THE LEGENDARY DEMON-EATING TENGU.
I'M SURE HE'S A LOT LIKE ME.
WHICH MEANS HE MUST BE WRETCHED.

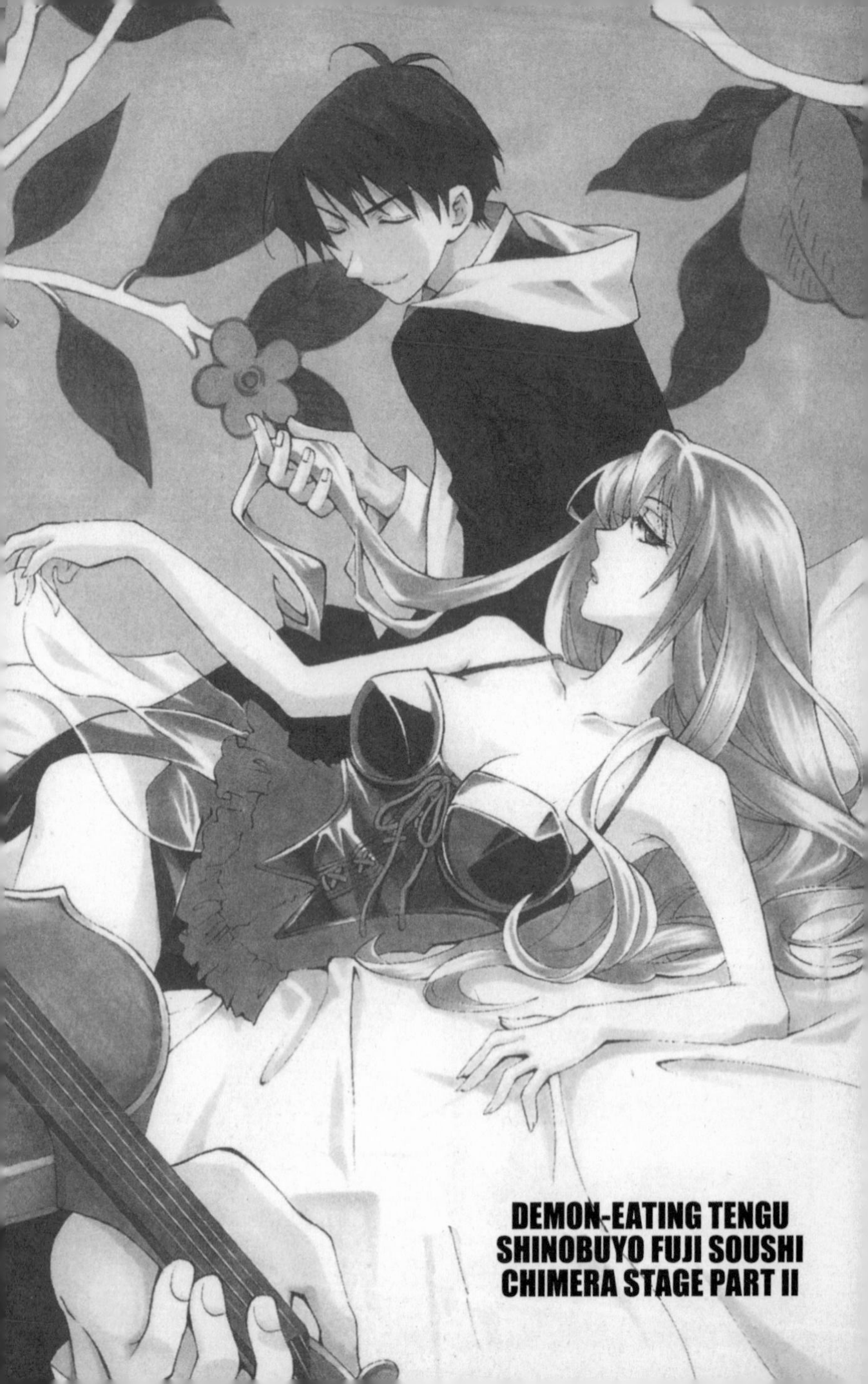

DEMON-EATING TENGU SHINOBUYO FUJI SOUSHI CHIMERA STAGE PART II

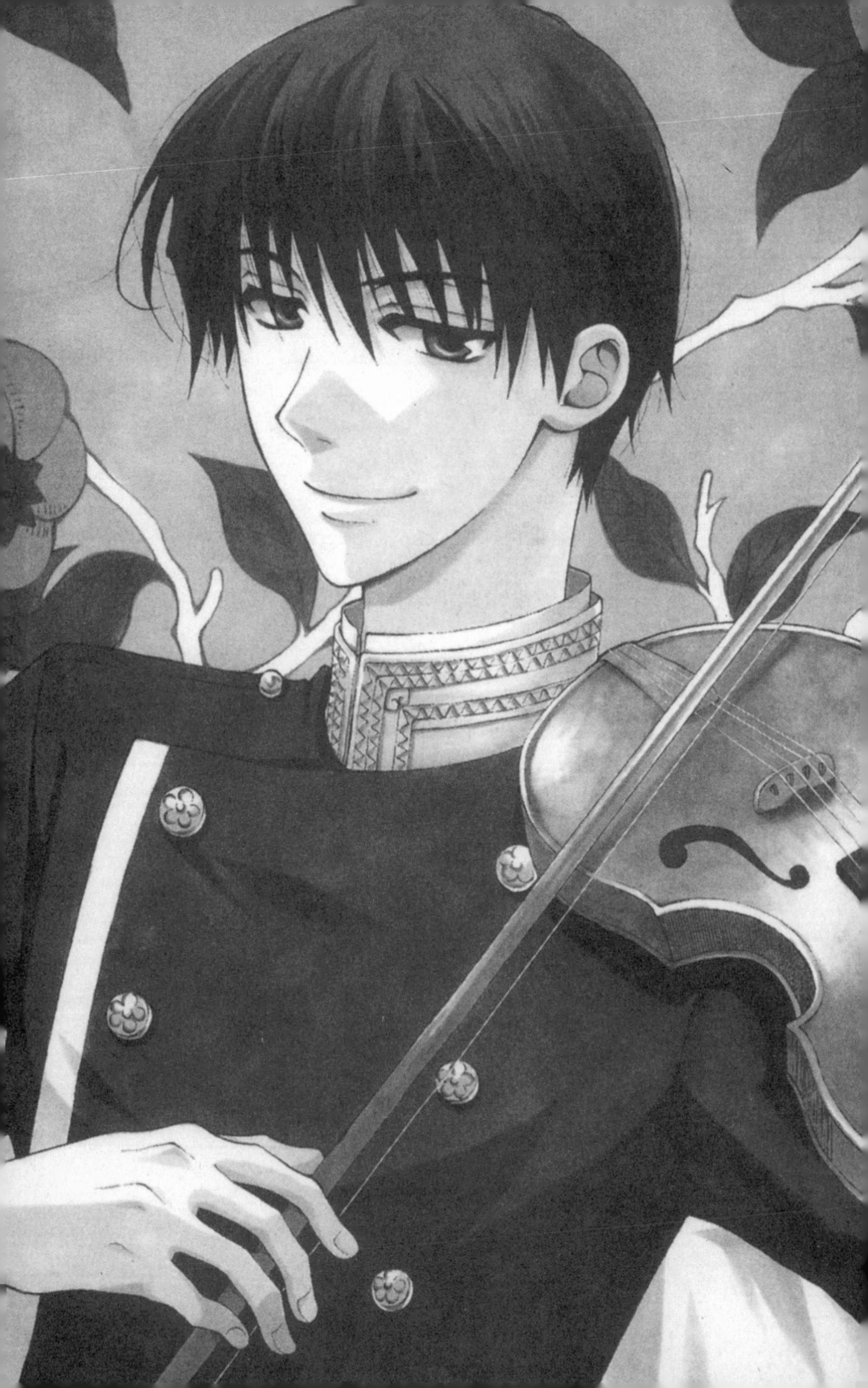

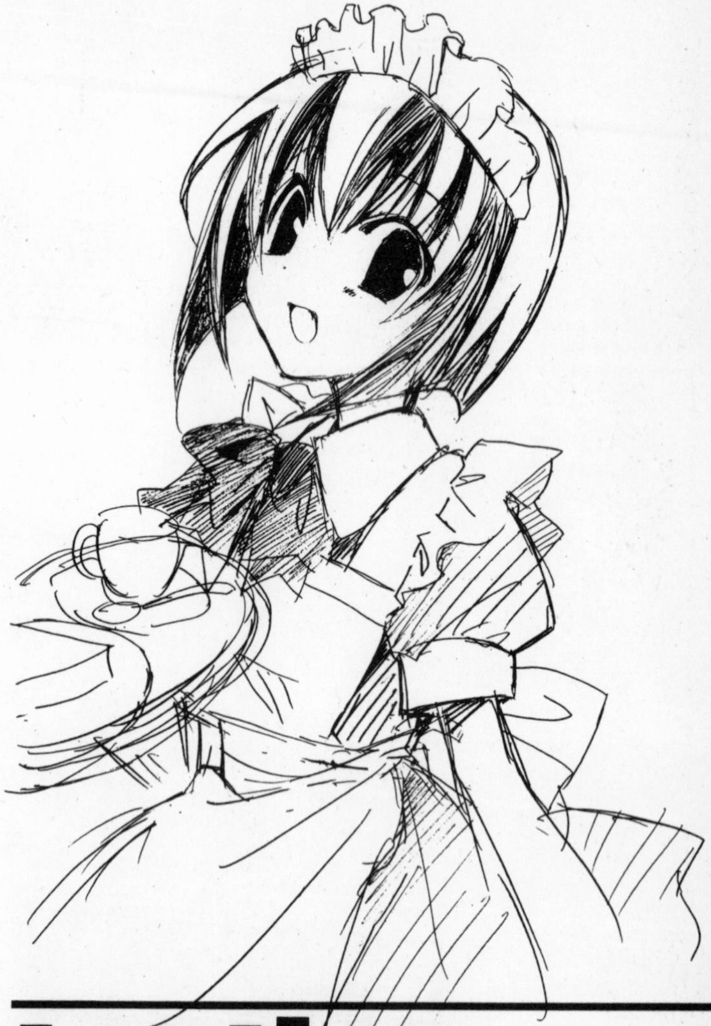

tactics

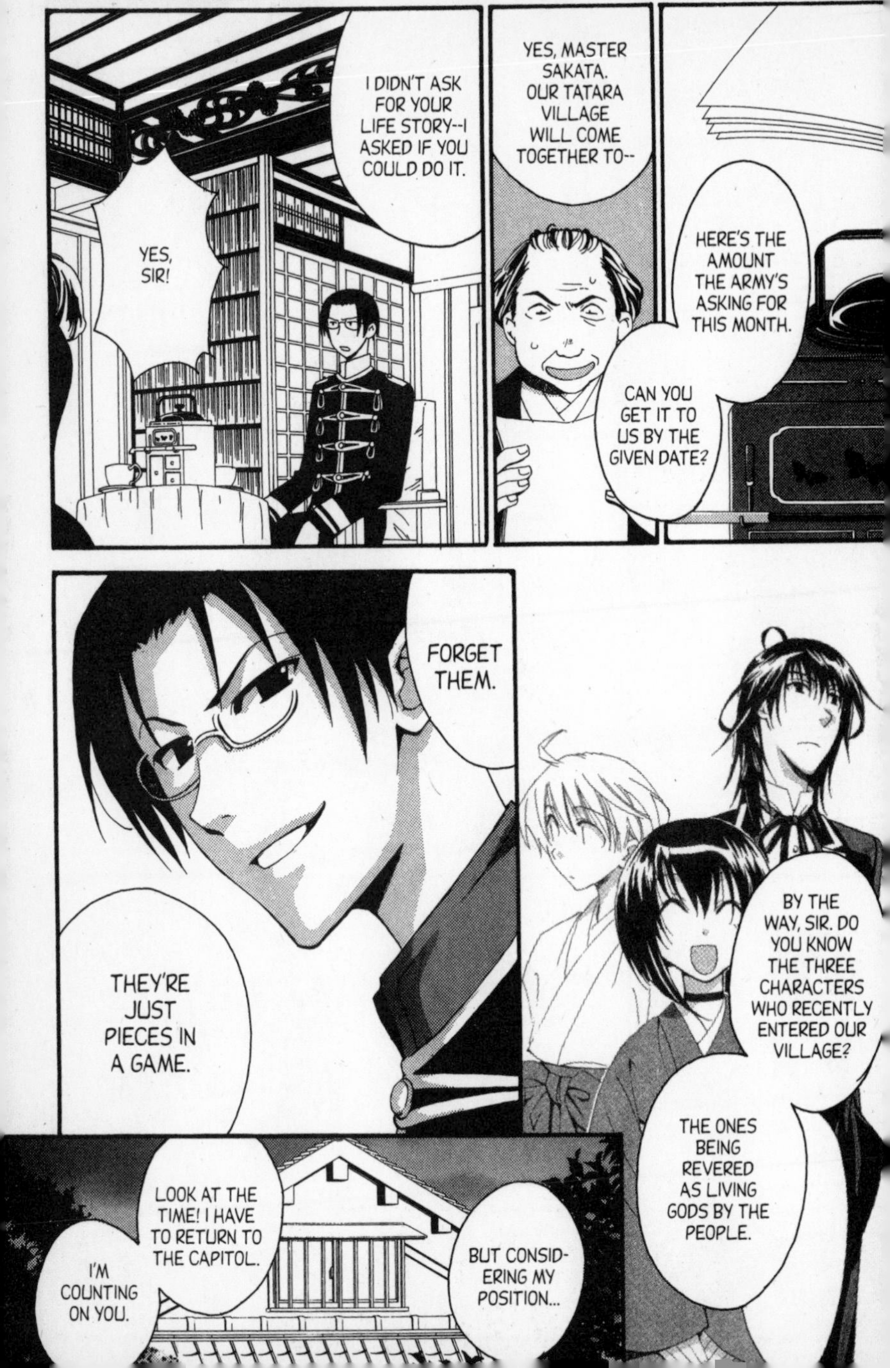
HERE'S THE AMOUNT THE ARMY'S ASKING FOR THIS MONTH.
CAN YOU GET IT TO US BY THE GIVEN DATE?
YES, MASTER SAKATA. OUR TATARA VILLAGE WILL COME TOGETHER TO--
I DIDN'T ASK FOR YOUR LIFE STORY--I ASKED IF YOU COULD DO IT.
YES, SIR!
BY THE WAY, SIR. DO YOU KNOW THE THREE CHARACTERS WHO RECENTLY ENTERED OUR VILLAGE?
THE ONES BEING REVERED AS LIVING GODS BY THE PEOPLE.
FORGET THEM.
THEY'RE JUST PIECES IN A GAME.
BUT CONSID-ERING MY POSITION...
LOOK AT THE TIME! I HAVE TO RETURN TO THE CAPITOL.
I'M COUNTING ON YOU.

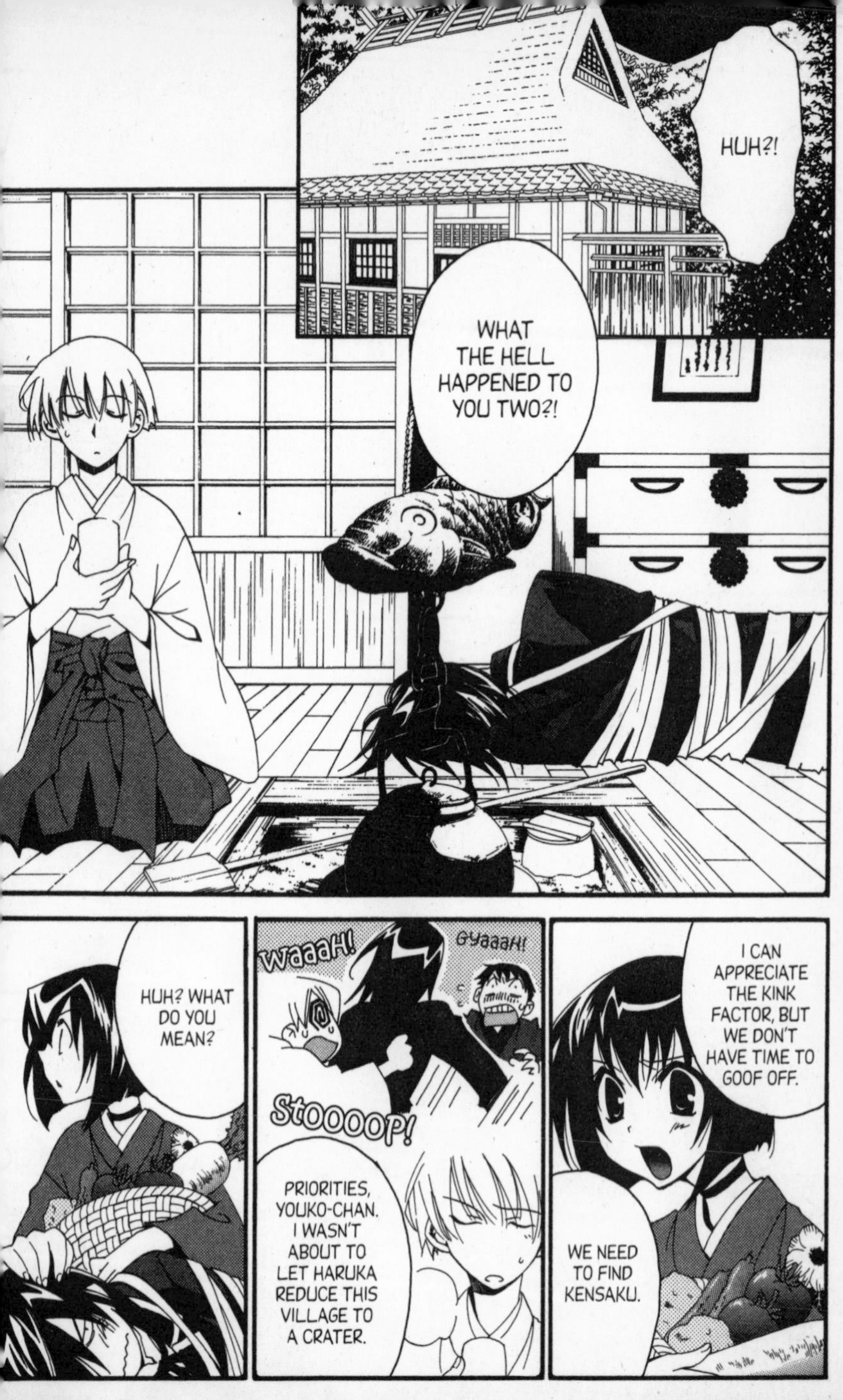
HUH?!
WHAT THE HELL HAPPENED TO YOU TWO?!
I CAN APPRECIATE THE KINK FACTOR, BUT WE DON'T HAVE TIME TO GOOF OFF.
WE NEED TO FIND KENSAKU.
GYaaaH!
WaaaH!
STOOOOOP!
PRIORITIES, YOUKO-CHAN. I WASN'T ABOUT TO LET HARUKA REDUCE THIS VILLAGE TO A CRATER.
HUH? WHAT DO YOU MEAN?

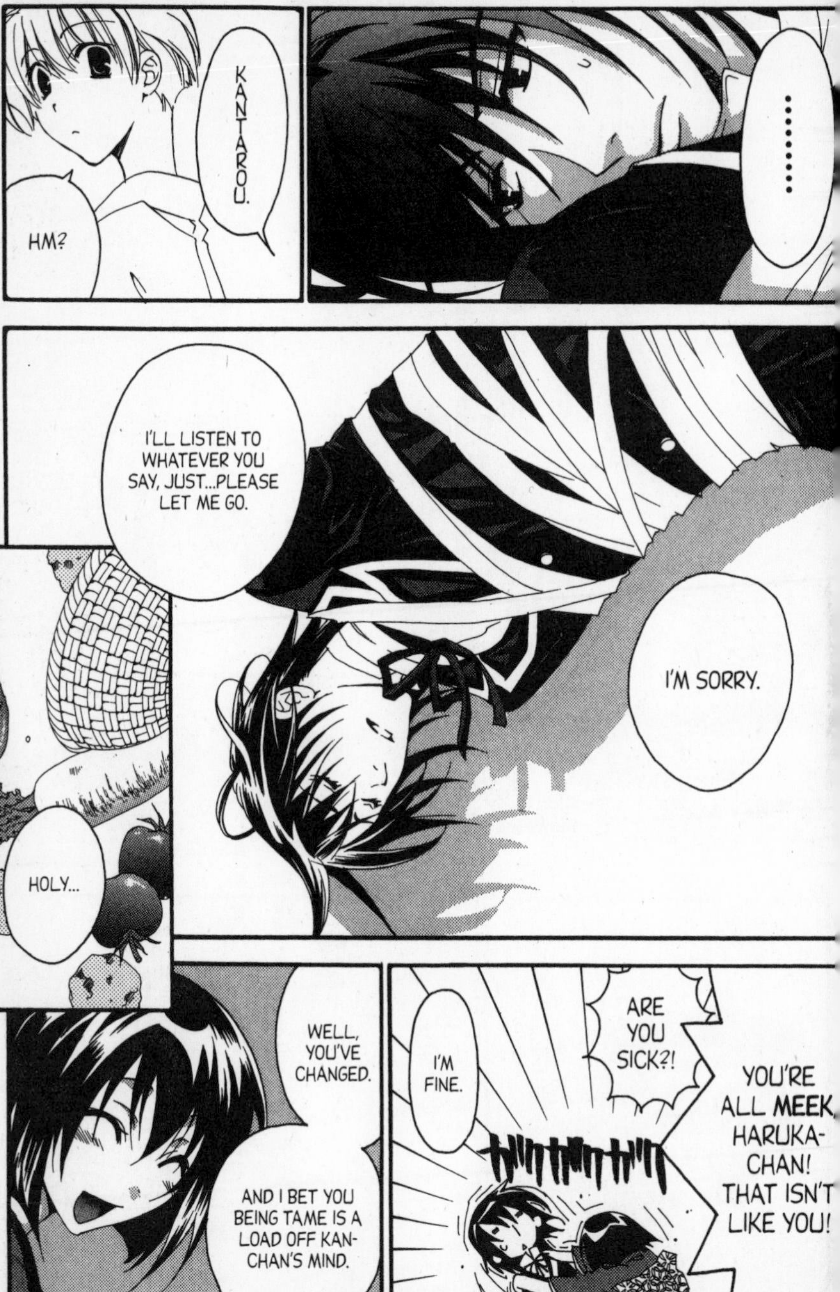
......
KANTAROU.
HM?
I'M SORRY.
I'LL LISTEN TO WHATEVER YOU SAY, JUST...PLEASE LET ME GO.
HOLY...
ARE YOU SICK?!
YOU'RE ALL MEEK HARUKA-CHAN! THAT ISN'T LIKE YOU!
I'M FINE.
WELL, YOU'VE CHANGED.
AND I BET YOU BEING TAME IS A LOAD OFF KAN-CHAN'S MIND.

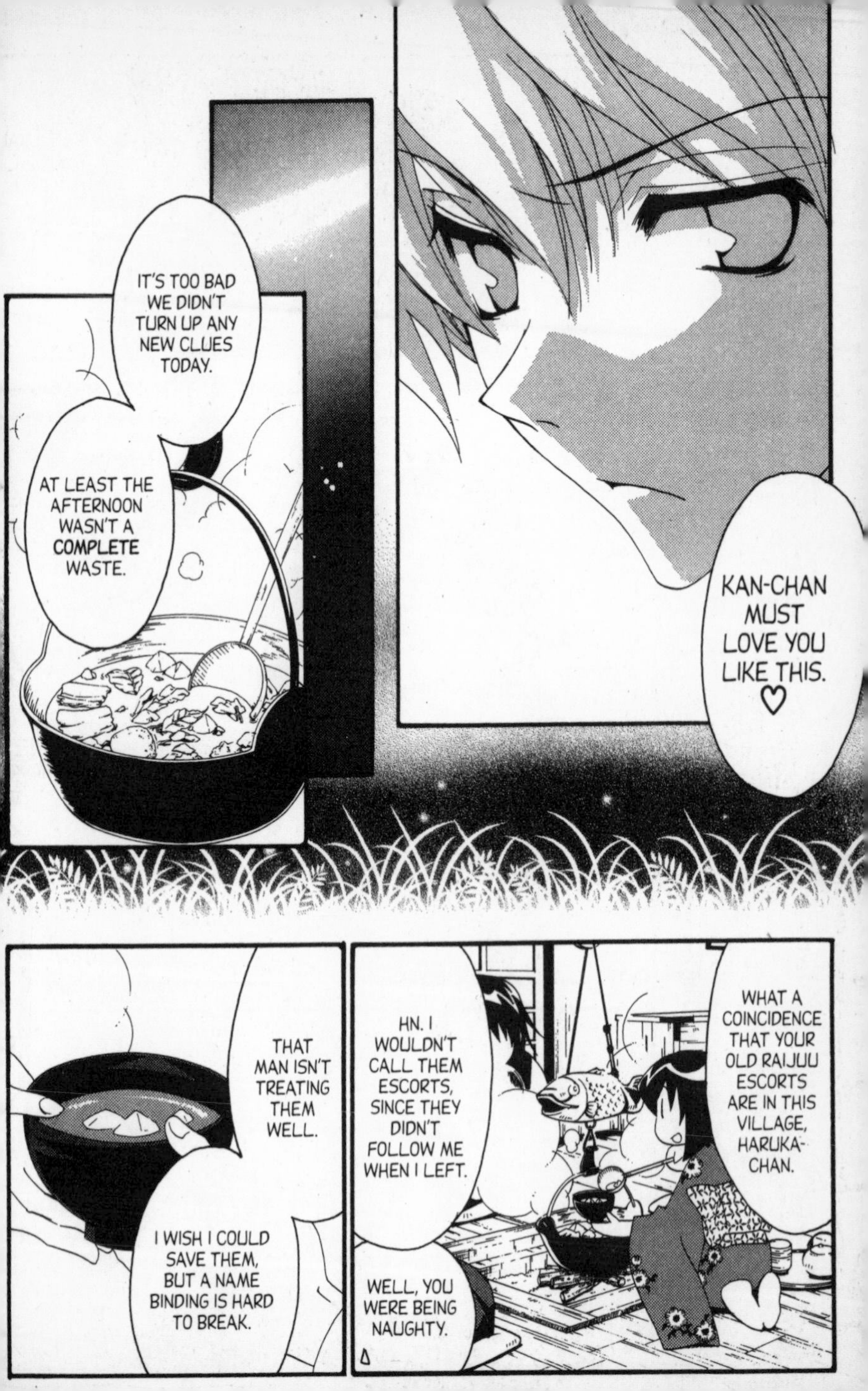
KAN-CHAN MUST LOVE YOU LIKE THIS. ♡
IT'S TOO BAD WE DIDN'T TURN UP ANY NEW CLUES TODAY.
AT LEAST THE AFTERNOON WASN'T A **COMPLETE** WASTE.
WHAT A COINCIDENCE THAT YOUR OLD RAIJUU ESCORTS ARE IN THIS VILLAGE, HARUKA-CHAN.
HN. I WOULDN'T CALL THEM ESCORTS, SINCE THEY DIDN'T FOLLOW ME WHEN I LEFT.
WELL, YOU WERE BEING NAUGHTY.
THAT MAN ISN'T TREATING THEM WELL.
I WISH I COULD SAVE THEM, BUT A NAME BINDING IS HARD TO BREAK.

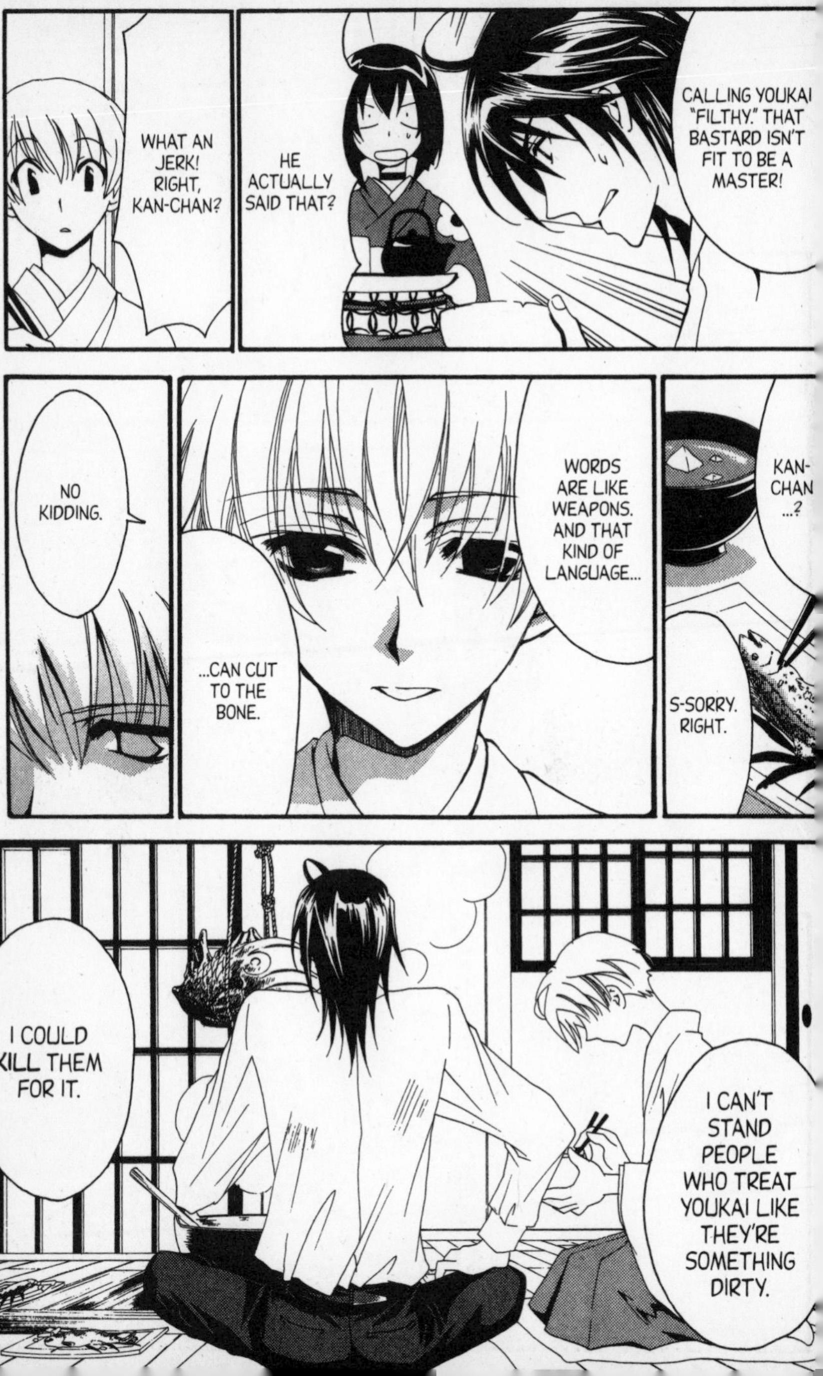
CALLING YOUKAI "FILTHY." THAT BASTARD ISN'T FIT TO BE A MASTER!
HE ACTUALLY SAID THAT?
WHAT AN JERK! RIGHT, KAN-CHAN?
KAN-CHAN ...?
S-SORRY. RIGHT.
WORDS ARE LIKE WEAPONS. AND THAT KIND OF LANGUAGE...
...CAN CUT TO THE BONE.
NO KIDDING.
I CAN'T STAND PEOPLE WHO TREAT YOUKAI LIKE THEY'RE SOMETHING DIRTY.
I COULD KILL THEM FOR IT.

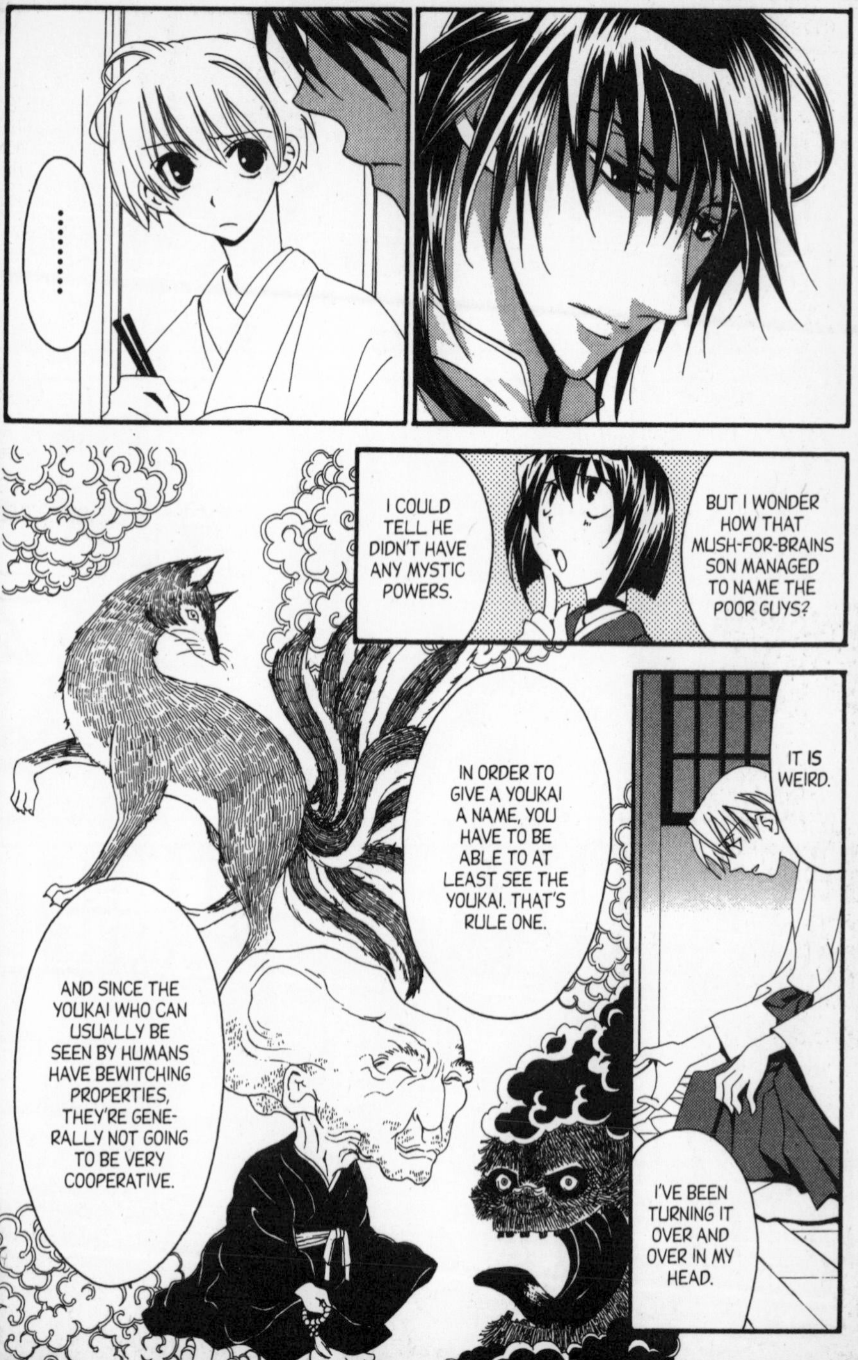

....
I COULD TELL HE DIDN'T HAVE ANY MYSTIC POWERS.
BUT I WONDER HOW THAT MUSH-FOR-BRAINS SON MANAGED TO NAME THE POOR GUYS?
IT IS WEIRD.
I'VE BEEN TURNING IT OVER AND OVER IN MY HEAD.
IN ORDER TO GIVE A YOUKAI A NAME, YOU HAVE TO BE ABLE TO AT LEAST SEE THE YOUKAI. THAT'S RULE ONE.
AND SINCE THE YOUKAI WHO CAN USUALLY BE SEEN BY HUMANS HAVE BEWITCHING PROPERTIES, THEY'RE GENE-RALLY NOT GOING TO BE VERY COOPERATIVE.

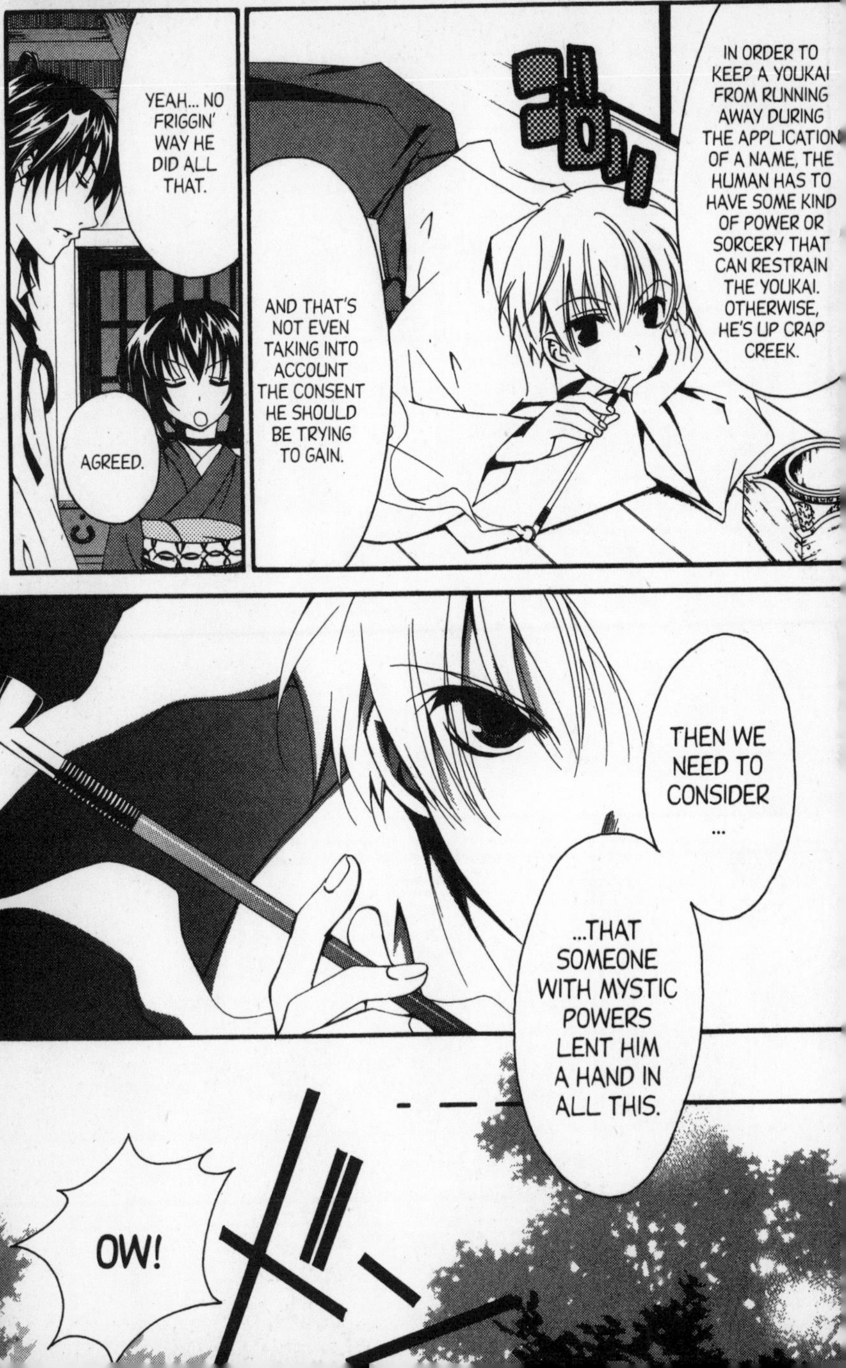
IN ORDER TO KEEP A YOUKAI FROM RUNNING AWAY DURING THE APPLICATION OF A NAME, THE HUMAN HAS TO HAVE SOME KIND OF POWER OR SORCERY THAT CAN RESTRAIN THE YOUKAI. OTHERWISE, HE'S UP CRAP CREEK.
AND THAT'S NOT EVEN TAKING INTO ACCOUNT THE CONSENT HE SHOULD BE TRYING TO GAIN.
YEAH... NO FRIGGIN' WAY HE DID ALL THAT.
AGREED.
THEN WE NEED TO CONSIDER ...
...THAT SOMEONE WITH MYSTIC POWERS LENT HIM A HAND IN ALL THIS.
OW!

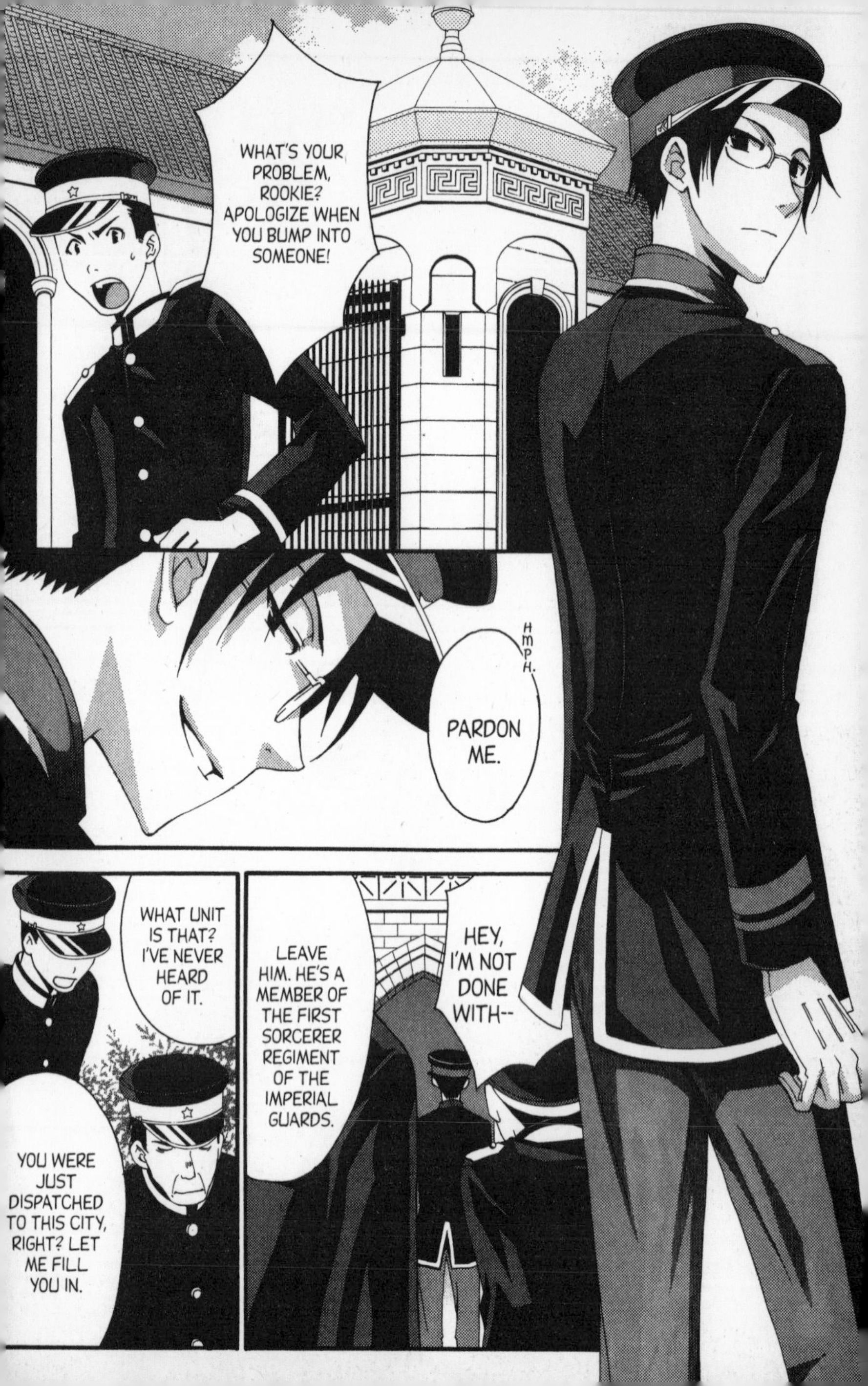
WHAT'S YOUR PROBLEM, ROOKIE? APOLOGIZE WHEN YOU BUMP INTO SOMEONE!
HMPH.
PARDON ME.
HEY, I'M NOT DONE WITH--
LEAVE HIM. HE'S A MEMBER OF THE FIRST SORCERER REGIMENT OF THE IMPERIAL GUARDS.
WHAT UNIT IS THAT? I'VE NEVER HEARD OF IT.
YOU WERE JUST DISPATCHED TO THIS CITY, RIGHT? LET ME FILL YOU IN.

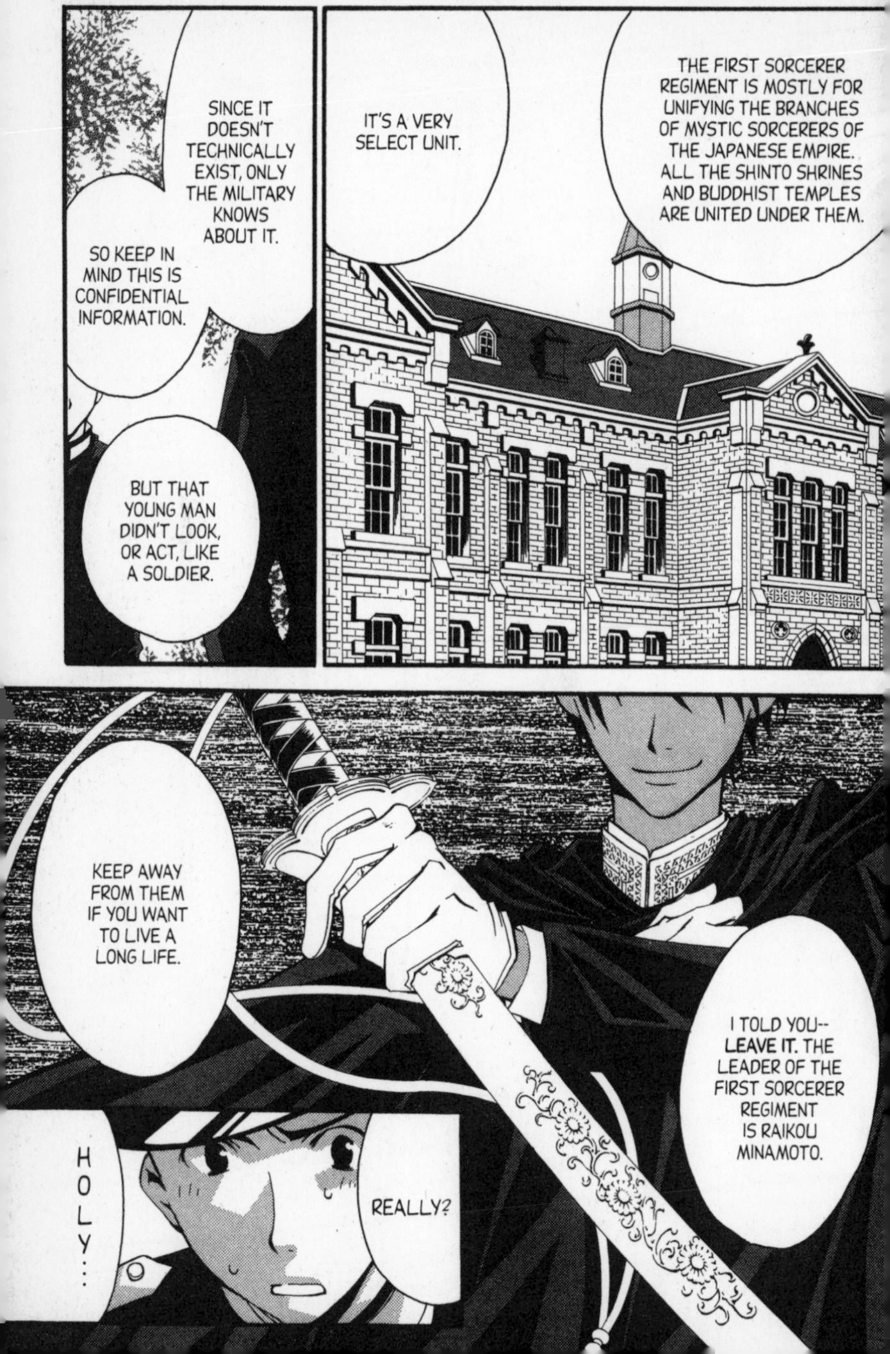
THE FIRST SORCERER REGIMENT IS MOSTLY FOR UNIFYING THE BRANCHES OF MYSTIC SORCERERS OF THE JAPANESE EMPIRE. ALL THE SHINTO SHRINES AND BUDDHIST TEMPLES ARE UNITED UNDER THEM.
IT'S A VERY SELECT UNIT.
SINCE IT DOESN'T TECHNICALLY EXIST, ONLY THE MILITARY KNOWS ABOUT IT.
SO KEEP IN MIND THIS IS CONFIDENTIAL INFORMATION.
BUT THAT YOUNG MAN DIDN'T LOOK, OR ACT, LIKE A SOLDIER.
I TOLD YOU-- **LEAVE IT.** THE LEADER OF THE FIRST SORCERER REGIMENT IS RAIKOU MINAMOTO.
KEEP AWAY FROM THEM IF YOU WANT TO LIVE A LONG LIFE.
REALLY?
HOLY...

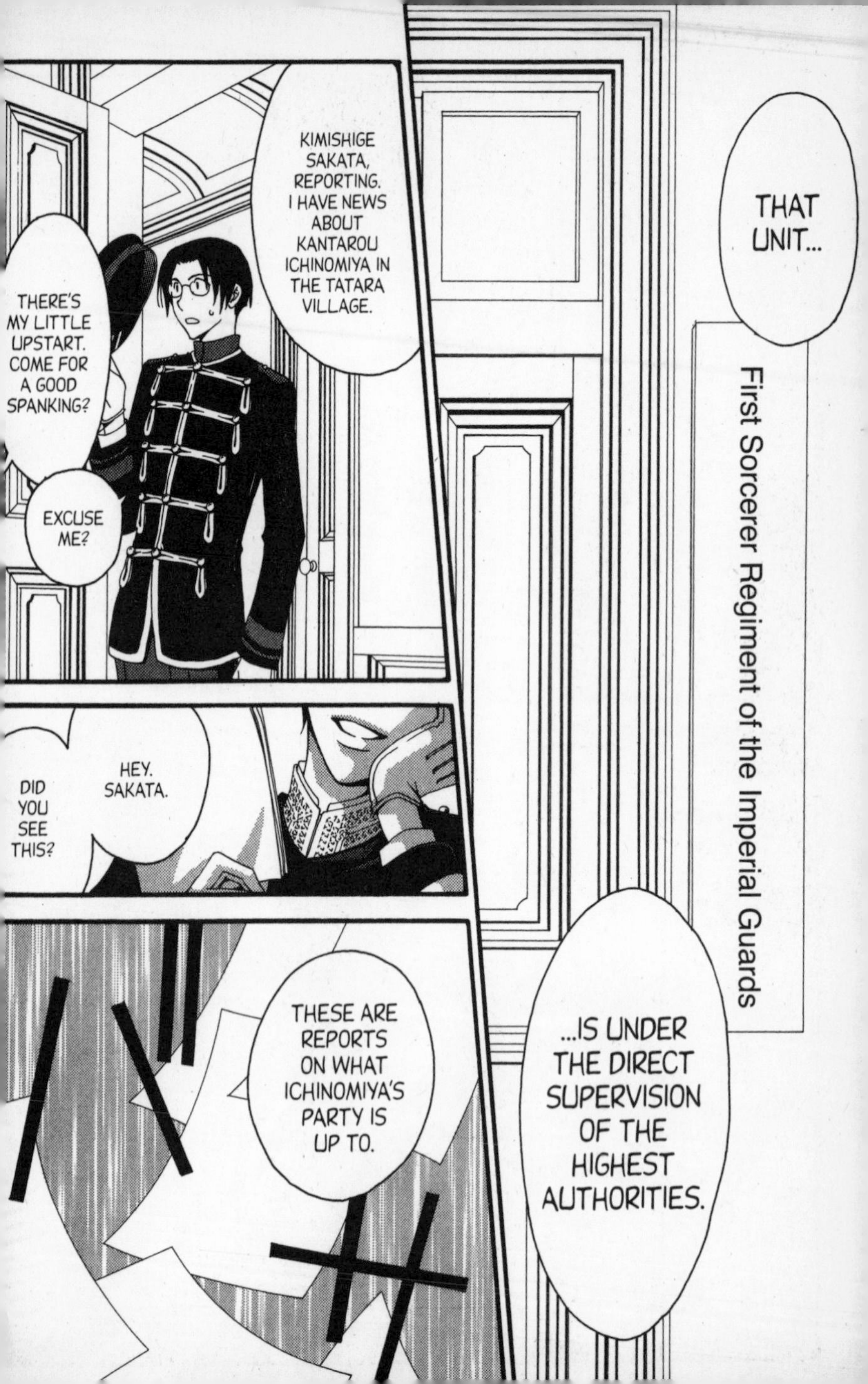
THAT UNIT...
First Sorcerer Regiment of the Imperial Guards
...IS UNDER THE DIRECT SUPERVISION OF THE HIGHEST AUTHORITIES.
KIMISHIGE SAKATA, REPORTING. I HAVE NEWS ABOUT KANTAROU ICHINOMIYA IN THE TATARA VILLAGE.
THERE'S MY LITTLE UPSTART. COME FOR A GOOD SPANKING?
EXCUSE ME?
HEY. SAKATA.
DID YOU SEE THIS?
THESE ARE REPORTS ON WHAT ICHINOMIYA'S PARTY IS UP TO.

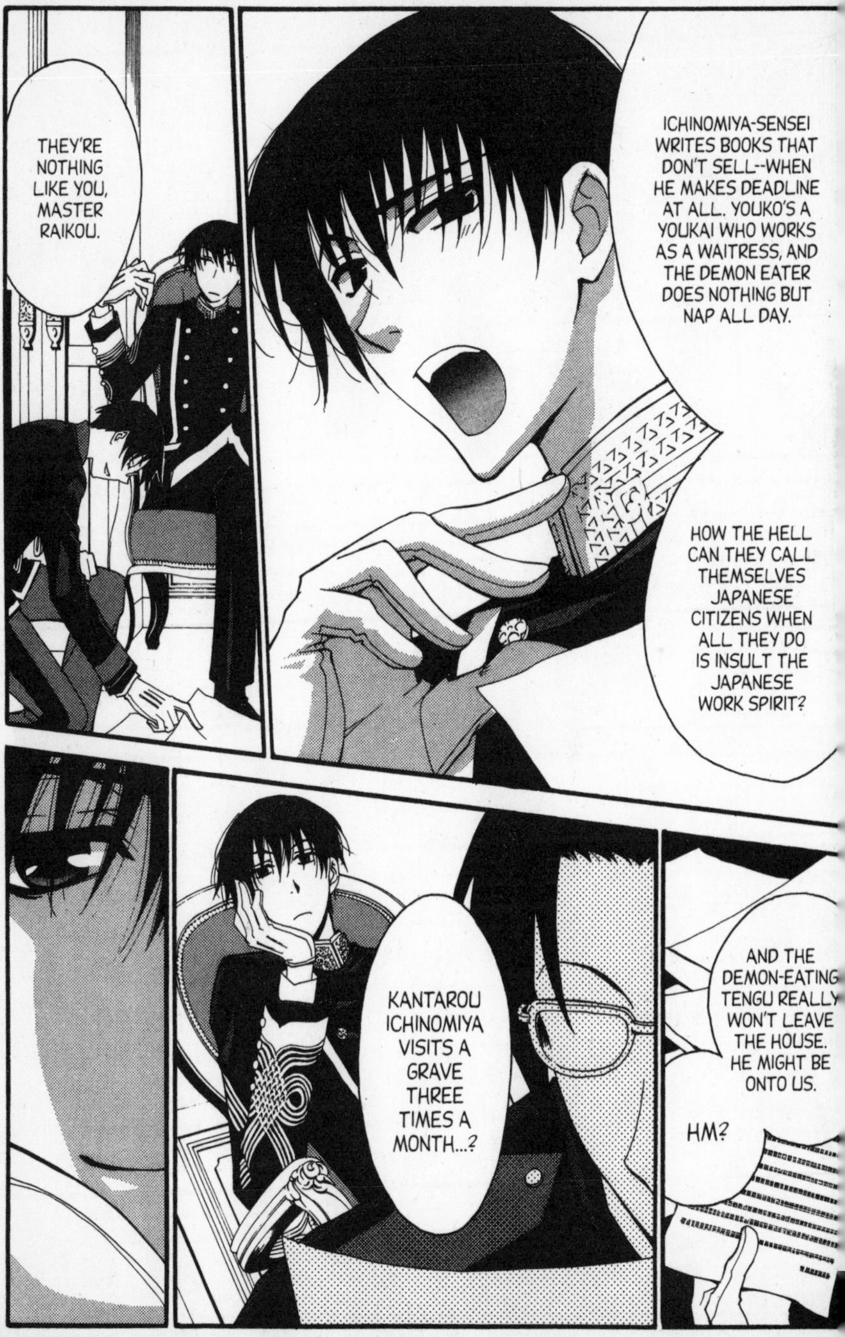
ICHINOMIYA-SENSEI WRITES BOOKS THAT DON'T SELL--WHEN HE MAKES DEADLINE AT ALL. YOUKO'S A YOUKAI WHO WORKS AS A WAITRESS, AND THE DEMON EATER DOES NOTHING BUT NAP ALL DAY.
HOW THE HELL CAN THEY CALL THEMSELVES JAPANESE CITIZENS WHEN ALL THEY DO IS INSULT THE JAPANESE WORK SPIRIT?
THEY'RE NOTHING LIKE YOU, MASTER RAIKOU.
AND THE DEMON-EATING TENGU REALLY WON'T LEAVE THE HOUSE. HE MIGHT BE ONTO US.
HM?
KANTAROU ICHINOMIYA VISITS A GRAVE THREE TIMES A MONTH...?

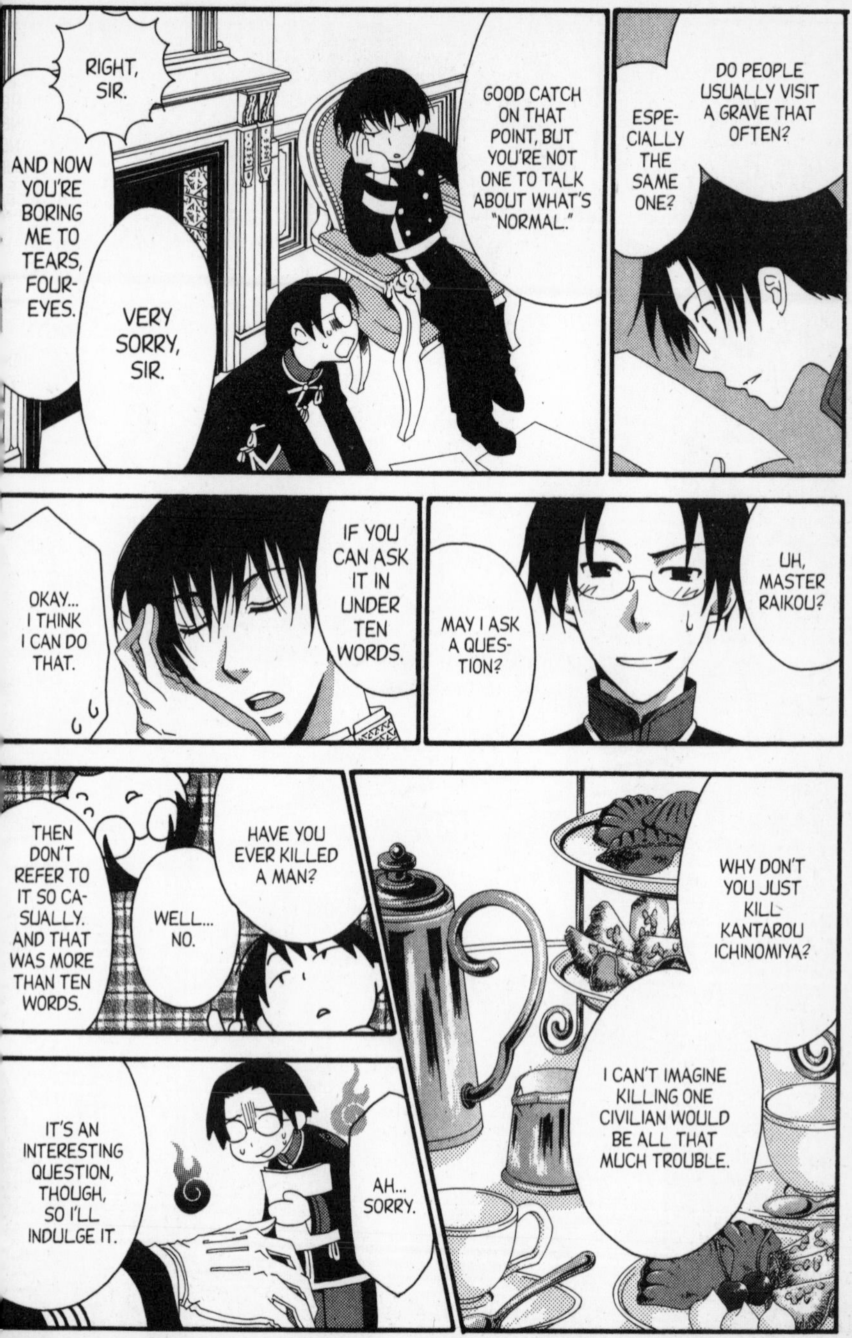
DO PEOPLE USUALLY VISIT A GRAVE THAT OFTEN?
ESPECIALLY THE SAME ONE?
GOOD CATCH ON THAT POINT, BUT YOU'RE NOT ONE TO TALK ABOUT WHAT'S "NORMAL."
RIGHT, SIR.
AND NOW YOU'RE BORING ME TO TEARS, FOUR-EYES.
VERY SORRY, SIR.
UH, MASTER RAIKOU?
MAY I ASK A QUESTION?
IF YOU CAN ASK IT IN UNDER TEN WORDS.
OKAY... I THINK I CAN DO THAT.
WHY DON'T YOU JUST KILL KANTAROU ICHINOMIYA?
I CAN'T IMAGINE KILLING ONE CIVILIAN WOULD BE ALL THAT MUCH TROUBLE.
HAVE YOU EVER KILLED A MAN?
WELL... NO.
THEN DON'T REFER TO IT SO CASUALLY. AND THAT WAS MORE THAN TEN WORDS.
AH... SORRY.
IT'S AN INTERESTING QUESTION, THOUGH, SO I'LL INDULGE IT.

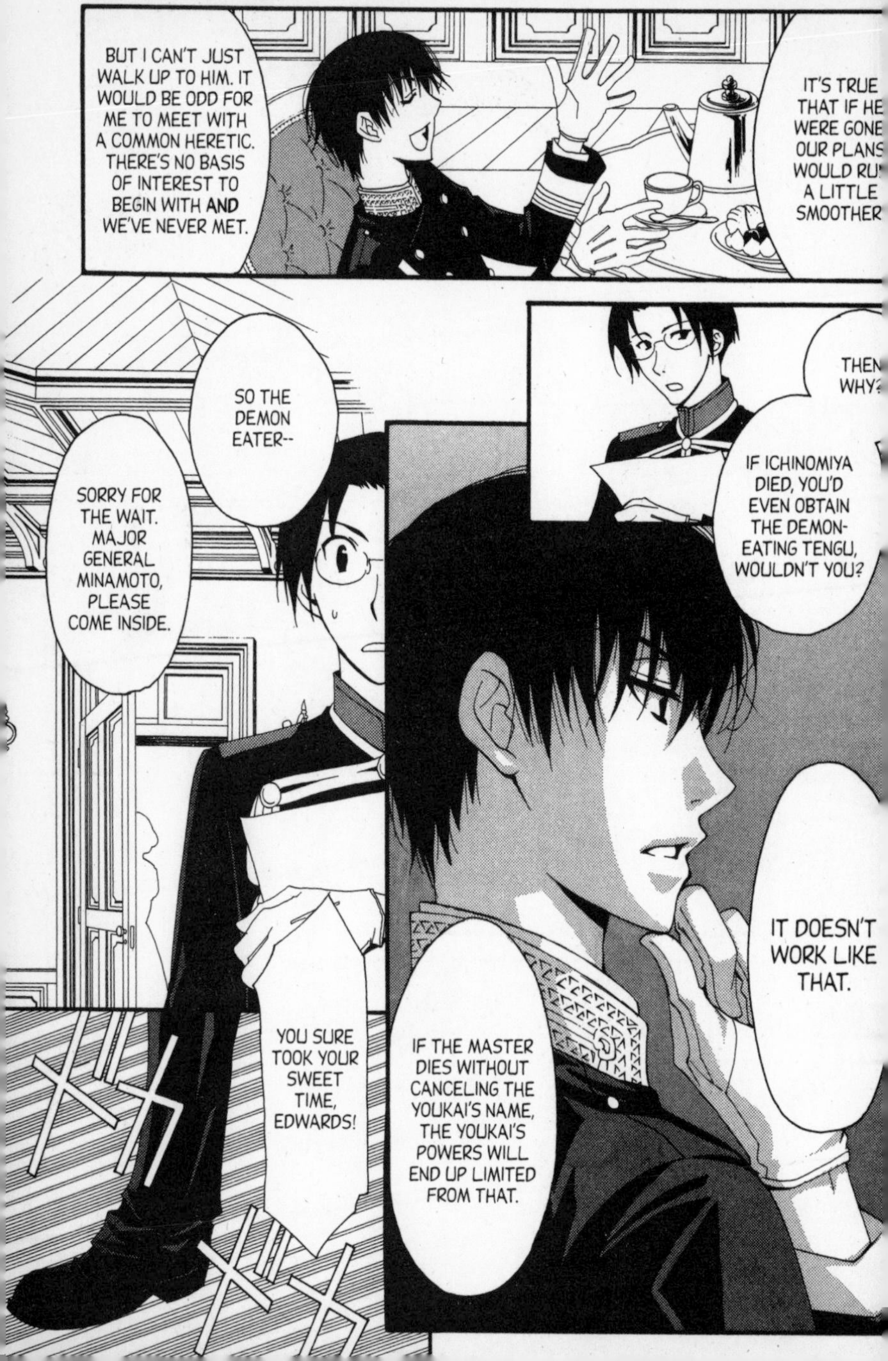
IT'S TRUE THAT IF HE WERE GONE OUR PLANS WOULD RU A LITTLE SMOOTHER
BUT I CAN'T JUST WALK UP TO HIM. IT WOULD BE ODD FOR ME TO MEET WITH A COMMON HERETIC. THERE'S NO BASIS OF INTEREST TO BEGIN WITH AND WE'VE NEVER MET.
THEN WHY?
IF ICHINOMIYA DIED, YOU'D EVEN OBTAIN THE DEMON-EATING TENGU, WOULDN'T YOU?
IT DOESN'T WORK LIKE THAT.
IF THE MASTER DIES WITHOUT CANCELING THE YOUKAI'S NAME, THE YOUKAI'S POWERS WILL END UP LIMITED FROM THAT.
SO THE DEMON EATER--
SORRY FOR THE WAIT. MAJOR GENERAL MINAMOTO, PLEASE COME INSIDE.
YOU SURE TOOK YOUR SWEET TIME, EDWARDS!

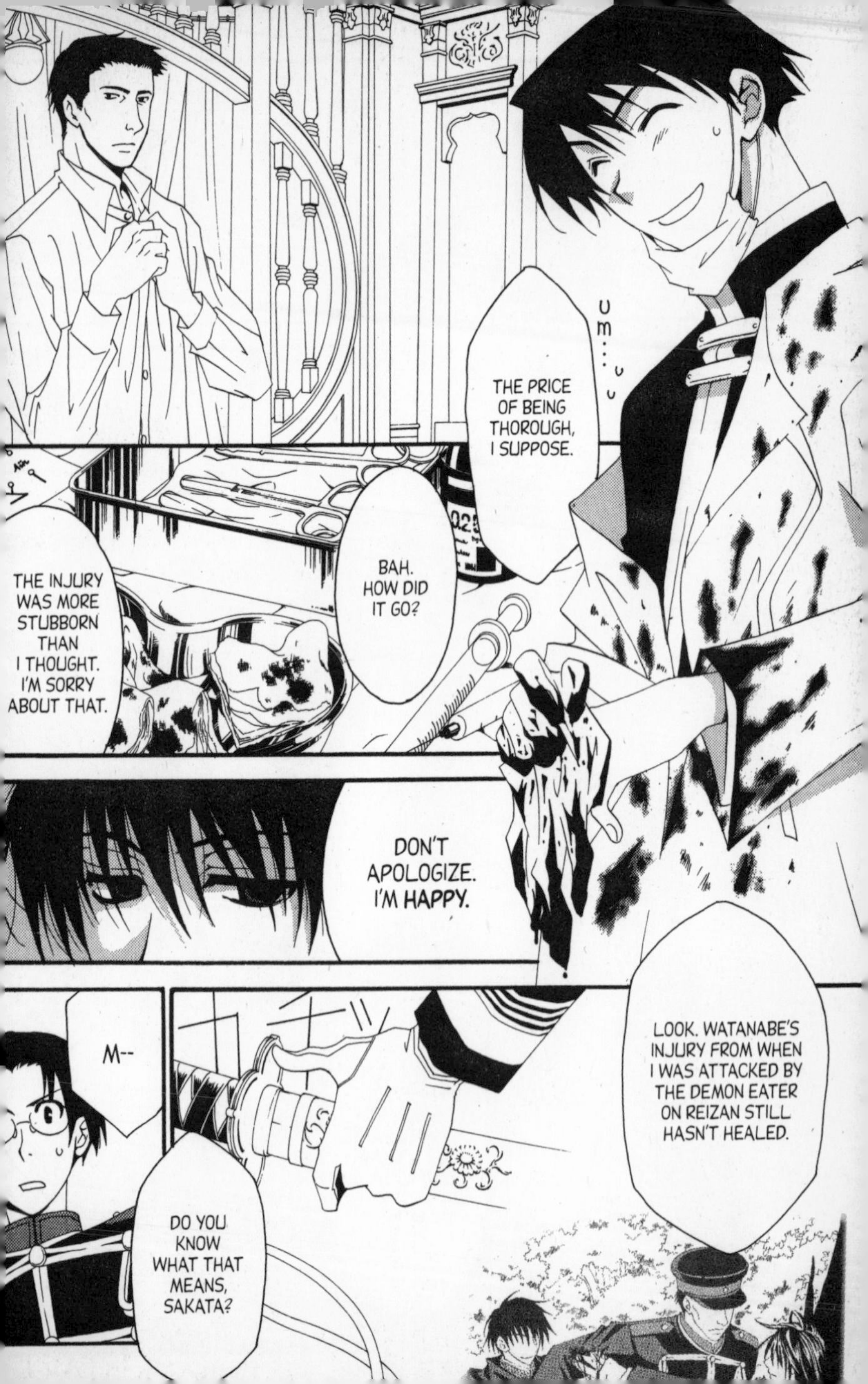
UM...
THE PRICE OF BEING THOROUGH, I SUPPOSE.
BAH. HOW DID IT GO?
THE INJURY WAS MORE STUBBORN THAN I THOUGHT. I'M SORRY ABOUT THAT.
DON'T APOLOGIZE. I'M **HAPPY**.
LOOK. WATANABE'S INJURY FROM WHEN I WAS ATTACKED BY THE DEMON EATER ON REIZAN STILL HASN'T HEALED.
M--
DO YOU KNOW WHAT THAT MEANS, SAKATA?

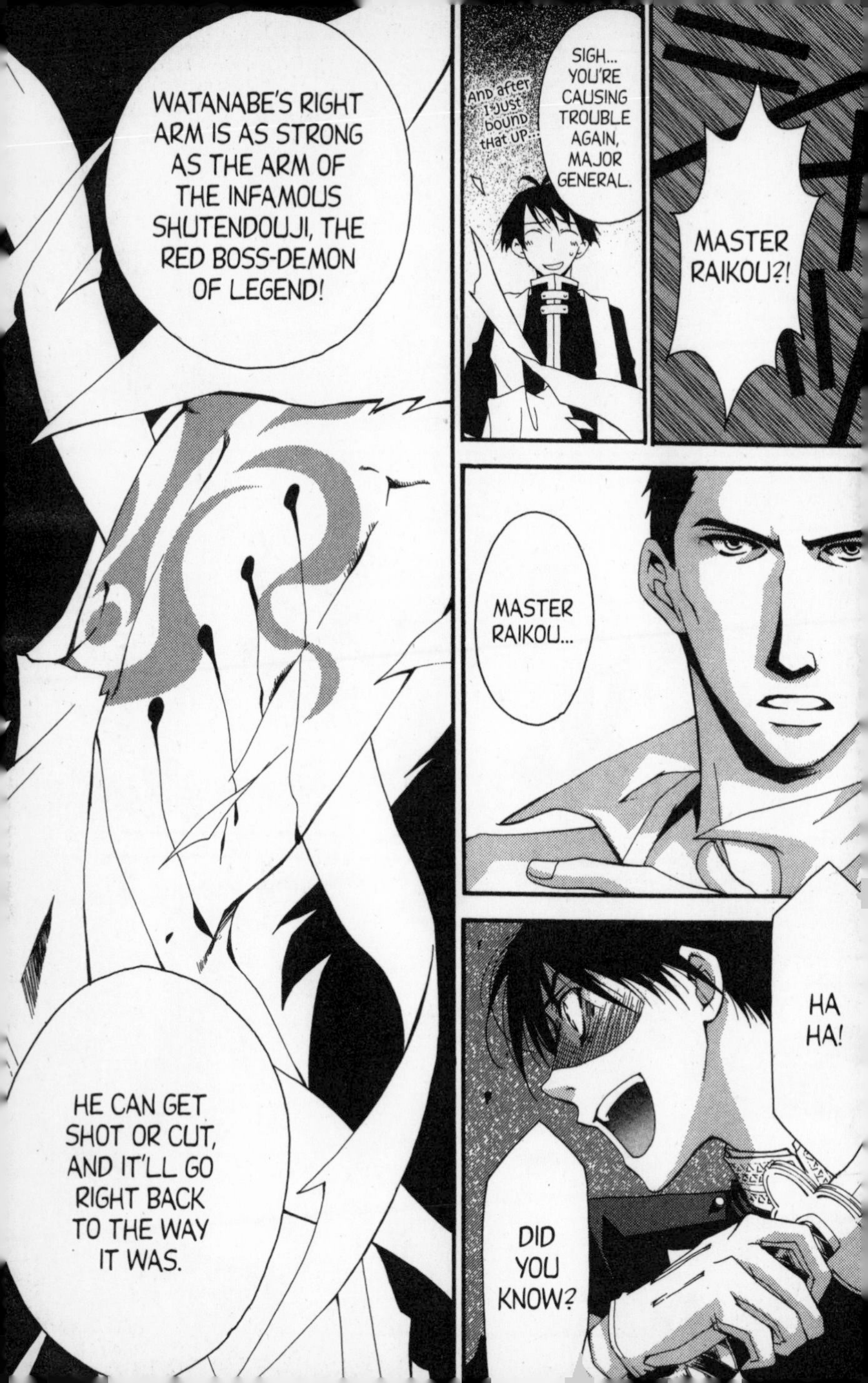
MASTER RAIKOU?!
SIGH... YOU'RE CAUSING TROUBLE AGAIN, MAJOR GENERAL.
And after I just bound that up...
MASTER RAIKOU...
HA HA!
DID YOU KNOW?
WATANABE'S RIGHT ARM IS AS STRONG AS THE ARM OF THE INFAMOUS SHUTENDOUJI, THE RED BOSS-DEMON OF LEGEND!
HE CAN GET SHOT OR CUT, AND IT'LL GO RIGHT BACK TO THE WAY IT WAS.

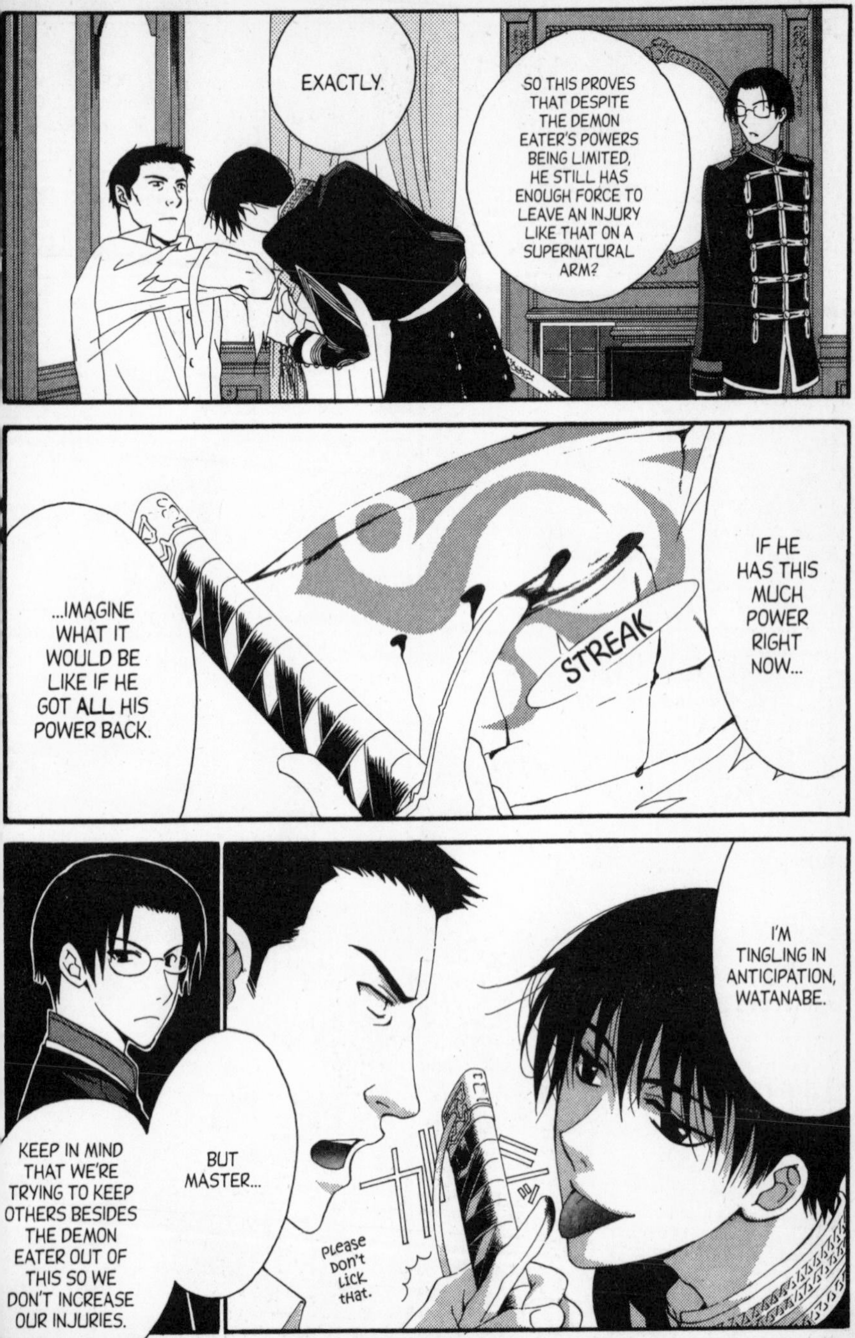

SO THIS PROVES THAT DESPITE THE DEMON EATER'S POWERS BEING LIMITED, HE STILL HAS ENOUGH FORCE TO LEAVE AN INJURY LIKE THAT ON A SUPERNATURAL ARM?
EXACTLY.
IF HE HAS THIS MUCH POWER RIGHT NOW...
STREAK
...IMAGINE WHAT IT WOULD BE LIKE IF HE GOT ALL HIS POWER BACK.
I'M TINGLING IN ANTICIPATION, WATANABE.
BUT MASTER...
Please don't lick that.
KEEP IN MIND THAT WE'RE TRYING TO KEEP OTHERS BESIDES THE DEMON EATER OUT OF THIS SO WE DON'T INCREASE OUR INJURIES.

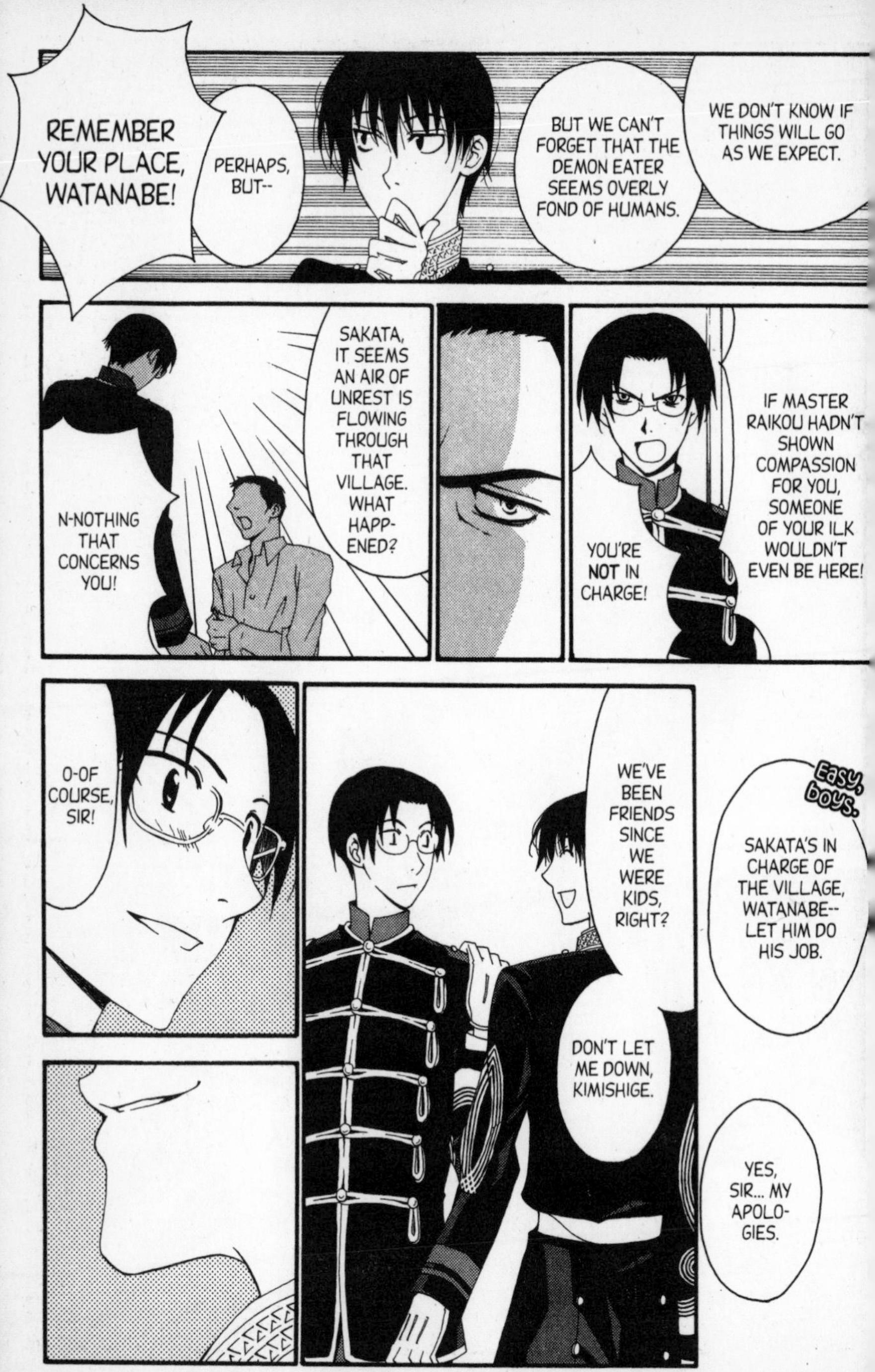
WE DON'T KNOW IF THINGS WILL GO AS WE EXPECT.
BUT WE CAN'T FORGET THAT THE DEMON EATER SEEMS OVERLY FOND OF HUMANS.
PERHAPS, BUT--
REMEMBER YOUR PLACE, WATANABE!
IF MASTER RAIKOU HADN'T SHOWN COMPASSION FOR YOU, SOMEONE OF YOUR ILK WOULDN'T EVEN BE HERE!
YOU'RE **NOT** IN CHARGE!
SAKATA, IT SEEMS AN AIR OF UNREST IS FLOWING THROUGH THAT VILLAGE. WHAT HAPP-ENED?
N-NOTHING THAT CONCERNS YOU!
Easy, boys.
SAKATA'S IN CHARGE OF THE VILLAGE, WATANABE-- LET HIM DO HIS JOB.
WE'VE BEEN FRIENDS SINCE WE WERE KIDS, RIGHT?
DON'T LET ME DOWN, KIMISHIGE.
YES, SIR... MY APOLO-GIES.
O-OF COURSE, SIR!

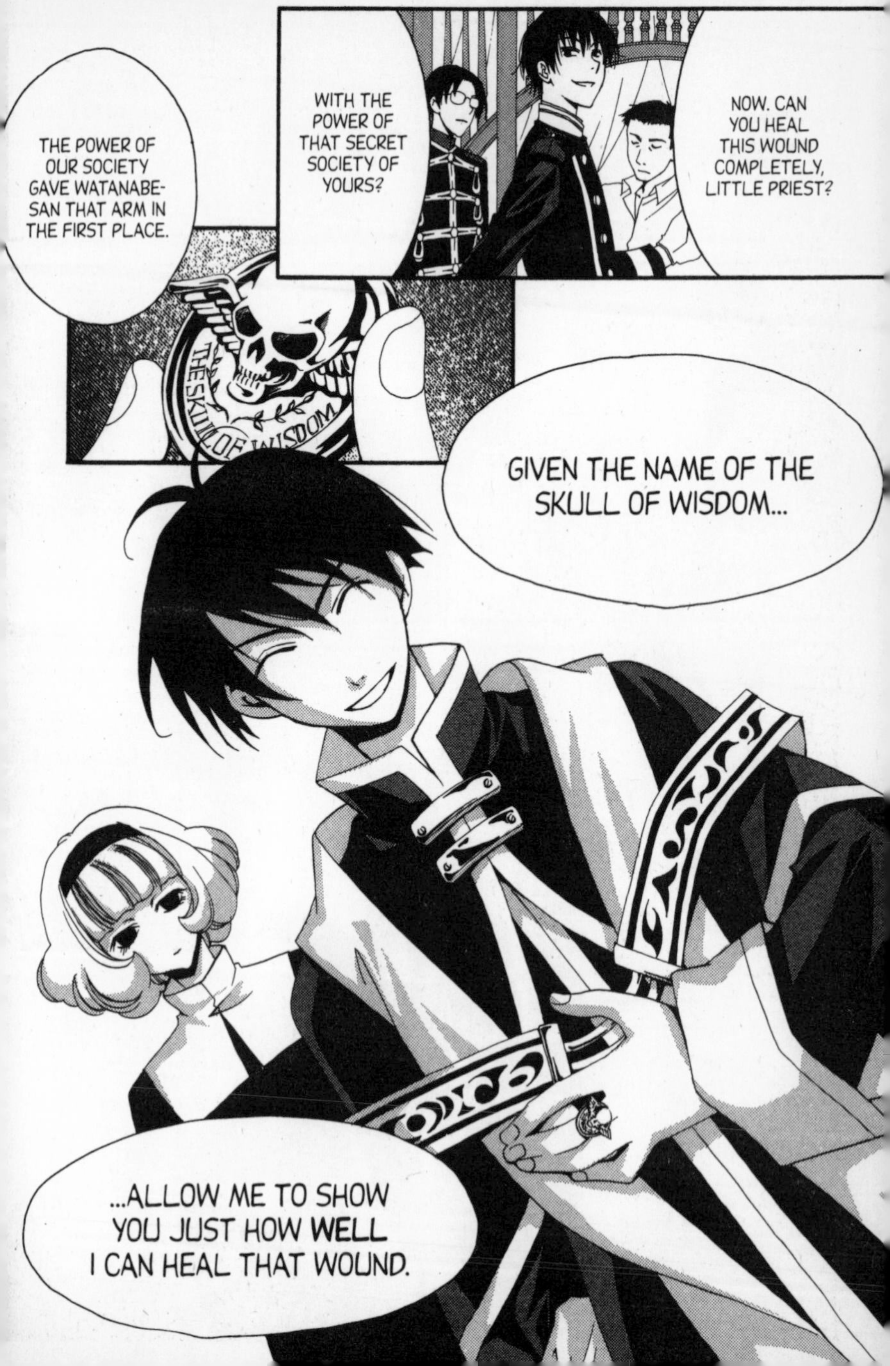
NOW. CAN YOU HEAL THIS WOUND COMPLETELY, LITTLE PRIEST?
WITH THE POWER OF THAT SECRET SOCIETY OF YOURS?
THE POWER OF OUR SOCIETY GAVE WATANABE-SAN THAT ARM IN THE FIRST PLACE.
THE SKULL OF WISDOM
GIVEN THE NAME OF THE SKULL OF WISDOM...
...ALLOW ME TO SHOW YOU JUST HOW WELL I CAN HEAL THAT WOUND.

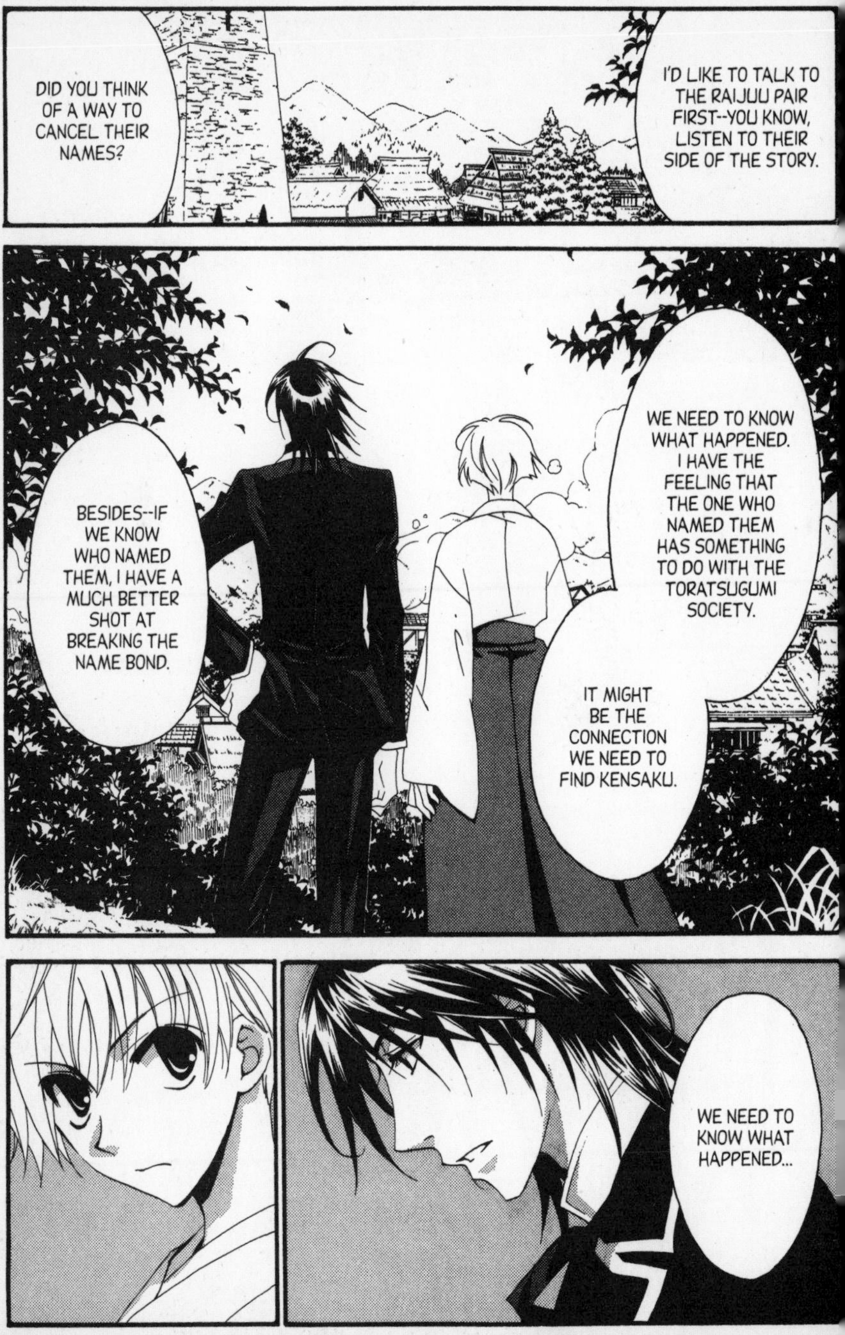
I'D LIKE TO TALK TO THE RAIJUU PAIR FIRST--YOU KNOW, LISTEN TO THEIR SIDE OF THE STORY.
DID YOU THINK OF A WAY TO CANCEL THEIR NAMES?
WE NEED TO KNOW WHAT HAPPENED. I HAVE THE FEELING THAT THE ONE WHO NAMED THEM HAS SOMETHING TO DO WITH THE TORATSUGUMI SOCIETY.
IT MIGHT BE THE CONNECTION WE NEED TO FIND KENSAKU.
BESIDES--IF WE KNOW WHO NAMED THEM, I HAVE A MUCH BETTER SHOT AT BREAKING THE NAME BOND.
WE NEED TO KNOW WHAT HAPPENED...

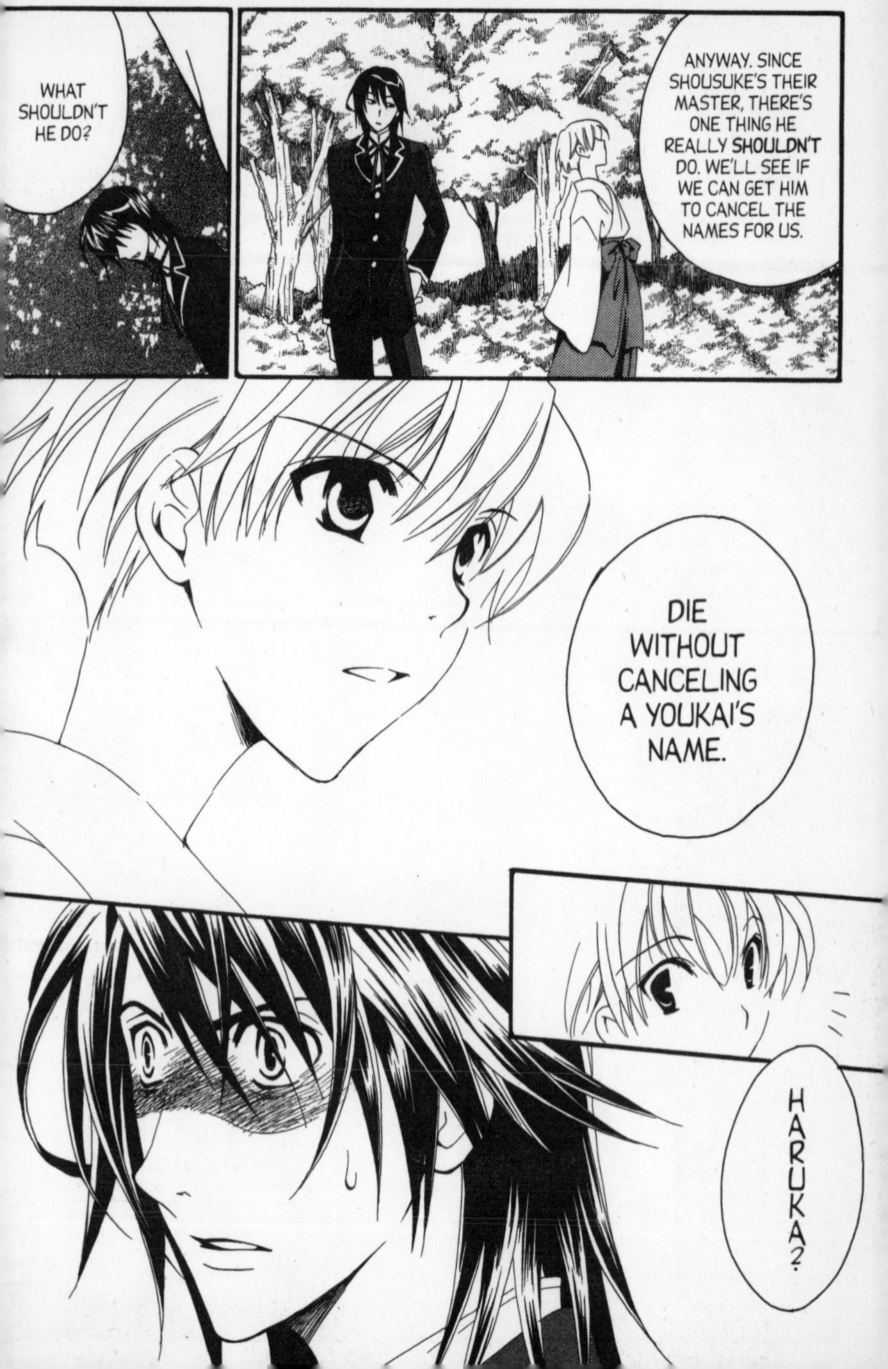
ANYWAY. SINCE SHOUSUKE'S THEIR MASTER, THERE'S ONE THING HE REALLY **SHOULDN'T** DO. WE'LL SEE IF WE CAN GET HIM TO CANCEL THE NAMES FOR US.
WHAT SHOULDN'T HE DO?
DIE WITHOUT CANCELING A YOUKAI'S NAME.
HARUKA?

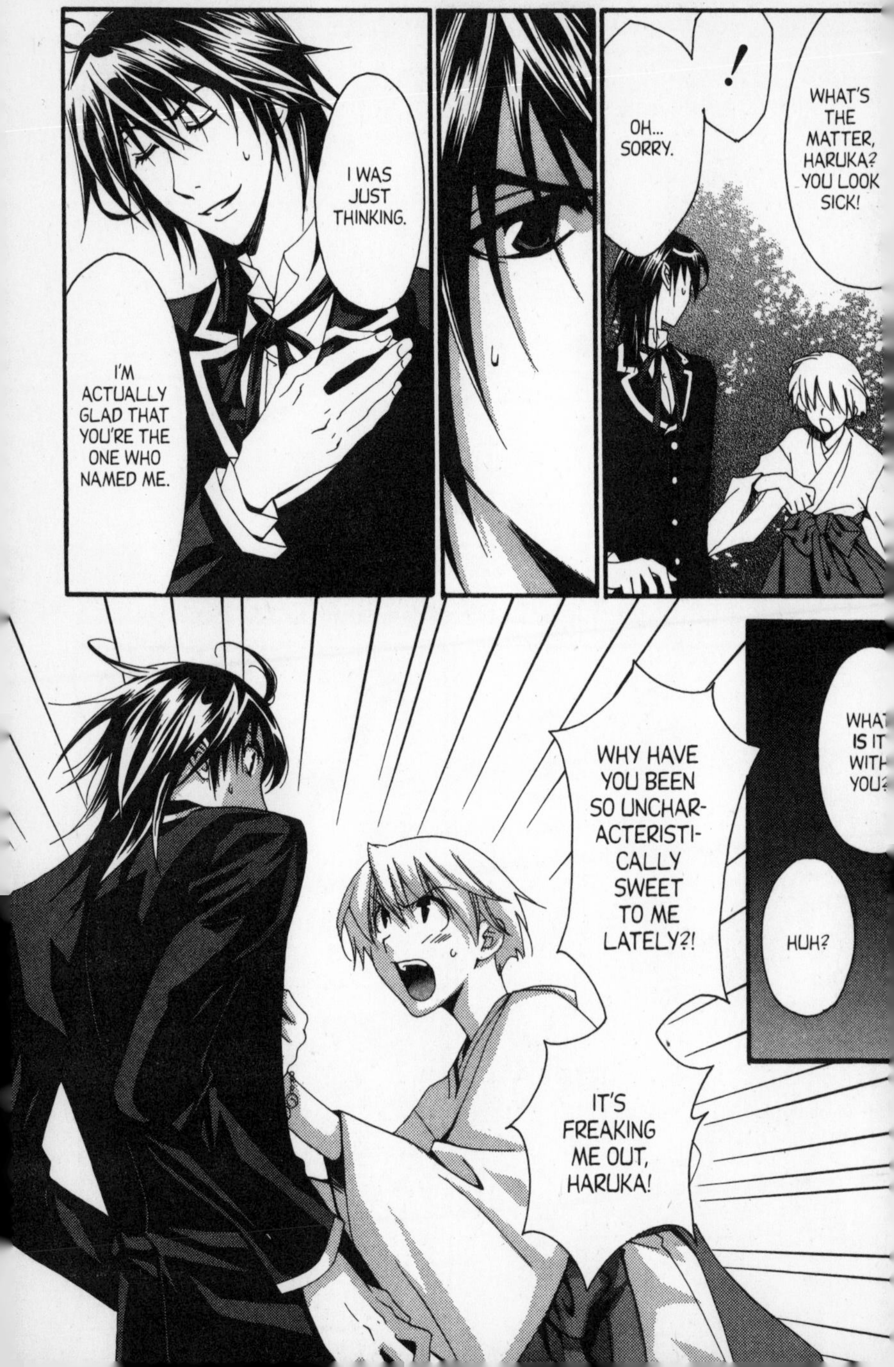
WHAT'S THE MATTER, HARUKA? YOU LOOK SICK!
!
OH... SORRY.
I WAS JUST THINKING.
I'M ACTUALLY GLAD THAT YOU'RE THE ONE WHO NAMED ME.
WHAT IS IT WITH YOU?
HUH?
WHY HAVE YOU BEEN SO UNCHARACTERISTICALLY SWEET TO ME LATELY?!
IT'S FREAKING ME OUT, HARUKA!

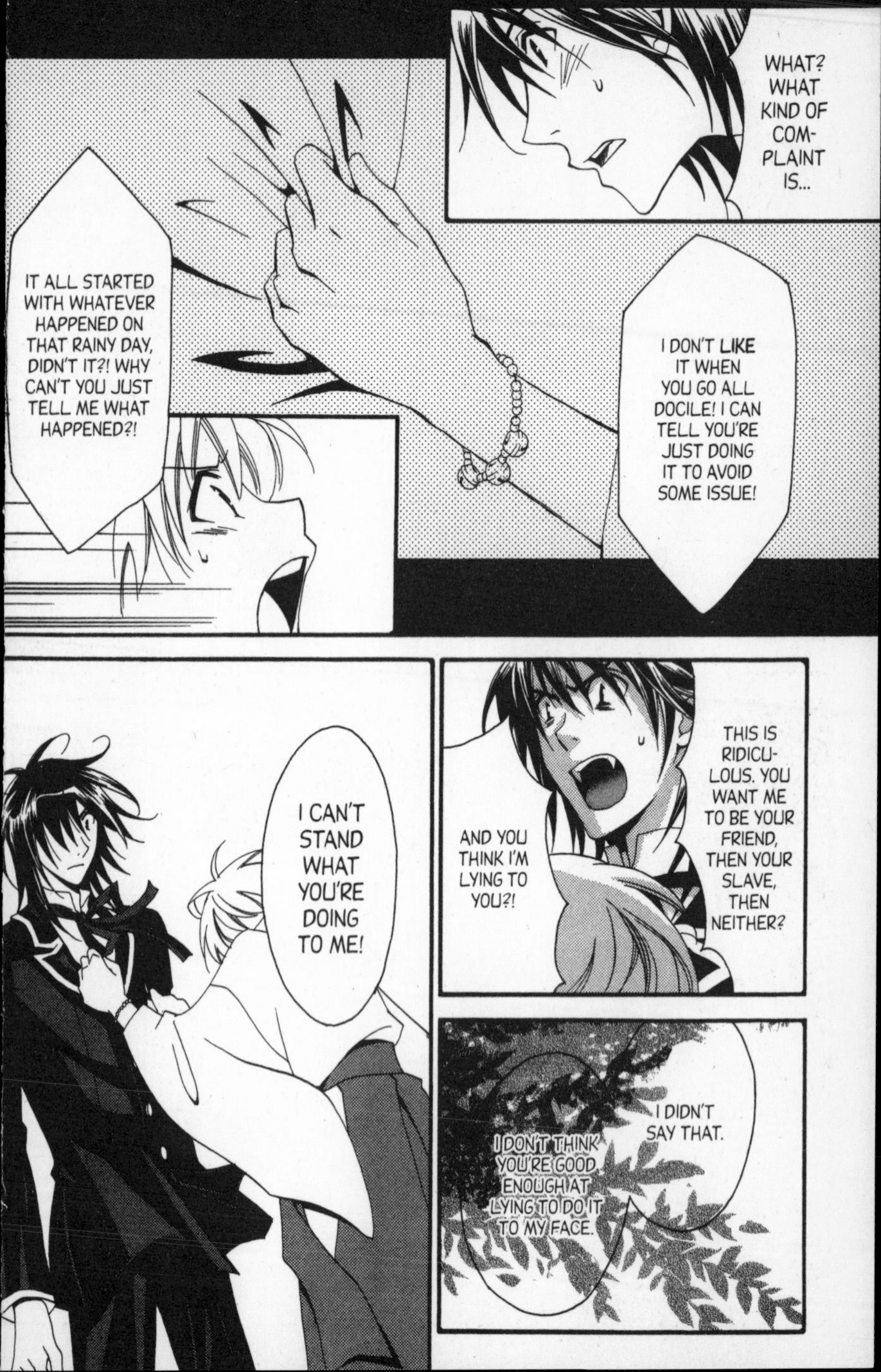
WHAT? WHAT KIND OF COM-PLAINT IS...
I DON'T LIKE IT WHEN YOU GO ALL DOCILE! I CAN TELL YOU'RE JUST DOING IT TO AVOID SOME ISSUE!
IT ALL STARTED WITH WHATEVER HAPPENED ON THAT RAINY DAY, DIDN'T IT?! WHY CAN'T YOU JUST TELL ME WHAT HAPPENED?!
THIS IS RIDICU-LOUS. YOU WANT ME TO BE YOUR FRIEND, THEN YOUR SLAVE, THEN NEITHER?
AND YOU THINK I'M LYING TO YOU?!
I DIDN'T SAY THAT.
I DON'T THINK YOU'RE GOOD ENOUGH AT LYING TO DO IT TO MY FACE.
I CAN'T STAND WHAT YOU'RE DOING TO ME!

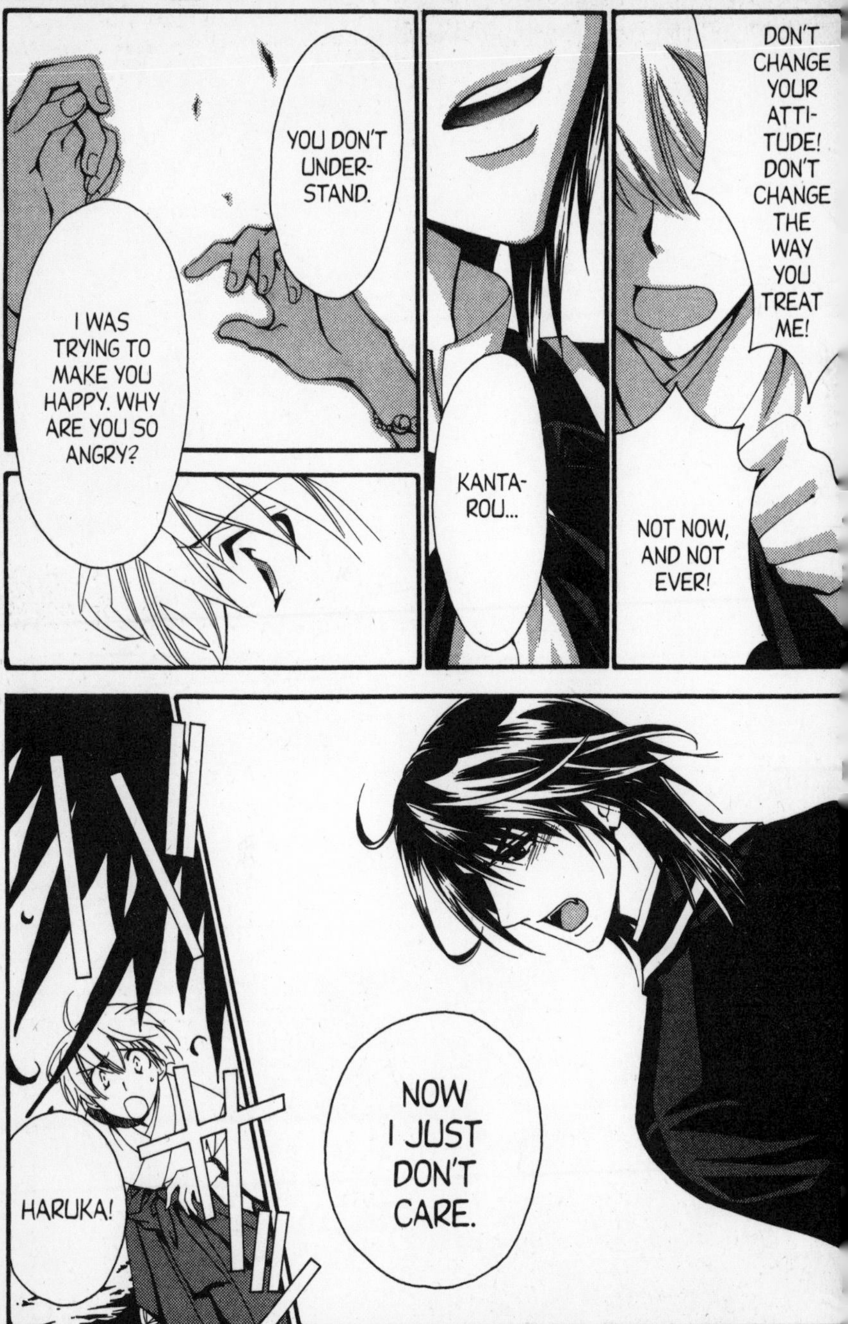
DON'T CHANGE YOUR ATTI-TUDE! DON'T CHANGE THE WAY YOU TREAT ME!
NOT NOW, AND NOT EVER!
KANTA-ROU...
YOU DON'T UNDER-STAND.
I WAS TRYING TO MAKE YOU HAPPY. WHY ARE YOU SO ANGRY?
NOW I JUST DON'T CARE.
HARUKA!

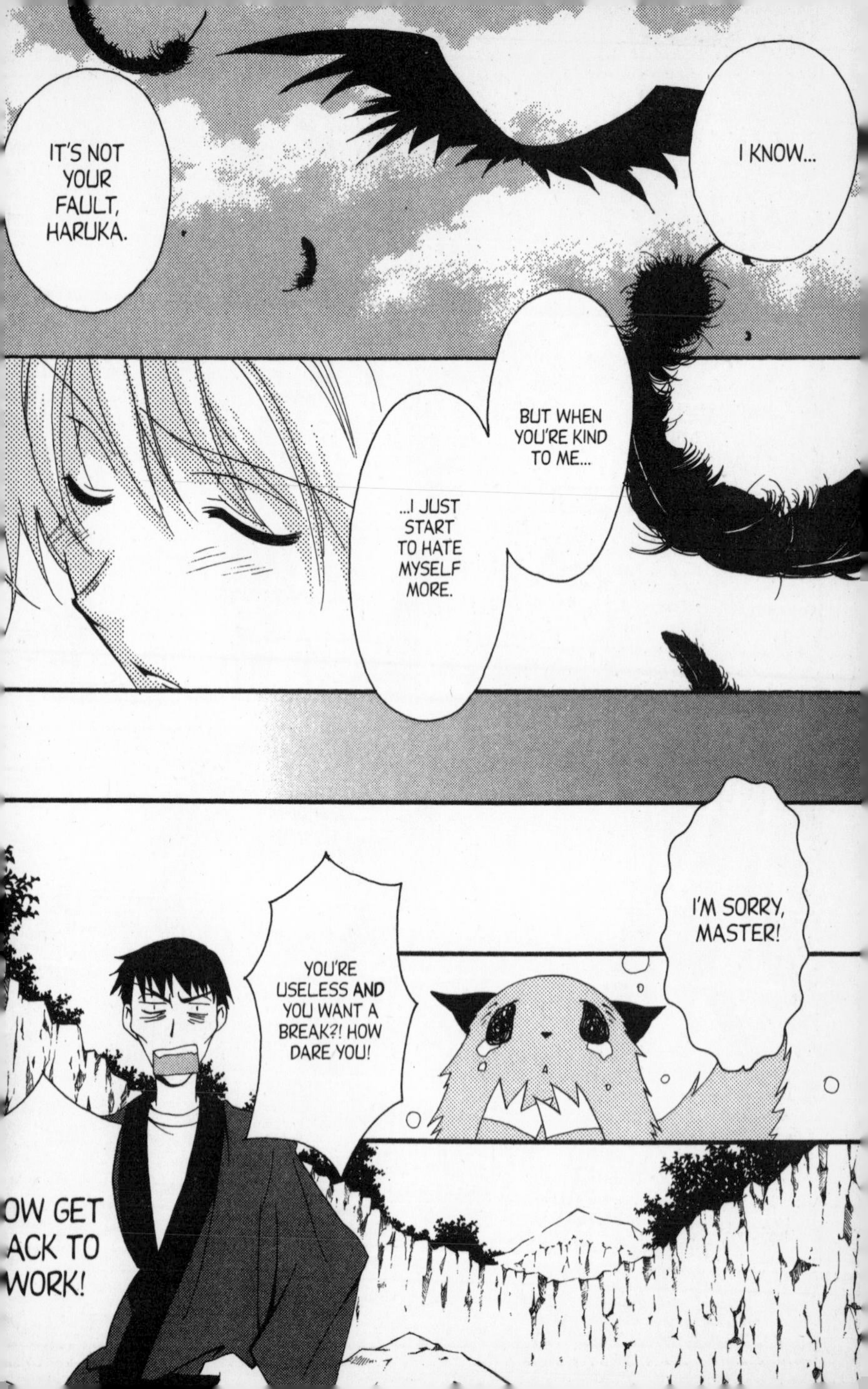
IT'S NOT YOUR FAULT, HARUKA.
I KNOW...
BUT WHEN YOU'RE KIND TO ME...
...I JUST START TO HATE MYSELF MORE.
I'M SORRY, MASTER!
YOU'RE USELESS AND YOU WANT A BREAK?! HOW DARE YOU!
OW GET ACK TO WORK!

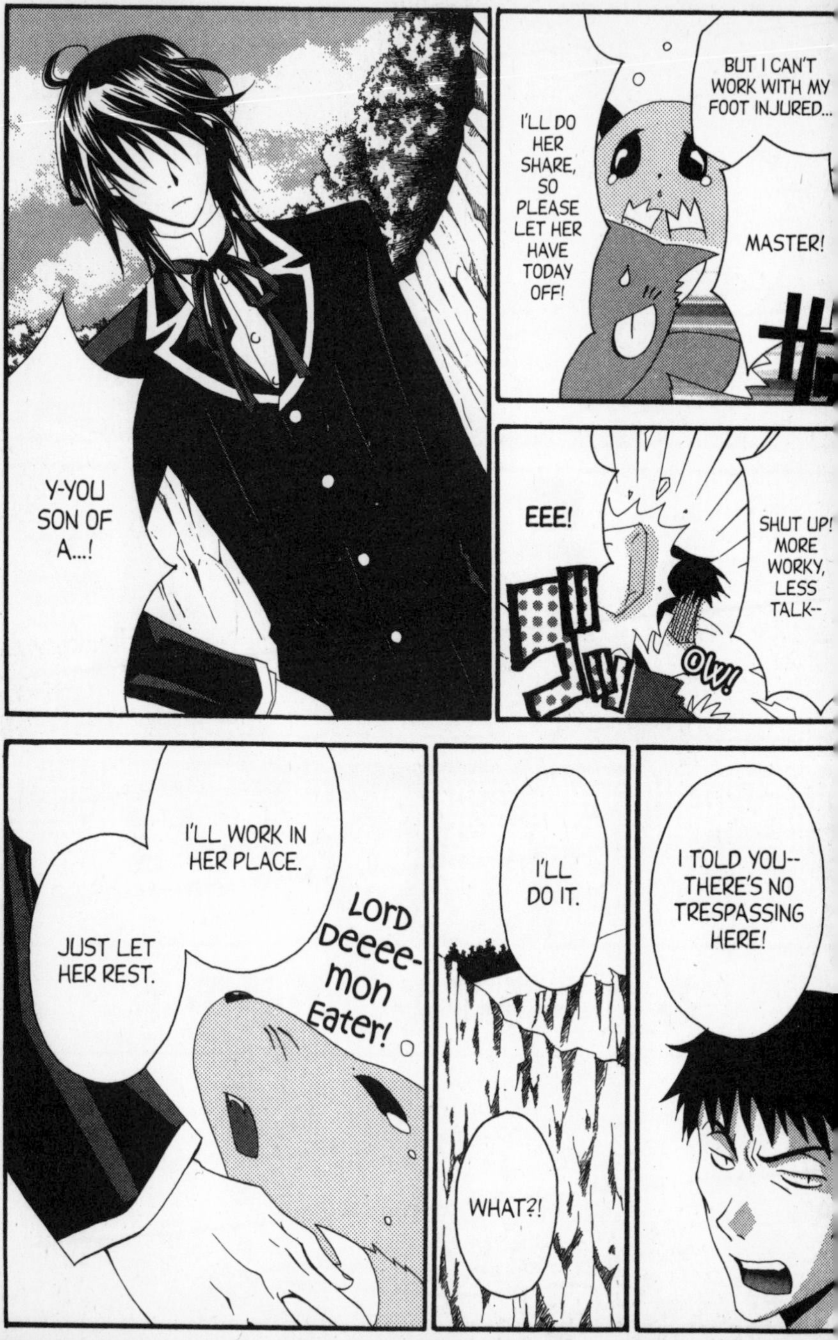
BUT I CAN'T WORK WITH MY FOOT INJURED...
I'LL DO HER SHARE, SO PLEASE LET HER HAVE TODAY OFF!
MASTER!
SHUT UP! MORE WORKY, LESS TALK--
EEE!
OW!
Y-YOU SON OF A...!
I TOLD YOU-- THERE'S NO TRESPASSING HERE!
I'LL DO IT.
WHAT?!
I'LL WORK IN HER PLACE.
JUST LET HER REST.
Lord Deeeee-mon Eater!

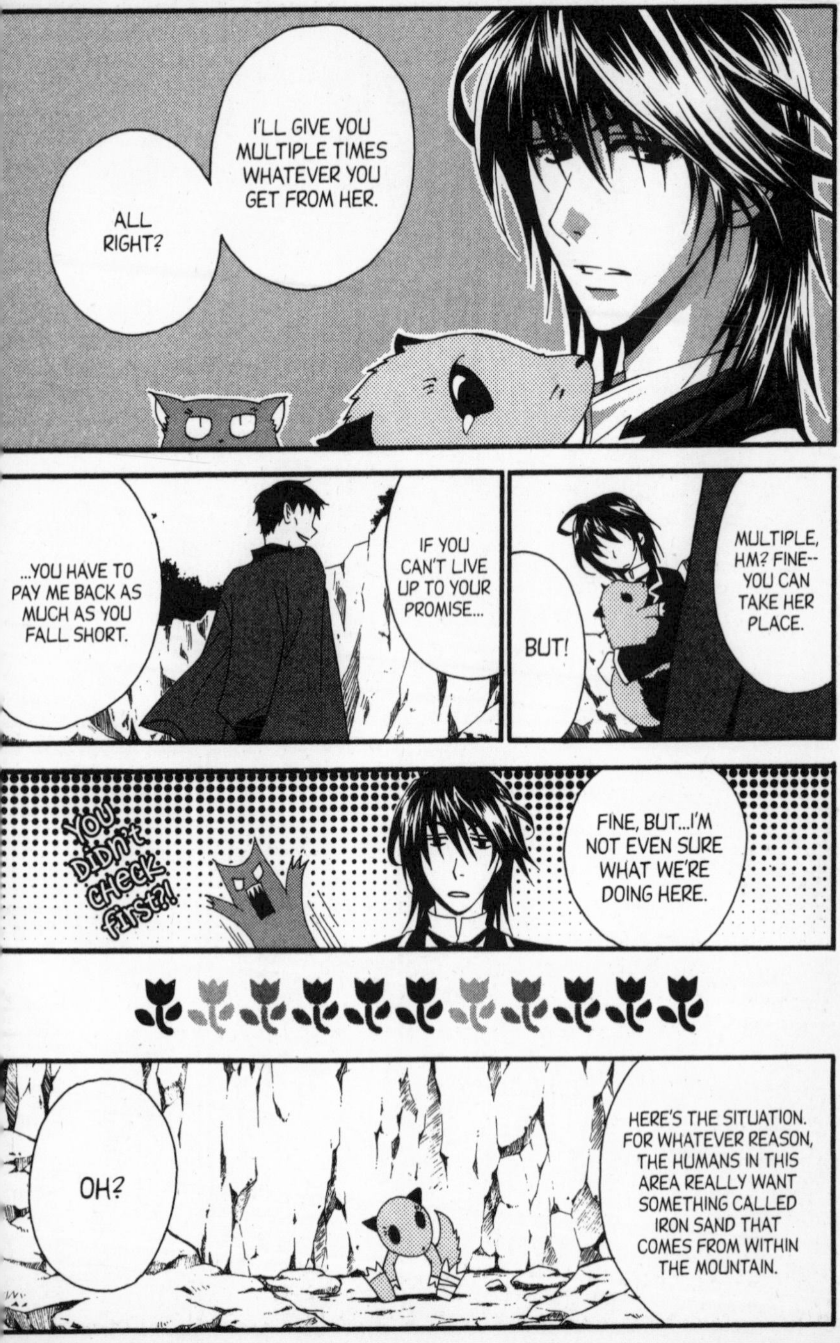
I'LL GIVE YOU MULTIPLE TIMES WHATEVER YOU GET FROM HER.
ALL RIGHT?
MULTIPLE, HM? FINE-- YOU CAN TAKE HER PLACE.
BUT!
IF YOU CAN'T LIVE UP TO YOUR PROMISE...
...YOU HAVE TO PAY ME BACK AS MUCH AS YOU FALL SHORT.
FINE, BUT...I'M NOT EVEN SURE WHAT WE'RE DOING HERE.
YOU DIDN'T CHECK FIRST?!
HERE'S THE SITUATION. FOR WHATEVER REASON, THE HUMANS IN THIS AREA REALLY WANT SOMETHING CALLED IRON SAND THAT COMES FROM WITHIN THE MOUNTAIN.
OH?

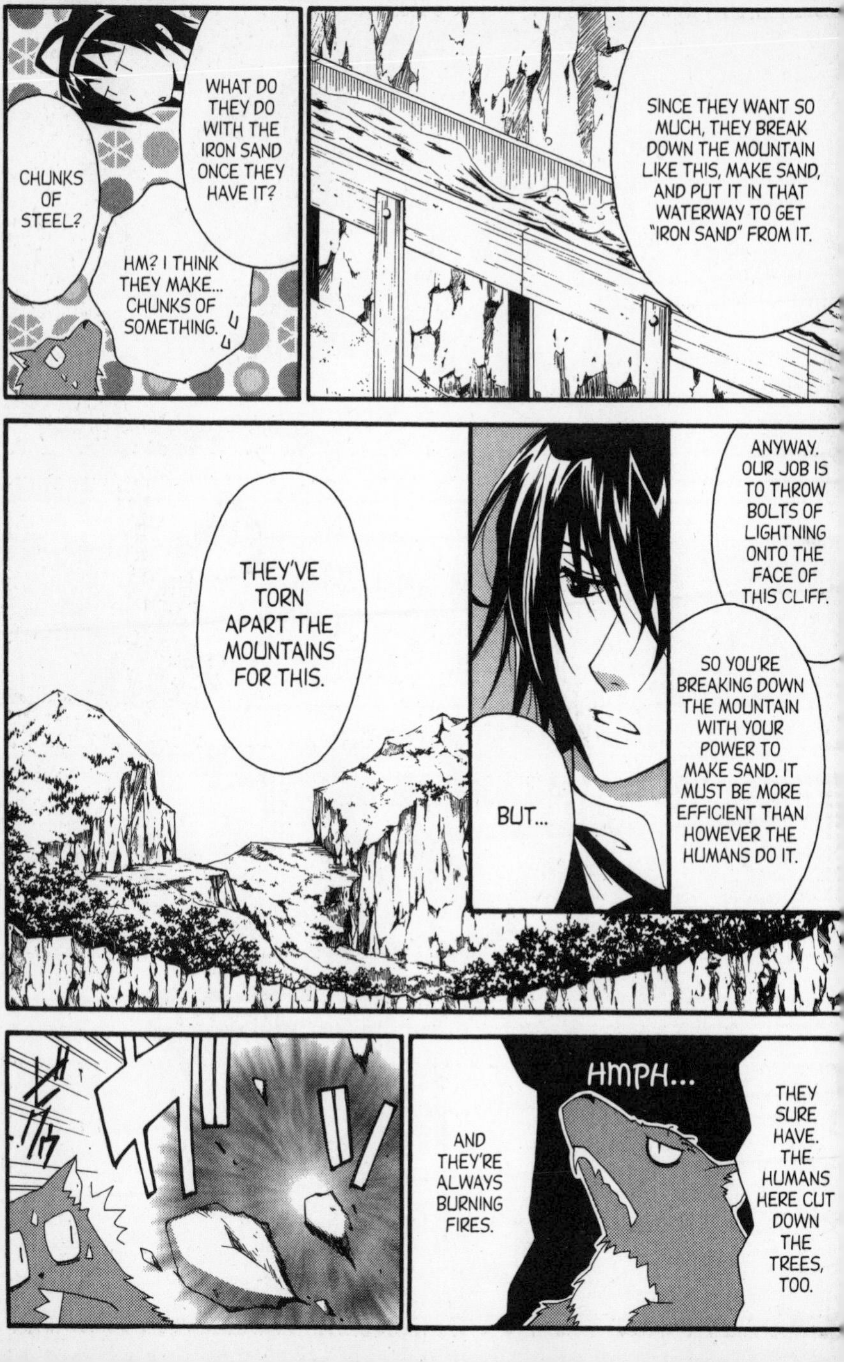
SINCE THEY WANT SO MUCH, THEY BREAK DOWN THE MOUNTAIN LIKE THIS, MAKE SAND, AND PUT IT IN THAT WATERWAY TO GET "IRON SAND" FROM IT.
WHAT DO THEY DO WITH THE IRON SAND ONCE THEY HAVE IT?
HM? I THINK THEY MAKE... CHUNKS OF SOMETHING.
CHUNKS OF STEEL?
ANYWAY. OUR JOB IS TO THROW BOLTS OF LIGHTNING ONTO THE FACE OF THIS CLIFF.
SO YOU'RE BREAKING DOWN THE MOUNTAIN WITH YOUR POWER TO MAKE SAND. IT MUST BE MORE EFFICIENT THAN HOWEVER THE HUMANS DO IT.
BUT...
THEY'VE TORN APART THE MOUNTAINS FOR THIS.
HMPH...
THEY SURE HAVE. THE HUMANS HERE CUT DOWN THE TREES, TOO.
AND THEY'RE ALWAYS BURNING FIRES.

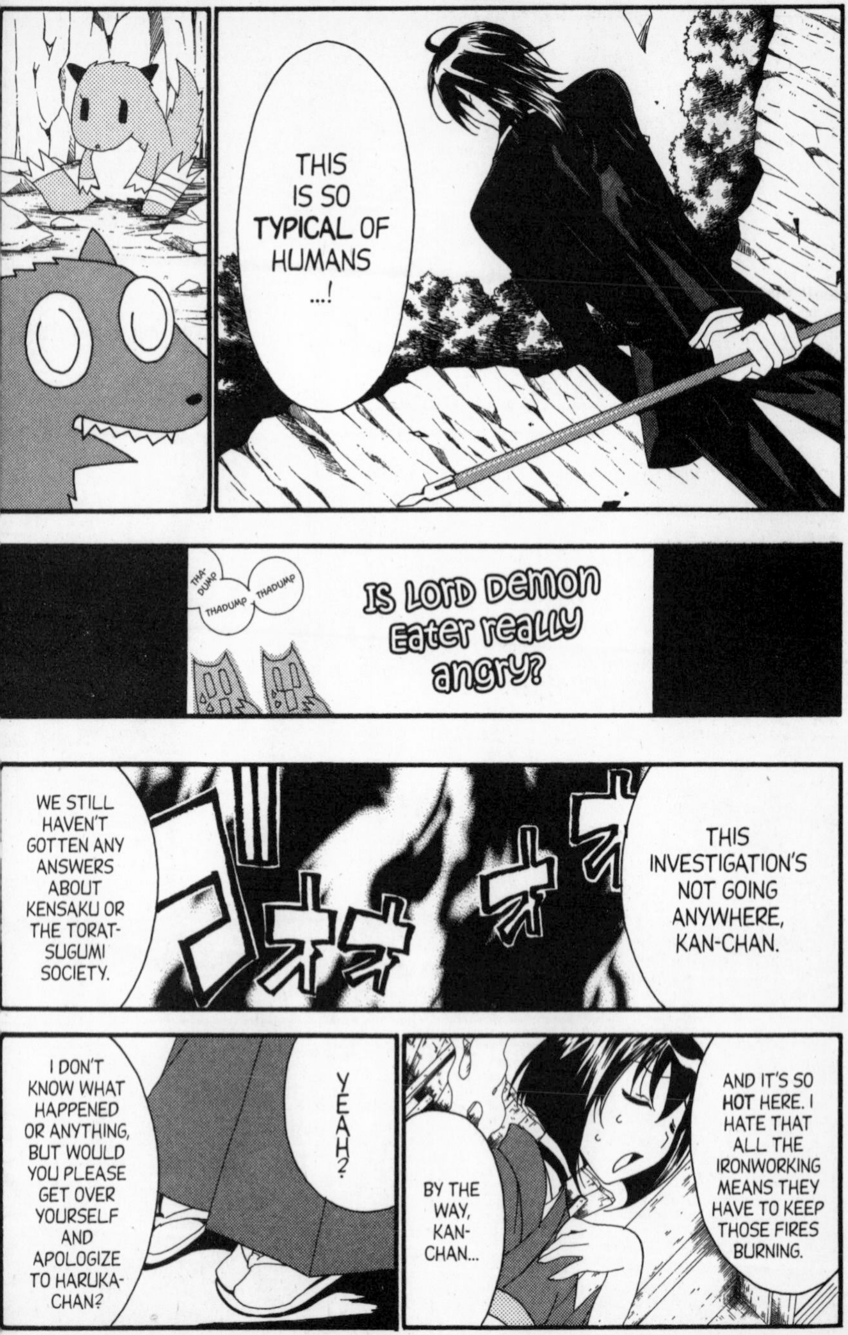
THIS IS SO TYPICAL OF HUMANS ...!
IS LORD DEMON EATER REALLY ANGRY?
THADUMP THADUMP
THA-DUMP
THIS INVESTIGATION'S NOT GOING ANYWHERE, KAN-CHAN.
WE STILL HAVEN'T GOTTEN ANY ANSWERS ABOUT KENSAKU OR THE TORAT-SUGUMI SOCIETY.
AND IT'S SO HOT HERE. I HATE THAT ALL THE IRONWORKING MEANS THEY HAVE TO KEEP THOSE FIRES BURNING.
BY THE WAY, KAN-CHAN...
YEAH?
I DON'T KNOW WHAT HAPPENED OR ANYTHING, BUT WOULD YOU PLEASE GET OVER YOURSELF AND APOLOGIZE TO HARUKA-CHAN?

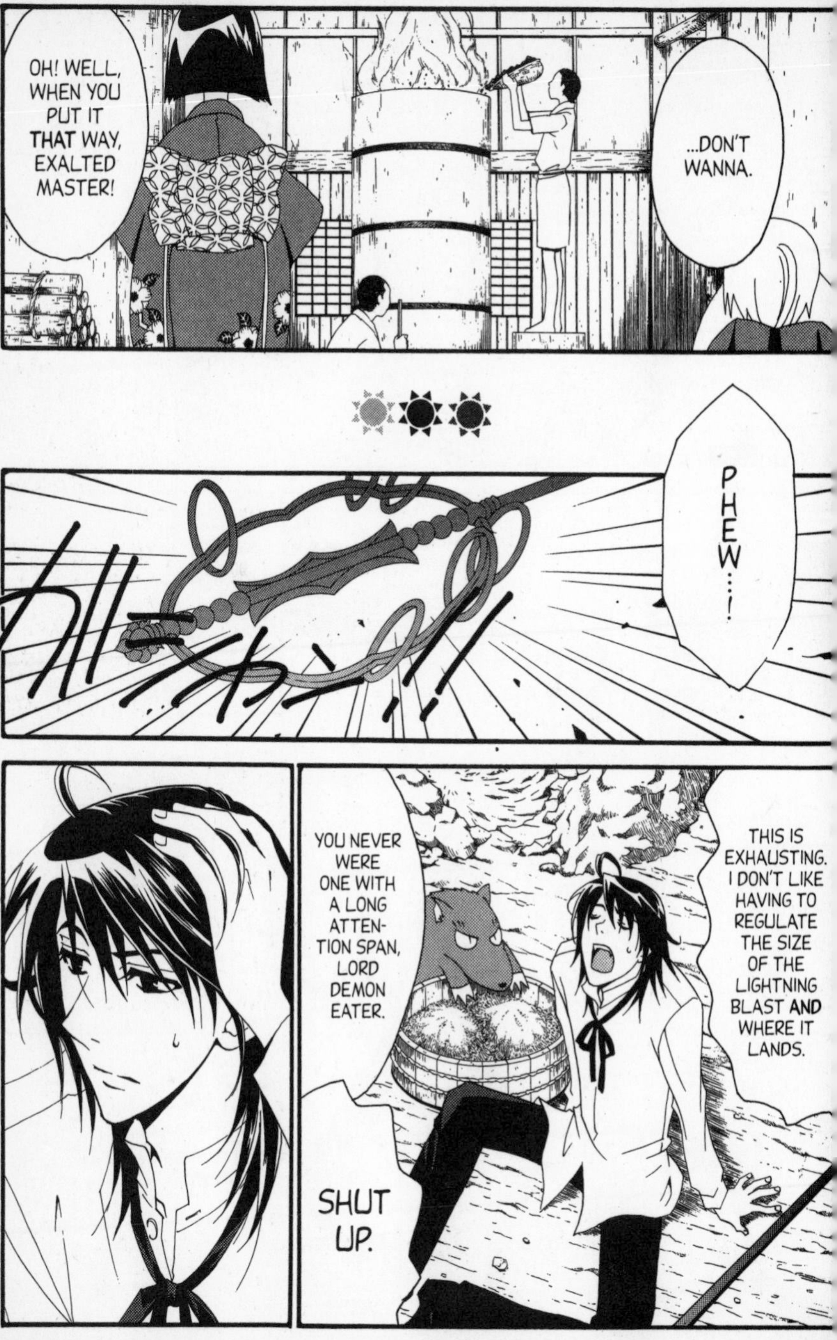
...DON'T WANNA.
OH! WELL, WHEN YOU PUT IT THAT WAY, EXALTED MASTER!
PHEW...!
THIS IS EXHAUSTING. I DON'T LIKE HAVING TO REGULATE THE SIZE OF THE LIGHTNING BLAST AND WHERE IT LANDS.
YOU NEVER WERE ONE WITH A LONG ATTEN-TION SPAN, LORD DEMON EATER.
SHUT UP.

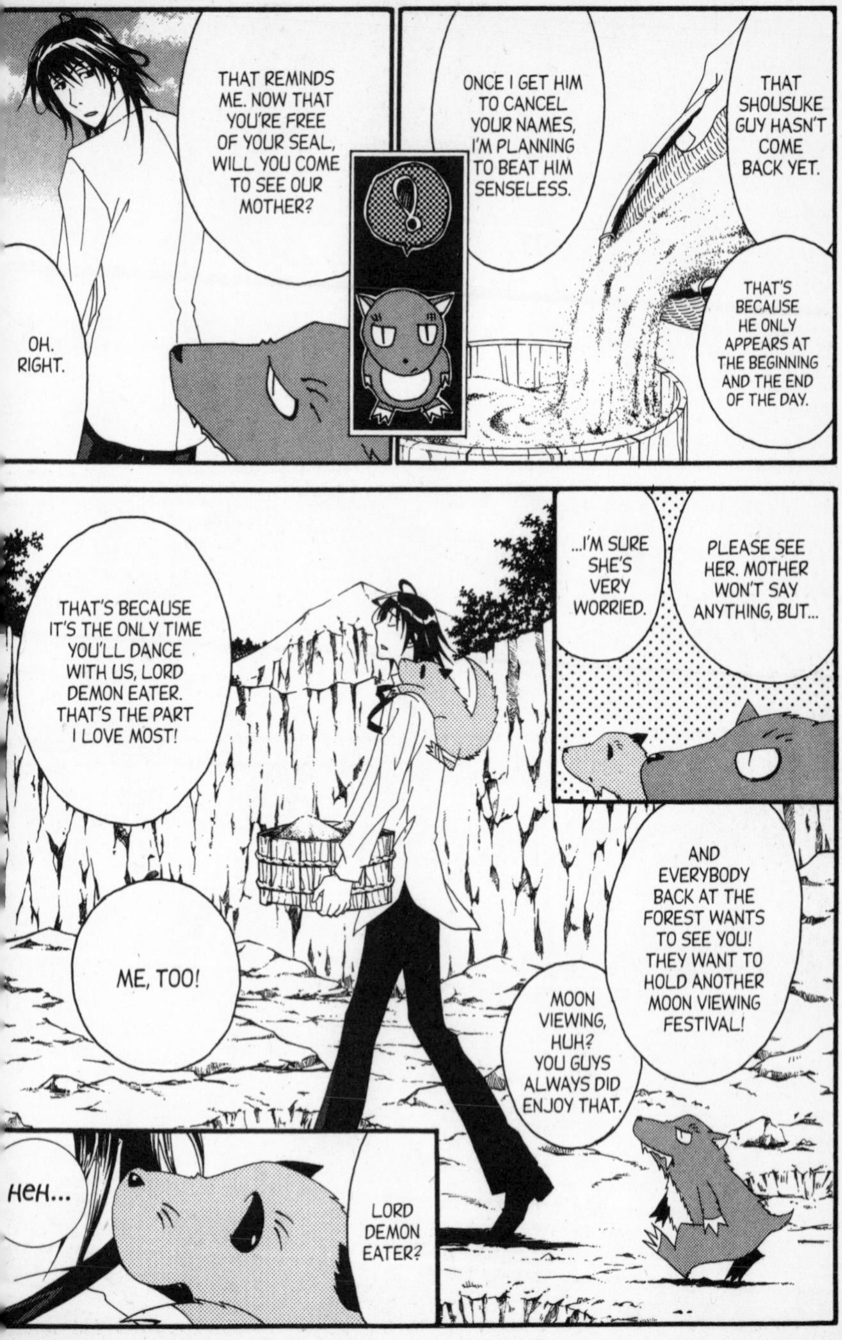
THAT SHOUSUKE GUY HASN'T COME BACK YET.
THAT'S BECAUSE HE ONLY APPEARS AT THE BEGINNING AND THE END OF THE DAY.
ONCE I GET HIM TO CANCEL YOUR NAMES, I'M PLANNING TO BEAT HIM SENSELESS.
?
THAT REMINDS ME. NOW THAT YOU'RE FREE OF YOUR SEAL, WILL YOU COME TO SEE OUR MOTHER?
OH. RIGHT.
PLEASE SEE HER. MOTHER WON'T SAY ANYTHING, BUT...
...I'M SURE SHE'S VERY WORRIED.
AND EVERYBODY BACK AT THE FOREST WANTS TO SEE YOU! THEY WANT TO HOLD ANOTHER MOON VIEWING FESTIVAL!
MOON VIEWING, HUH? YOU GUYS ALWAYS DID ENJOY THAT.
THAT'S BECAUSE IT'S THE ONLY TIME YOU'LL DANCE WITH US, LORD DEMON EATER. THAT'S THE PART I LOVE MOST!
ME, TOO!
LORD DEMON EATER?
HEH...

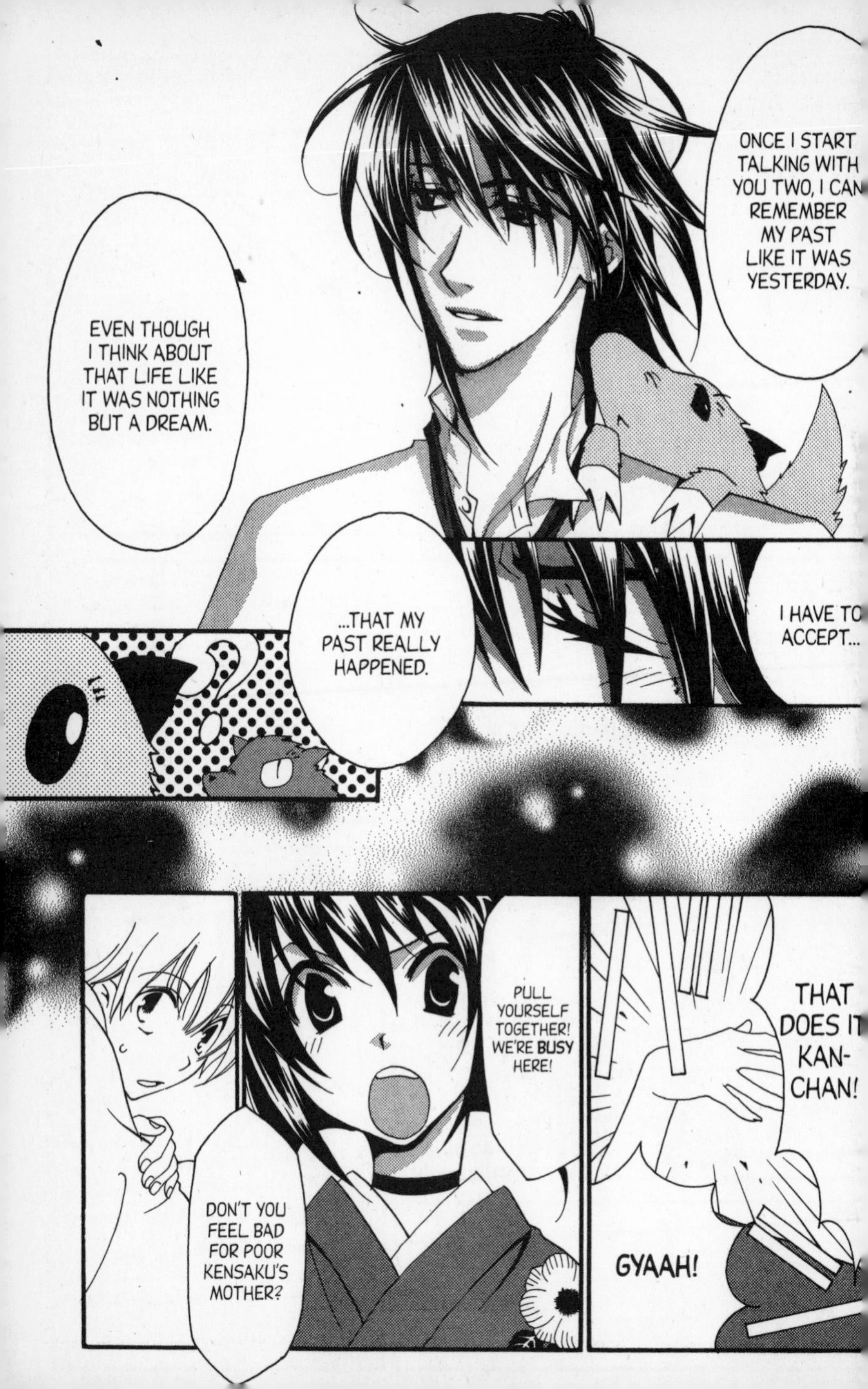
ONCE I START TALKING WITH YOU TWO, I CAN REMEMBER MY PAST LIKE IT WAS YESTERDAY.
EVEN THOUGH I THINK ABOUT THAT LIFE LIKE IT WAS NOTHING BUT A DREAM.
I HAVE TO ACCEPT...
...THAT MY PAST REALLY HAPPENED.
THAT DOES IT KAN-CHAN!
GYAAH!
PULL YOURSELF TOGETHER! WE'RE BUSY HERE!
DON'T YOU FEEL BAD FOR POOR KENSAKU'S MOTHER?

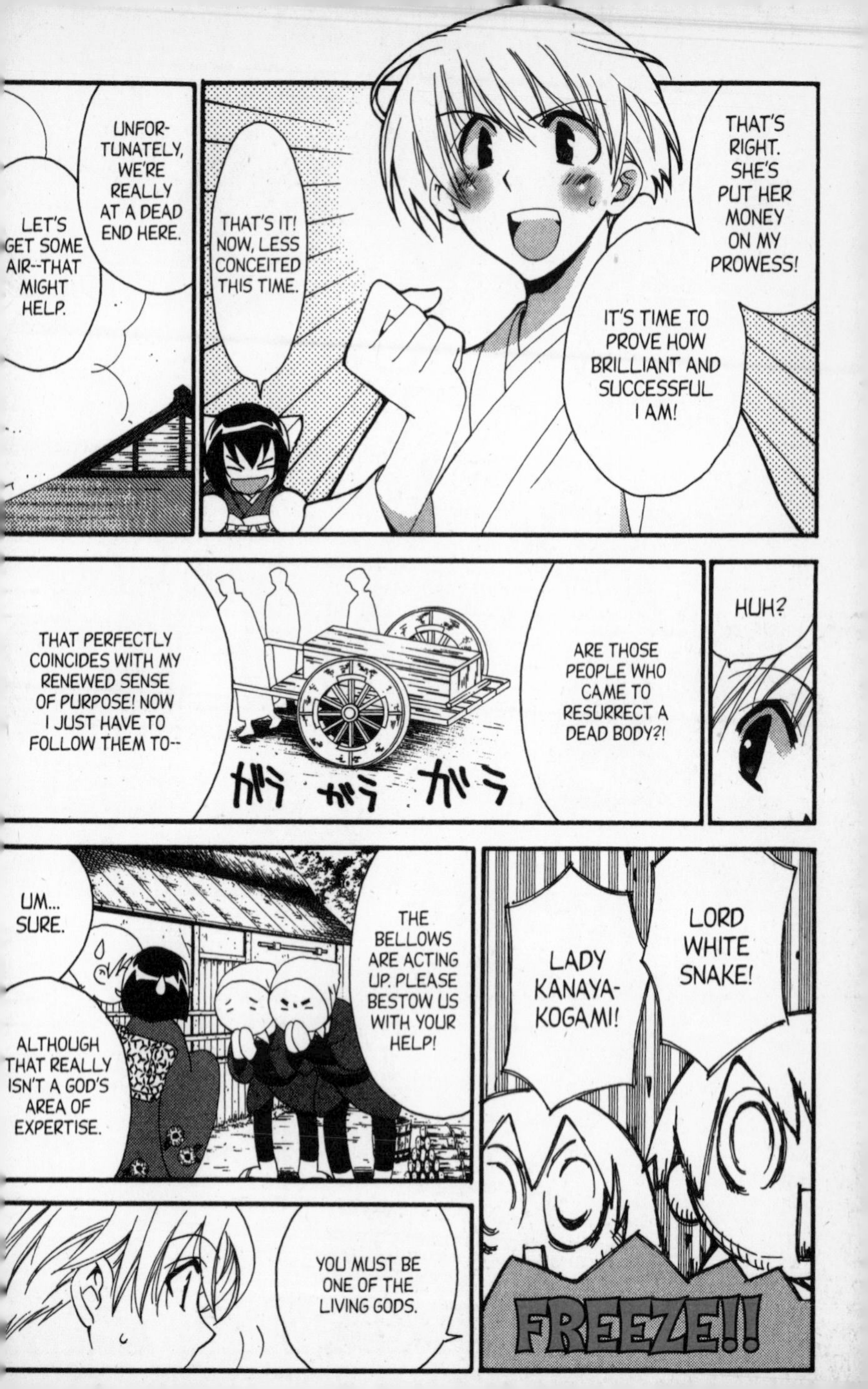

THAT'S RIGHT. SHE'S PUT HER MONEY ON MY PROWESS!
IT'S TIME TO PROVE HOW BRILLIANT AND SUCCESSFUL I AM!
THAT'S IT! NOW, LESS CONCEITED THIS TIME.
UNFOR-TUNATELY, WE'RE REALLY AT A DEAD END HERE.
LET'S GET SOME AIR--THAT MIGHT HELP.
...
...
HUH?
ARE THOSE PEOPLE WHO CAME TO RESURRECT A DEAD BODY?!
ガラ ガラ ガラ
THAT PERFECTLY COINCIDES WITH MY RENEWED SENSE OF PURPOSE! NOW I JUST HAVE TO FOLLOW THEM TO--
LORD WHITE SNAKE!
LADY KANAYA-KOGAMI!
FREEZE!!
THE BELLOWS ARE ACTING UP. PLEASE BESTOW US WITH YOUR HELP!
UM... SURE.
ALTHOUGH THAT REALLY ISN'T A GOD'S AREA OF EXPERTISE.
YOU MUST BE ONE OF THE LIVING GODS.

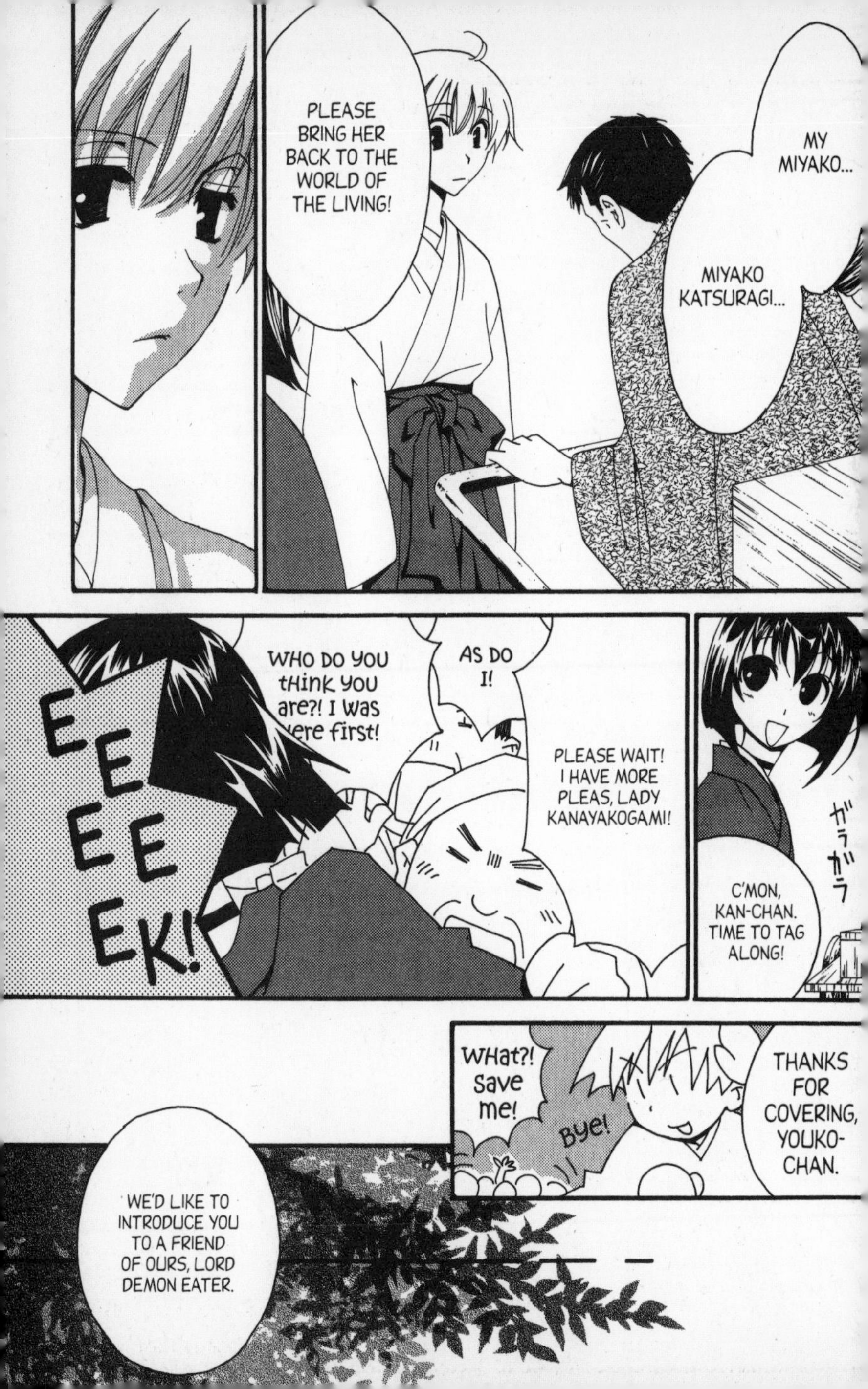

MY MIYAKO...
MIYAKO KATSURAGI...
PLEASE BRING HER BACK TO THE WORLD OF THE LIVING!
C'MON, KAN-CHAN. TIME TO TAG ALONG!
ガラガラ
PLEASE WAIT! I HAVE MORE PLEAS, LADY KANAYAKOGAMI!
AS DO I!
WHO DO YOU tHINK YOU are?! I WAS ere first!
EEEEEK!
THANKS FOR COVERING, YOUKO-CHAN.
BYe!
WHAt?! Save me!
WE'D LIKE TO INTRODUCE YOU TO A FRIEND OF OURS, LORD DEMON EATER.

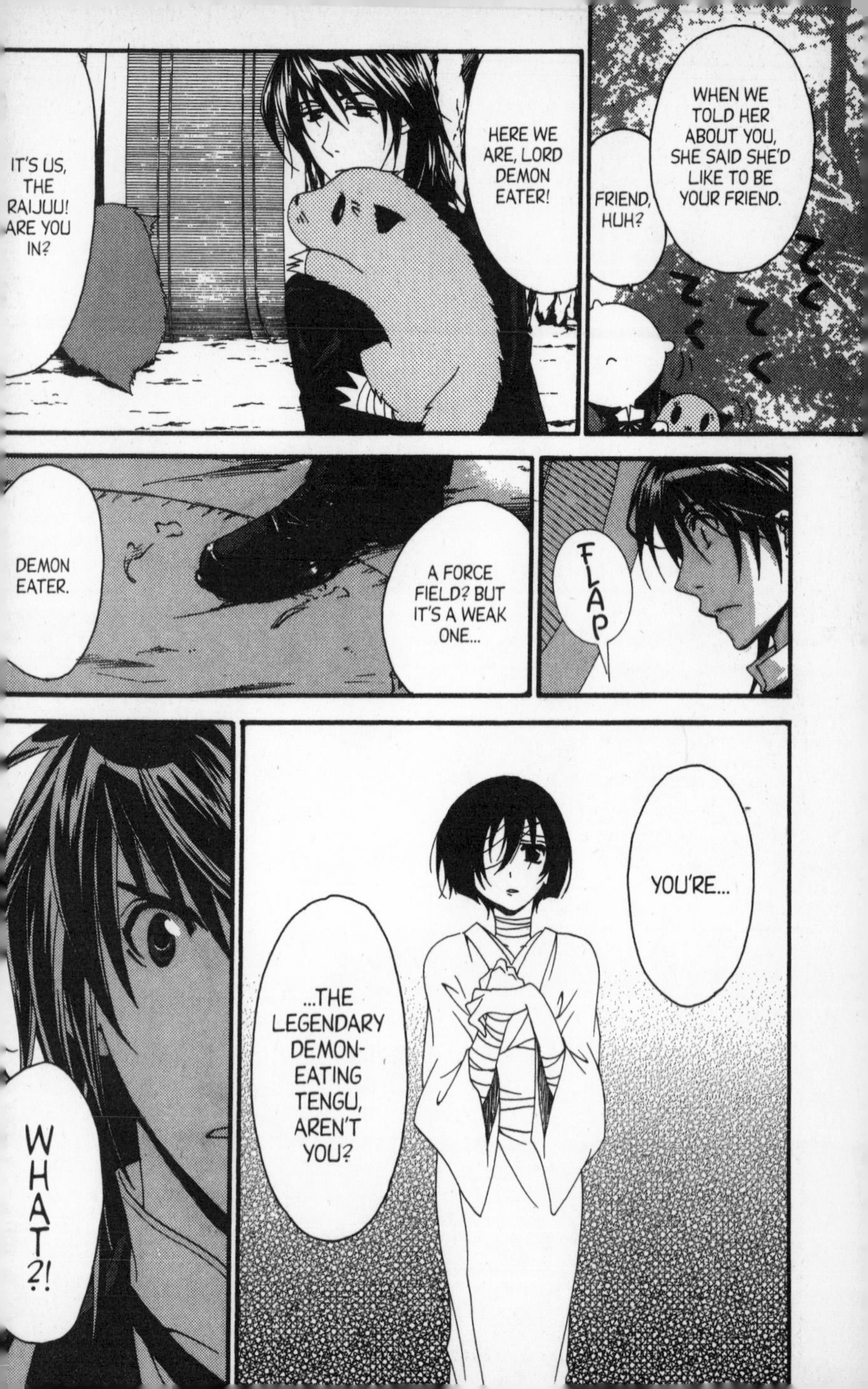
WHEN WE TOLD HER ABOUT YOU, SHE SAID SHE'D LIKE TO BE YOUR FRIEND.
FRIEND, HUH?
HERE WE ARE, LORD DEMON EATER!
IT'S US, THE RAIJUU! ARE YOU IN?
FLAP
A FORCE FIELD? BUT IT'S A WEAK ONE...
DEMON EATER.
YOU'RE...
...THE LEGENDARY DEMON-EATING TENGU, AREN'T YOU?
WHAT?!

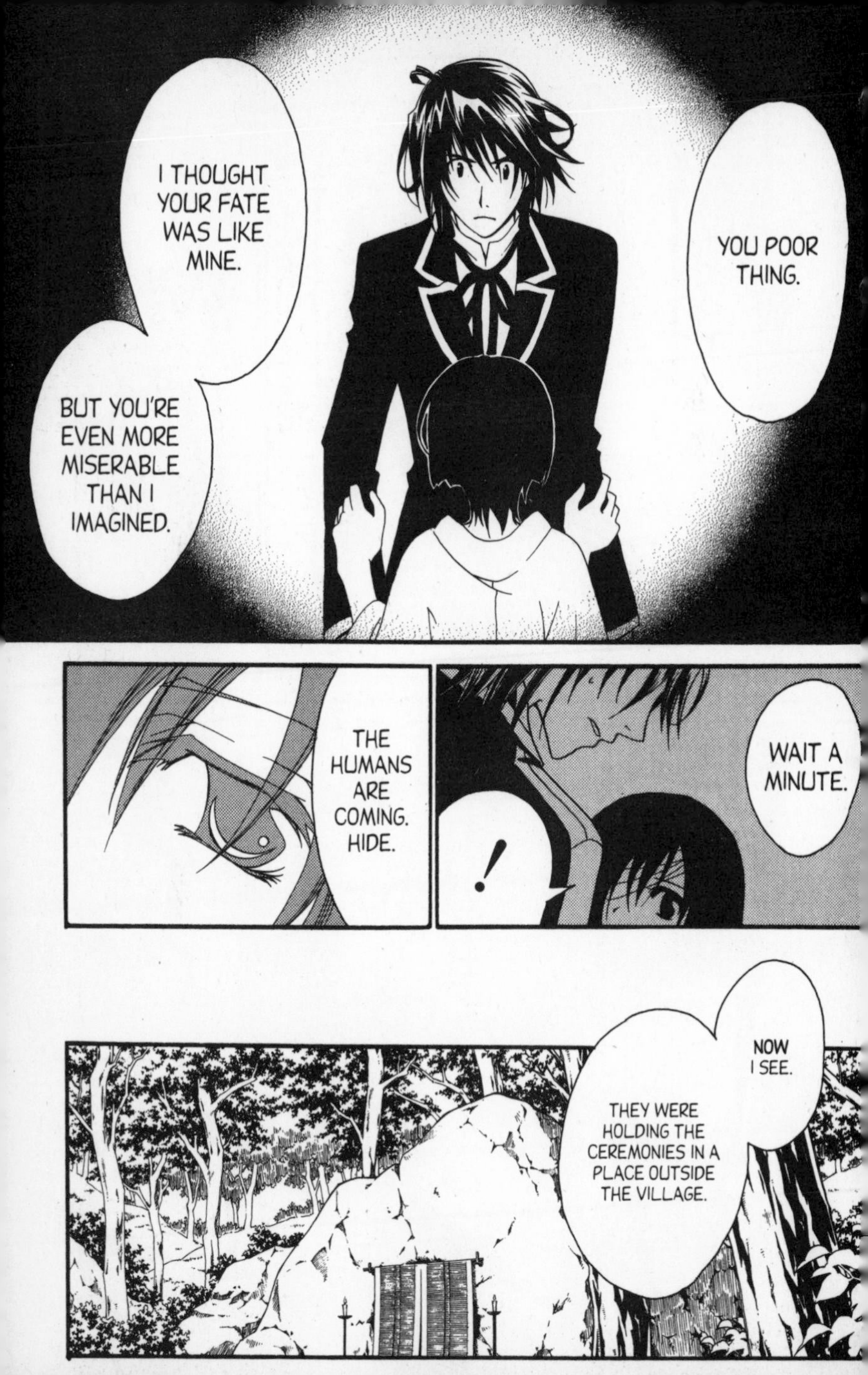
YOU POOR THING.
I THOUGHT YOUR FATE WAS LIKE MINE.
BUT YOU'RE EVEN MORE MISERABLE THAN I IMAGINED.
WAIT A MINUTE.
!
THE HUMANS ARE COMING. HIDE.
NOW I SEE.
THEY WERE HOLDING THE CEREMONIES IN A PLACE OUTSIDE THE VILLAGE.

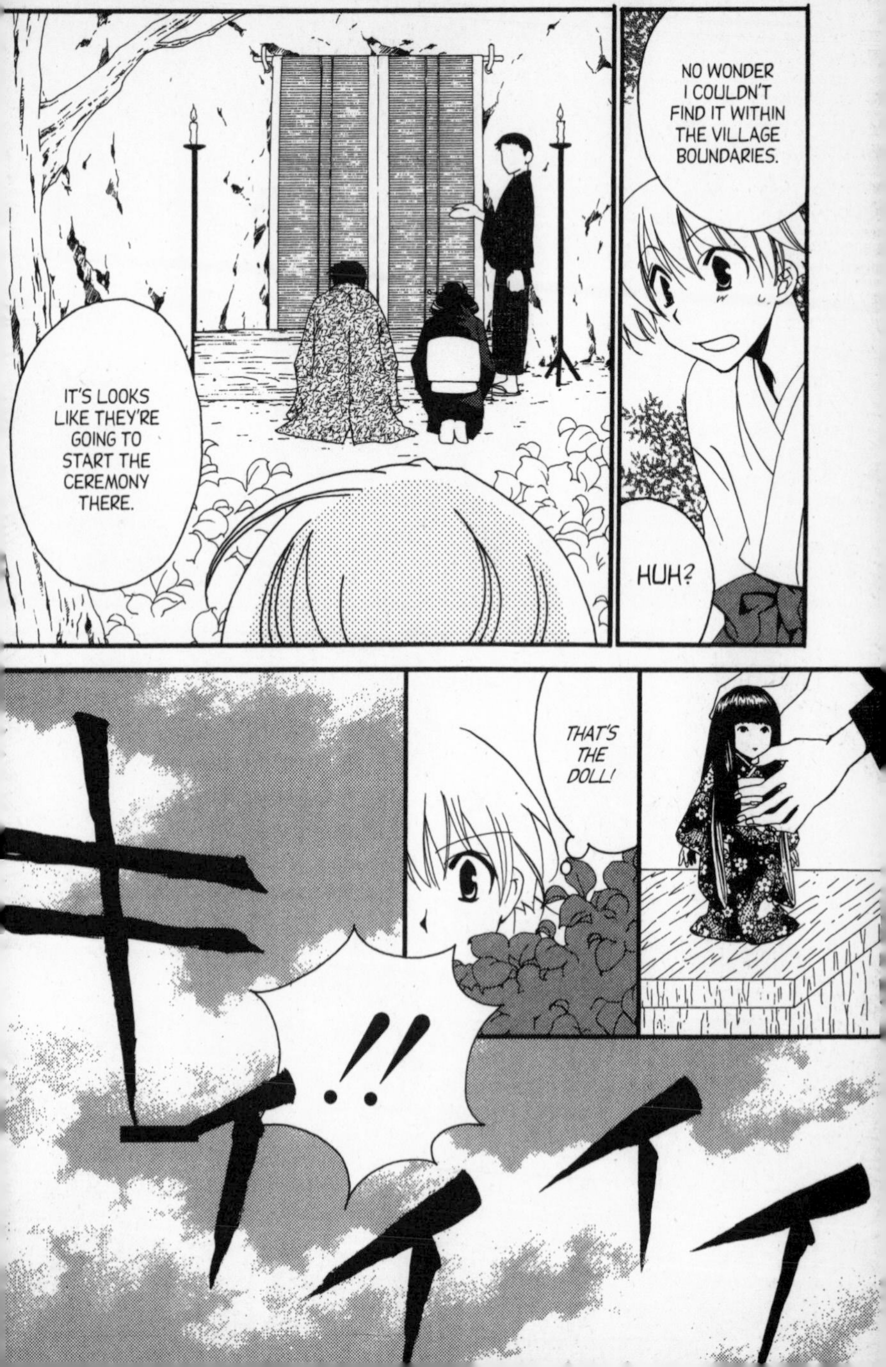
NO WONDER I COULDN'T FIND IT WITHIN THE VILLAGE BOUNDARIES.
HUH?
IT'S LOOKS LIKE THEY'RE GOING TO START THE CEREMONY THERE.
THAT'S THE DOLL!
!!

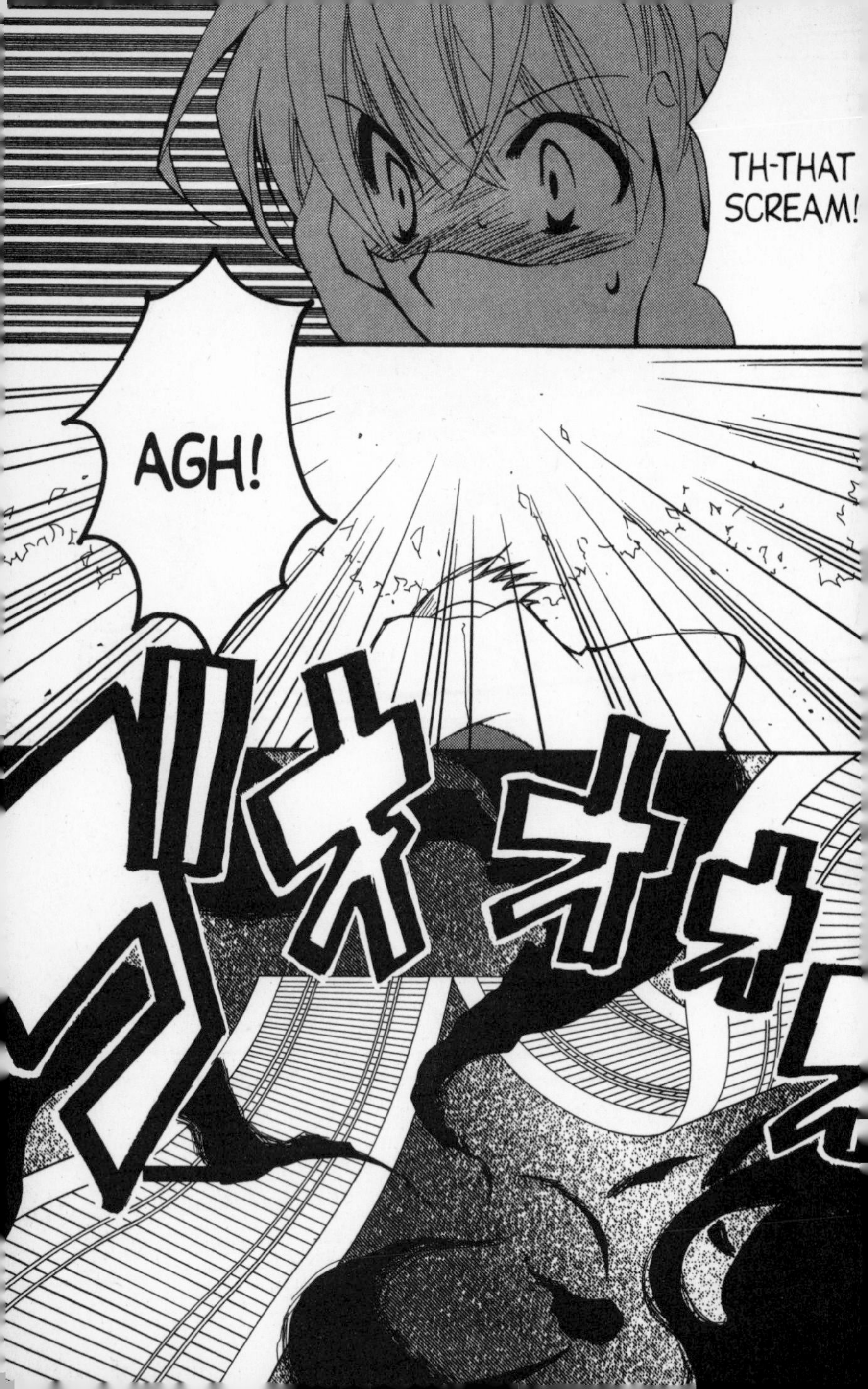
TH-THAT SCREAM!
AGH!

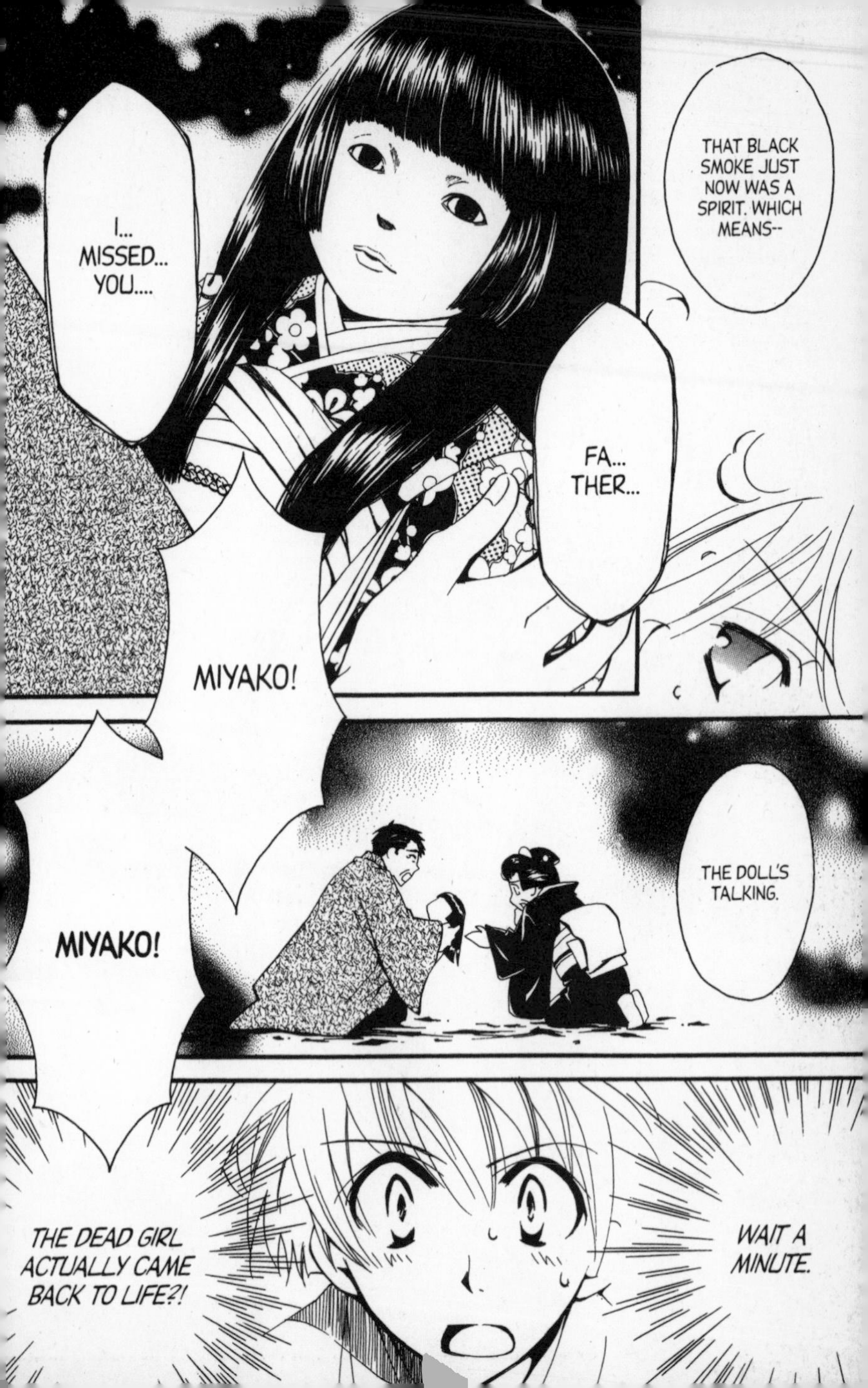

THAT BLACK SMOKE JUST NOW WAS A SPIRIT. WHICH MEANS--
FA... THER...
I... MISSED... YOU....
MIYAKO!
THE DOLL'S TALKING.
MIYAKO!
WAIT A MINUTE.
THE DEAD GIRL ACTUALLY CAME BACK TO LIFE?!

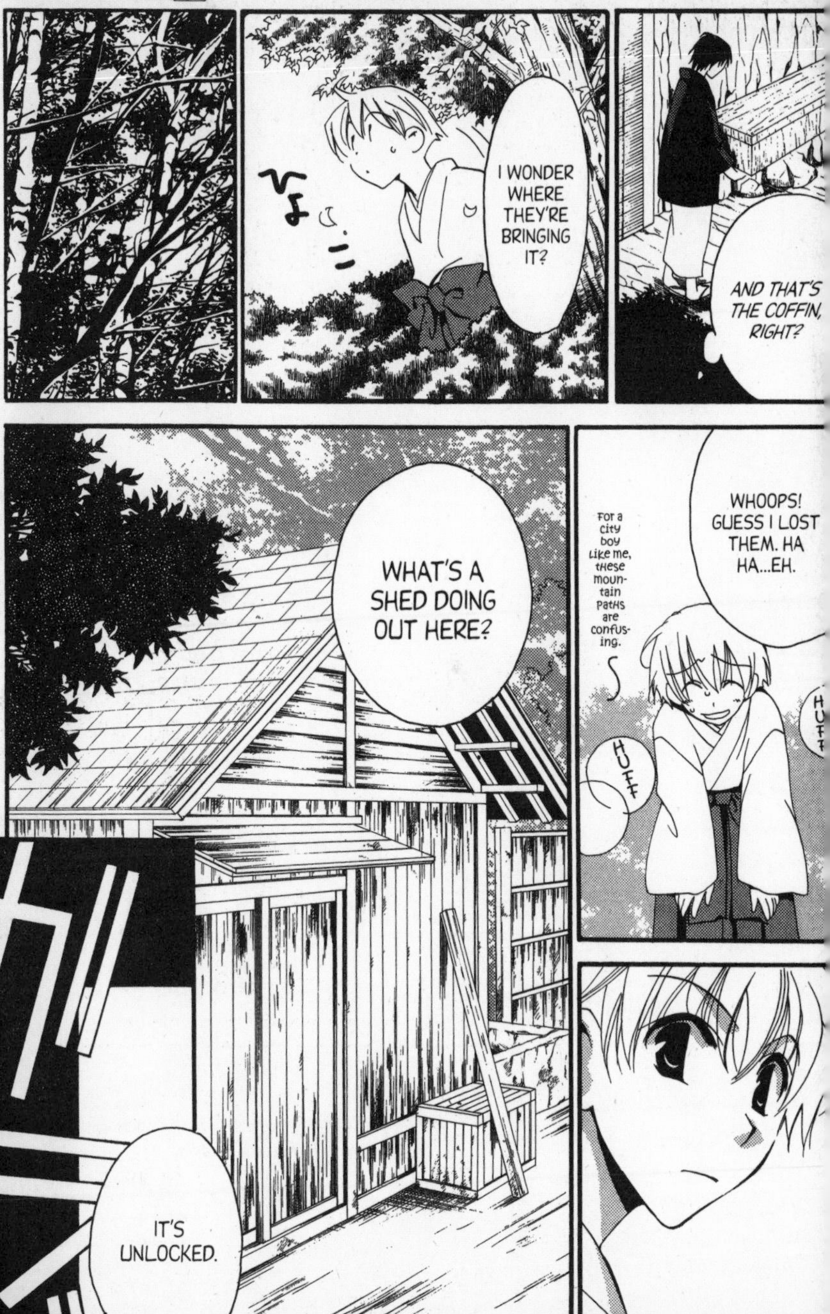
AND THAT'S THE COFFIN, RIGHT?
I WONDER WHERE THEY'RE BRINGING IT?
WHOOPS! GUESS I LOST THEM. HA HA...EH.
For a city boy like me, these mountain paths are confusing.
HUFF
HUFF
WHAT'S A SHED DOING OUT HERE?
IT'S UNLOCKED.

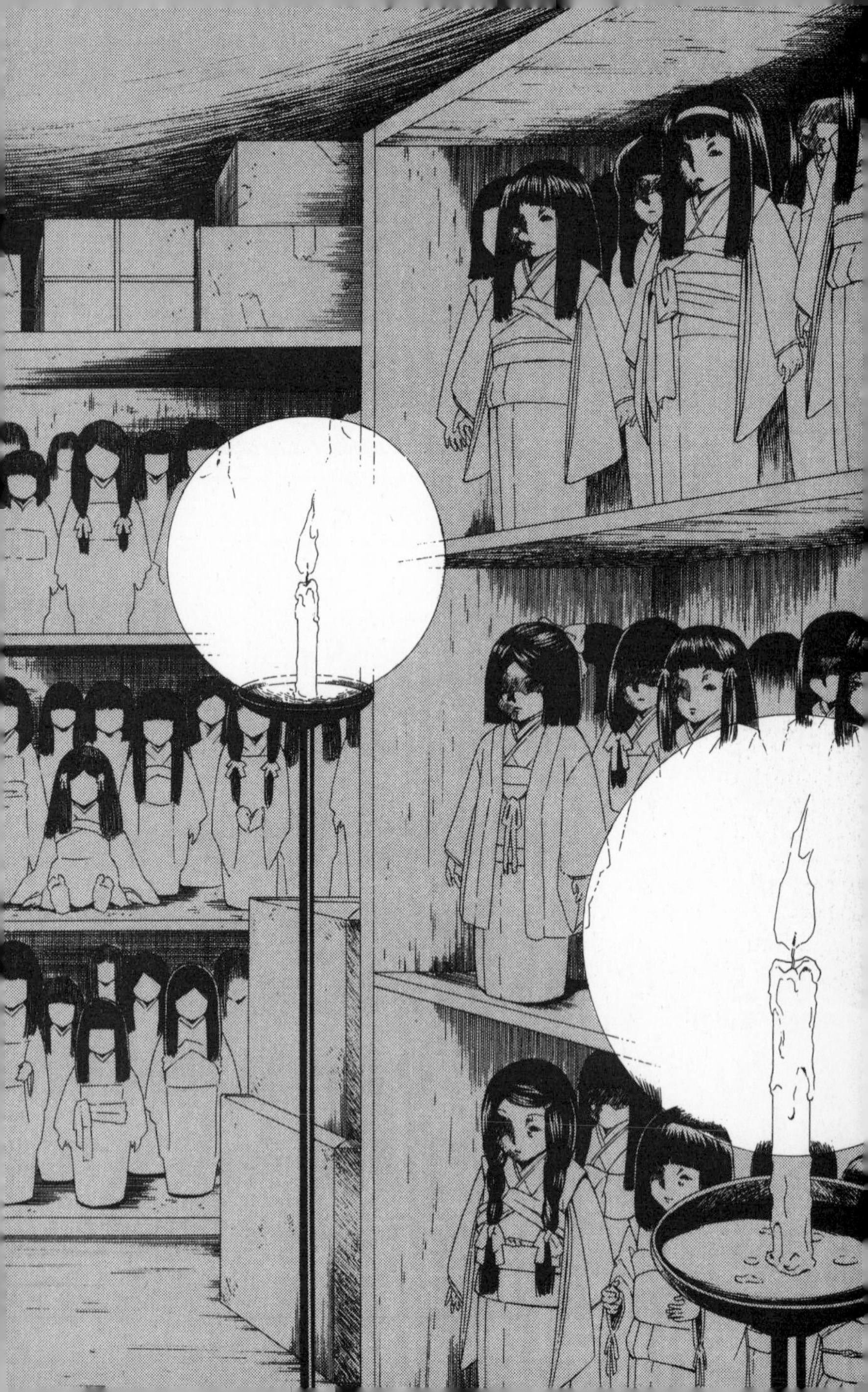

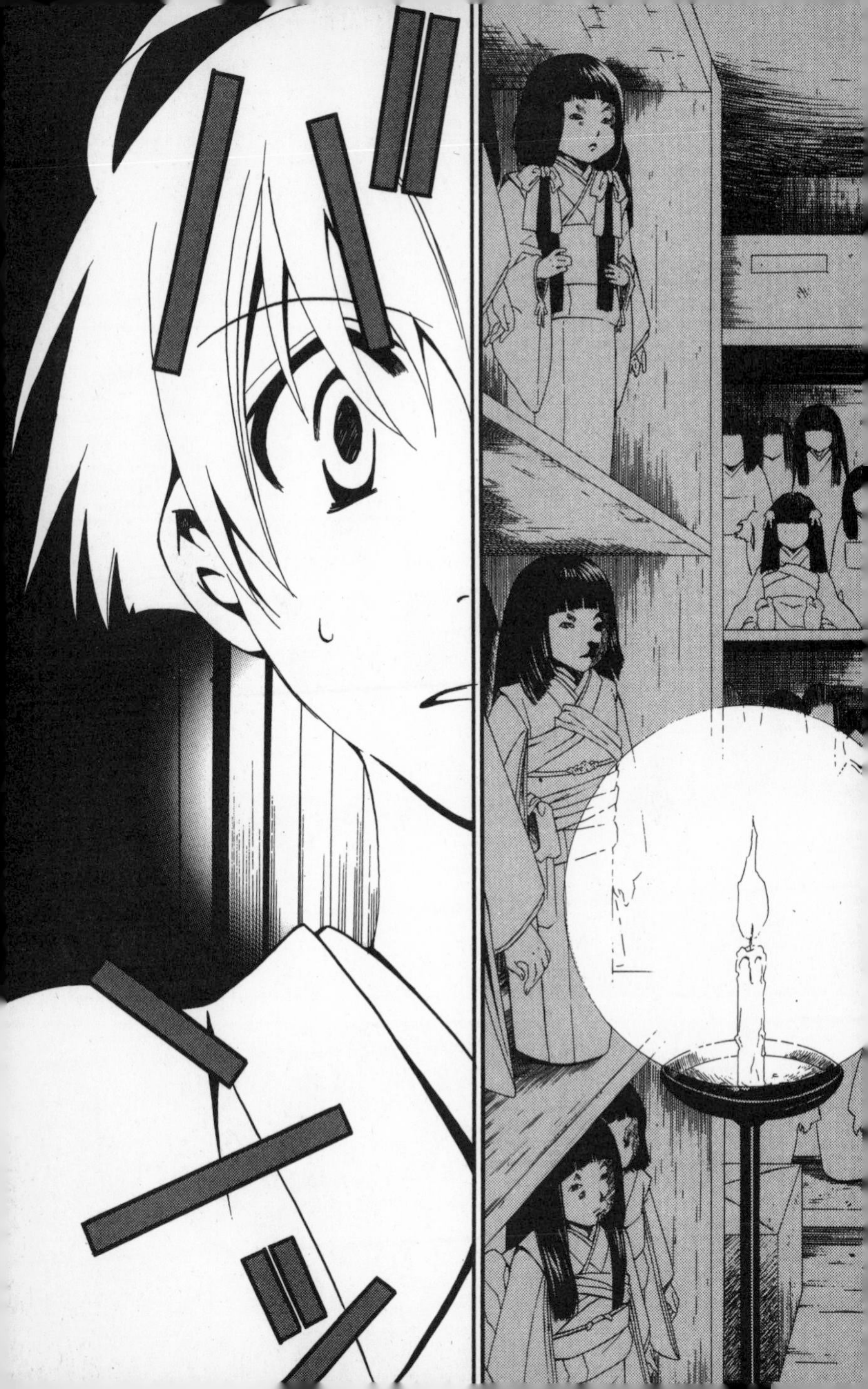

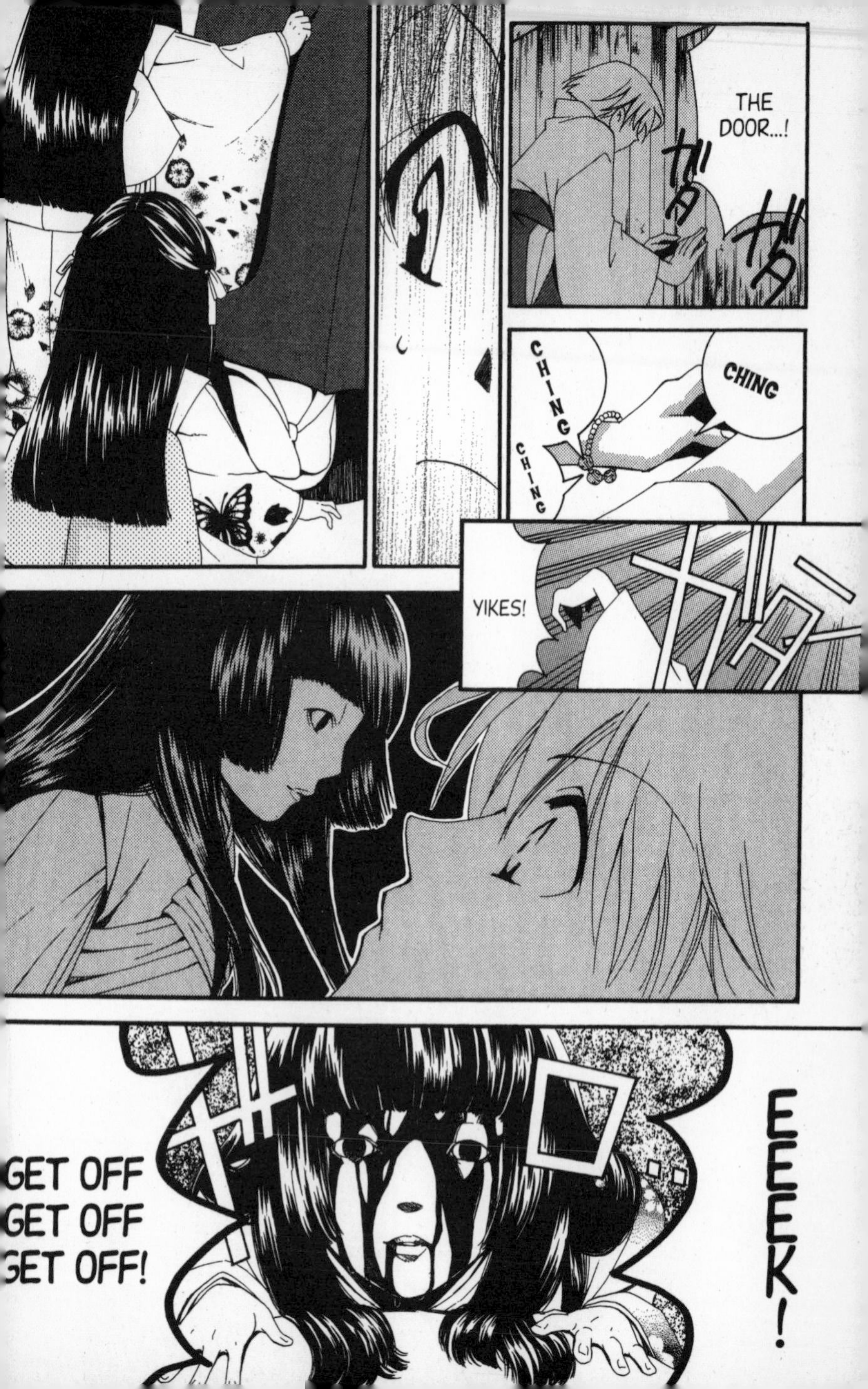
THE DOOR...!
CHING
CHING
CHING
YIKES!
EEEEK!
GET OFF
GET OFF
GET OFF!

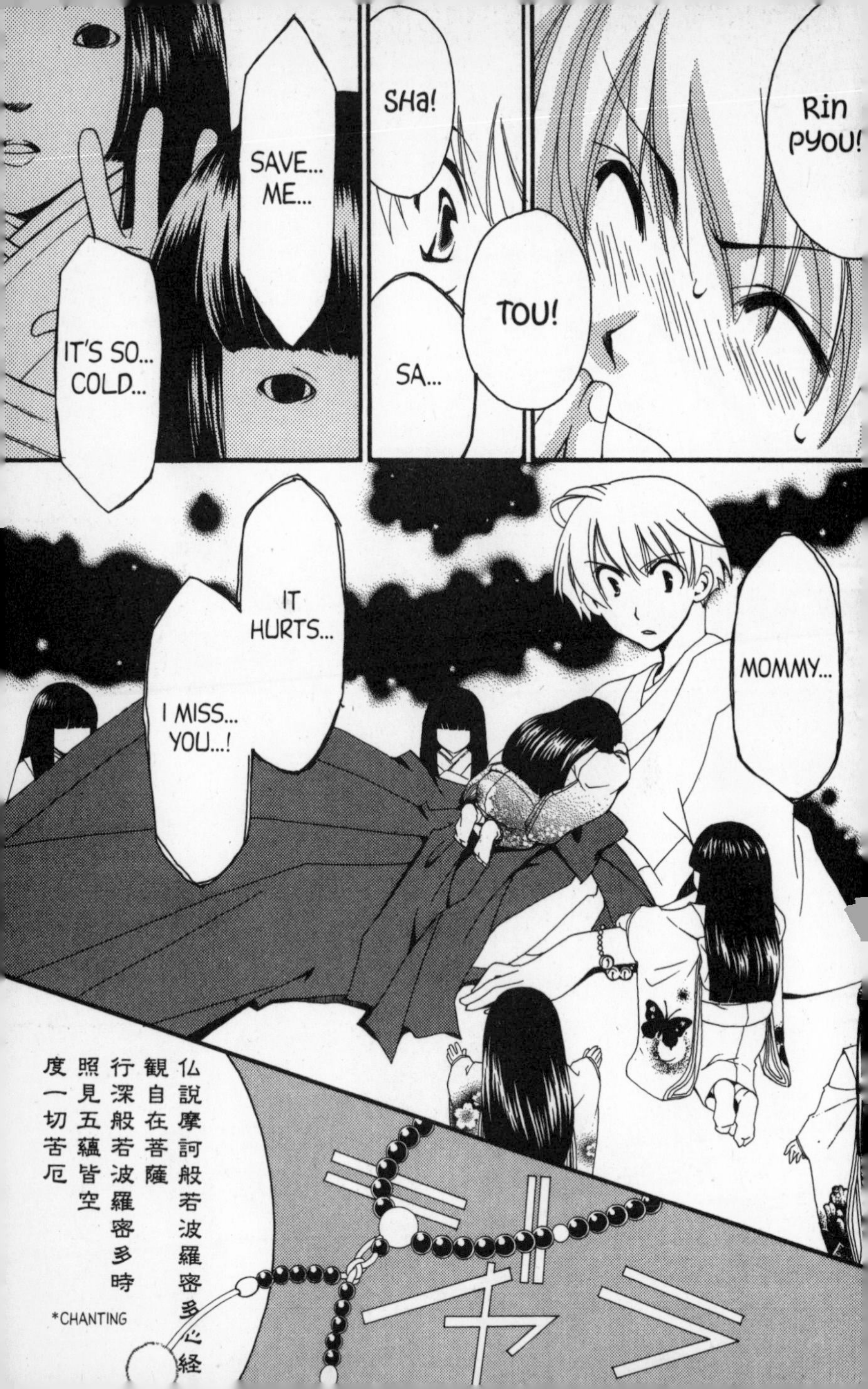
Rin pyou!
TOU!
SHA!
SA...
SAVE... ME...
IT'S SO... COLD...
MOMMY...
IT HURTS...
I MISS... YOU...!
仏説摩訶般若波羅密多心経
観自在菩薩
行深般若波羅密多時
照見五蘊皆空
度一切苦厄
*CHANTING
ジャラ

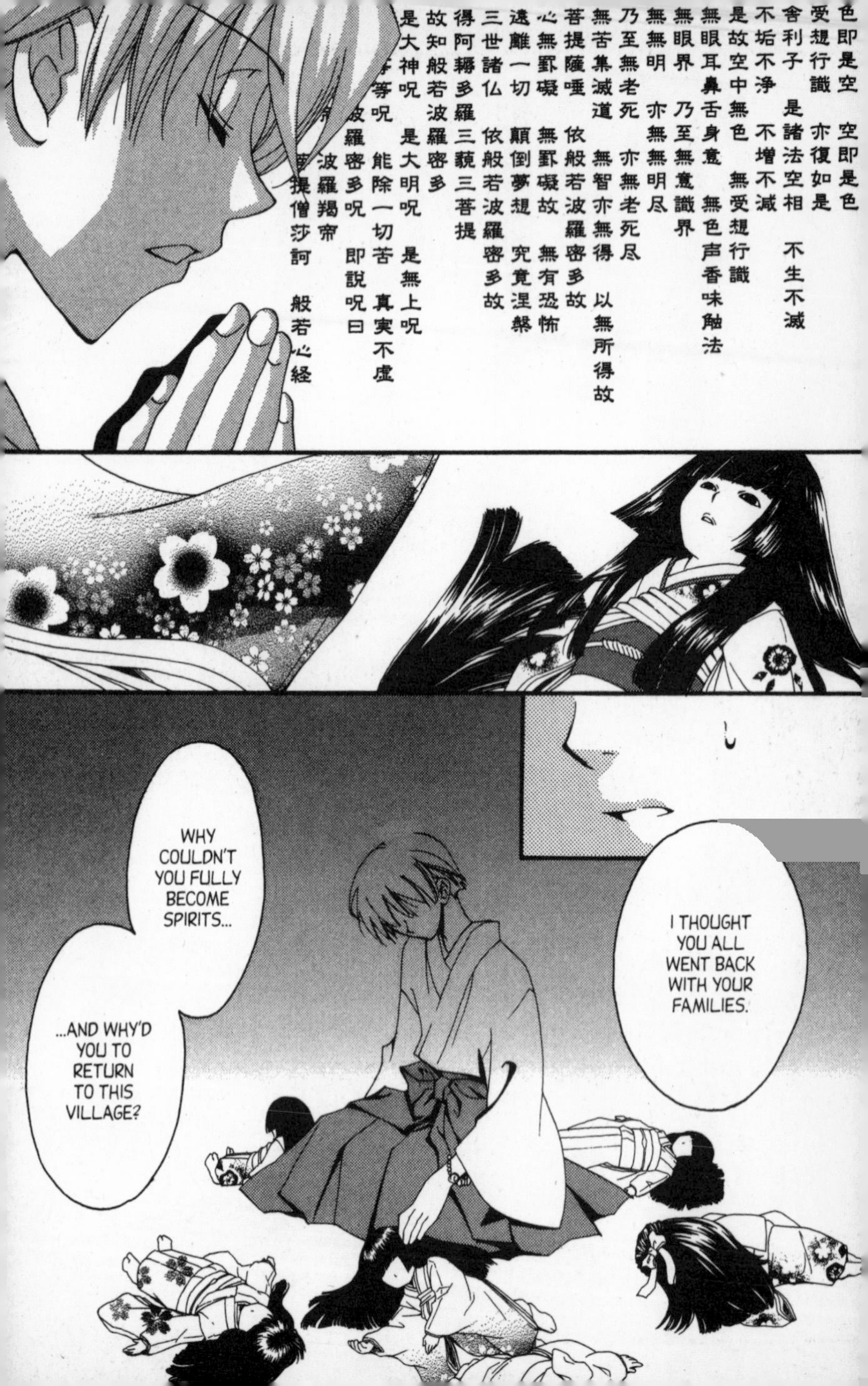
色即是空　空即是色
受想行識　亦復如是
舎利子　是諸法空相　不生不滅
不垢不浄　不増不減
是故空中無色　無受想行識
無眼耳鼻舌身意　無色声香味触法
無眼界　乃至無意識界
無無明　亦無無明尽
乃至無老死　亦無老死尽
無苦集滅道　無智亦無得　以無所得故
菩提薩唾　依般若波羅蜜多故
心無罣礙　無罣礙故　無有恐怖
遠離一切　顛倒夢想　究竟涅槃
三世諸仏　依般若波羅蜜多故
得阿耨多羅三藐三菩提
故知般若波羅蜜多
是大神呪　是大明呪　是無上呪
等等呪　能除一切苦　真実不虚
波羅蜜多呪　即説呪曰
波羅羯帝
提僧莎訶　般若心経
し
I THOUGHT YOU ALL WENT BACK WITH YOUR FAMILIES.
WHY COULDN'T YOU FULLY BECOME SPIRITS...
...AND WHY'D YOU TO RETURN TO THIS VILLAGE?

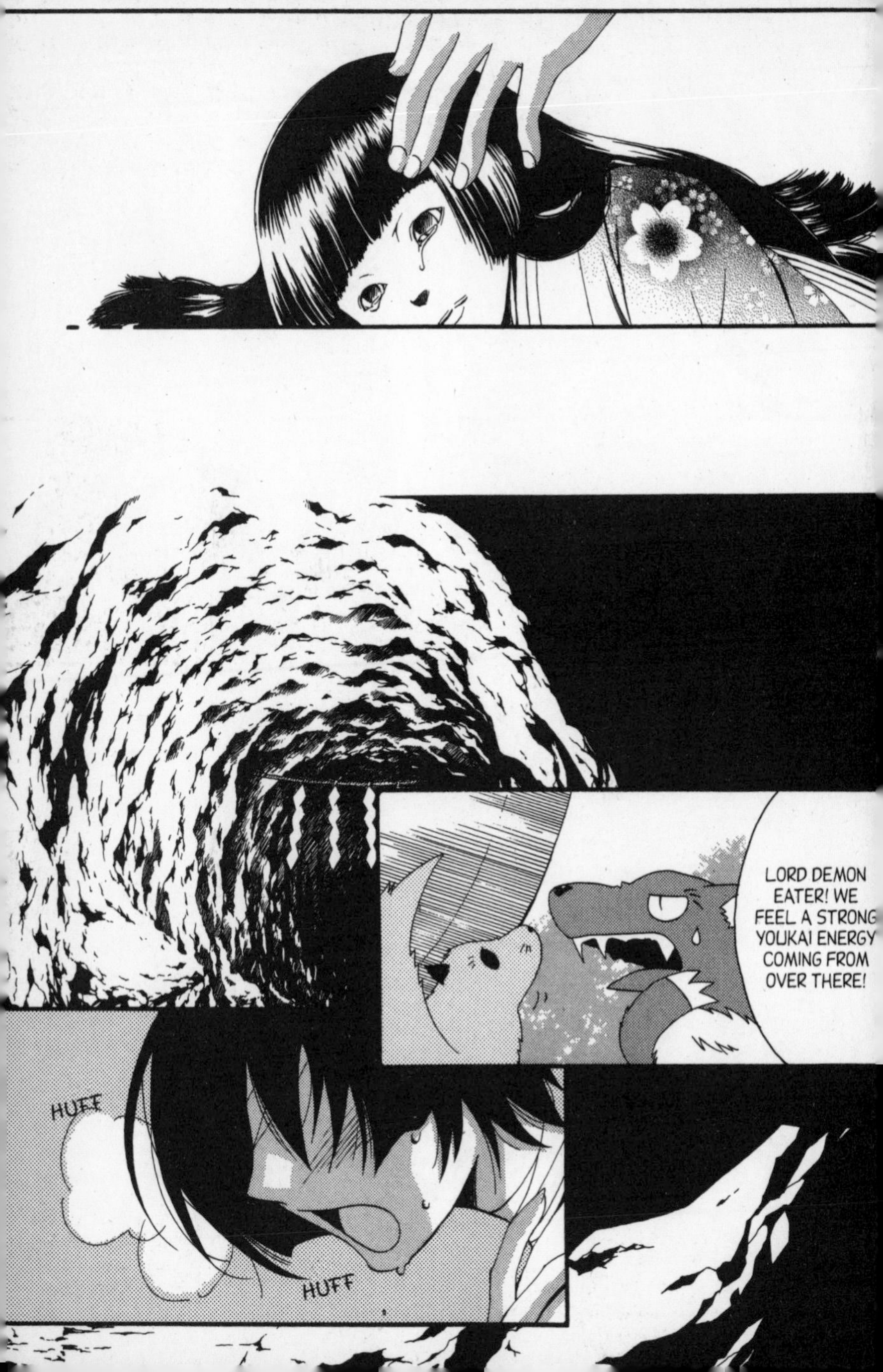
LORD DEMON EATER! WE FEEL A STRONG YOUKAI ENERGY COMING FROM OVER THERE!
HUFF
HUFF

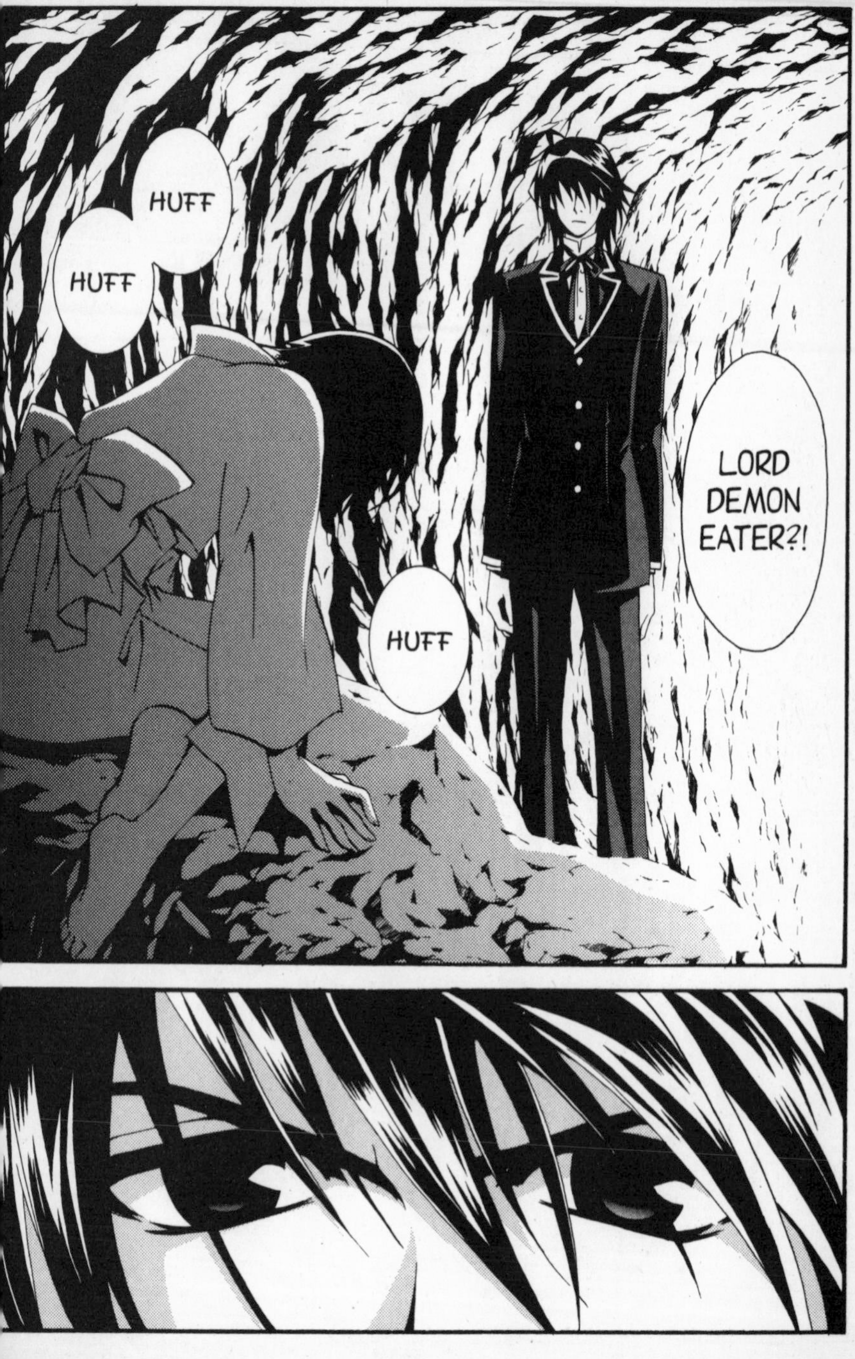
LORD DEMON EATER?!
HUFF
HUFF
HUFF

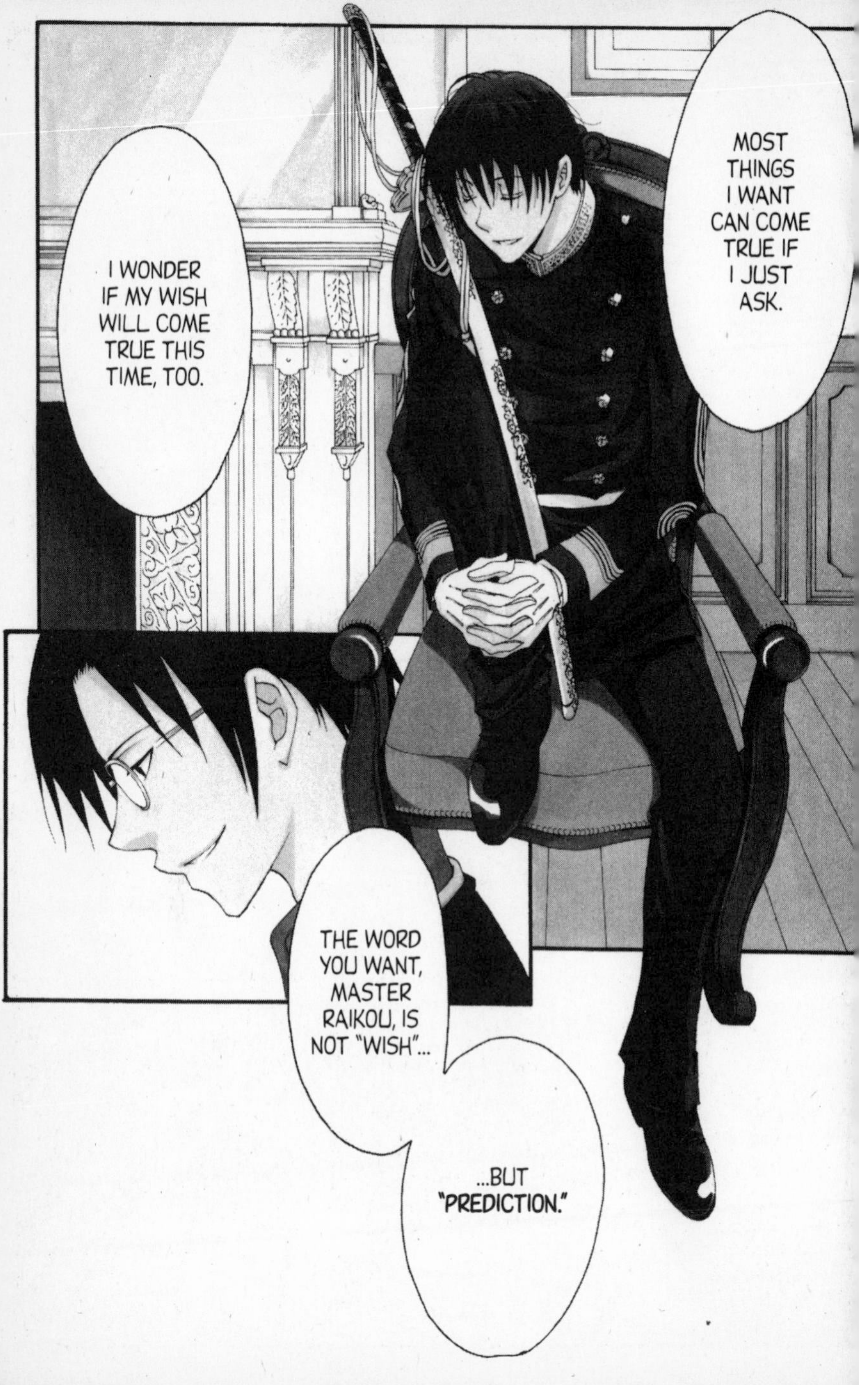
MOST THINGS I WANT CAN COME TRUE IF I JUST ASK.
I WONDER IF MY WISH WILL COME TRUE THIS TIME, TOO.
THE WORD YOU WANT, MASTER RAIKOU, IS NOT "WISH"...
...BUT "PREDICTION."

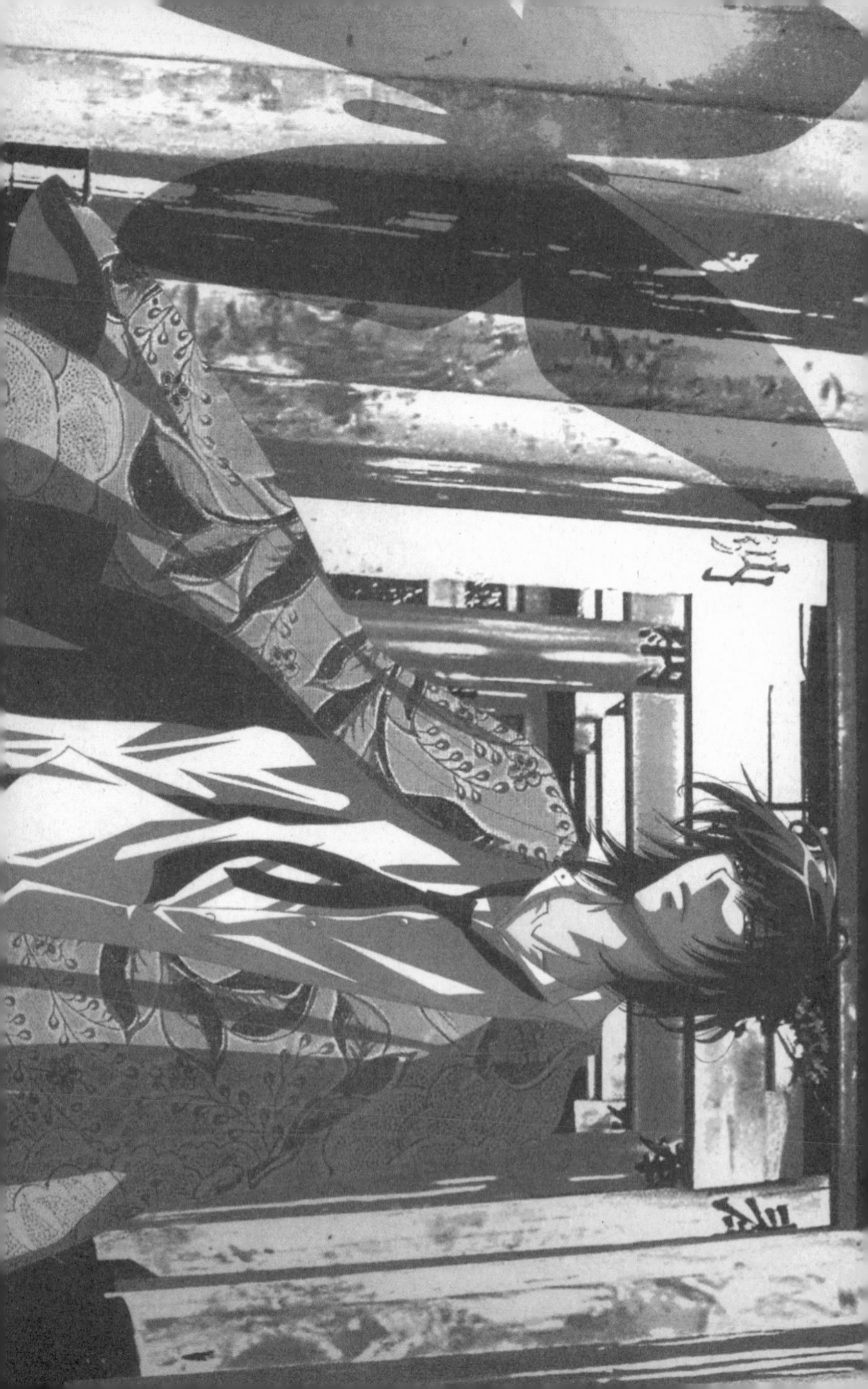

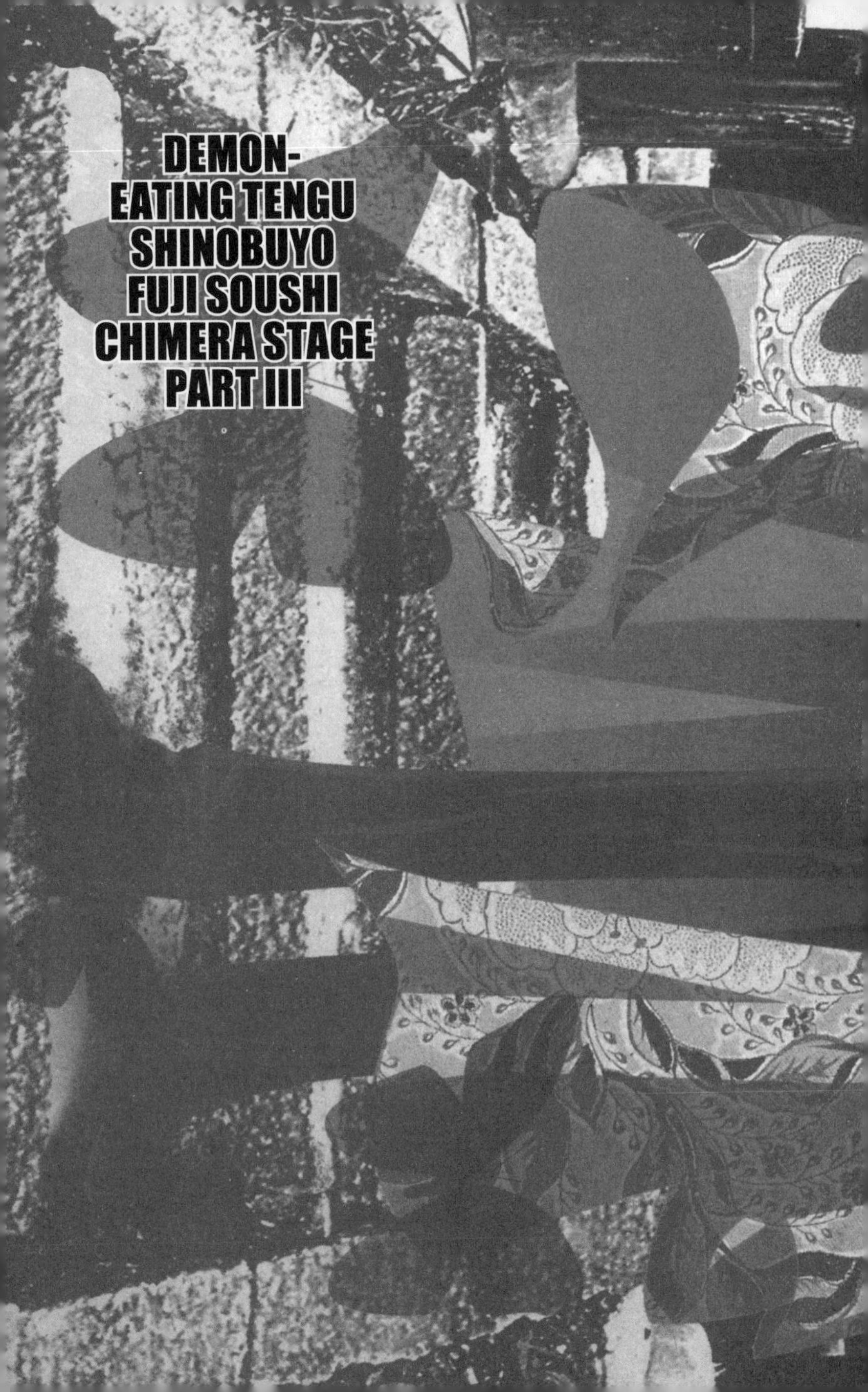
DEMON-
EATING TENGU
SHINOBUYO
FUJI SOUSHI
CHIMERA STAGE
PART III

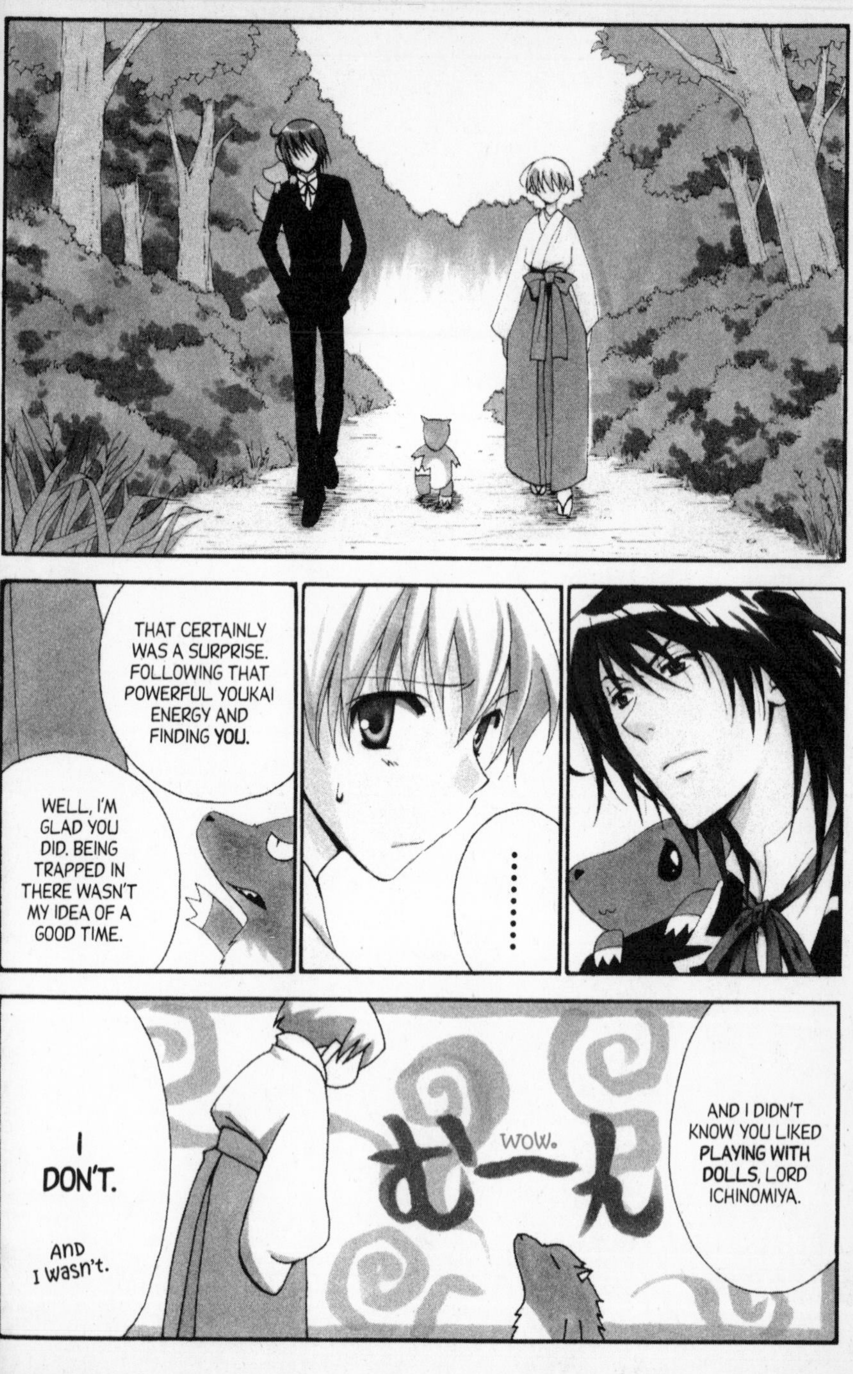
......
THAT CERTAINLY WAS A SURPRISE. FOLLOWING THAT POWERFUL YOUKAI ENERGY AND FINDING **YOU**.
WELL, I'M GLAD YOU DID. BEING TRAPPED IN THERE WASN'T MY IDEA OF A GOOD TIME.
AND I DIDN'T KNOW YOU LIKED **PLAYING WITH DOLLS**, LORD ICHINOMIYA.
WOW.
むーん
I DON'T.
And I wasn't.

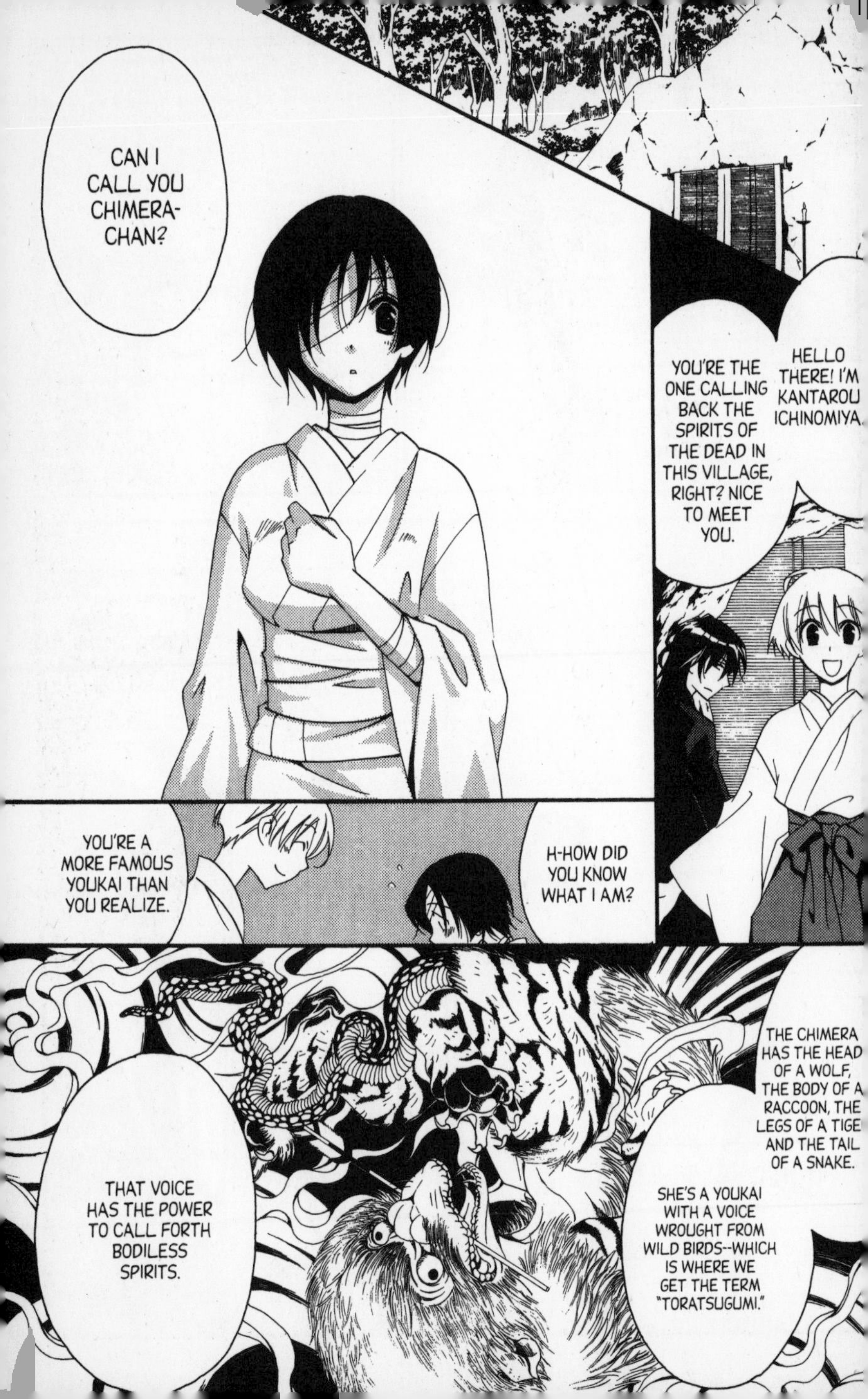
HELLO THERE! I'M KANTAROU ICHINOMIYA.
YOU'RE THE ONE CALLING BACK THE SPIRITS OF THE DEAD IN THIS VILLAGE, RIGHT? NICE TO MEET YOU.
CAN I CALL YOU CHIMERA-CHAN?
H-HOW DID YOU KNOW WHAT I AM?
YOU'RE A MORE FAMOUS YOUKAI THAN YOU REALIZE.
THE CHIMERA HAS THE HEAD OF A WOLF, THE BODY OF A RACCOON, THE LEGS OF A TIGE AND THE TAIL OF A SNAKE.
SHE'S A YOUKAI WITH A VOICE WROUGHT FROM WILD BIRDS--WHICH IS WHERE WE GET THE TERM "TORATSUGUMI."
THAT VOICE HAS THE POWER TO CALL FORTH BODILESS SPIRITS.

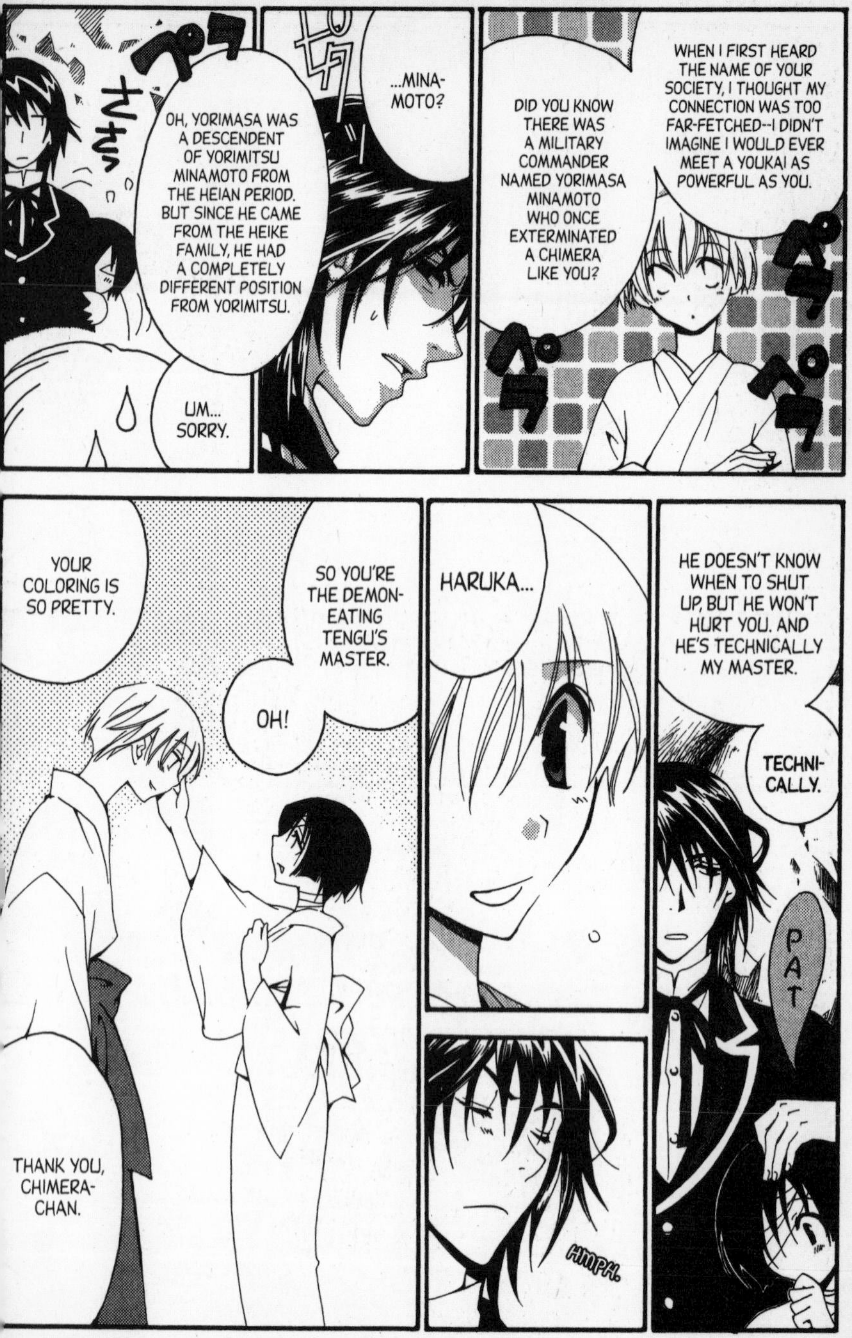
WHEN I FIRST HEARD THE NAME OF YOUR SOCIETY, I THOUGHT MY CONNECTION WAS TOO FAR-FETCHED--I DIDN'T IMAGINE I WOULD EVER MEET A YOUKAI AS POWERFUL AS YOU.
DID YOU KNOW THERE WAS A MILITARY COMMANDER NAMED YORIMASA MINAMOTO WHO ONCE EXTERMINATED A CHIMERA LIKE YOU?
...MINA-MOTO?
OH, YORIMASA WAS A DESCENDENT OF YORIMITSU MINAMOTO FROM THE HEIAN PERIOD. BUT SINCE HE CAME FROM THE HEIKE FAMILY, HE HAD A COMPLETELY DIFFERENT POSITION FROM YORIMITSU.
UM... SORRY.
HE DOESN'T KNOW WHEN TO SHUT UP, BUT HE WON'T HURT YOU. AND HE'S TECHNICALLY MY MASTER.
TECHNI-CALLY.
PAT
HARUKA...
HMPH.
SO YOU'RE THE DEMON-EATING TENGU'S MASTER.
YOUR COLORING IS SO PRETTY.
OH!
THANK YOU, CHIMERA-CHAN.

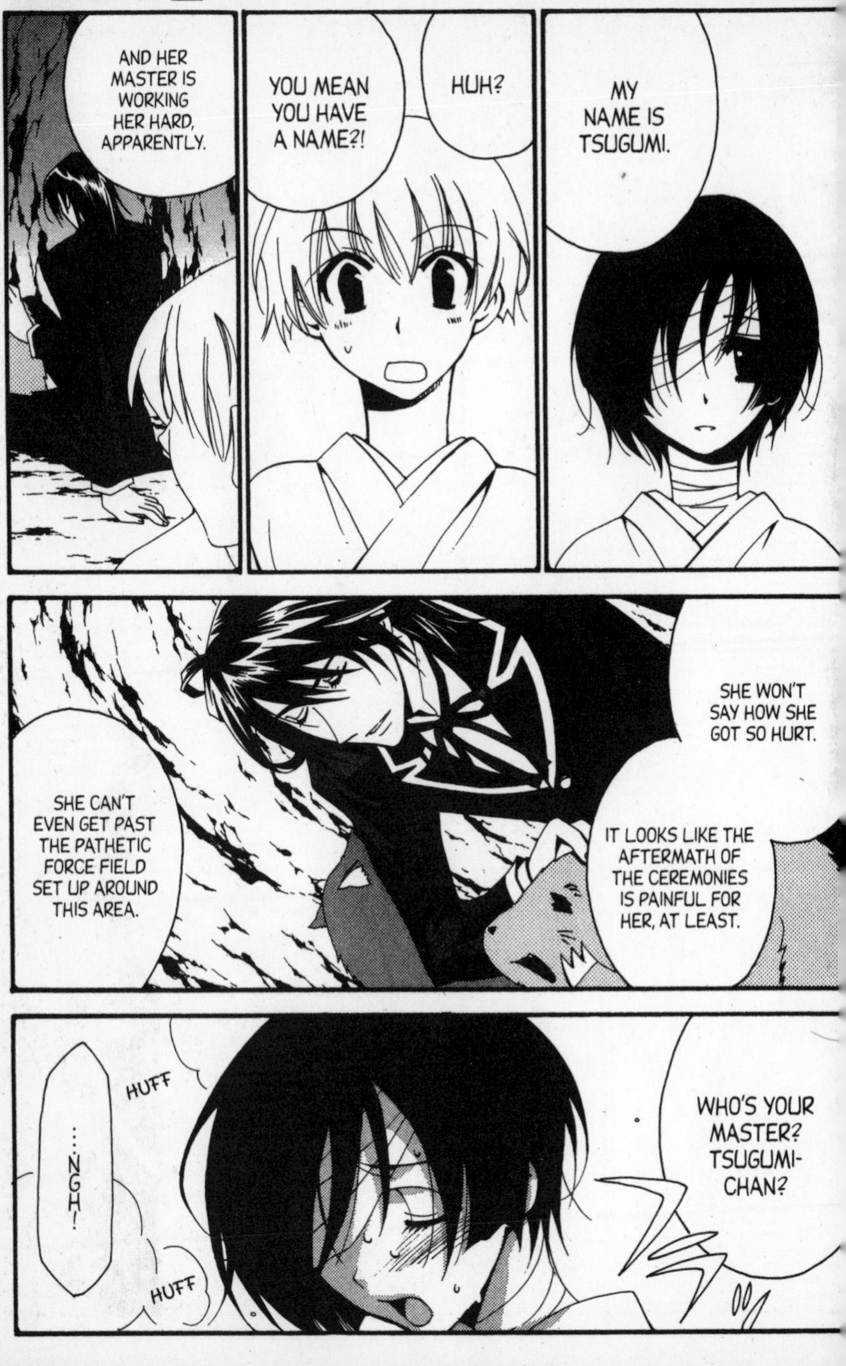
MY NAME IS TSUGUMI.
HUH?
YOU MEAN YOU HAVE A NAME?!
AND HER MASTER IS WORKING HER HARD, APPARENTLY.
SHE WON'T SAY HOW SHE GOT SO HURT.
IT LOOKS LIKE THE AFTERMATH OF THE CEREMONIES IS PAINFUL FOR HER, AT LEAST.
SHE CAN'T EVEN GET PAST THE PATHETIC FORCE FIELD SET UP AROUND THIS AREA.
WHO'S YOUR MASTER? TSUGUMI-CHAN?
HUFF
...NGH!
HUFF

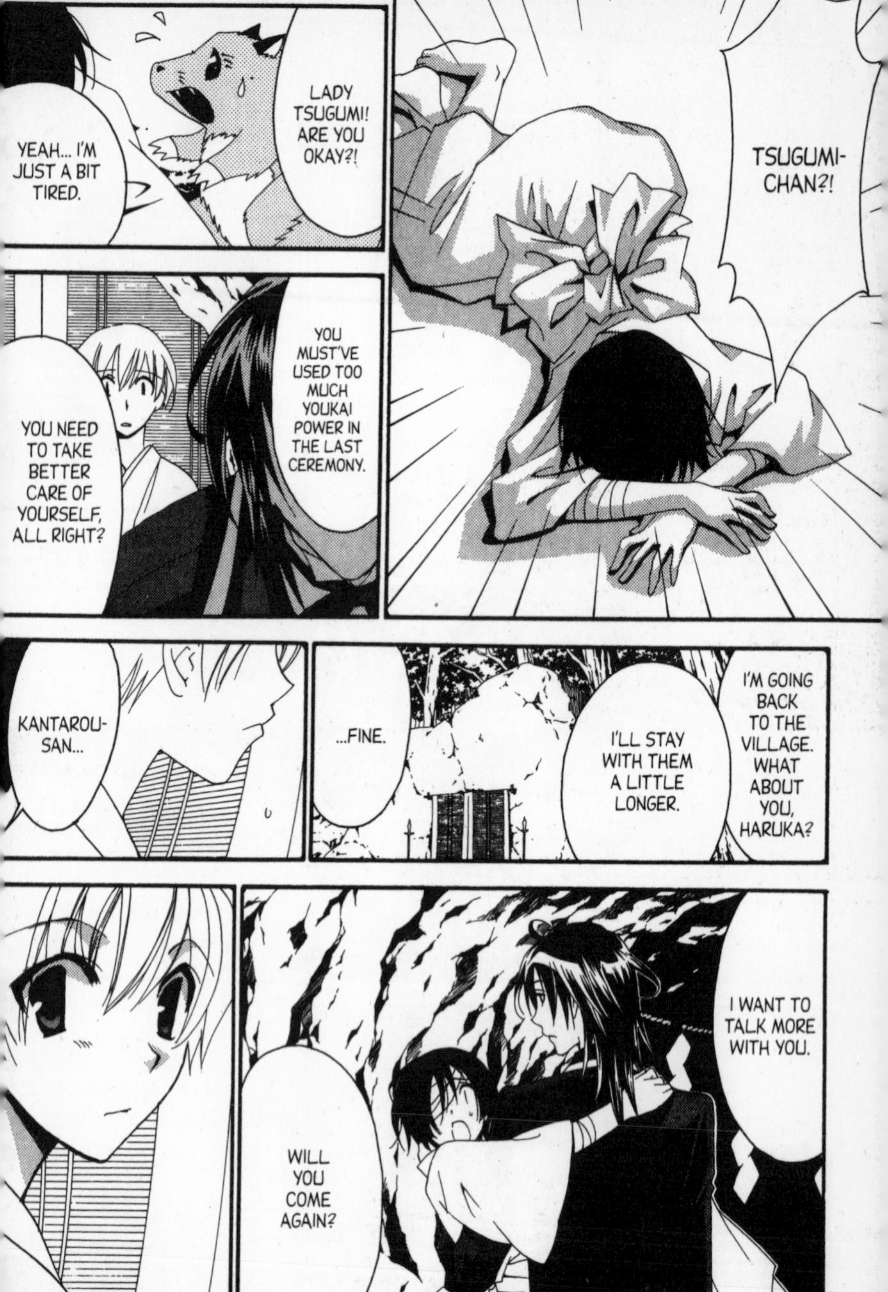
TSUGUMI-CHAN?!
LADY TSUGUMI! ARE YOU OKAY?!
YEAH... I'M JUST A BIT TIRED.
YOU MUST'VE USED TOO MUCH YOUKAI POWER IN THE LAST CEREMONY.
YOU NEED TO TAKE BETTER CARE OF YOURSELF, ALL RIGHT?
I'M GOING BACK TO THE VILLAGE. WHAT ABOUT YOU, HARUKA?
I'LL STAY WITH THEM A LITTLE LONGER.
...FINE.
KANTAROU-SAN...
I WANT TO TALK MORE WITH YOU.
WILL YOU COME AGAIN?

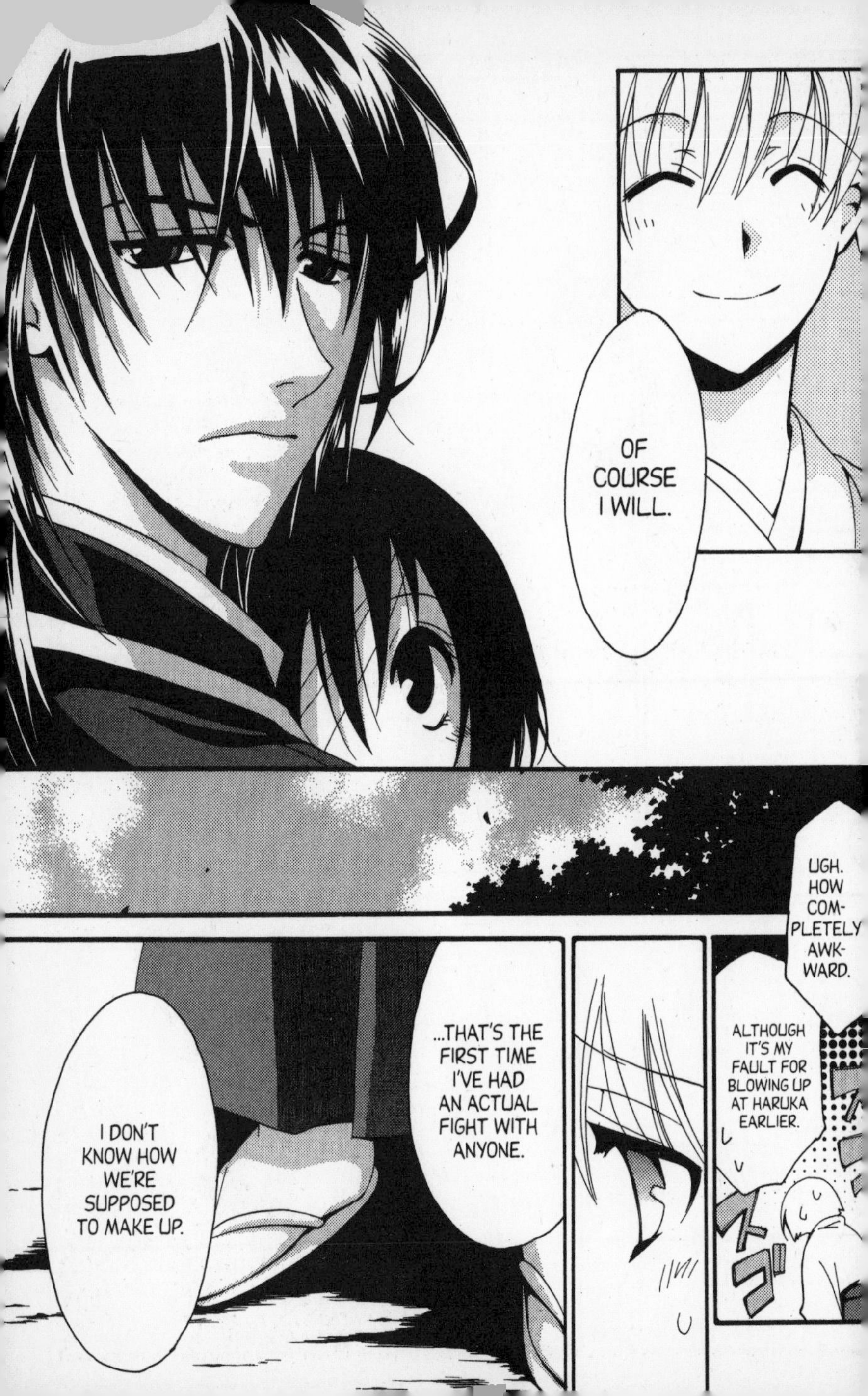
OF COURSE I WILL.
UGH. HOW COMPLETELY AWKWARD.
ALTHOUGH IT'S MY FAULT FOR BLOWING UP AT HARUKA EARLIER.
...THAT'S THE FIRST TIME I'VE HAD AN ACTUAL FIGHT WITH ANYONE.
I DON'T KNOW HOW WE'RE SUPPOSED TO MAKE UP.

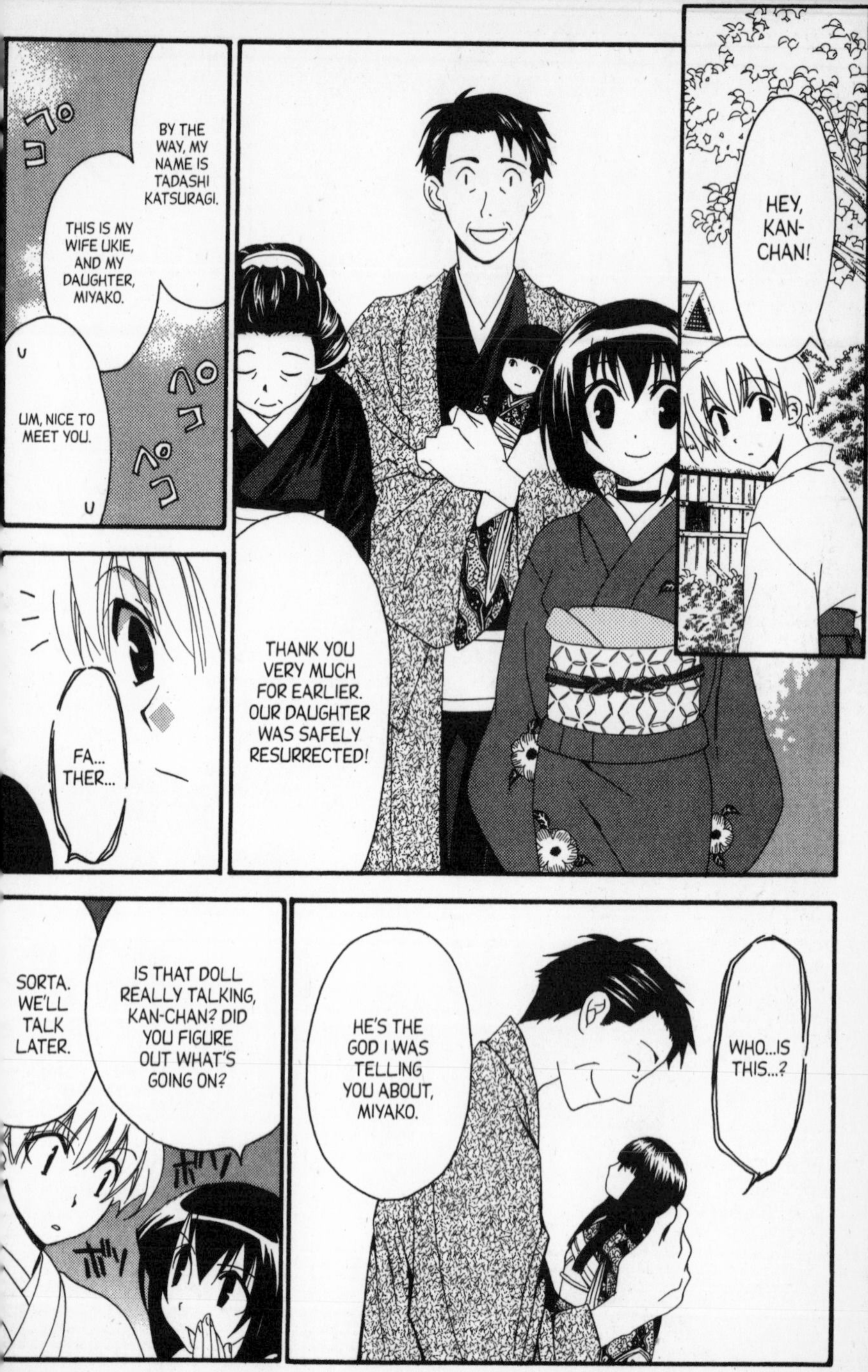
HEY, KAN-CHAN!
THANK YOU VERY MUCH FOR EARLIER. OUR DAUGHTER WAS SAFELY RESURRECTED!
BY THE WAY, MY NAME IS TADASHI KATSURAGI.
THIS IS MY WIFE UKIE, AND MY DAUGHTER, MIYAKO.
ペコ
UM, NICE TO MEET YOU.
ペコ
ペコ
FA... THER...
WHO...IS THIS...?
HE'S THE GOD I WAS TELLING YOU ABOUT, MIYAKO.
IS THAT DOLL REALLY TALKING, KAN-CHAN? DID YOU FIGURE OUT WHAT'S GOING ON?
SORTA. WE'LL TALK LATER.
ボソ
ボソ

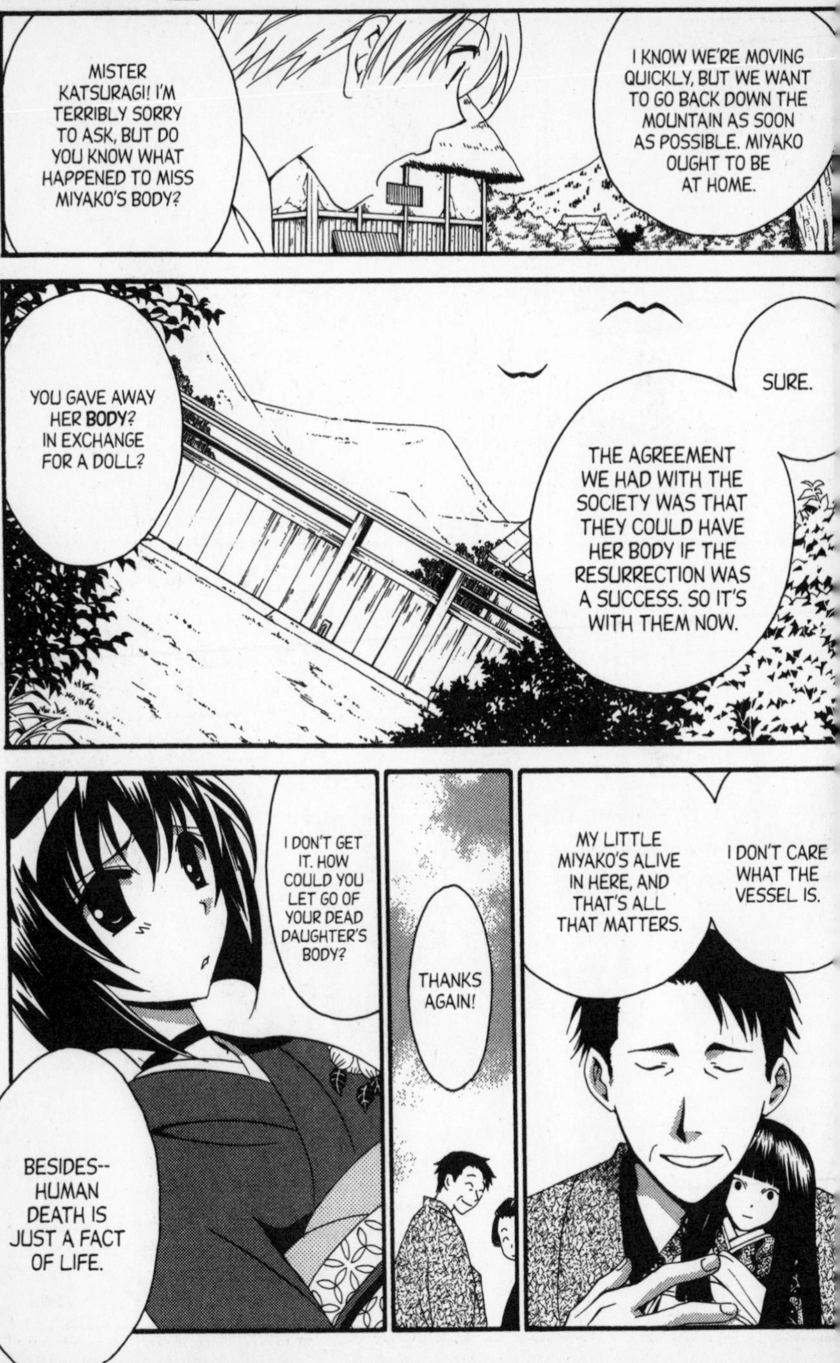
I KNOW WE'RE MOVING QUICKLY, BUT WE WANT TO GO BACK DOWN THE MOUNTAIN AS SOON AS POSSIBLE. MIYAKO OUGHT TO BE AT HOME.
MISTER KATSURAGI! I'M TERRIBLY SORRY TO ASK, BUT DO YOU KNOW WHAT HAPPENED TO MISS MIYAKO'S BODY?
SURE.
THE AGREEMENT WE HAD WITH THE SOCIETY WAS THAT THEY COULD HAVE HER BODY IF THE RESURRECTION WAS A SUCCESS. SO IT'S WITH THEM NOW.
YOU GAVE AWAY HER **BODY**? IN EXCHANGE FOR A DOLL?
I DON'T CARE WHAT THE VESSEL IS.
MY LITTLE MIYAKO'S ALIVE IN HERE, AND THAT'S ALL THAT MATTERS.
THANKS AGAIN!
I DON'T GET IT. HOW COULD YOU LET GO OF YOUR DEAD DAUGHTER'S BODY?
BESIDES-- HUMAN DEATH IS JUST A FACT OF LIFE.

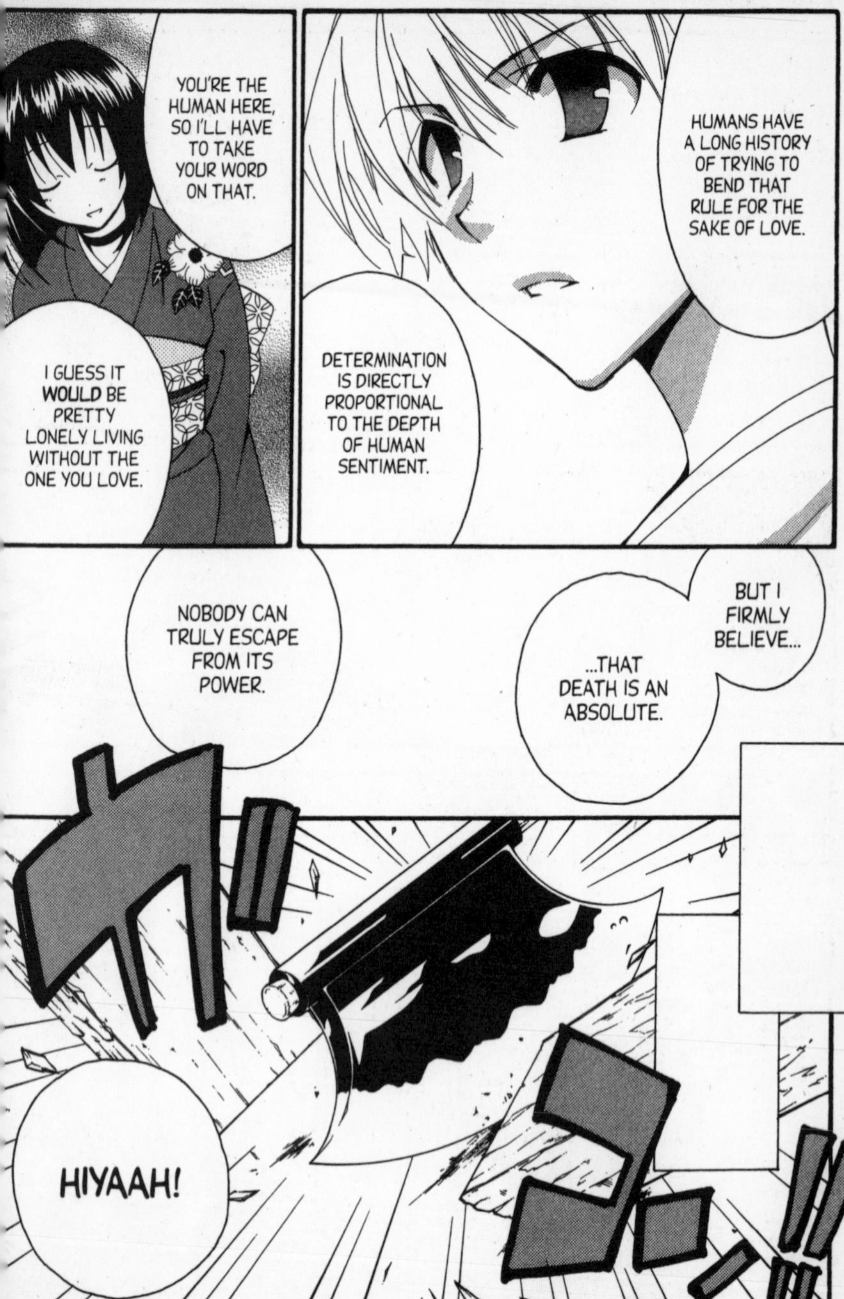
HUMANS HAVE A LONG HISTORY OF TRYING TO BEND THAT RULE FOR THE SAKE OF LOVE.
DETERMINATION IS DIRECTLY PROPORTIONAL TO THE DEPTH OF HUMAN SENTIMENT.
YOU'RE THE HUMAN HERE, SO I'LL HAVE TO TAKE YOUR WORD ON THAT.
I GUESS IT WOULD BE PRETTY LONELY LIVING WITHOUT THE ONE YOU LOVE.
BUT I FIRMLY BELIEVE...
...THAT DEATH IS AN ABSOLUTE.
NOBODY CAN TRULY ESCAPE FROM ITS POWER.
HIYAAH!

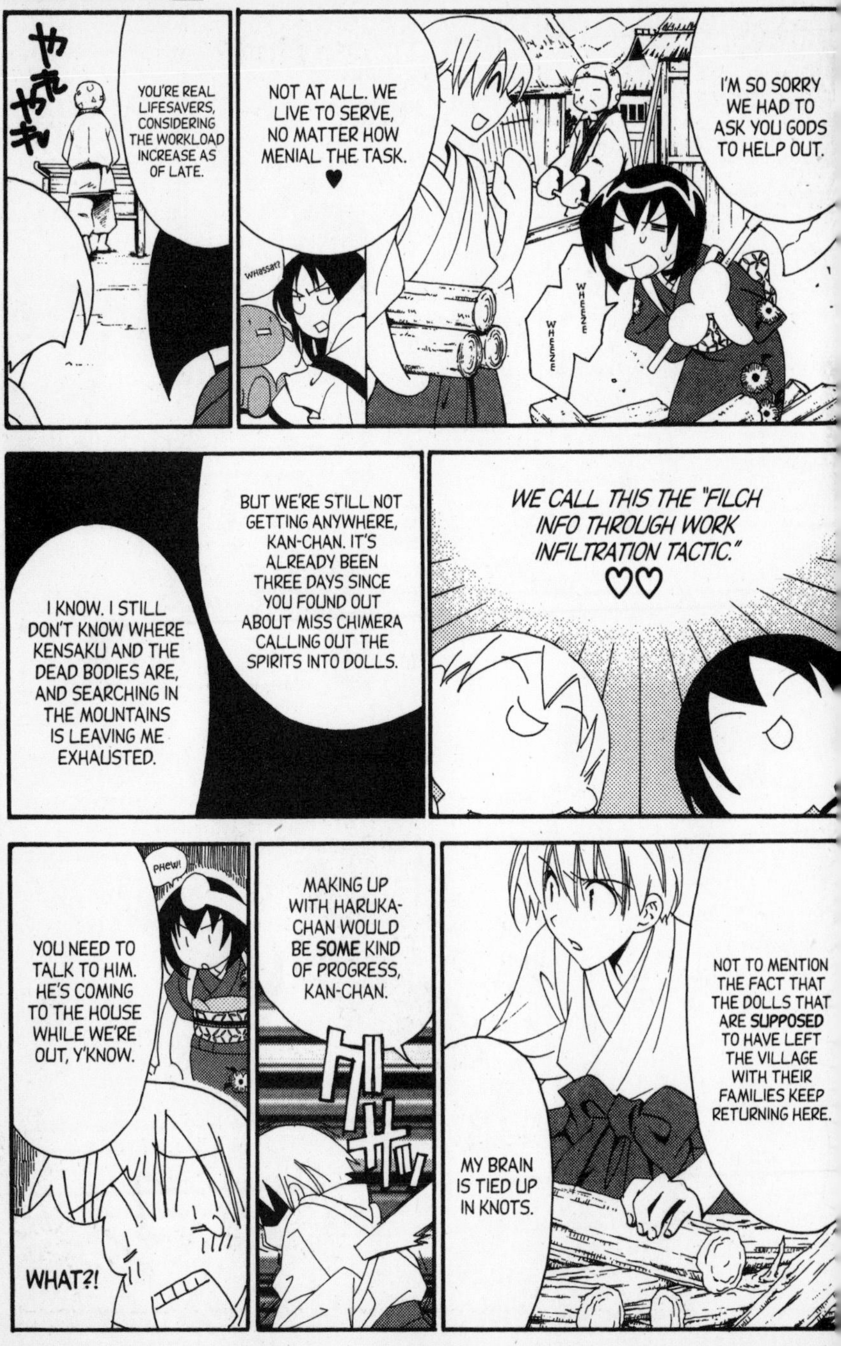
I'M SO SORRY WE HAD TO ASK YOU GODS TO HELP OUT.
WHEEZE
WHEEZE
NOT AT ALL. WE LIVE TO SERVE, NO MATTER HOW MENIAL THE TASK. ♥
WHASSAT?
YOU'RE REAL LIFESAVERS, CONSIDERING THE WORKLOAD INCREASE AS OF LATE.
WE CALL THIS THE "FILCH INFO THROUGH WORK INFILTRATION TACTIC." ♡♡
BUT WE'RE STILL NOT GETTING ANYWHERE, KAN-CHAN. IT'S ALREADY BEEN THREE DAYS SINCE YOU FOUND OUT ABOUT MISS CHIMERA CALLING OUT THE SPIRITS INTO DOLLS.
I KNOW. I STILL DON'T KNOW WHERE KENSAKU AND THE DEAD BODIES ARE, AND SEARCHING IN THE MOUNTAINS IS LEAVING ME EXHAUSTED.
NOT TO MENTION THE FACT THAT THE DOLLS THAT ARE SUPPOSED TO HAVE LEFT THE VILLAGE WITH THEIR FAMILIES KEEP RETURNING HERE.
MY BRAIN IS TIED UP IN KNOTS.
MAKING UP WITH HARUKA-CHAN WOULD BE SOME KIND OF PROGRESS, KAN-CHAN.
PHEW!
YOU NEED TO TALK TO HIM. HE'S COMING TO THE HOUSE WHILE WE'RE OUT, Y'KNOW.
WHAT?!

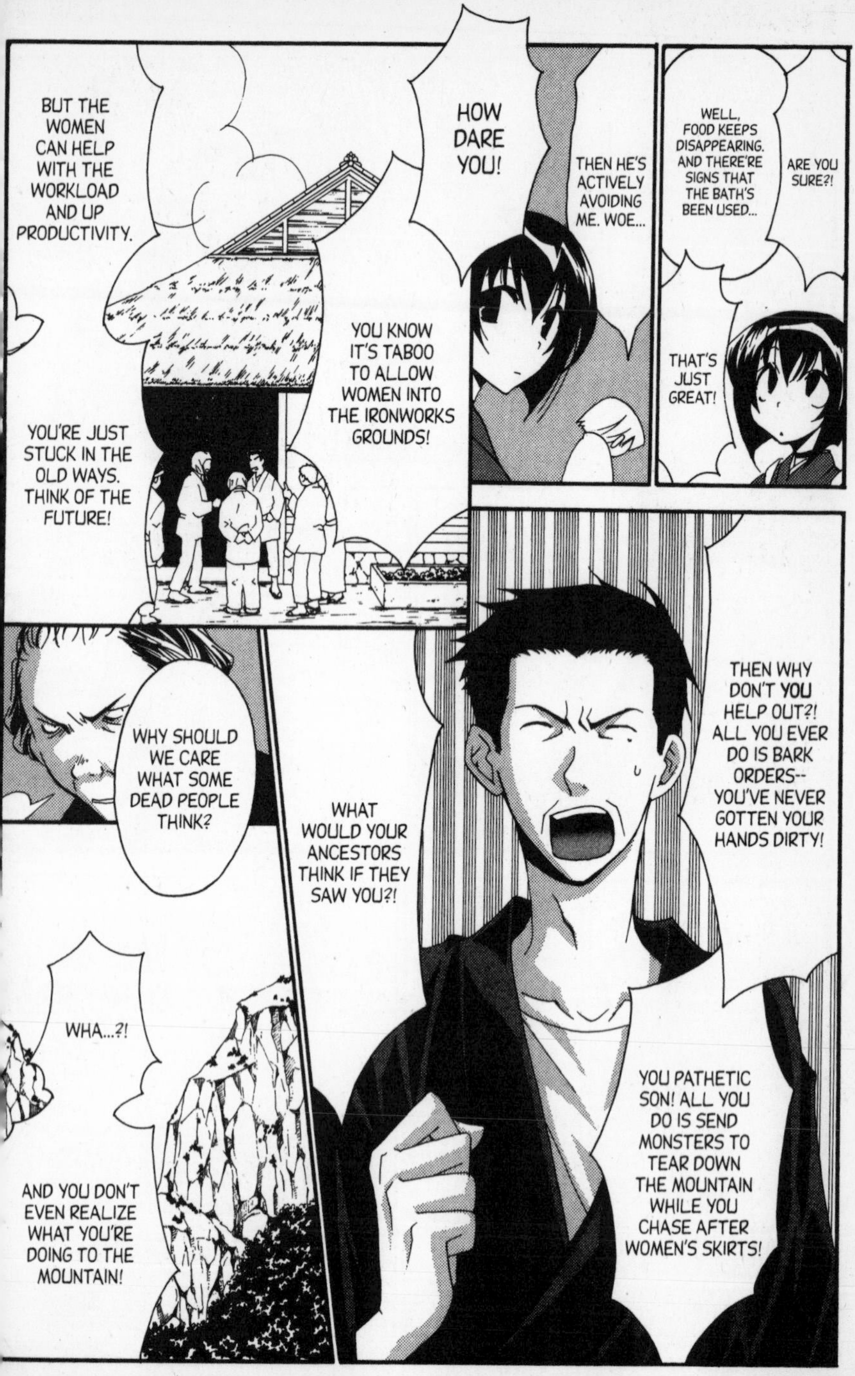
ARE YOU SURE?!
WELL, FOOD KEEPS DISAPPEARING. AND THERE'RE SIGNS THAT THE BATH'S BEEN USED...
THAT'S JUST GREAT!
THEN HE'S ACTIVELY AVOIDING ME. WOE...
HOW DARE YOU!
YOU KNOW IT'S TABOO TO ALLOW WOMEN INTO THE IRONWORKS GROUNDS!
BUT THE WOMEN CAN HELP WITH THE WORKLOAD AND UP PRODUCTIVITY.
YOU'RE JUST STUCK IN THE OLD WAYS. THINK OF THE FUTURE!
THEN WHY DON'T YOU HELP OUT?! ALL YOU EVER DO IS BARK ORDERS-- YOU'VE NEVER GOTTEN YOUR HANDS DIRTY!
YOU PATHETIC SON! ALL YOU DO IS SEND MONSTERS TO TEAR DOWN THE MOUNTAIN WHILE YOU CHASE AFTER WOMEN'S SKIRTS!
WHAT WOULD YOUR ANCESTORS THINK IF THEY SAW YOU?!
WHY SHOULD WE CARE WHAT SOME DEAD PEOPLE THINK?
WHA...?!
AND YOU DON'T EVEN REALIZE WHAT YOU'RE DOING TO THE MOUNTAIN!

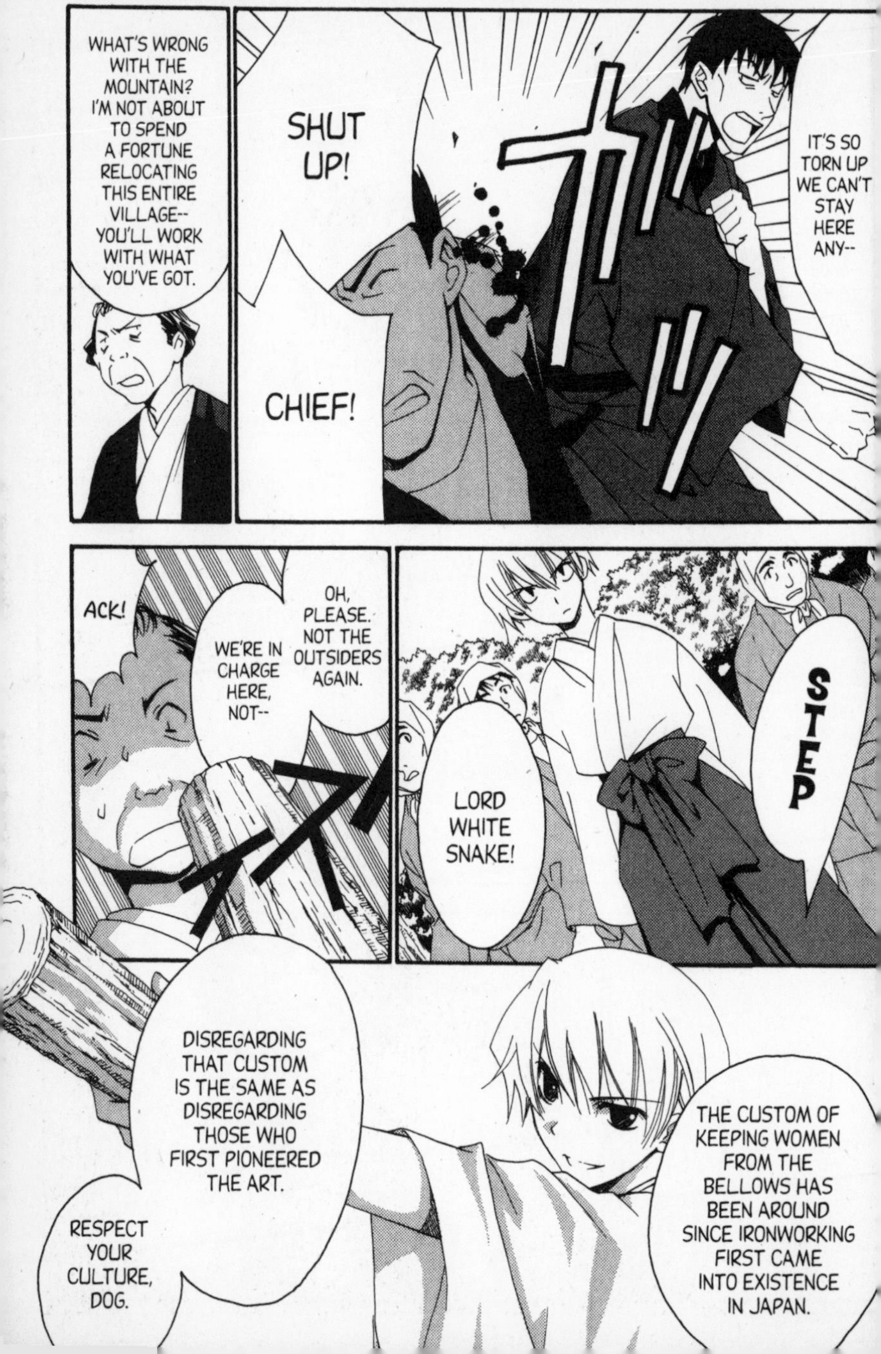
IT'S SO TORN UP WE CAN'T STAY HERE ANY--
SHUT UP!
CHIEF!
WHAT'S WRONG WITH THE MOUNTAIN? I'M NOT ABOUT TO SPEND A FORTUNE RELOCATING THIS ENTIRE VILLAGE-- YOU'LL WORK WITH WHAT YOU'VE GOT.
STEP
LORD WHITE SNAKE!
OH, PLEASE. NOT THE OUTSIDERS AGAIN.
WE'RE IN CHARGE HERE, NOT--
ACK!
THE CUSTOM OF KEEPING WOMEN FROM THE BELLOWS HAS BEEN AROUND SINCE IRONWORKING FIRST CAME INTO EXISTENCE IN JAPAN.
DISREGARDING THAT CUSTOM IS THE SAME AS DISREGARDING THOSE WHO FIRST PIONEERED THE ART.
RESPECT YOUR CULTURE, DOG.

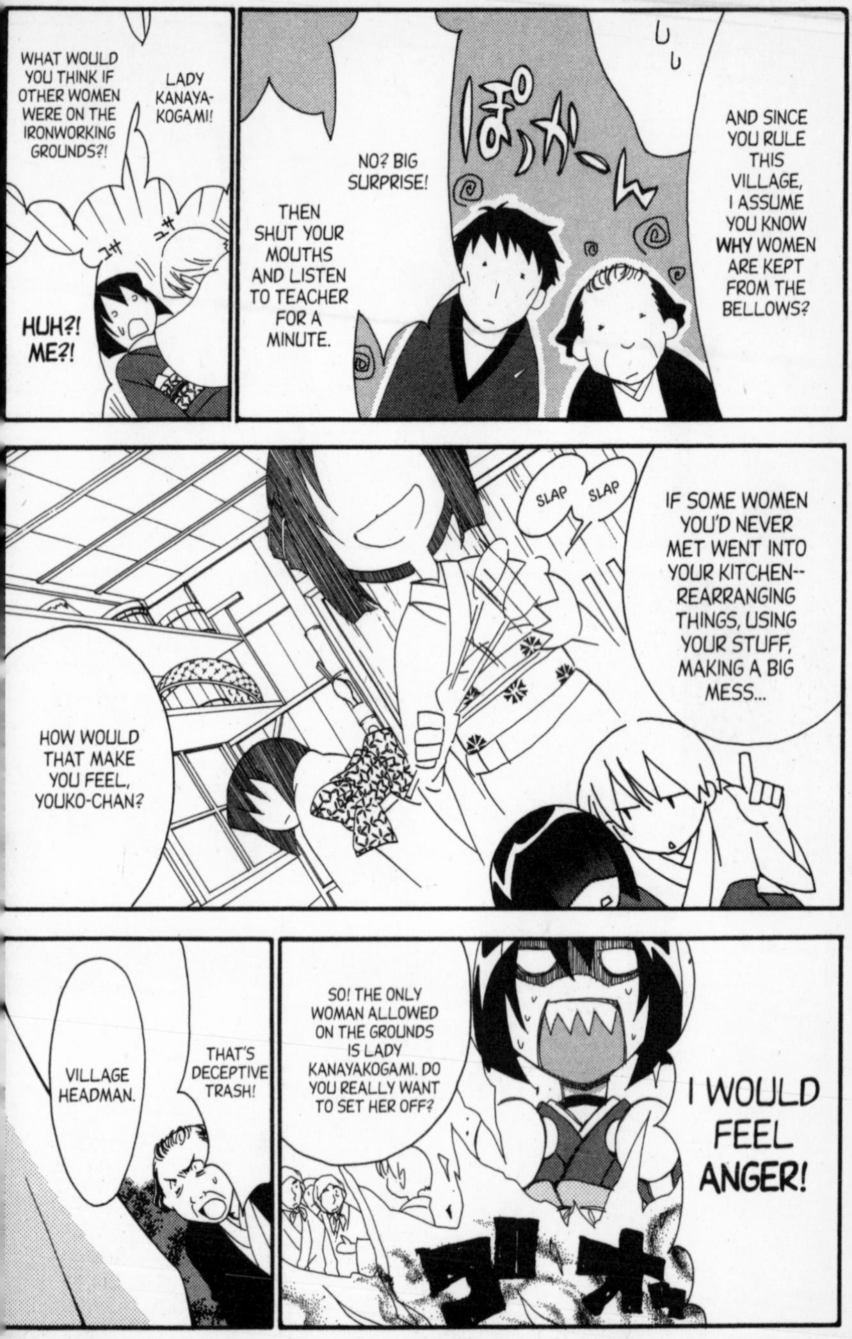
AND SINCE YOU RULE THIS VILLAGE, I ASSUME YOU KNOW **WHY** WOMEN ARE KEPT FROM THE BELLOWS?
ぽっかーん
NO? BIG SURPRISE!
THEN SHUT YOUR MOUTHS AND LISTEN TO TEACHER FOR A MINUTE.
LADY KANAYA-KOGAMI!
WHAT WOULD YOU THINK IF OTHER WOMEN WERE ON THE IRONWORKING GROUNDS?!
ユサ ユサ
HUH?! ME?!
IF SOME WOMEN YOU'D NEVER MET WENT INTO YOUR KITCHEN-- REARRANGING THINGS, USING YOUR STUFF, MAKING A BIG MESS...
SLAP SLAP
HOW WOULD THAT MAKE YOU FEEL, YOUKO-CHAN?
I WOULD FEEL ANGER!
SO! THE ONLY WOMAN ALLOWED ON THE GROUNDS IS LADY KANAYAKOGAMI. DO YOU REALLY WANT TO SET HER OFF?
THAT'S DECEPTIVE TRASH!
VILLAGE HEADMAN.

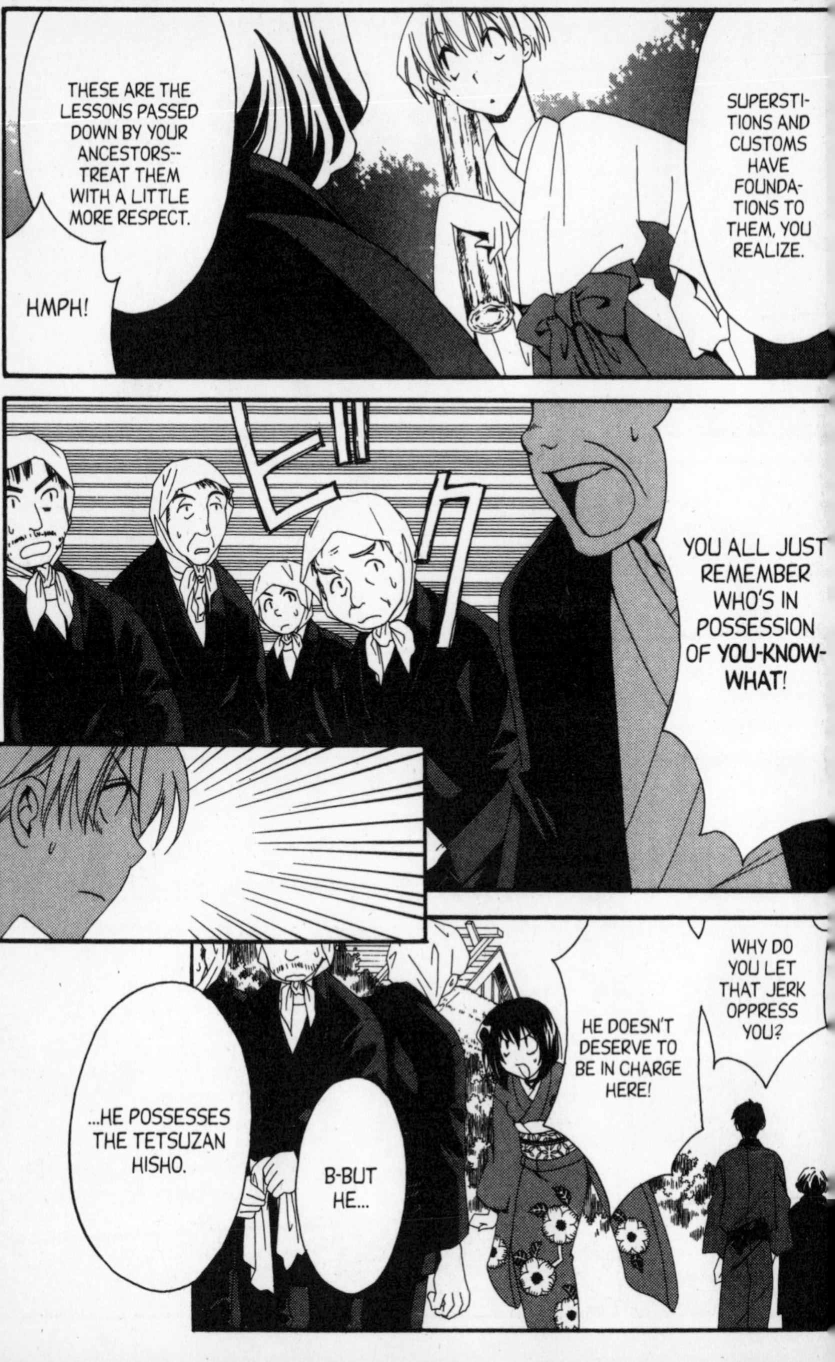
SUPERSTITIONS AND CUSTOMS HAVE FOUNDATIONS TO THEM, YOU REALIZE.
THESE ARE THE LESSONS PASSED DOWN BY YOUR ANCESTORS-- TREAT THEM WITH A LITTLE MORE RESPECT.
HMPH!
YOU ALL JUST REMEMBER WHO'S IN POSSESSION OF **YOU-KNOW-WHAT**!
ビク
WHY DO YOU LET THAT JERK OPPRESS YOU?
HE DOESN'T DESERVE TO BE IN CHARGE HERE!
B-BUT HE...
...HE POSSESSES THE TETSUZAN HISHO.

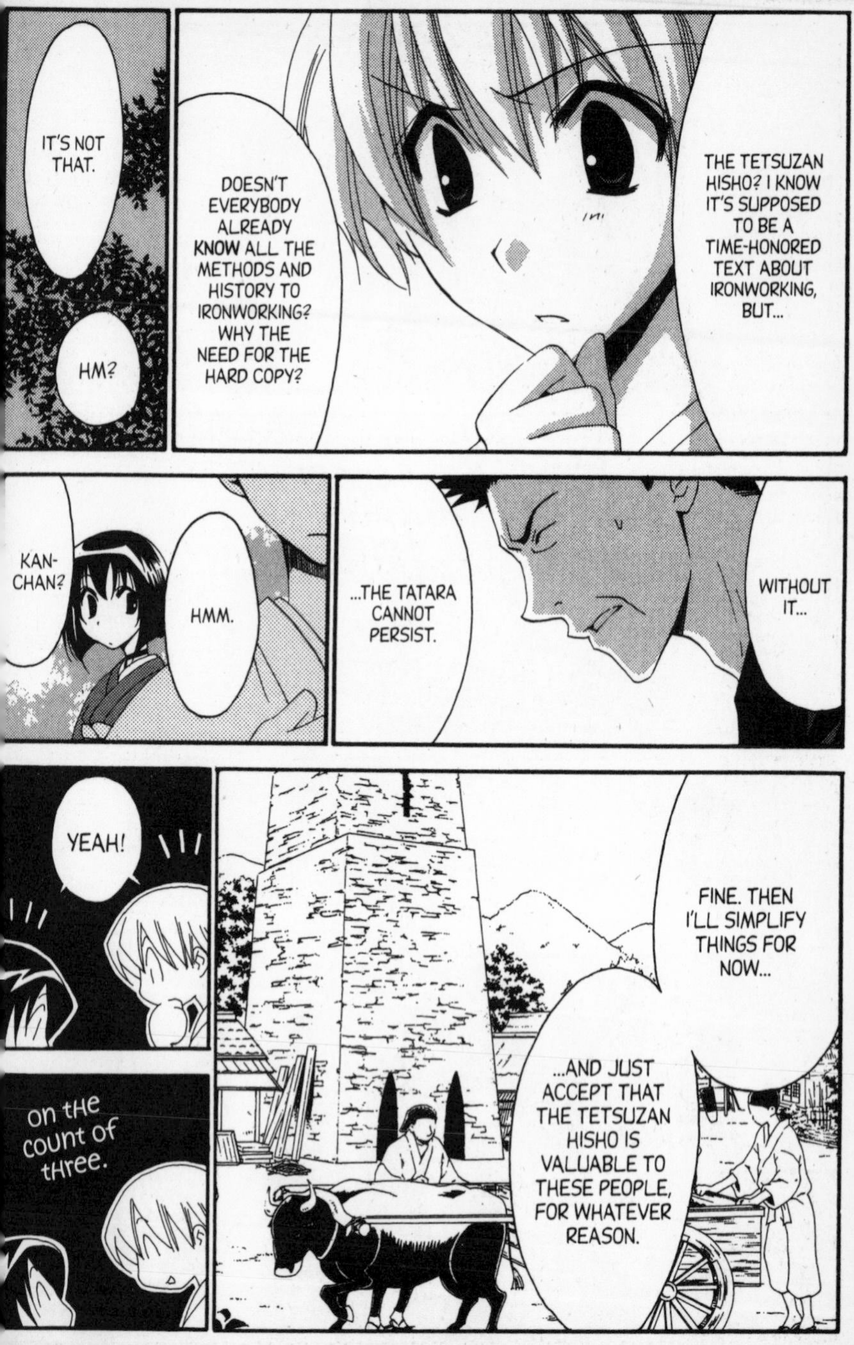
THE TETSUZAN HISHO? I KNOW IT'S SUPPOSED TO BE A TIME-HONORED TEXT ABOUT IRONWORKING, BUT...
DOESN'T EVERYBODY ALREADY KNOW ALL THE METHODS AND HISTORY TO IRONWORKING? WHY THE NEED FOR THE HARD COPY?
IT'S NOT THAT.
HM?
WITHOUT IT...
...THE TATARA CANNOT PERSIST.
HMM.
KAN-CHAN?
FINE. THEN I'LL SIMPLIFY THINGS FOR NOW...
...AND JUST ACCEPT THAT THE TETSUZAN HISHO IS VALUABLE TO THESE PEOPLE, FOR WHATEVER REASON.
YEAH!
on the count of three.

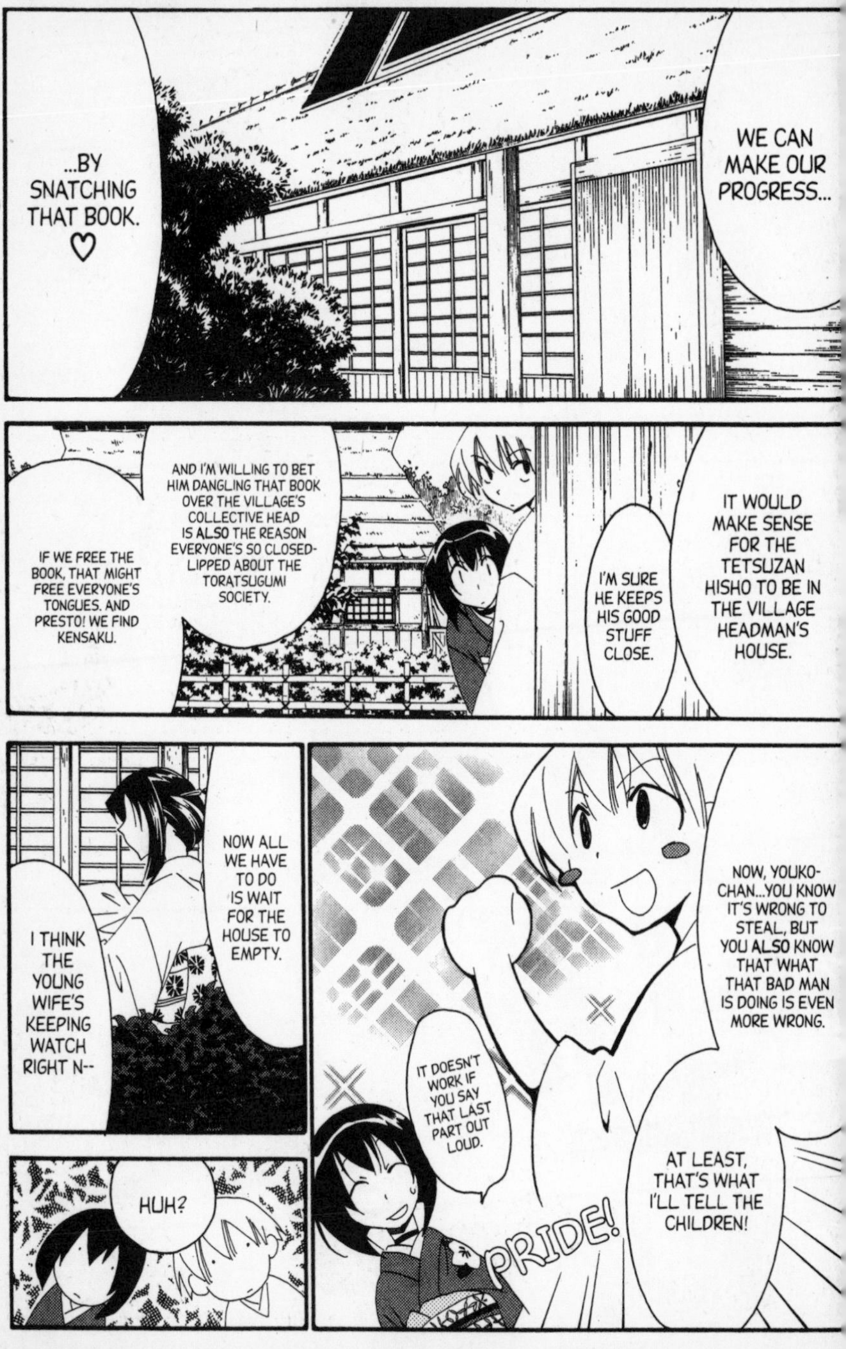
WE CAN MAKE OUR PROGRESS...
...BY SNATCHING THAT BOOK. ♡
IT WOULD MAKE SENSE FOR THE TETSUZAN HISHO TO BE IN THE VILLAGE HEADMAN'S HOUSE.
I'M SURE HE KEEPS HIS GOOD STUFF CLOSE.
AND I'M WILLING TO BET HIM DANGLING THAT BOOK OVER THE VILLAGE'S COLLECTIVE HEAD IS ALSO THE REASON EVERYONE'S SO CLOSED-LIPPED ABOUT THE TORATSUGUMI SOCIETY.
IF WE FREE THE BOOK, THAT MIGHT FREE EVERYONE'S TONGUES. AND PRESTO! WE FIND KENSAKU.
NOW, YOUKO-CHAN...YOU KNOW IT'S WRONG TO STEAL, BUT YOU ALSO KNOW THAT WHAT THAT BAD MAN IS DOING IS EVEN MORE WRONG.
AT LEAST, THAT'S WHAT I'LL TELL THE CHILDREN!
PRIDE!
IT DOESN'T WORK IF YOU SAY THAT LAST PART OUT LOUD.
NOW ALL WE HAVE TO DO IS WAIT FOR THE HOUSE TO EMPTY.
I THINK THE YOUNG WIFE'S KEEPING WATCH RIGHT N--
HUH?

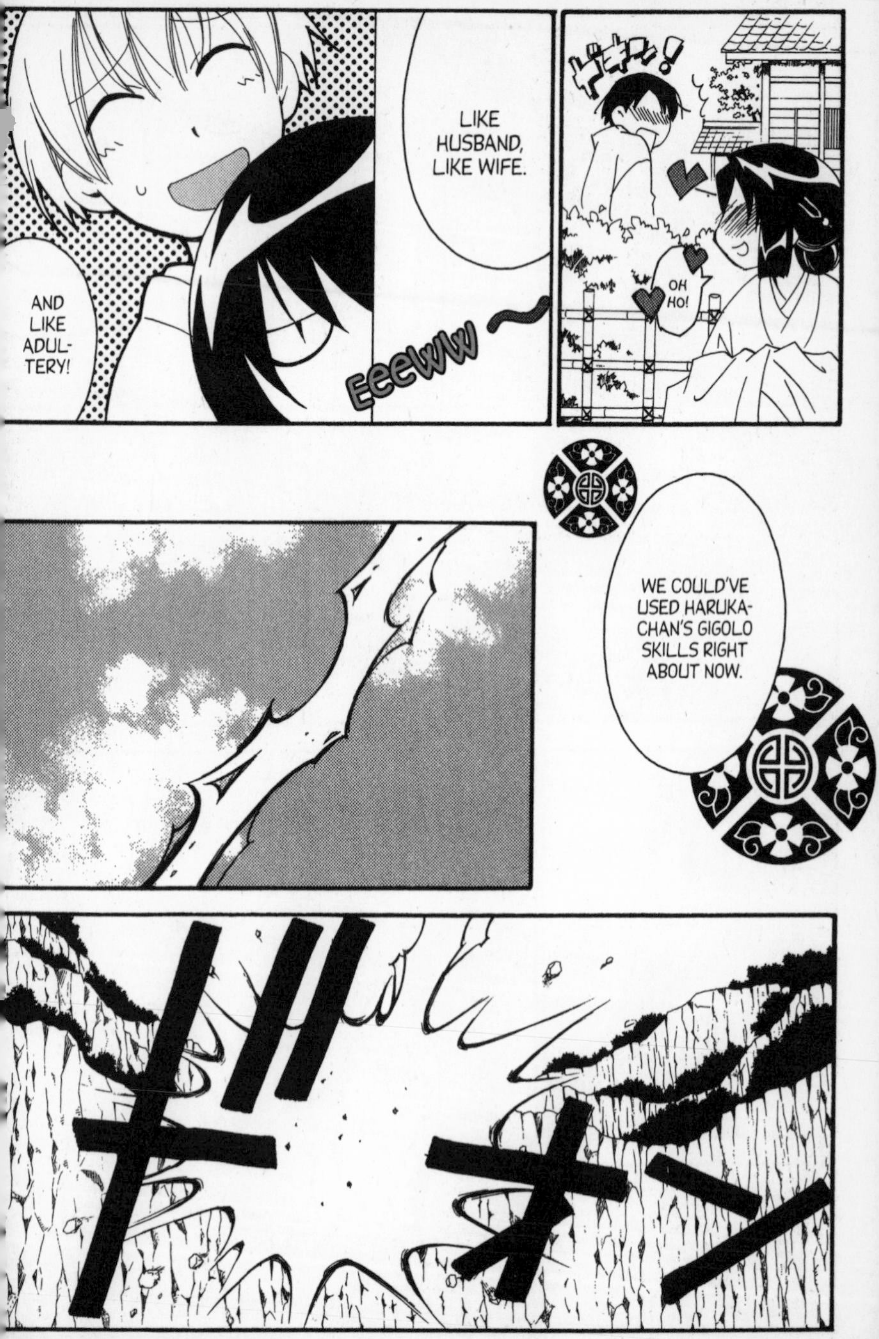
OH HO!
LIKE HUSBAND, LIKE WIFE.
EEEWW ~
AND LIKE ADULTERY!
WE COULD'VE USED HARUKA-CHAN'S GIGOLO SKILLS RIGHT ABOUT NOW.

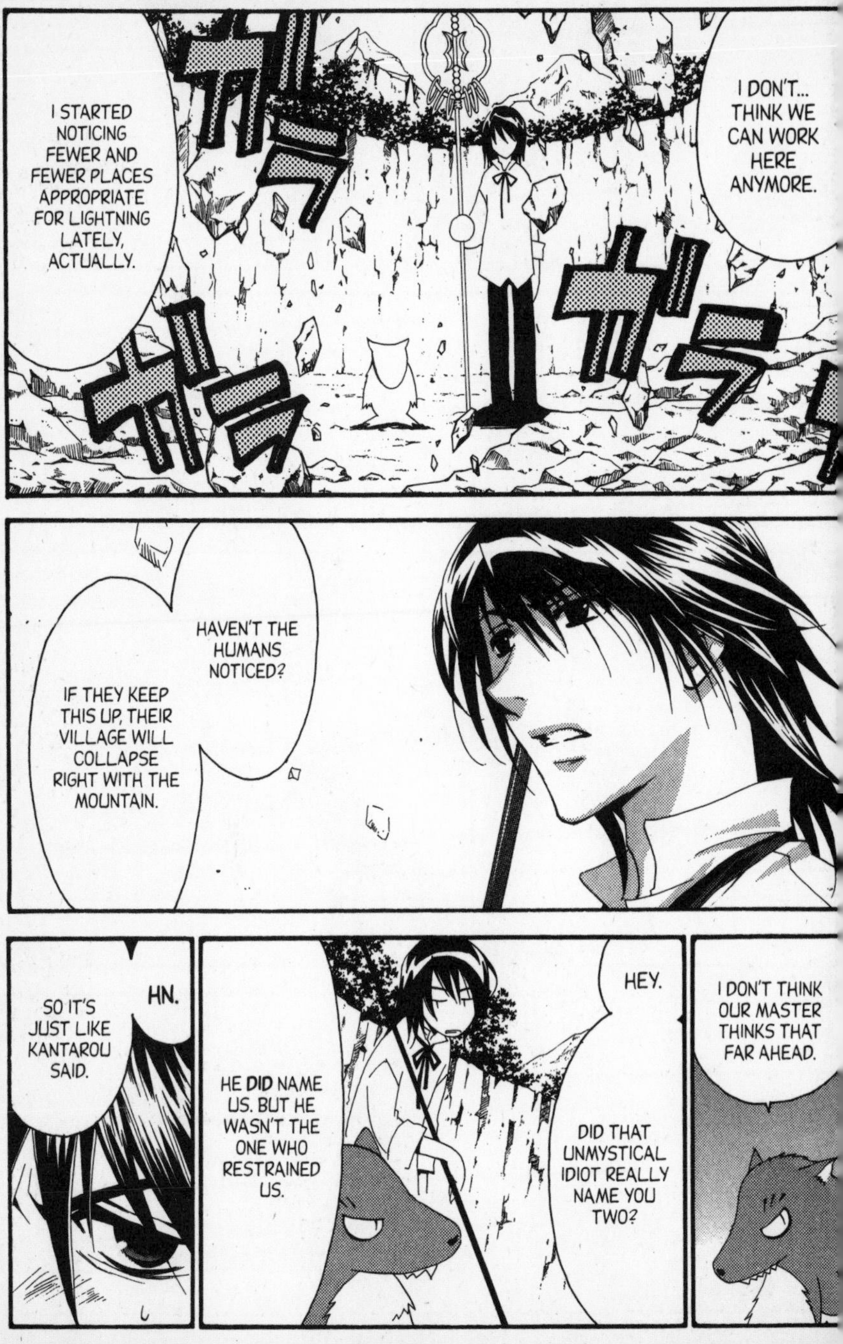
I DON'T... THINK WE CAN WORK HERE ANYMORE.
ガラッ
ガラ
I STARTED NOTICING FEWER AND FEWER PLACES APPROPRIATE FOR LIGHTNING LATELY, ACTUALLY.
ガラ
HAVEN'T THE HUMANS NOTICED?
IF THEY KEEP THIS UP, THEIR VILLAGE WILL COLLAPSE RIGHT WITH THE MOUNTAIN.
I DON'T THINK OUR MASTER THINKS THAT FAR AHEAD.
HEY.
DID THAT UNMYSTICAL IDIOT REALLY NAME YOU TWO?
HE **DID** NAME US. BUT HE WASN'T THE ONE WHO RESTRAINED US.
HN.
SO IT'S JUST LIKE KANTAROU SAID.

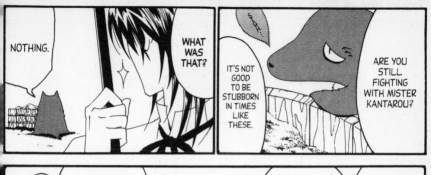

ARE YOU STILL FIGHTING WITH MISTER KANTAROU?
IT'S NOT GOOD TO BE STUBBORN IN TIMES LIKE THESE.
WHAT WAS THAT?
NOTHING.
WHAT WAS THE SORCERER WHO RESTRAINED YOU LIKE?
HM? HE LOOKED A LOT LIKE YOU, LORD DEMON EATER.
SO HE WAS WEARING WESTERN CLOTHES. ANYTHING ELSE?
WELL...
UM...
YESTERDAY WE ATE RADISH LEAVES WITH MILLET AND WHEAT. ♡
I FORGOT THAT YOU TWO HAVE TINY BRAINS.
YOU'RE ONE TO TALK, SIR.
GOOD WORK OUT HERE!
I BROUGHT A SNACK FOR YOU.

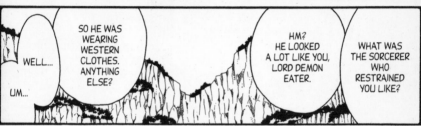

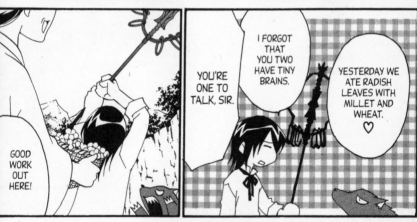

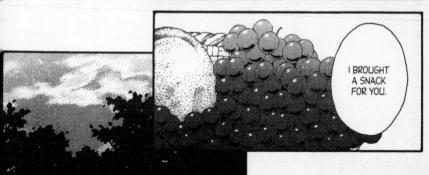

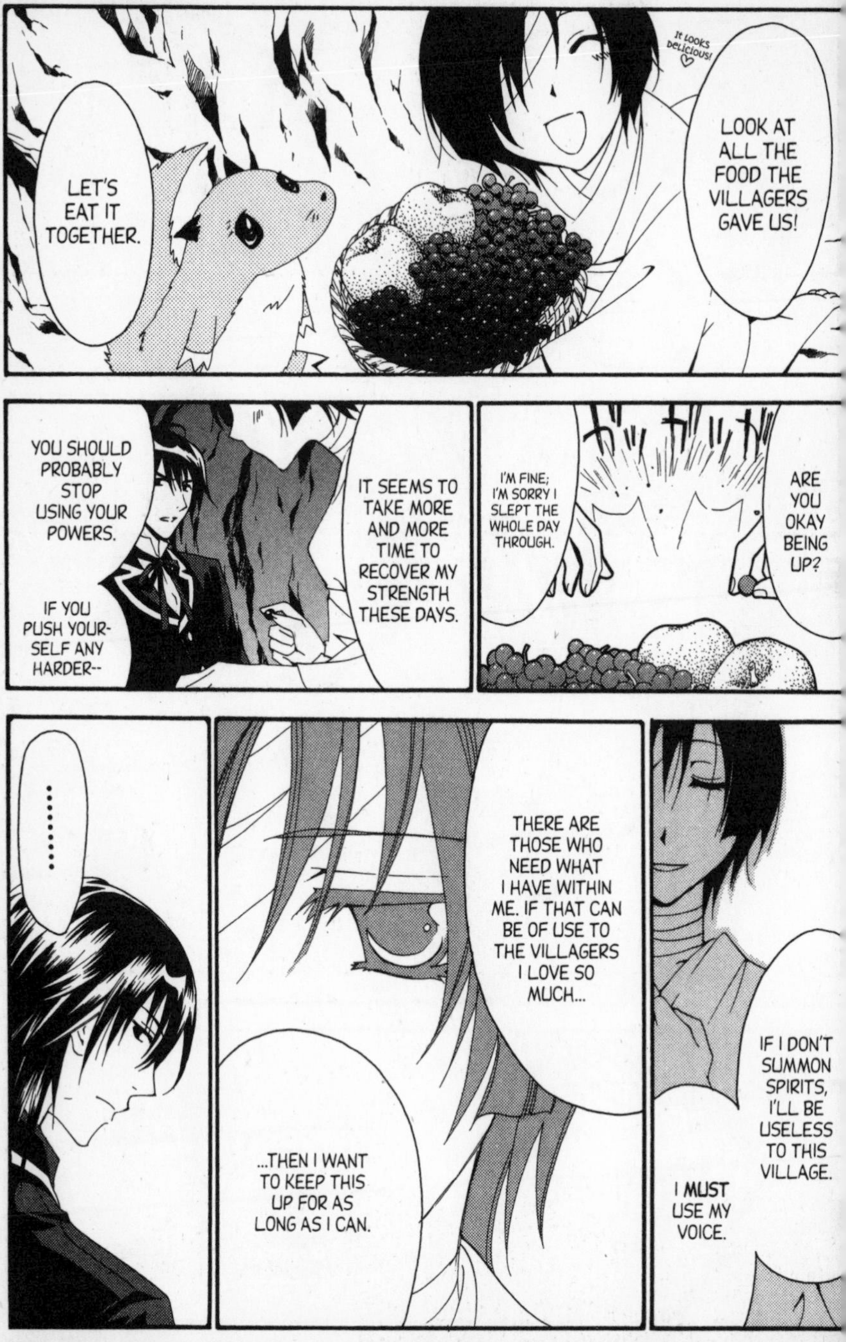
It looks delicious! ♡
LOOK AT ALL THE FOOD THE VILLAGERS GAVE US!
LET'S EAT IT TOGETHER.
ARE YOU OKAY BEING UP?
I'M FINE; I'M SORRY I SLEPT THE WHOLE DAY THROUGH.
IT SEEMS TO TAKE MORE AND MORE TIME TO RECOVER MY STRENGTH THESE DAYS.
YOU SHOULD PROBABLY STOP USING YOUR POWERS.
IF YOU PUSH YOURSELF ANY HARDER--
IF I DON'T SUMMON SPIRITS, I'LL BE USELESS TO THIS VILLAGE.
I **MUST** USE MY VOICE.
THERE ARE THOSE WHO NEED WHAT I HAVE WITHIN ME. IF THAT CAN BE OF USE TO THE VILLAGERS I LOVE SO MUCH...
...THEN I WANT TO KEEP THIS UP FOR AS LONG AS I CAN.
....

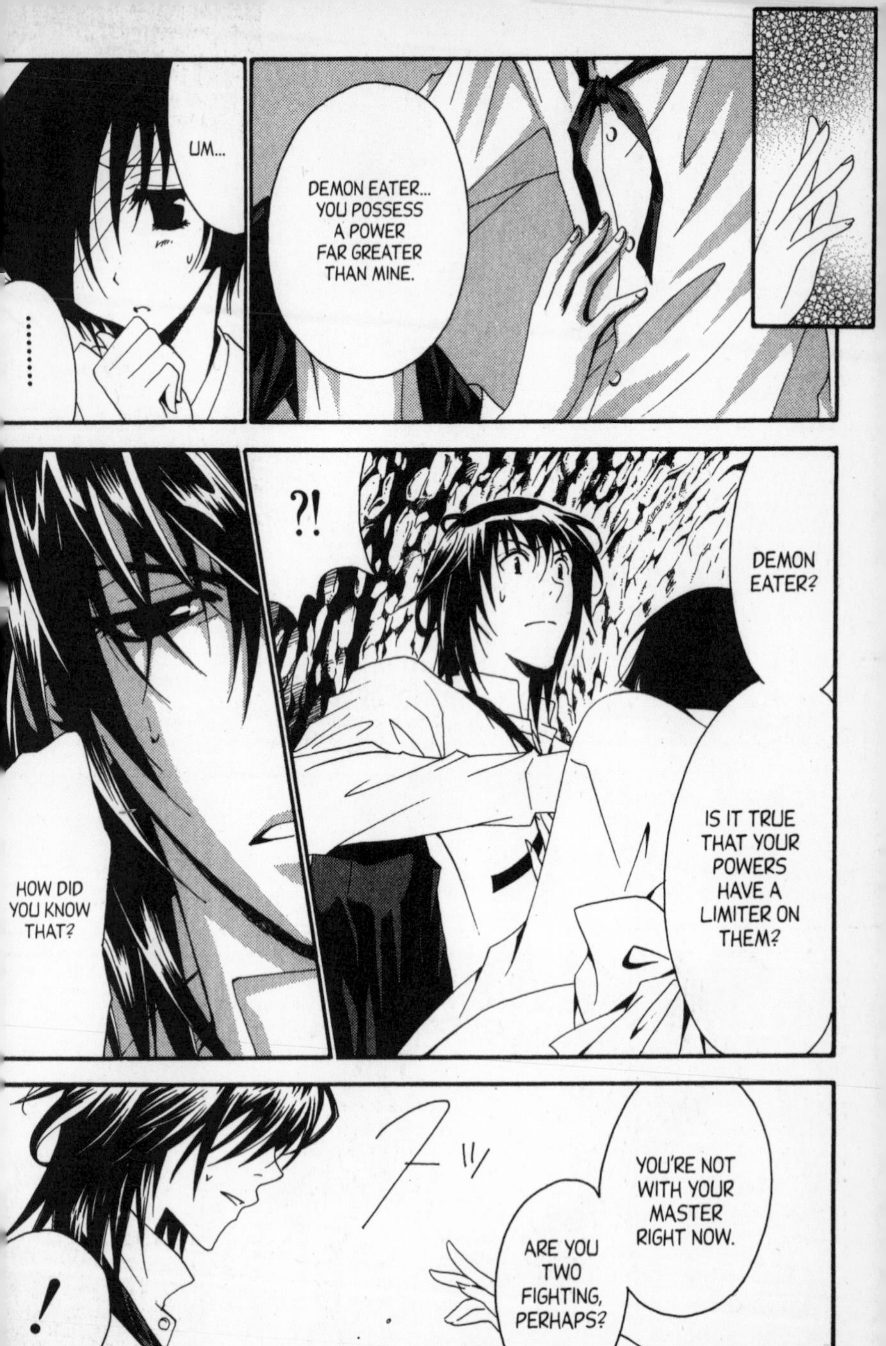
DEMON EATER... YOU POSSESS A POWER FAR GREATER THAN MINE.
UM...
......
DEMON EATER?
IS IT TRUE THAT YOUR POWERS HAVE A LIMITER ON THEM?
?!
HOW DID YOU KNOW THAT?
YOU'RE NOT WITH YOUR MASTER RIGHT NOW.
ARE YOU TWO FIGHTING, PERHAPS?
!

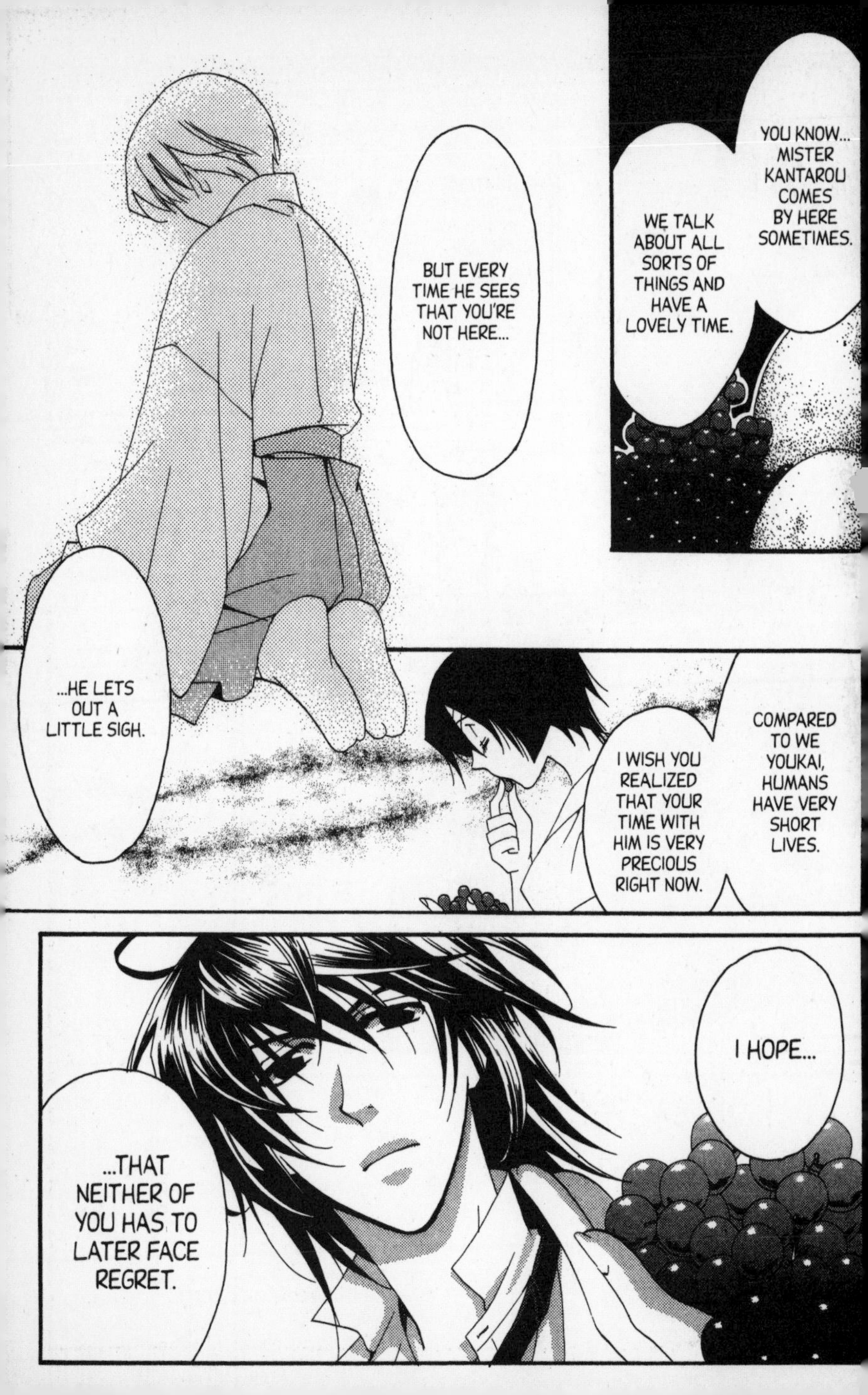
YOU KNOW... MISTER KANTAROU COMES BY HERE SOMETIMES.
WE TALK ABOUT ALL SORTS OF THINGS AND HAVE A LOVELY TIME.
BUT EVERY TIME HE SEES THAT YOU'RE NOT HERE...
...HE LETS OUT A LITTLE SIGH.
COMPARED TO WE YOUKAI, HUMANS HAVE VERY SHORT LIVES.
I WISH YOU REALIZED THAT YOUR TIME WITH HIM IS VERY PRECIOUS RIGHT NOW.
I HOPE...
...THAT NEITHER OF YOU HAS TO LATER FACE REGRET.

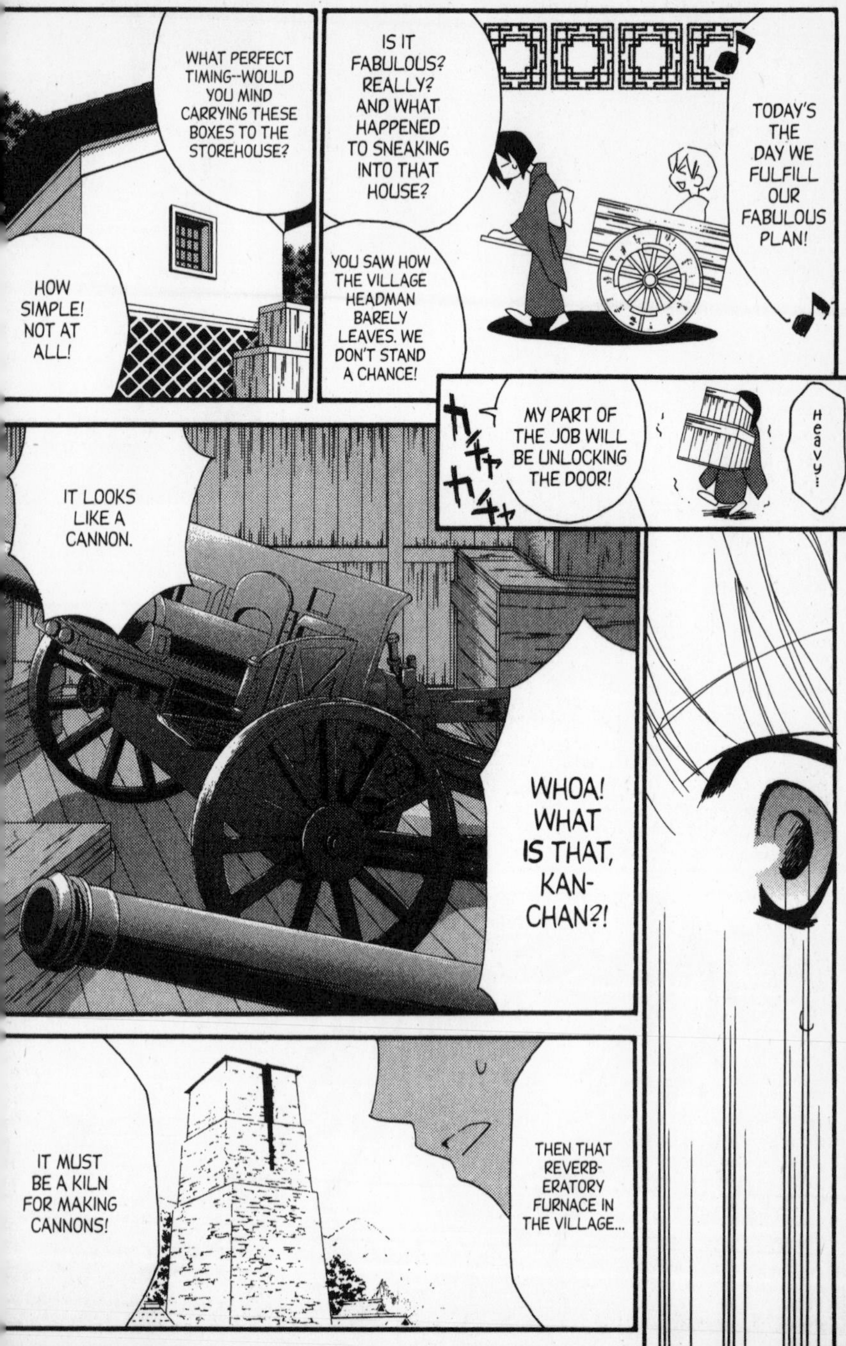
TODAY'S THE DAY WE FULFILL OUR FABULOUS PLAN!
IS IT FABULOUS? REALLY? AND WHAT HAPPENED TO SNEAKING INTO THAT HOUSE?
YOU SAW HOW THE VILLAGE HEADMAN BARELY LEAVES. WE DON'T STAND A CHANCE!
WHAT PERFECT TIMING--WOULD YOU MIND CARRYING THESE BOXES TO THE STOREHOUSE?
HOW SIMPLE! NOT AT ALL!
Heavy...
MY PART OF THE JOB WILL BE UNLOCKING THE DOOR!
カチャ カチャ
WHOA! WHAT IS THAT, KAN-CHAN?!
IT LOOKS LIKE A CANNON.
THEN THAT REVERBERATORY FURNACE IN THE VILLAGE...
IT MUST BE A KILN FOR MAKING CANNONS!

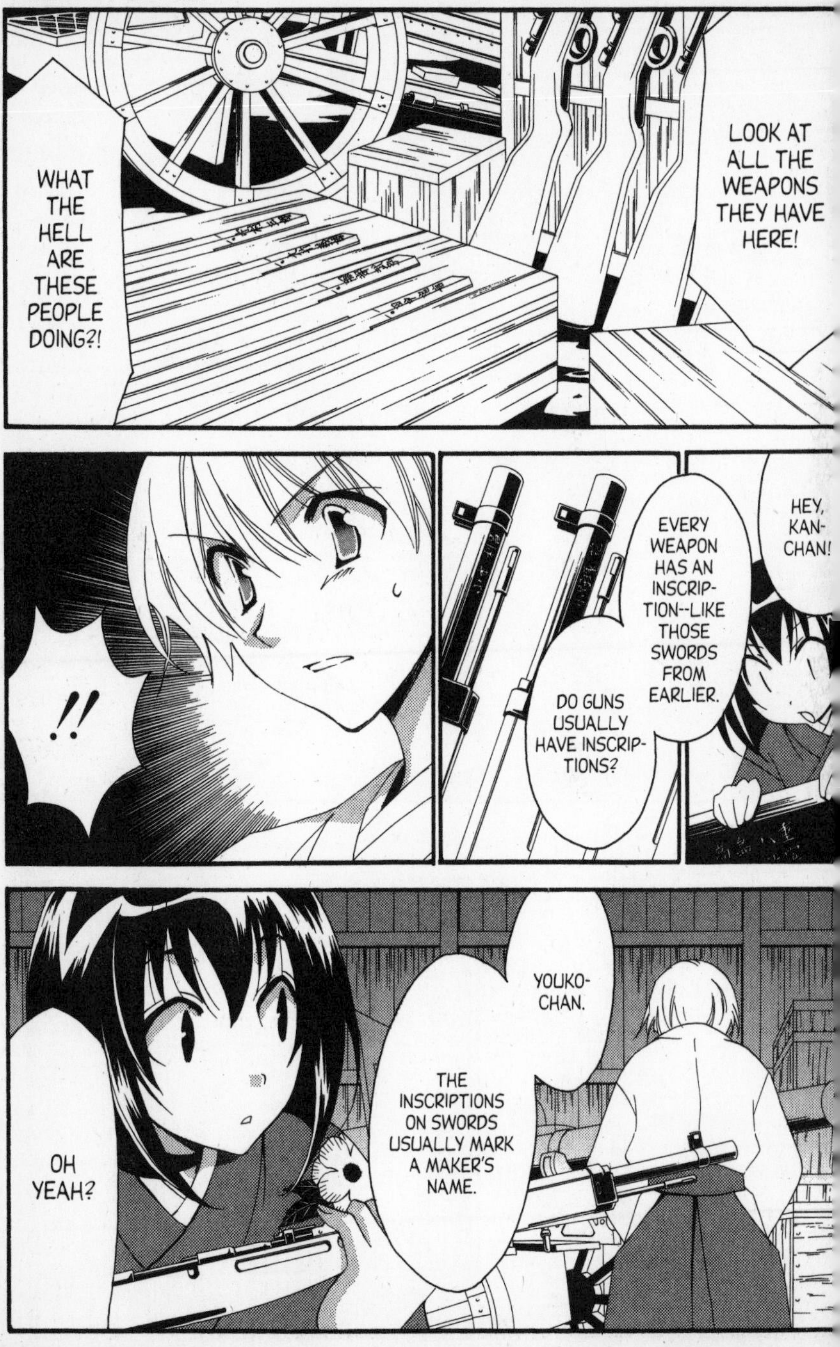
LOOK AT ALL THE WEAPONS THEY HAVE HERE!
WHAT THE HELL ARE THESE PEOPLE DOING?!
HEY, KAN-CHAN!
EVERY WEAPON HAS AN INSCRIPTION--LIKE THOSE SWORDS FROM EARLIER.
DO GUNS USUALLY HAVE INSCRIPTIONS?
!!
YOUKO-CHAN.
THE INSCRIPTIONS ON SWORDS USUALLY MARK A MAKER'S NAME.
OH YEAH?

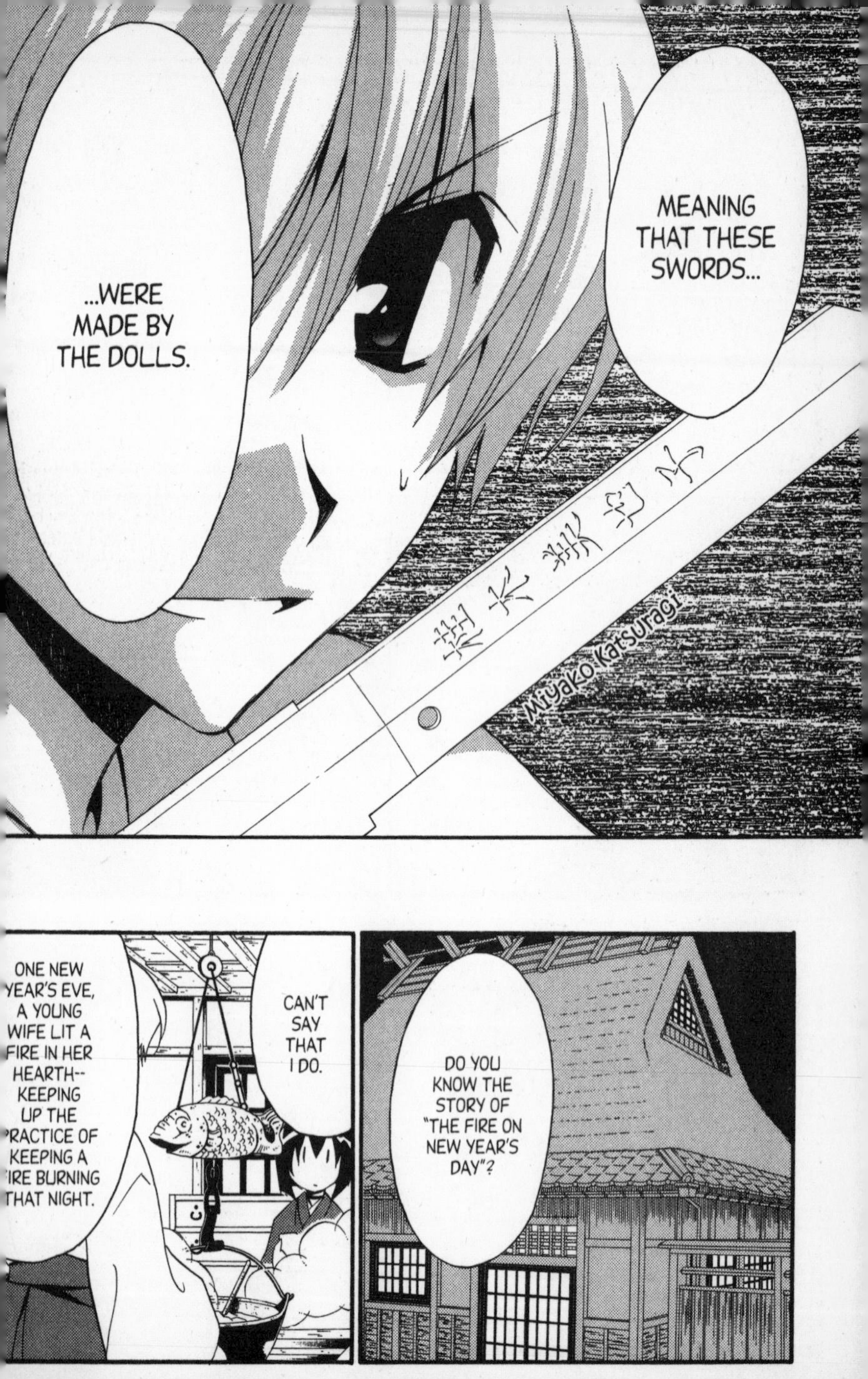
MEANING THAT THESE SWORDS...
...WERE MADE BY THE DOLLS.
Miyako Katsuragi
DO YOU KNOW THE STORY OF "THE FIRE ON NEW YEAR'S DAY"?
CAN'T SAY THAT I DO.
ONE NEW YEAR'S EVE, A YOUNG WIFE LIT A FIRE IN HER HEARTH-- KEEPING UP THE PRACTICE OF KEEPING A FIRE BURNING THAT NIGHT.

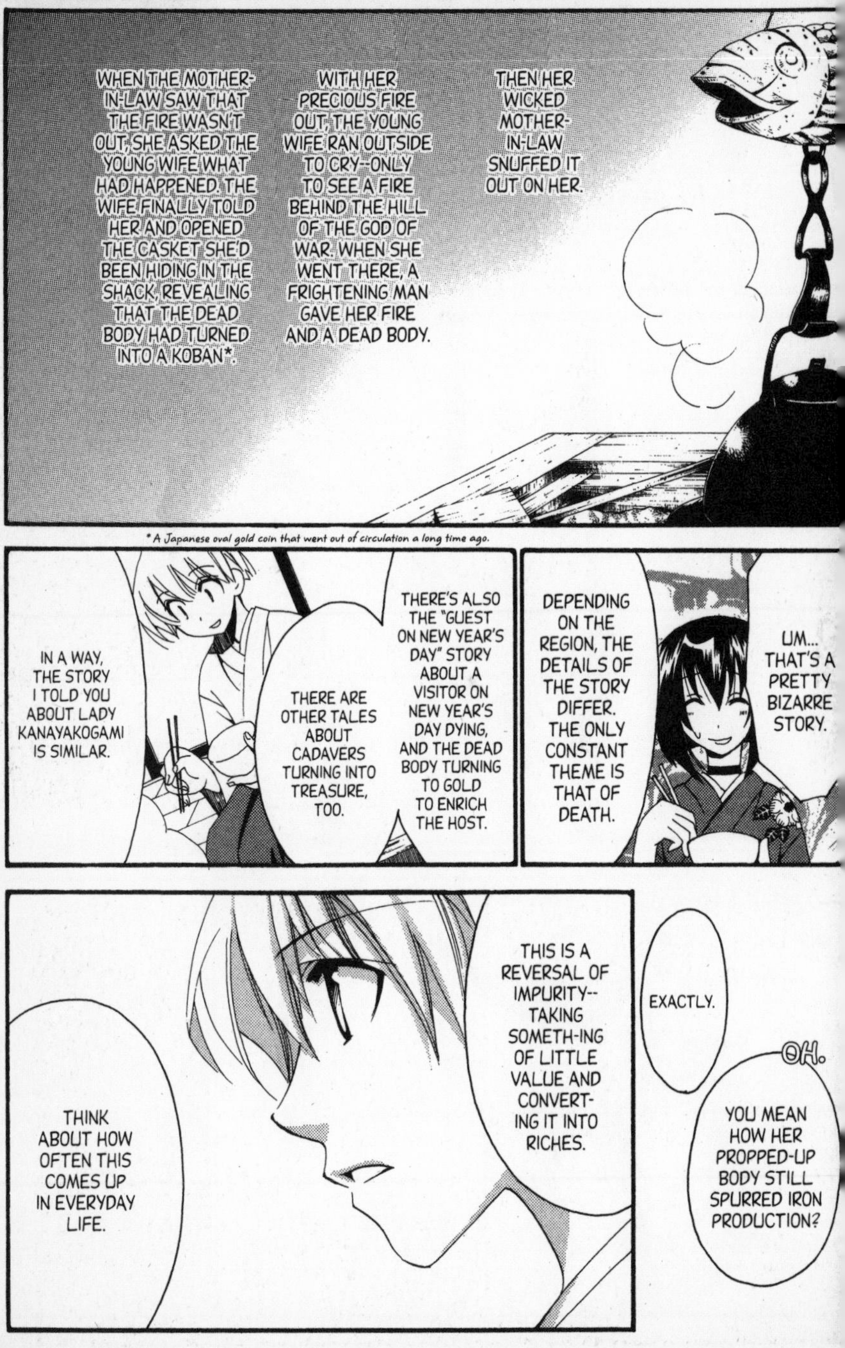
THEN HER WICKED MOTHER-IN-LAW SNUFFED IT OUT ON HER.
WITH HER PRECIOUS FIRE OUT, THE YOUNG WIFE RAN OUTSIDE TO CRY--ONLY TO SEE A FIRE BEHIND THE HILL OF THE GOD OF WAR. WHEN SHE WENT THERE, A FRIGHTENING MAN GAVE HER FIRE AND A DEAD BODY.
WHEN THE MOTHER-IN-LAW SAW THAT THE FIRE WASN'T OUT, SHE ASKED THE YOUNG WIFE WHAT HAD HAPPENED. THE WIFE FINALLY TOLD HER AND OPENED THE CASKET SHE'D BEEN HIDING IN THE SHACK, REVEALING THAT THE DEAD BODY HAD TURNED INTO A KOBAN*.
*A Japanese oval gold coin that went out of circulation a long time ago.
UM... THAT'S A PRETTY BIZARRE STORY.
DEPENDING ON THE REGION, THE DETAILS OF THE STORY DIFFER. THE ONLY CONSTANT THEME IS THAT OF DEATH.
THERE'S ALSO THE "GUEST ON NEW YEAR'S DAY" STORY ABOUT A VISITOR ON NEW YEAR'S DAY DYING, AND THE DEAD BODY TURNING TO GOLD TO ENRICH THE HOST.
THERE ARE OTHER TALES ABOUT CADAVERS TURNING INTO TREASURE, TOO.
IN A WAY, THE STORY I TOLD YOU ABOUT LADY KANAYAKOGAMI IS SIMILAR.
OH.
YOU MEAN HOW HER PROPPED-UP BODY STILL SPURRED IRON PRODUCTION?
EXACTLY.
THIS IS A REVERSAL OF IMPURITY--TAKING SOMETH-ING OF LITTLE VALUE AND CONVERT-ING IT INTO RICHES.
THINK ABOUT HOW OFTEN THIS COMES UP IN EVERYDAY LIFE.

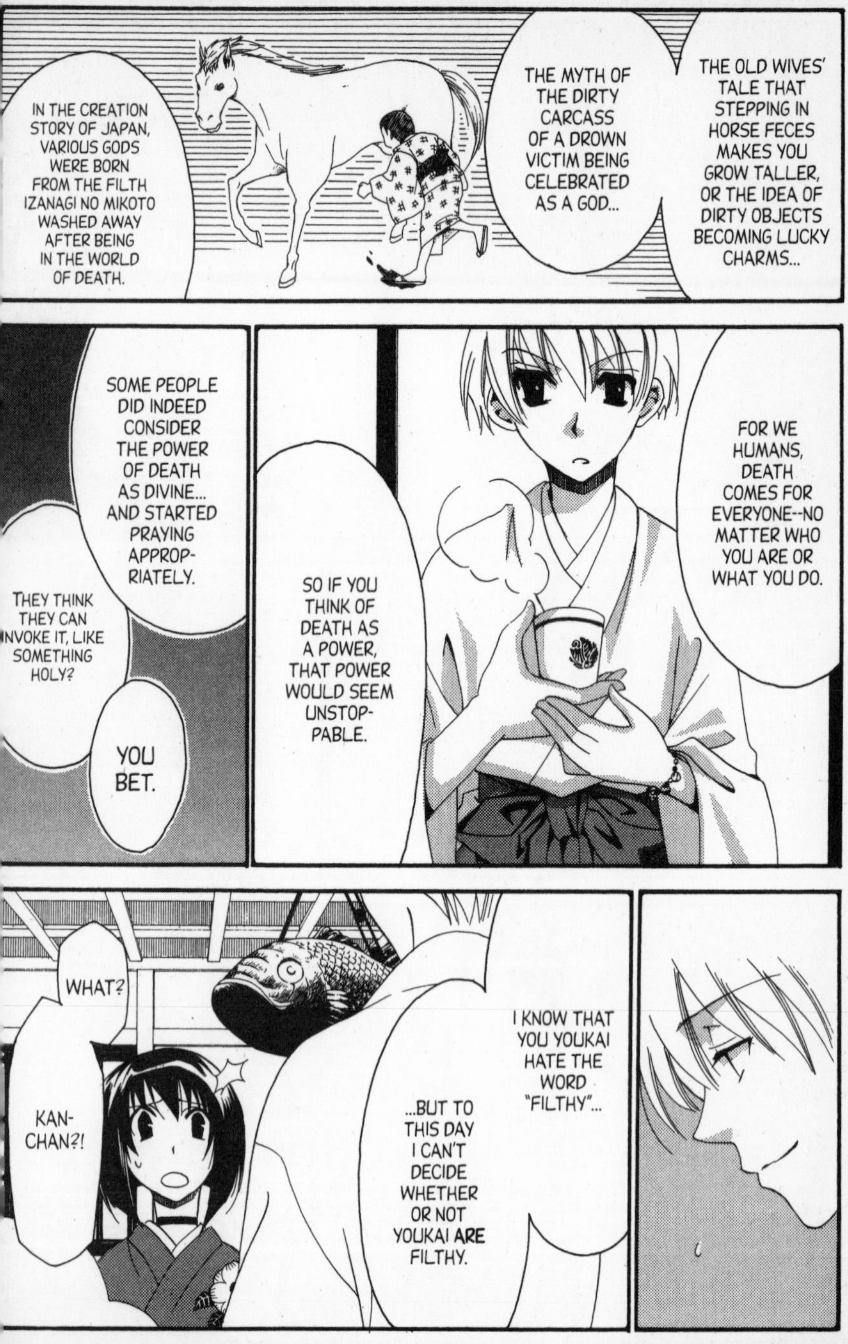
THE OLD WIVES' TALE THAT STEPPING IN HORSE FECES MAKES YOU GROW TALLER, OR THE IDEA OF DIRTY OBJECTS BECOMING LUCKY CHARMS...
THE MYTH OF THE DIRTY CARCASS OF A DROWN VICTIM BEING CELEBRATED AS A GOD...
IN THE CREATION STORY OF JAPAN, VARIOUS GODS WERE BORN FROM THE FILTH IZANAGI NO MIKOTO WASHED AWAY AFTER BEING IN THE WORLD OF DEATH.
FOR WE HUMANS, DEATH COMES FOR EVERYONE--NO MATTER WHO YOU ARE OR WHAT YOU DO.
SO IF YOU THINK OF DEATH AS A POWER, THAT POWER WOULD SEEM UNSTOP-PABLE.
SOME PEOPLE DID INDEED CONSIDER THE POWER OF DEATH AS DIVINE... AND STARTED PRAYING APPROP-RIATELY.
THEY THINK THEY CAN NVOKE IT, LIKE SOMETHING HOLY?
YOU BET.
I KNOW THAT YOU YOUKAI HATE THE WORD "FILTHY"...
...BUT TO THIS DAY I CAN'T DECIDE WHETHER OR NOT YOUKAI **ARE** FILTHY.
WHAT?
KAN-CHAN?!

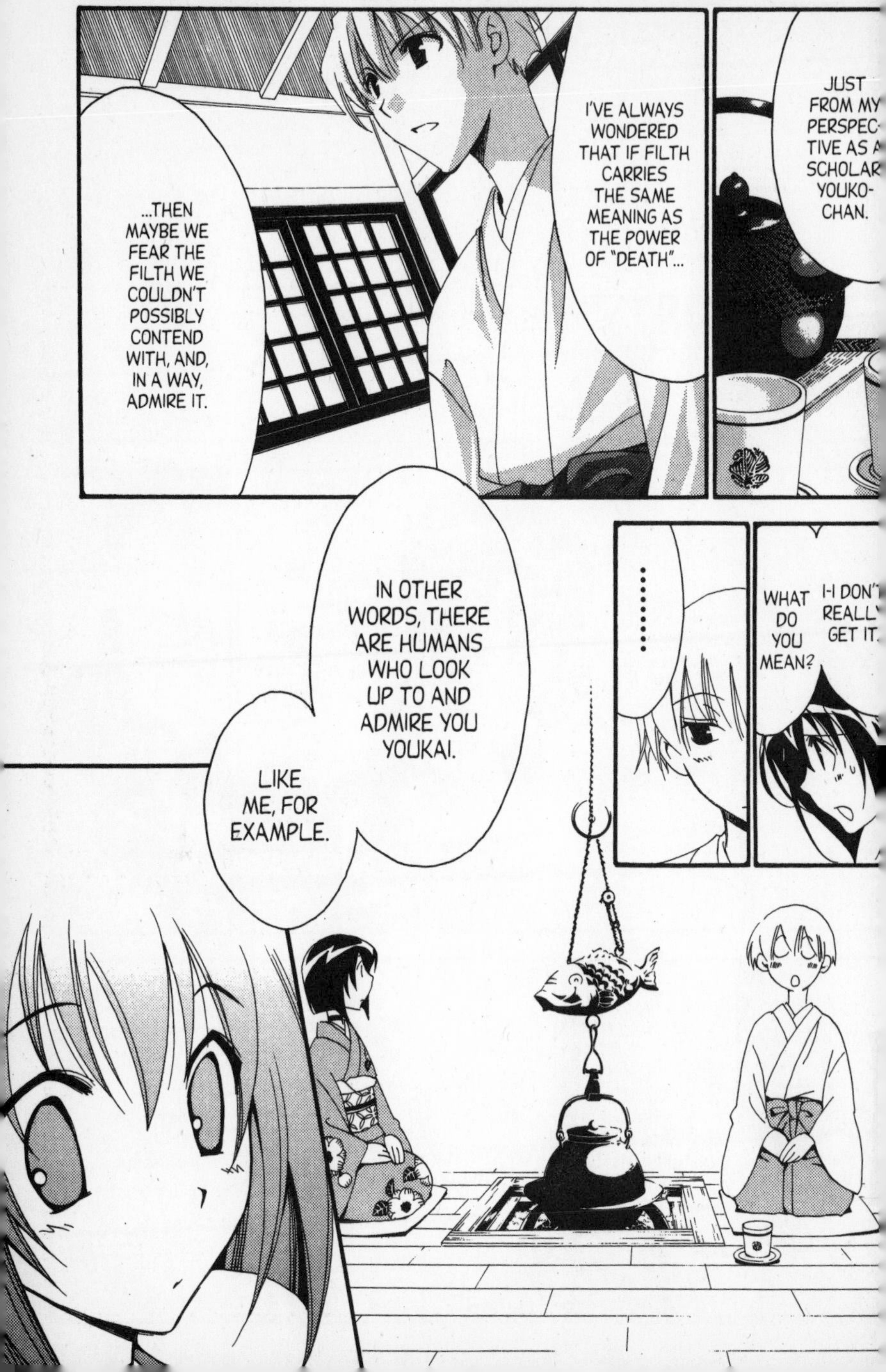
JUST FROM MY PERSPEC-TIVE AS A SCHOLAR YOUKO-CHAN.
I'VE ALWAYS WONDERED THAT IF FILTH CARRIES THE SAME MEANING AS THE POWER OF "DEATH"...
...THEN MAYBE WE FEAR THE FILTH WE COULDN'T POSSIBLY CONTEND WITH, AND, IN A WAY, ADMIRE IT.
I-I DON'T REALLY GET IT.
WHAT DO YOU MEAN?
....
IN OTHER WORDS, THERE ARE HUMANS WHO LOOK UP TO AND ADMIRE YOU YOUKAI.
LIKE ME, FOR EXAMPLE.

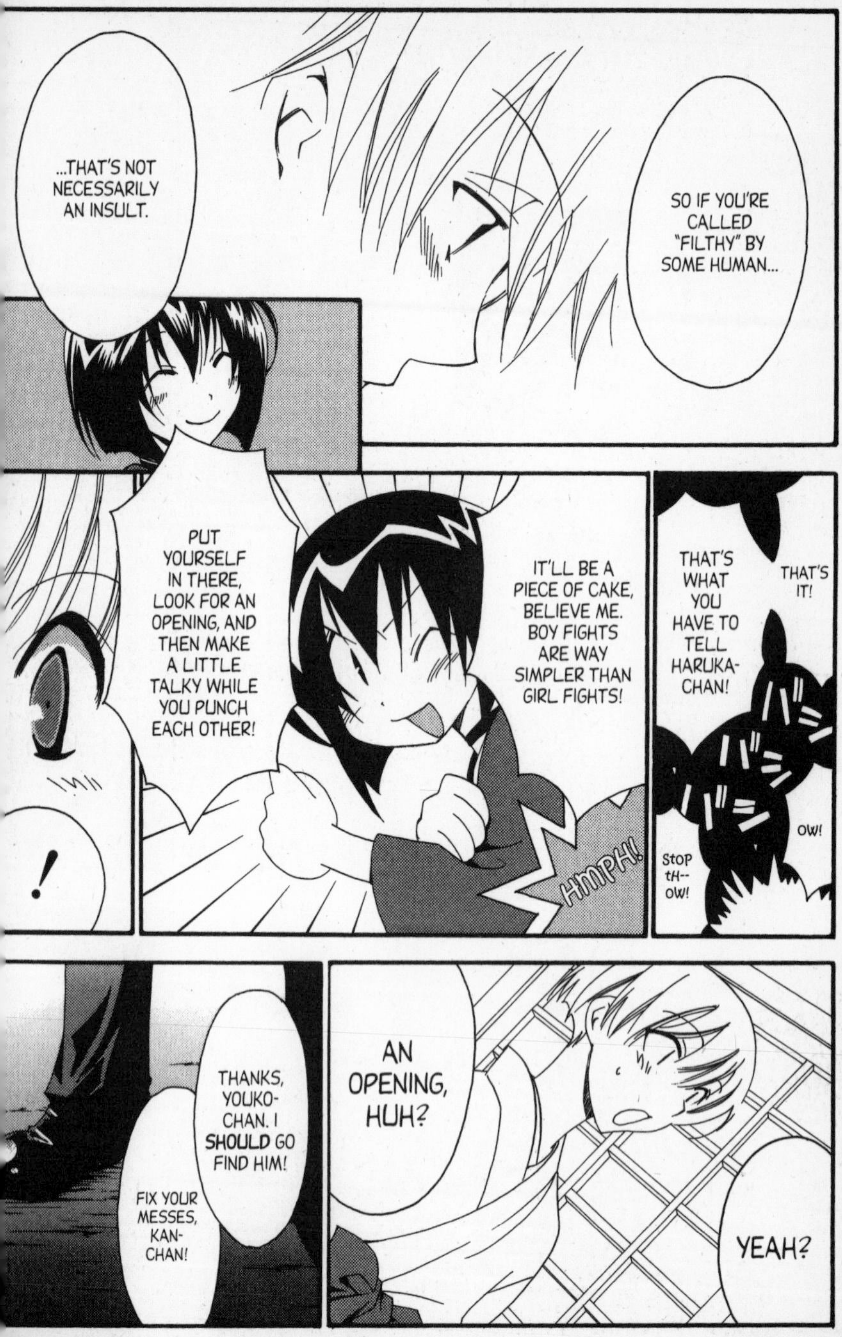
SO IF YOU'RE CALLED "FILTHY" BY SOME HUMAN...
...THAT'S NOT NECESSARILY AN INSULT.
THAT'S IT!
THAT'S WHAT YOU HAVE TO TELL HARUKA-CHAN!
OW!
Stop tH-- OW!
IT'LL BE A PIECE OF CAKE, BELIEVE ME. BOY FIGHTS ARE WAY SIMPLER THAN GIRL FIGHTS!
PUT YOURSELF IN THERE, LOOK FOR AN OPENING, AND THEN MAKE A LITTLE TALKY WHILE YOU PUNCH EACH OTHER!
HMPH!
!
AN OPENING, HUH?
YEAH?
THANKS, YOUKO-CHAN. I SHOULD GO FIND HIM!
FIX YOUR MESSES, KAN-CHAN!

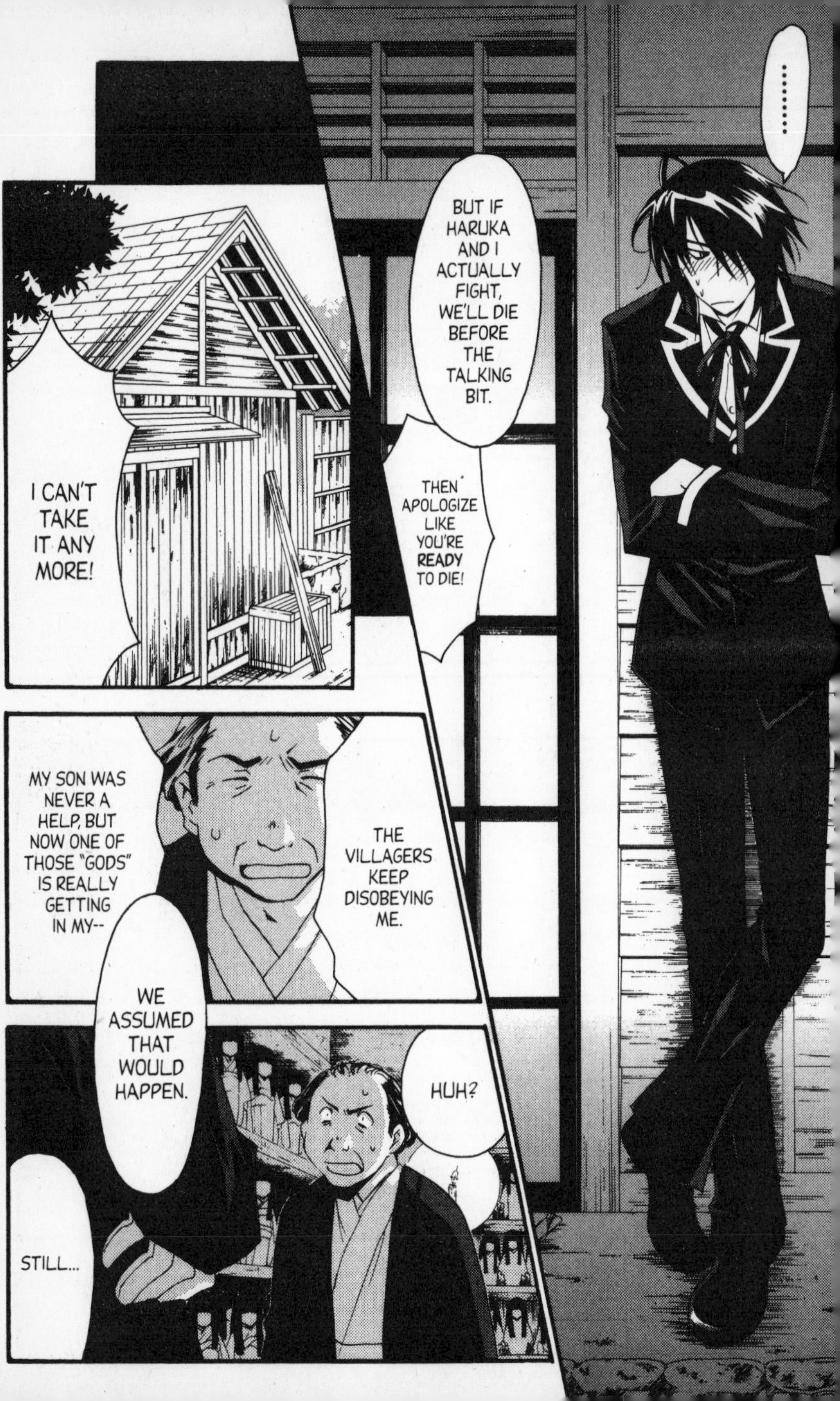
......
BUT IF HARUKA AND I ACTUALLY FIGHT, WE'LL DIE BEFORE THE TALKING BIT.
THEN APOLOGIZE LIKE YOU'RE READY TO DIE!
I CAN'T TAKE IT ANY MORE!
THE VILLAGERS KEEP DISOBEYING ME.
MY SON WAS NEVER A HELP, BUT NOW ONE OF THOSE "GODS" IS REALLY GETTING IN MY--
HUH?
WE ASSUMED THAT WOULD HAPPEN.
STILL...

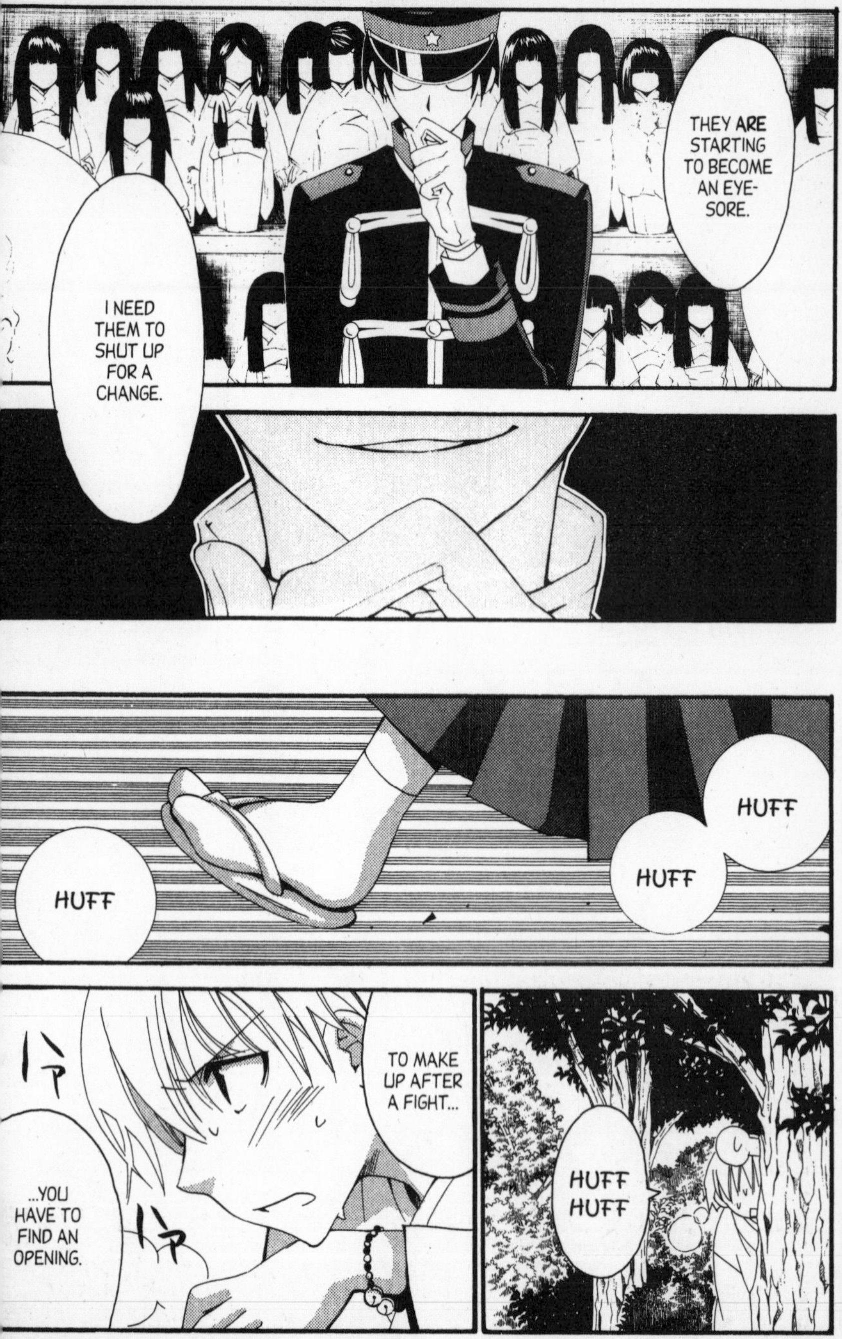
THEY ARE STARTING TO BECOME AN EYE-SORE.
I NEED THEM TO SHUT UP FOR A CHANGE.
HUFF
HUFF
HUFF
HUFF HUFF
TO MAKE UP AFTER A FIGHT...
ハァ
...YOU HAVE TO FIND AN OPENING.
ハァ

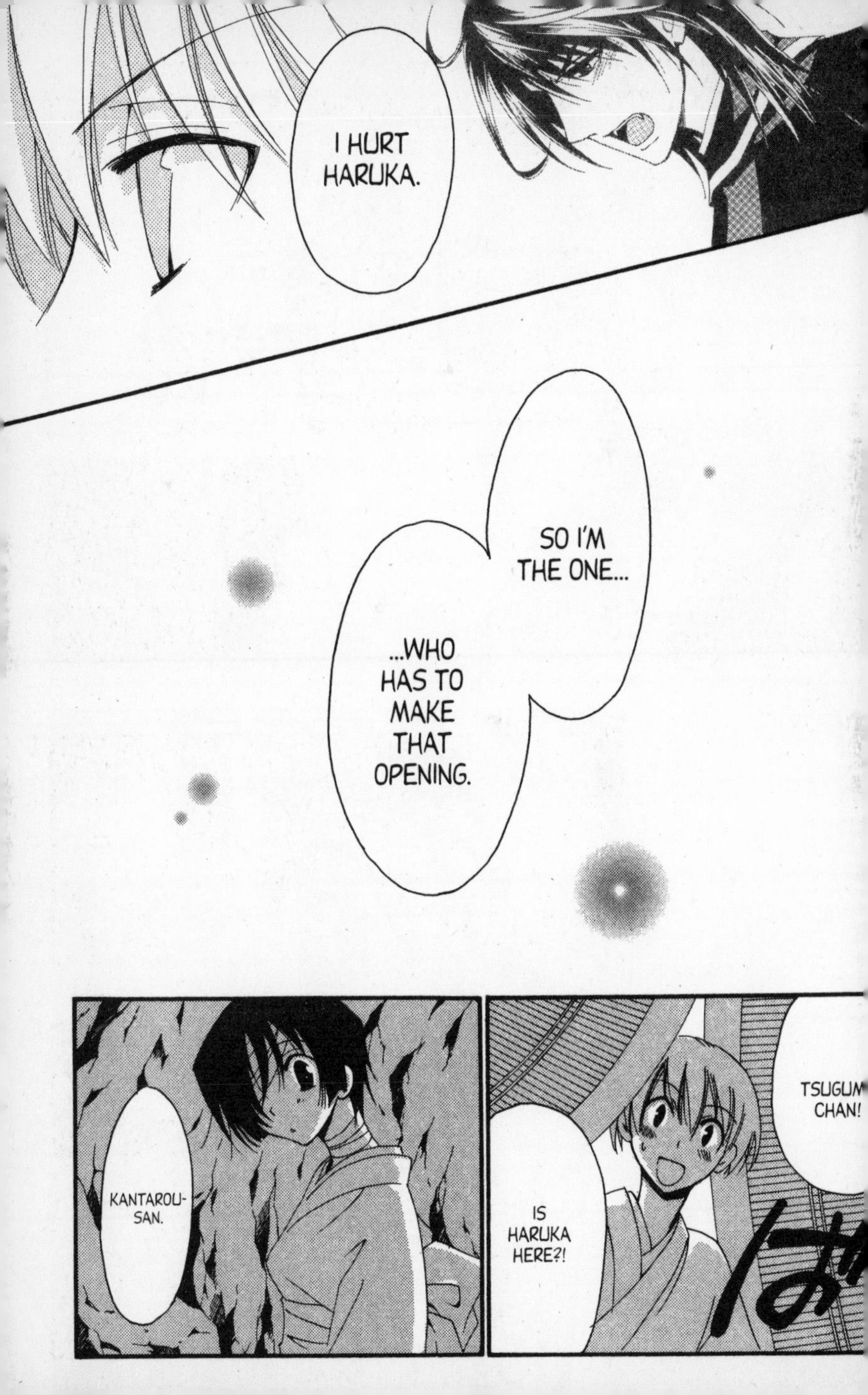
I HURT HARUKA.
SO I'M THE ONE...
...WHO HAS TO MAKE THAT OPENING.
TSUGUM CHAN!
IS HARUKA HERE?!
KANTAROU-SAN.

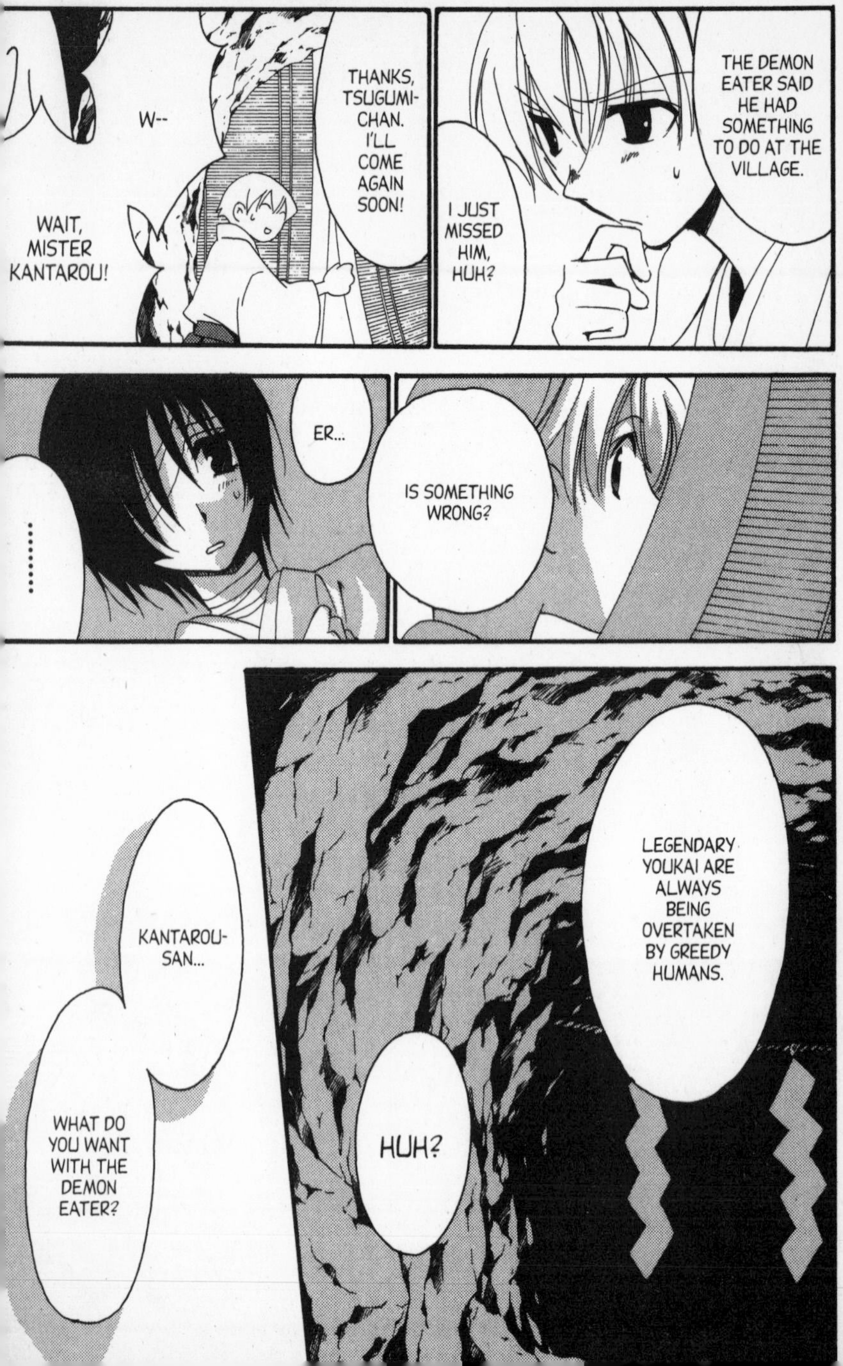
THE DEMON EATER SAID HE HAD SOMETHING TO DO AT THE VILLAGE.
I JUST MISSED HIM, HUH?
THANKS, TSUGUMI-CHAN. I'LL COME AGAIN SOON!
W--
WAIT, MISTER KANTAROU!
IS SOMETHING WRONG?
ER...
....
LEGENDARY YOUKAI ARE ALWAYS BEING OVERTAKEN BY GREEDY HUMANS.
HUH?
KANTAROU-SAN...
WHAT DO YOU WANT WITH THE DEMON EATER?

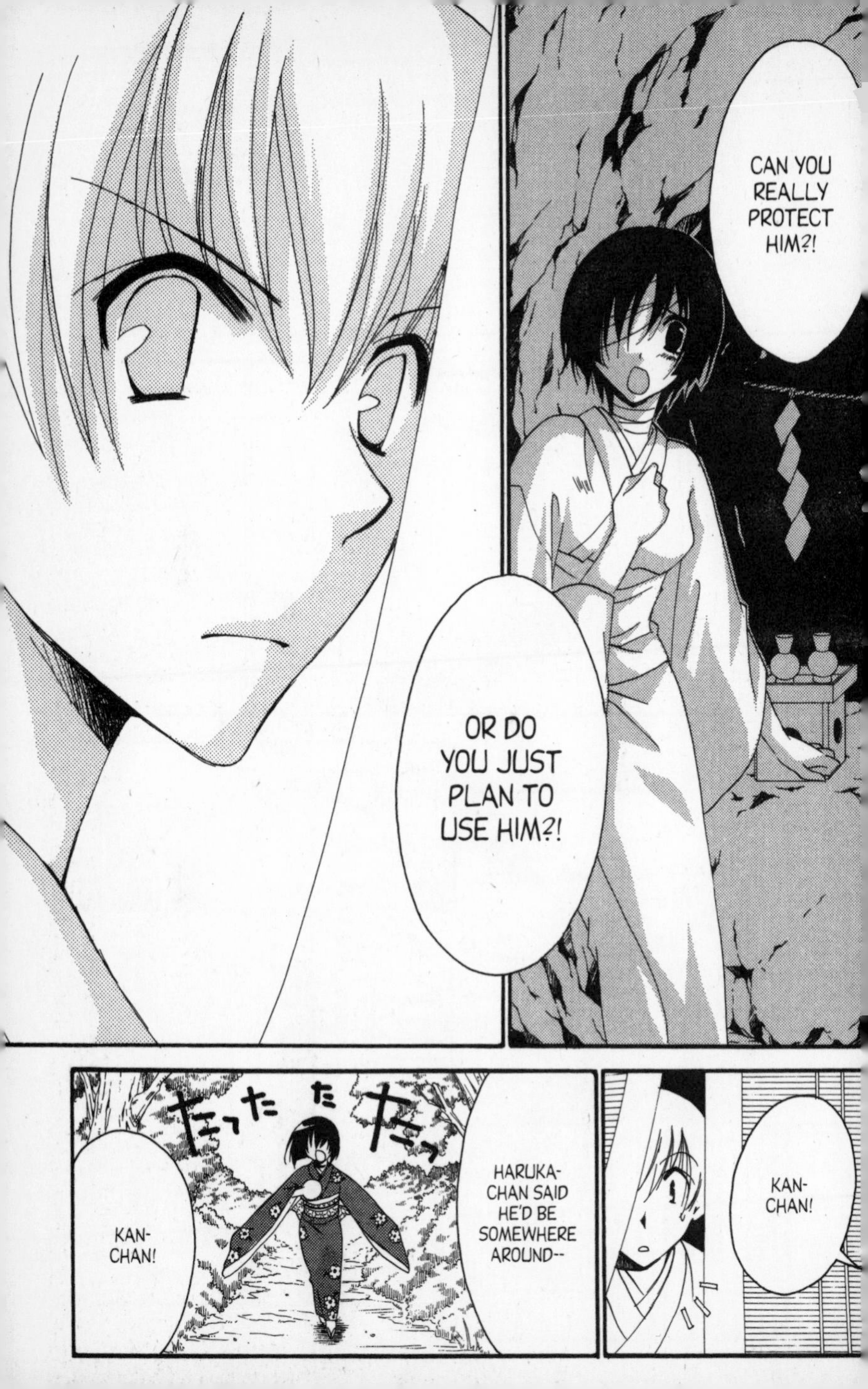
CAN YOU REALLY PROTECT HIM?!
OR DO YOU JUST PLAN TO USE HIM?!
KAN-CHAN!
たっ た た たっ
HARUKA-CHAN SAID HE'D BE SOMEWHERE AROUND--
KAN-CHAN!

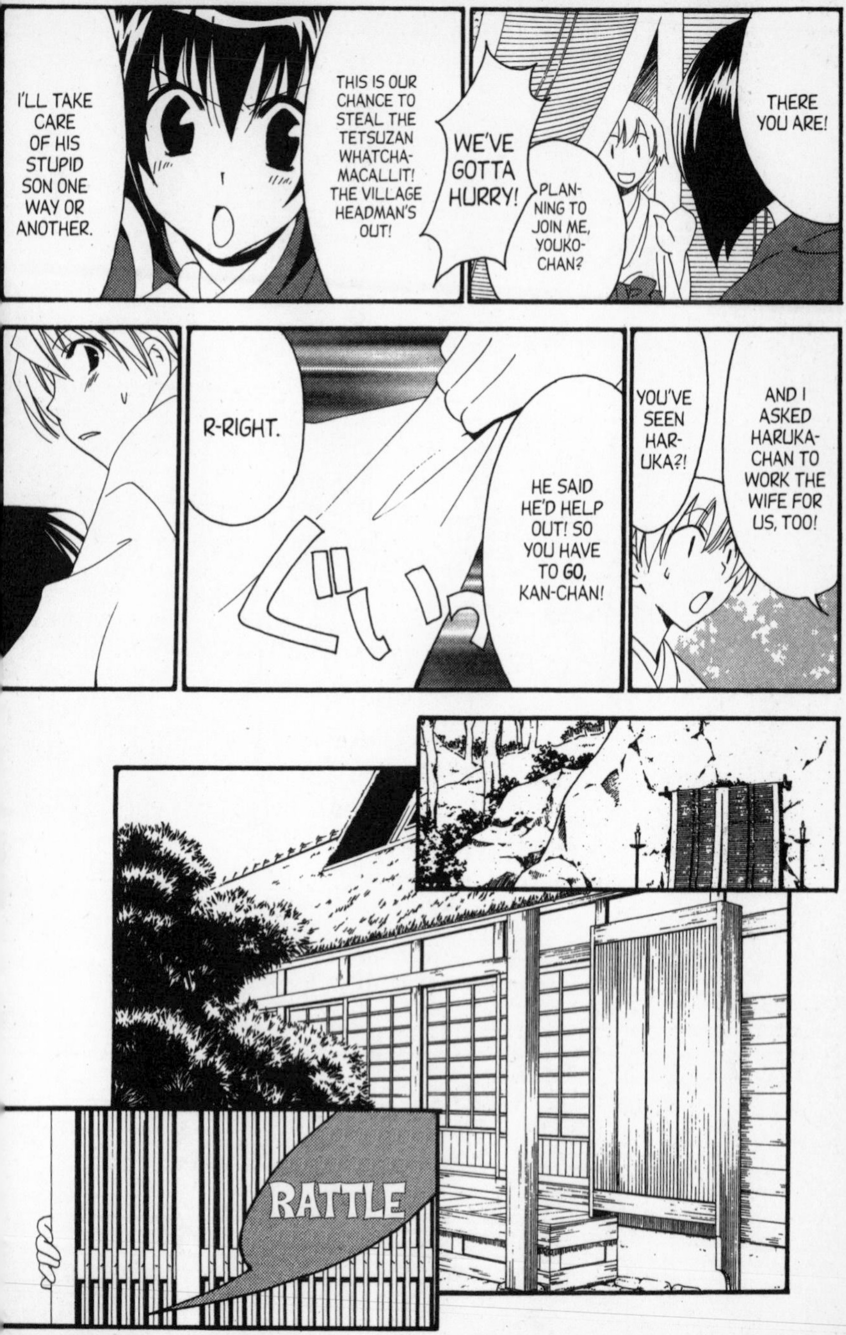
THERE YOU ARE!
PLANNING TO JOIN ME, YOUKO-CHAN?
WE'VE GOTTA HURRY!
THIS IS OUR CHANCE TO STEAL THE TETSUZAN WHATCHAMACALLIT! THE VILLAGE HEADMAN'S OUT!
I'LL TAKE CARE OF HIS STUPID SON ONE WAY OR ANOTHER.
AND I ASKED HARUKA-CHAN TO WORK THE WIFE FOR US, TOO!
YOU'VE SEEN HARUKA?!
HE SAID HE'D HELP OUT! SO YOU HAVE TO GO, KAN-CHAN!
R-RIGHT.
RATTLE

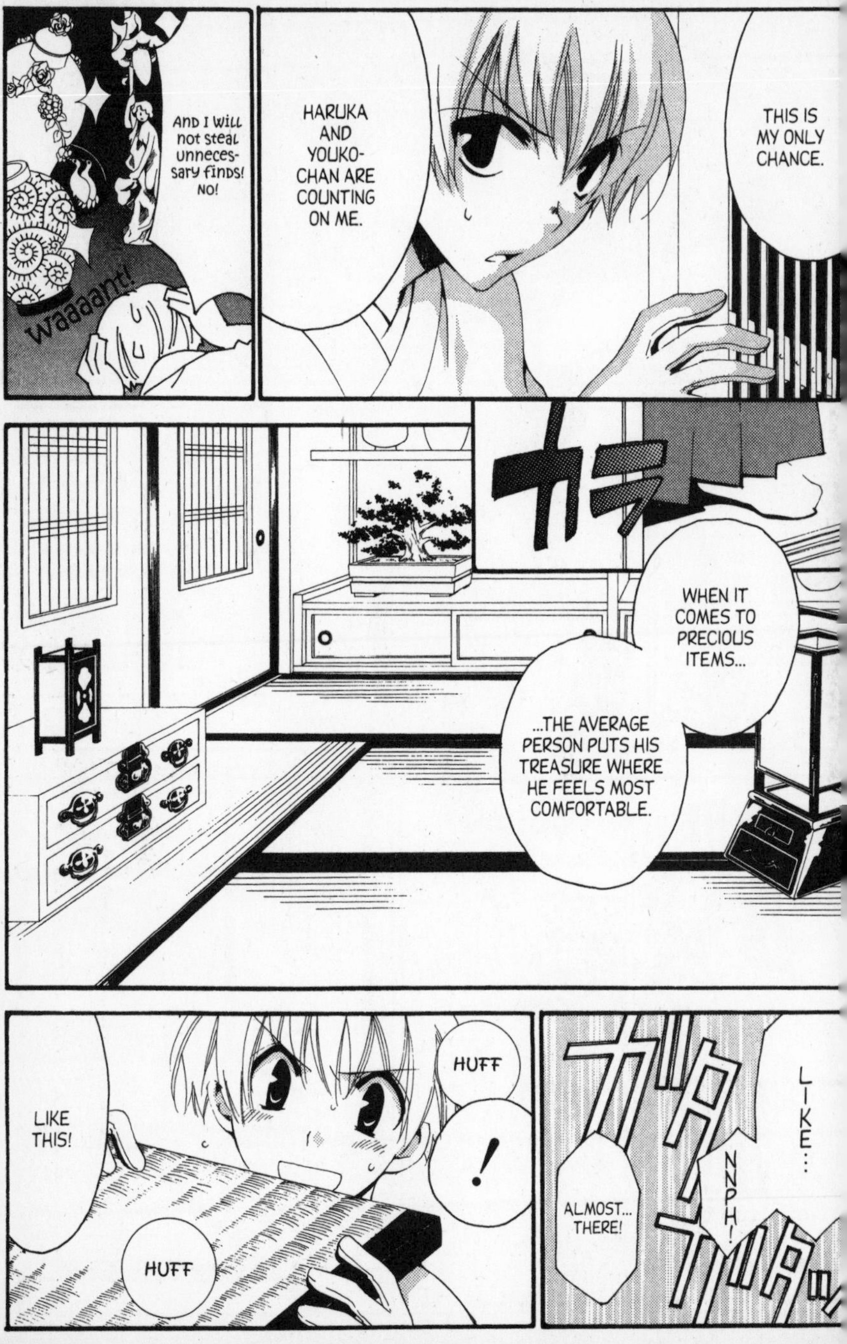
THIS IS MY ONLY CHANCE.
HARUKA AND YOUKO-CHAN ARE COUNTING ON ME.
And I will not steal unneces-sary finds! NO!
waaaant!
カラ
WHEN IT COMES TO PRECIOUS ITEMS...
...THE AVERAGE PERSON PUTS HIS TREASURE WHERE HE FEELS MOST COMFORTABLE.
LIKE...
NNPH!
ALMOST... THERE!
カタ
カタッ
HUFF
!
LIKE THIS!
HUFF

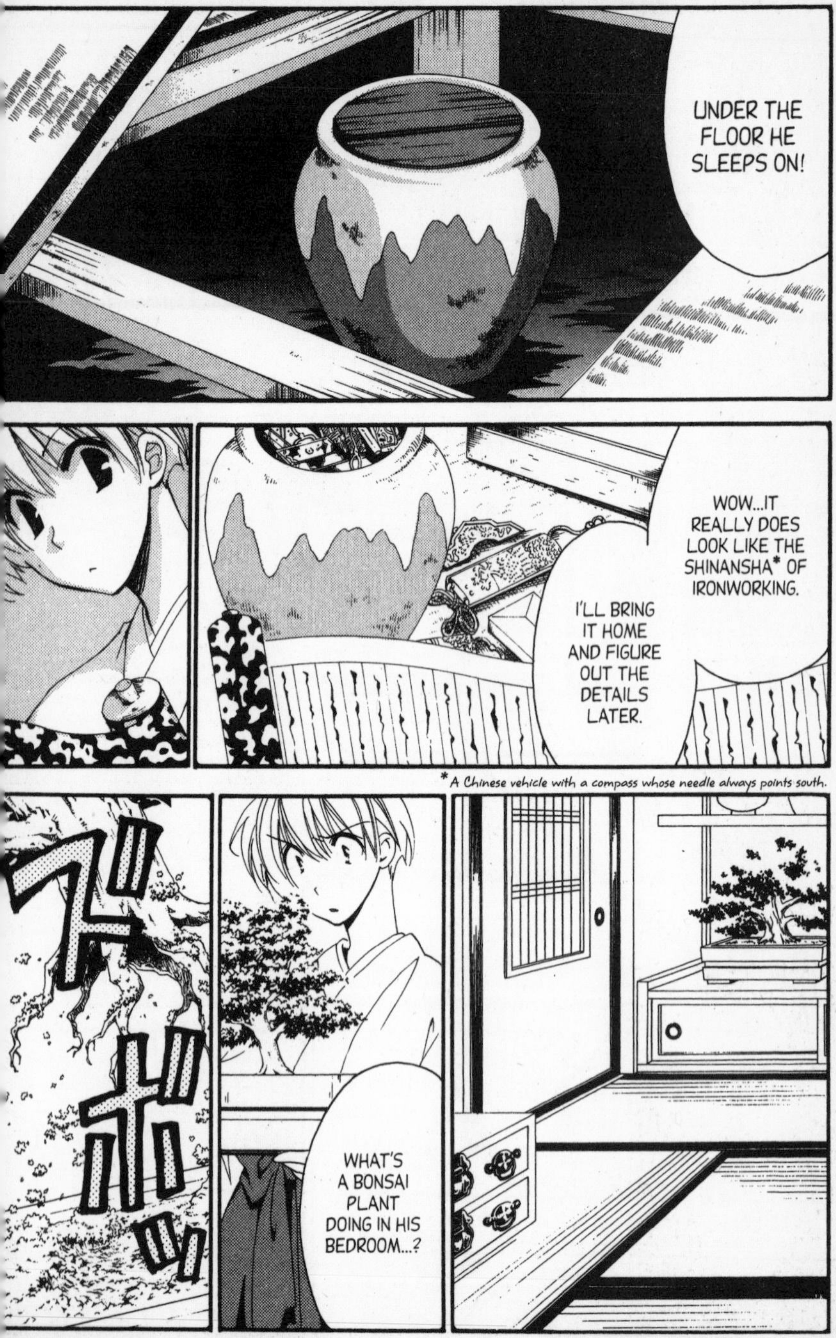
UNDER THE FLOOR HE SLEEPS ON!
WOW...IT REALLY DOES LOOK LIKE THE SHINANSHA* OF IRONWORKING.
I'LL BRING IT HOME AND FIGURE OUT THE DETAILS LATER.
WHAT'S A BONSAI PLANT DOING IN HIS BEDROOM...?
ズボッ
* A Chinese vehicle with a compass whose needle always points south.

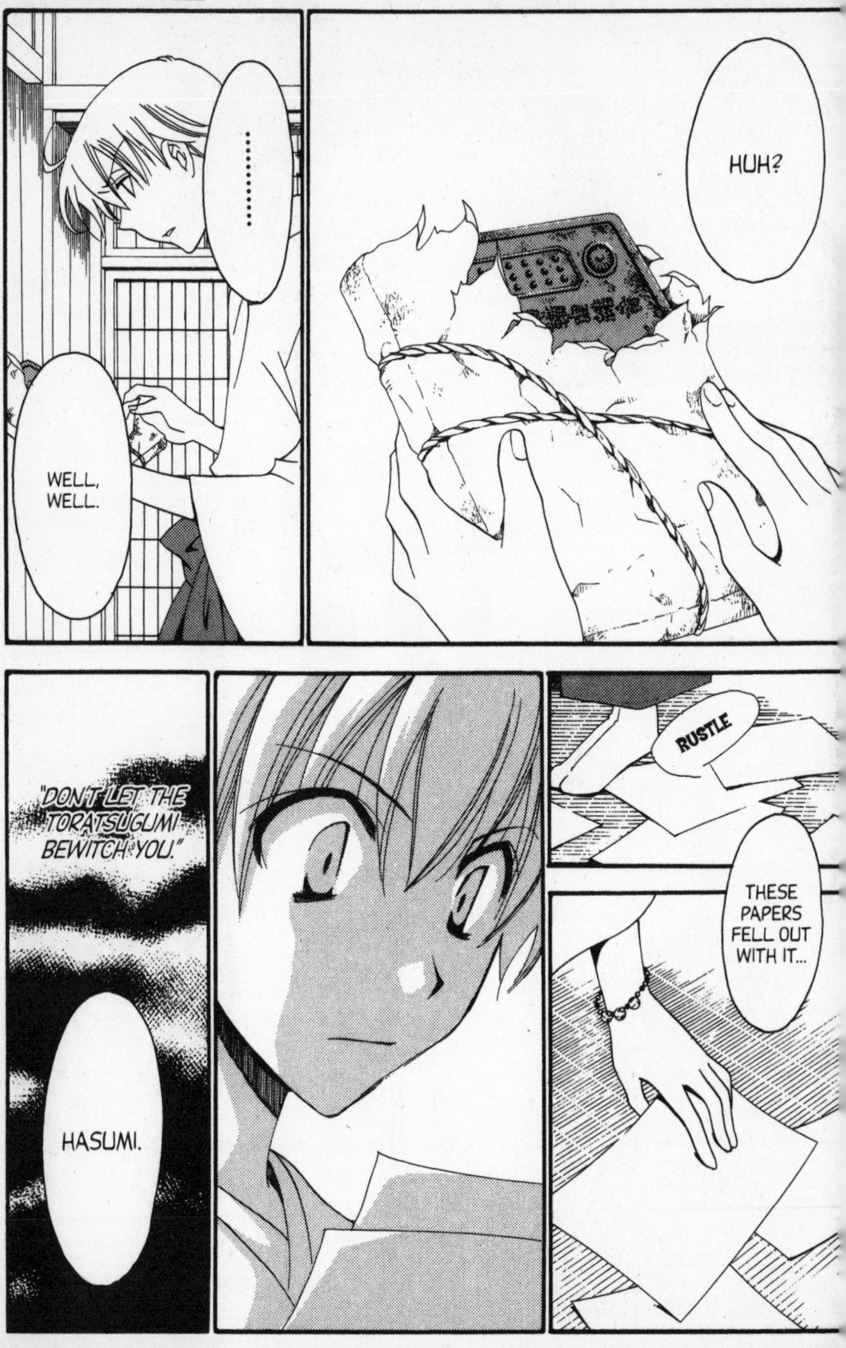
HUH?
......
WELL, WELL.
RUSTLE
THESE PAPERS FELL OUT WITH IT...
"DON'T LET THE TORATSUGUMI BEWITCH YOU."
HASUMI.

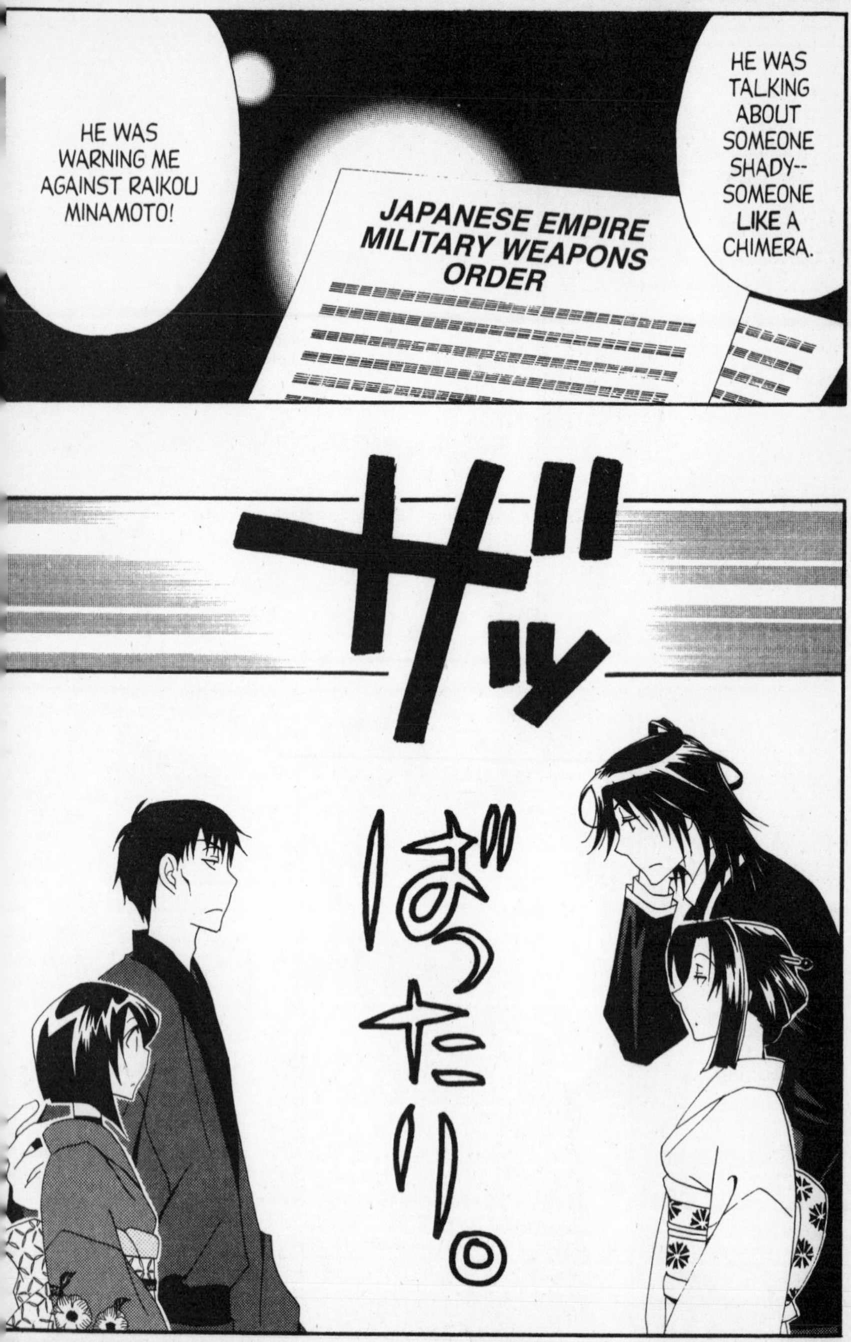
HE WAS TALKING ABOUT SOMEONE SHADY-- SOMEONE LIKE A CHIMERA.
HE WAS WARNING ME AGAINST RAIKOU MINAMOTO!
JAPANESE EMPIRE MILITARY WEAPONS ORDER
ザッ
ぱったり。

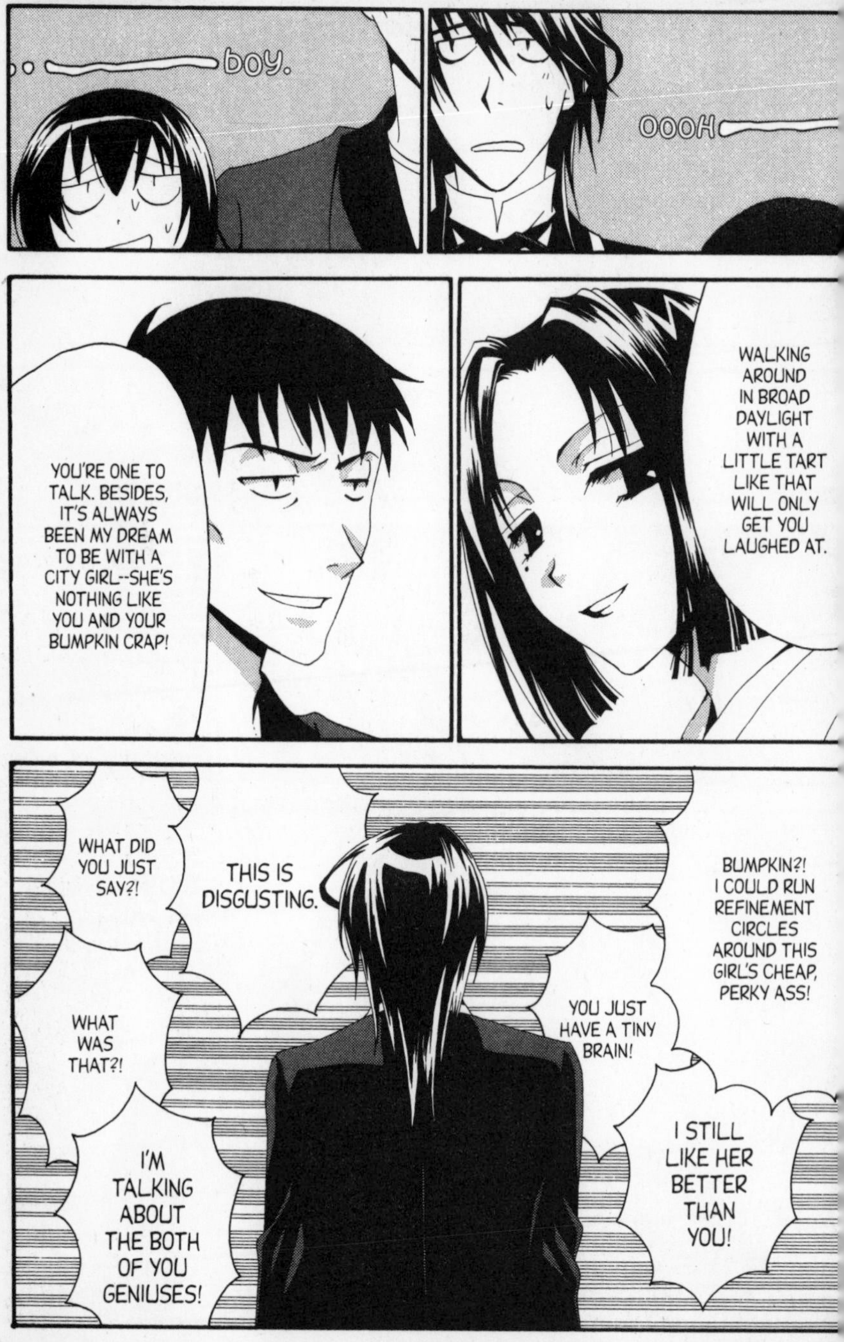
OOOH——
..——boy.
WALKING AROUND IN BROAD DAYLIGHT WITH A LITTLE TART LIKE THAT WILL ONLY GET YOU LAUGHED AT.
YOU'RE ONE TO TALK. BESIDES, IT'S ALWAYS BEEN MY DREAM TO BE WITH A CITY GIRL--SHE'S NOTHING LIKE YOU AND YOUR BUMPKIN CRAP!
BUMPKIN?! I COULD RUN REFINEMENT CIRCLES AROUND THIS GIRL'S CHEAP, PERKY ASS!
YOU JUST HAVE A TINY BRAIN!
I STILL LIKE HER BETTER THAN YOU!
THIS IS DISGUSTING.
WHAT DID YOU JUST SAY?!
WHAT WAS THAT?!
I'M TALKING ABOUT THE BOTH OF YOU GENIUSES!

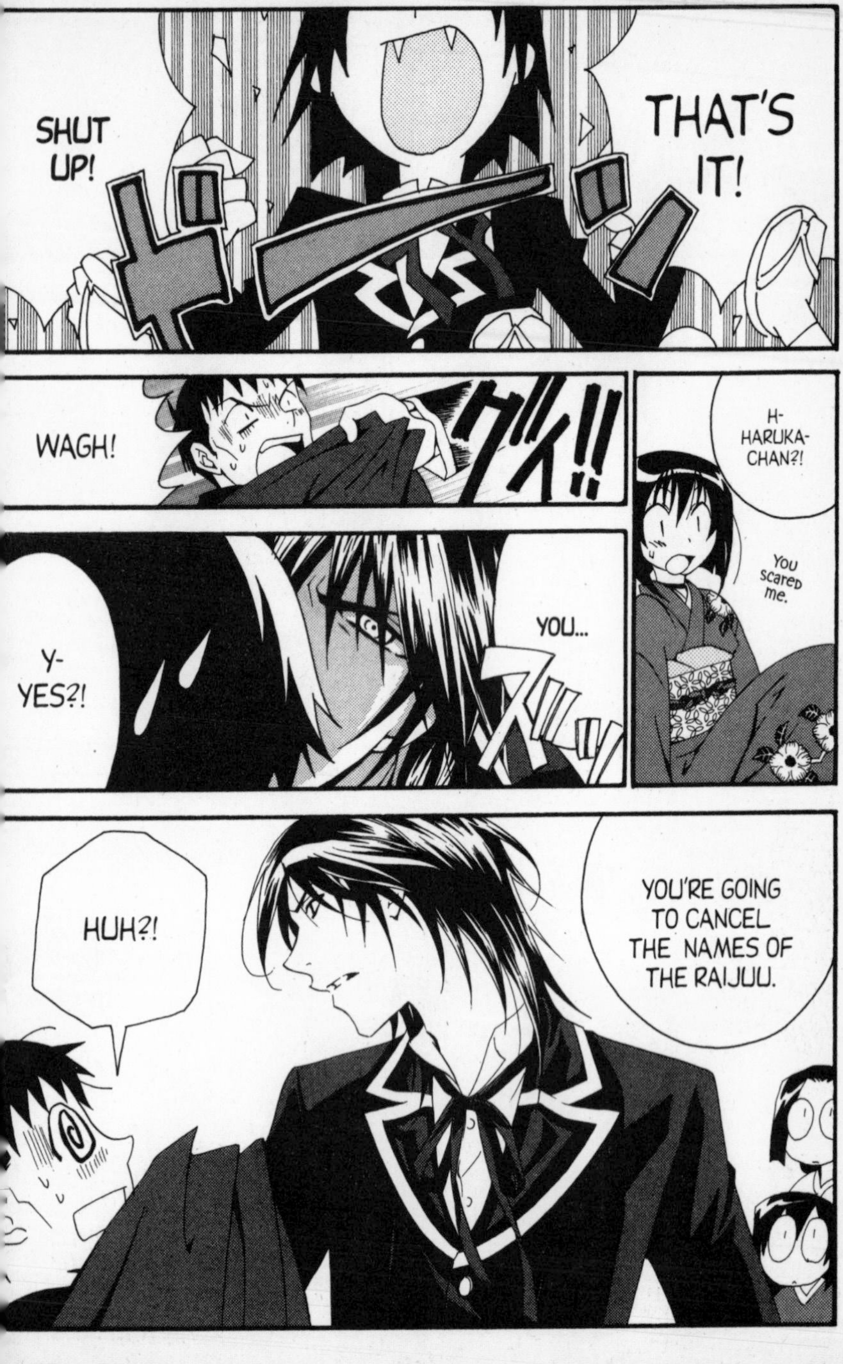
THAT'S IT!
SHUT UP!
H-HARUKA-CHAN?!
You scared me.
WAGH!
YOU...
Y-YES?!
YOU'RE GOING TO CANCEL THE NAMES OF THE RAIJUU.
HUH?!

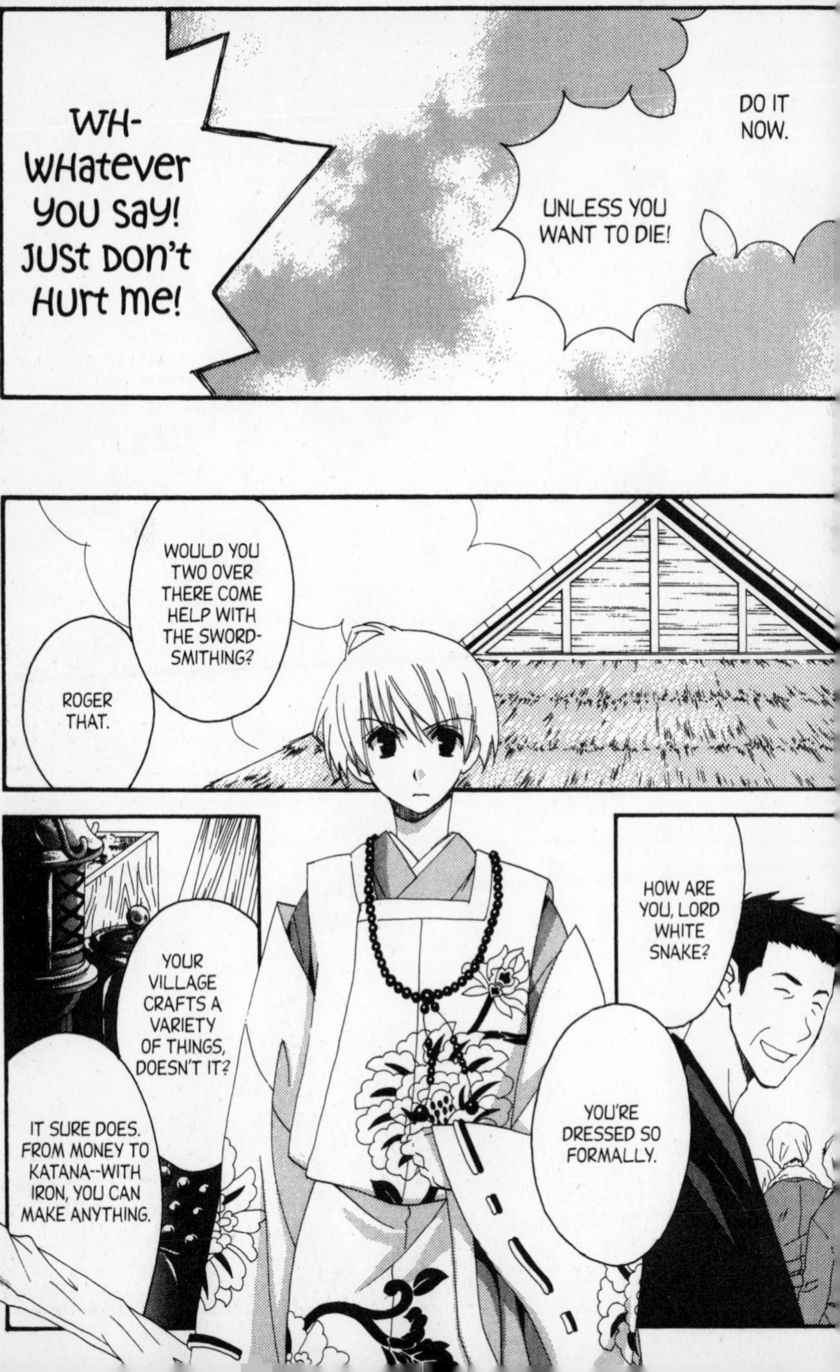
DO IT NOW.
UNLESS YOU WANT TO DIE!
WH-WHATEVER YOU SAY! JUST DON'T HURT ME!
WOULD YOU TWO OVER THERE COME HELP WITH THE SWORD-SMITHING?
ROGER THAT.
HOW ARE YOU, LORD WHITE SNAKE?
YOU'RE DRESSED SO FORMALLY.
YOUR VILLAGE CRAFTS A VARIETY OF THINGS, DOESN'T IT?
IT SURE DOES. FROM MONEY TO KATANA--WITH IRON, YOU CAN MAKE ANYTHING.

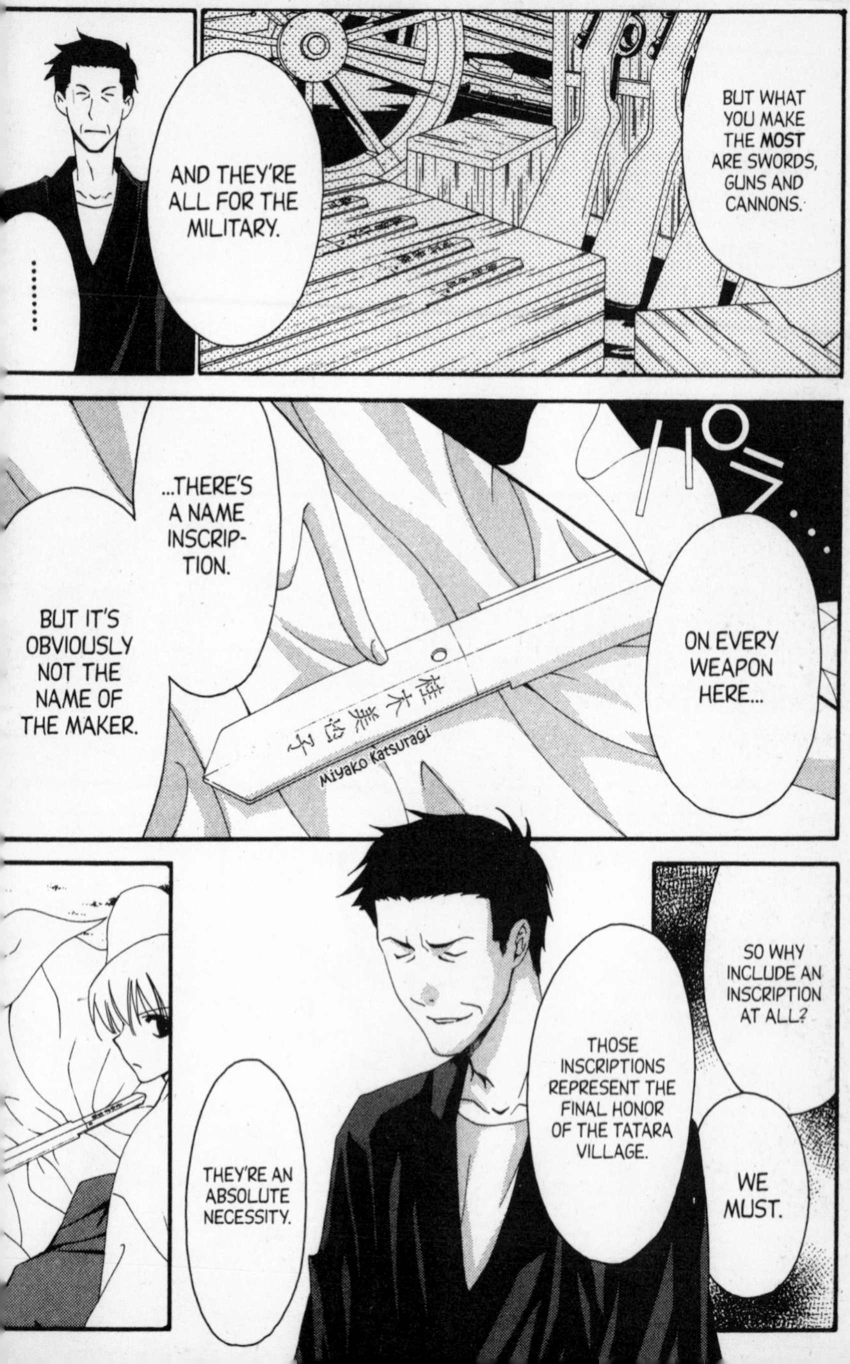
BUT WHAT YOU MAKE THE MOST ARE SWORDS, GUNS AND CANNONS.
AND THEY'RE ALL FOR THE MILITARY.
....
ON EVERY WEAPON HERE...
...THERE'S A NAME INSCRIPTION.
BUT IT'S OBVIOUSLY NOT THE NAME OF THE MAKER.
Miyako Katsuragi
SO WHY INCLUDE AN INSCRIPTION AT ALL?
WE MUST.
THOSE INSCRIPTIONS REPRESENT THE FINAL HONOR OF THE TATARA VILLAGE.
THEY'RE AN ABSOLUTE NECESSITY.

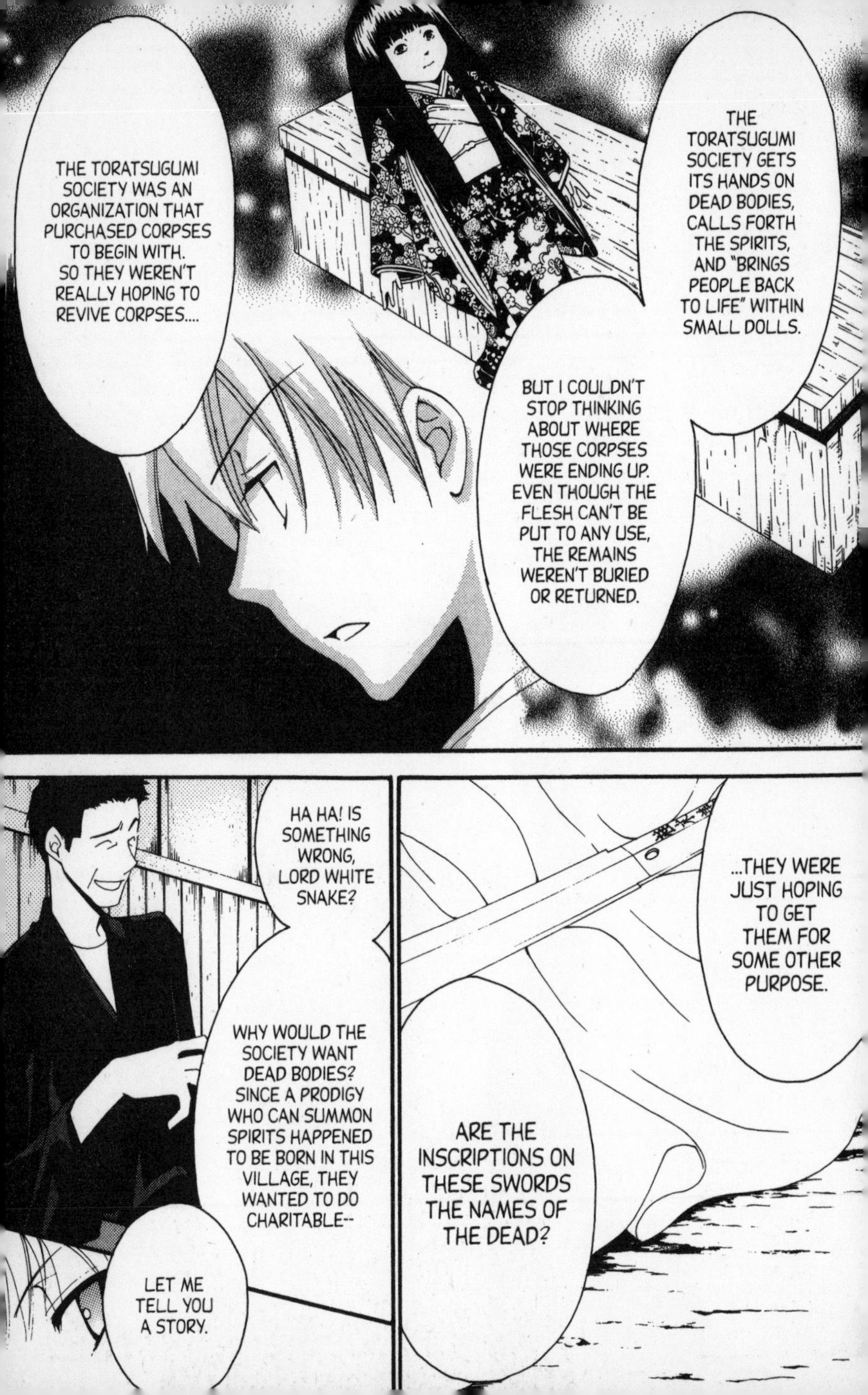
THE TORATSUGUMI SOCIETY GETS ITS HANDS ON DEAD BODIES, CALLS FORTH THE SPIRITS, AND "BRINGS PEOPLE BACK TO LIFE" WITHIN SMALL DOLLS.
BUT I COULDN'T STOP THINKING ABOUT WHERE THOSE CORPSES WERE ENDING UP. EVEN THOUGH THE FLESH CAN'T BE PUT TO ANY USE, THE REMAINS WEREN'T BURIED OR RETURNED.
THE TORATSUGUMI SOCIETY WAS AN ORGANIZATION THAT PURCHASED CORPSES TO BEGIN WITH. SO THEY WEREN'T REALLY HOPING TO REVIVE CORPSES....
...THEY WERE JUST HOPING TO GET THEM FOR SOME OTHER PURPOSE.
ARE THE INSCRIPTIONS ON THESE SWORDS THE NAMES OF THE DEAD?
HA HA! IS SOMETHING WRONG, LORD WHITE SNAKE?
WHY WOULD THE SOCIETY WANT DEAD BODIES? SINCE A PRODIGY WHO CAN SUMMON SPIRITS HAPPENED TO BE BORN IN THIS VILLAGE, THEY WANTED TO DO CHARITABLE--
LET ME TELL YOU A STORY.

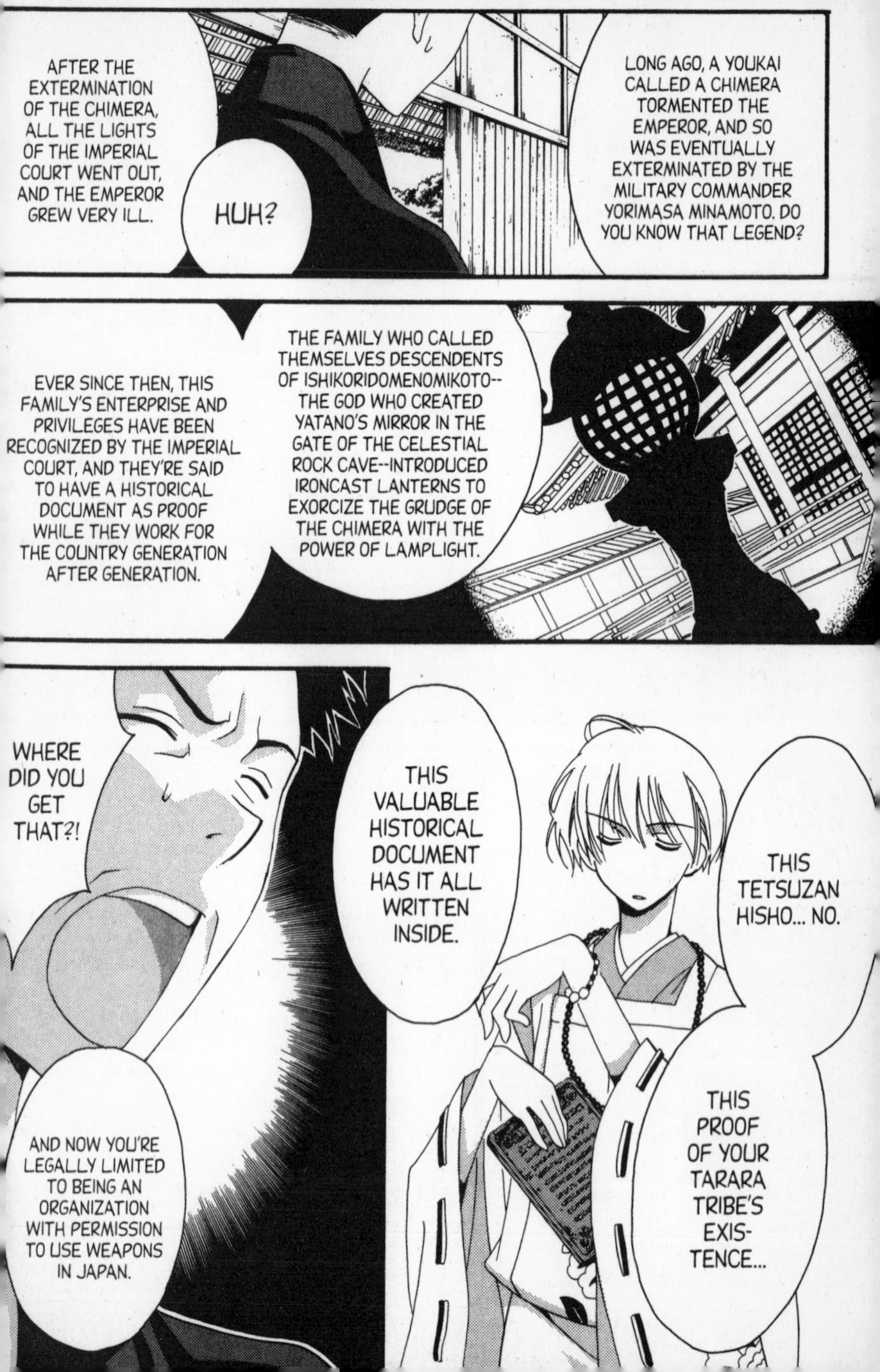
LONG AGO, A YOUKAI CALLED A CHIMERA TORMENTED THE EMPEROR, AND SO WAS EVENTUALLY EXTERMINATED BY THE MILITARY COMMANDER YORIMASA MINAMOTO. DO YOU KNOW THAT LEGEND?
HUH?
AFTER THE EXTERMINATION OF THE CHIMERA, ALL THE LIGHTS OF THE IMPERIAL COURT WENT OUT, AND THE EMPEROR GREW VERY ILL.
THE FAMILY WHO CALLED THEMSELVES DESCENDENTS OF ISHIKORIDOMENOMIKOTO--THE GOD WHO CREATED YATANO'S MIRROR IN THE GATE OF THE CELESTIAL ROCK CAVE--INTRODUCED IRONCAST LANTERNS TO EXORCIZE THE GRUDGE OF THE CHIMERA WITH THE POWER OF LAMPLIGHT.
EVER SINCE THEN, THIS FAMILY'S ENTERPRISE AND PRIVILEGES HAVE BEEN RECOGNIZED BY THE IMPERIAL COURT, AND THEY'RE SAID TO HAVE A HISTORICAL DOCUMENT AS PROOF WHILE THEY WORK FOR THE COUNTRY GENERATION AFTER GENERATION.
THIS TETSUZAN HISHO... NO.
THIS VALUABLE HISTORICAL DOCUMENT HAS IT ALL WRITTEN INSIDE.
THIS PROOF OF YOUR TARARA TRIBE'S EXIS-TENCE...
WHERE DID YOU GET THAT?!
AND NOW YOU'RE LEGALLY LIMITED TO BEING AN ORGANIZATION WITH PERMISSION TO USE WEAPONS IN JAPAN.

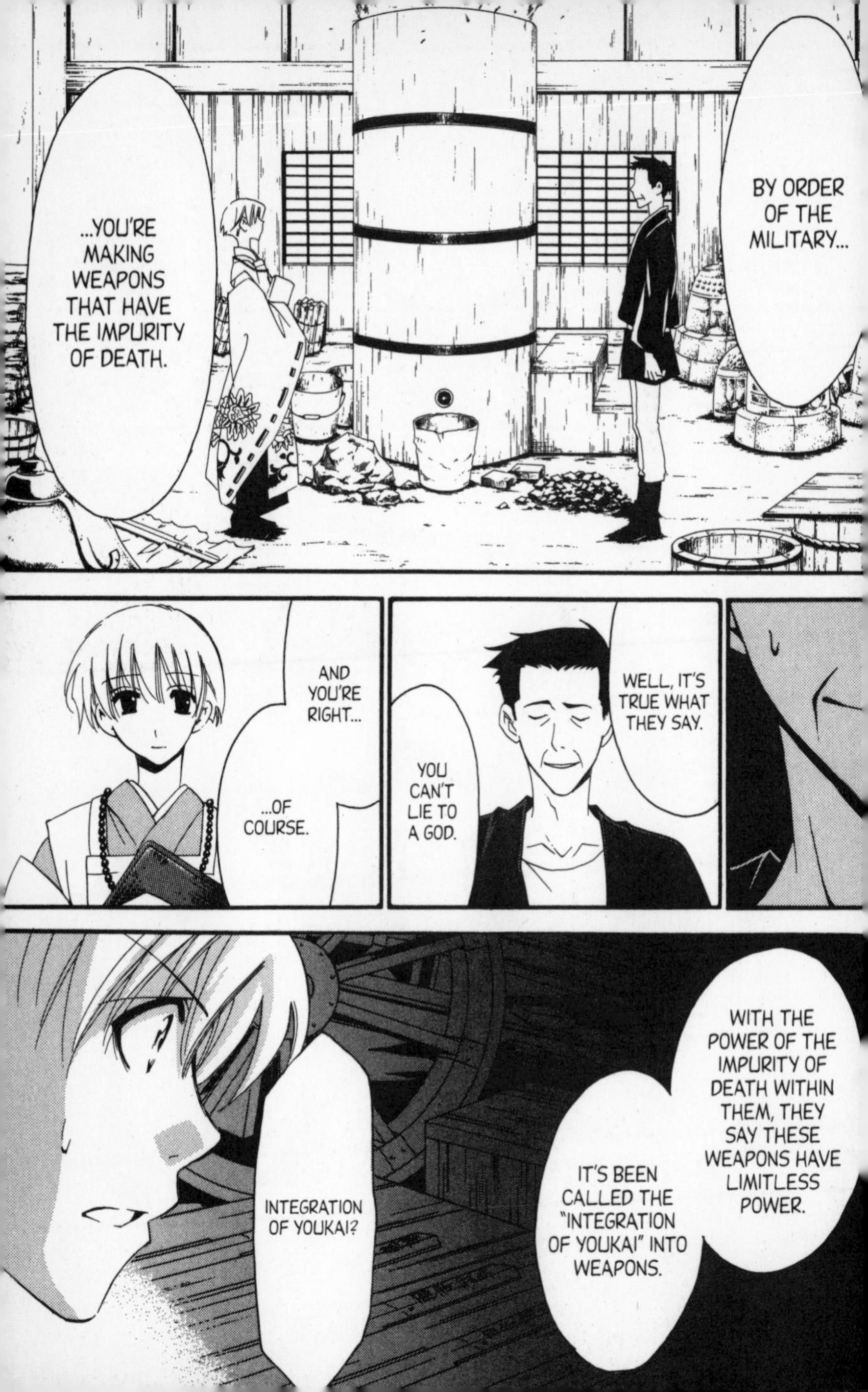
BY ORDER OF THE MILITARY...
...YOU'RE MAKING WEAPONS THAT HAVE THE IMPURITY OF DEATH.
WELL, IT'S TRUE WHAT THEY SAY.
YOU CAN'T LIE TO A GOD.
AND YOU'RE RIGHT...
...OF COURSE.
WITH THE POWER OF THE IMPURITY OF DEATH WITHIN THEM, THEY SAY THESE WEAPONS HAVE LIMITLESS POWER.
IT'S BEEN CALLED THE "INTEGRATION OF YOUKAI" INTO WEAPONS.
INTEGRATION OF YOUKAI?

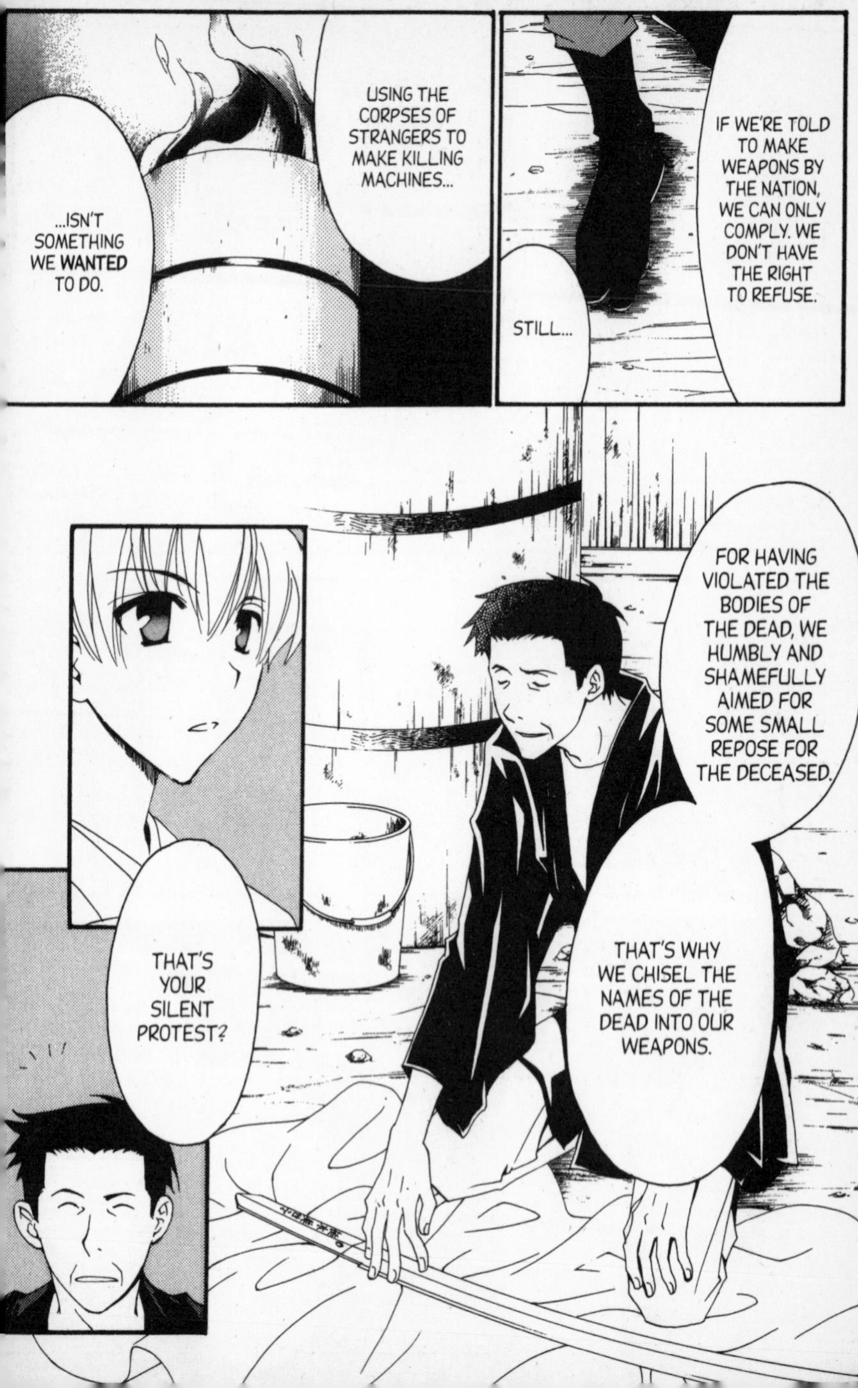
IF WE'RE TOLD TO MAKE WEAPONS BY THE NATION, WE CAN ONLY COMPLY. WE DON'T HAVE THE RIGHT TO REFUSE.
STILL...
USING THE CORPSES OF STRANGERS TO MAKE KILLING MACHINES...
...ISN'T SOMETHING WE **WANTED** TO DO.
FOR HAVING VIOLATED THE BODIES OF THE DEAD, WE HUMBLY AND SHAMEFULLY AIMED FOR SOME SMALL REPOSE FOR THE DECEASED.
THAT'S WHY WE CHISEL THE NAMES OF THE DEAD INTO OUR WEAPONS.
THAT'S YOUR SILENT PROTEST?

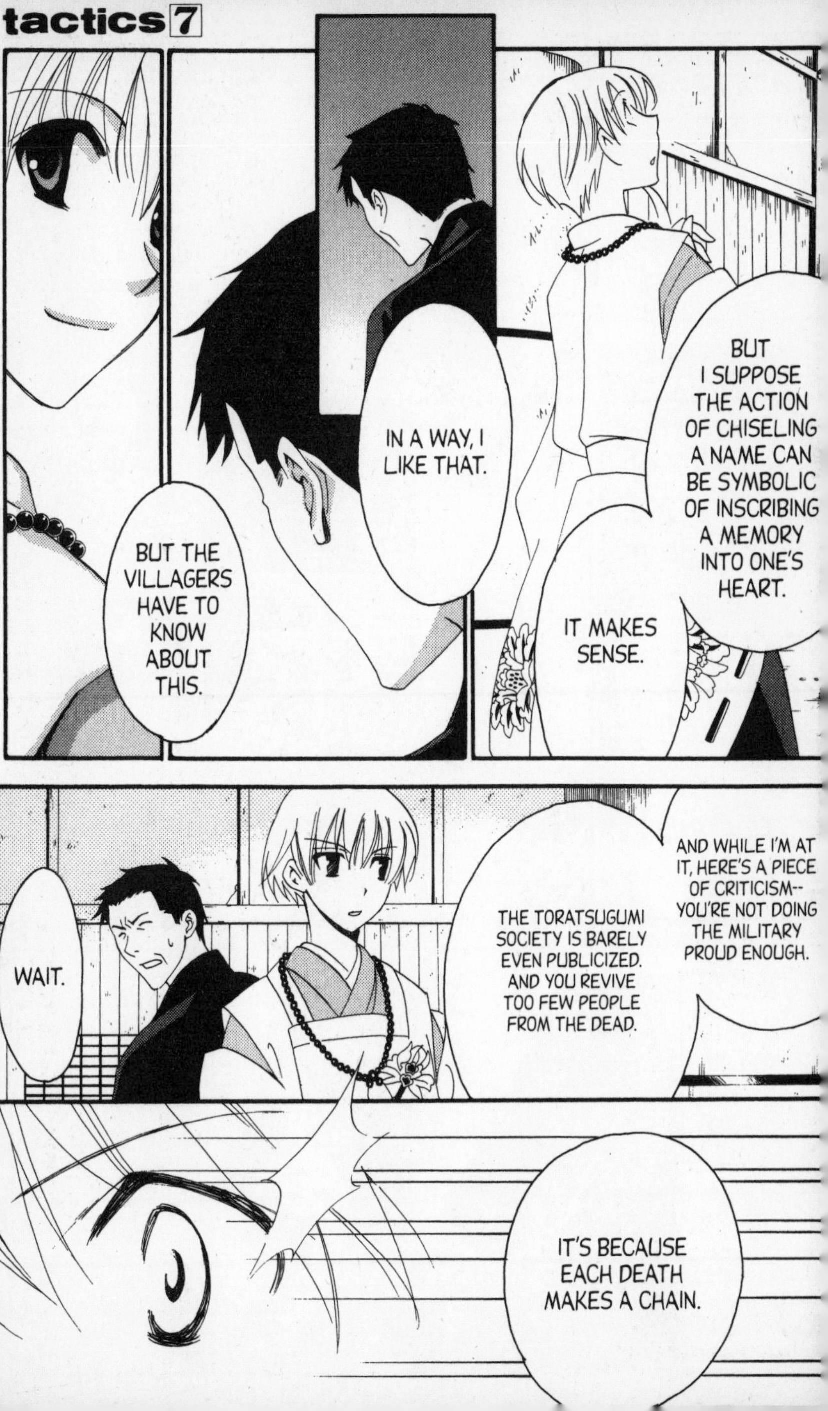
BUT I SUPPOSE THE ACTION OF CHISELING A NAME CAN BE SYMBOLIC OF INSCRIBING A MEMORY INTO ONE'S HEART.
IT MAKES SENSE.
IN A WAY, I LIKE THAT.
BUT THE VILLAGERS HAVE TO KNOW ABOUT THIS.
AND WHILE I'M AT IT, HERE'S A PIECE OF CRITICISM-- YOU'RE NOT DOING THE MILITARY PROUD ENOUGH.
THE TORATSUGUMI SOCIETY IS BARELY EVEN PUBLICIZED. AND YOU REVIVE TOO FEW PEOPLE FROM THE DEAD.
WAIT.
IT'S BECAUSE EACH DEATH MAKES A CHAIN.

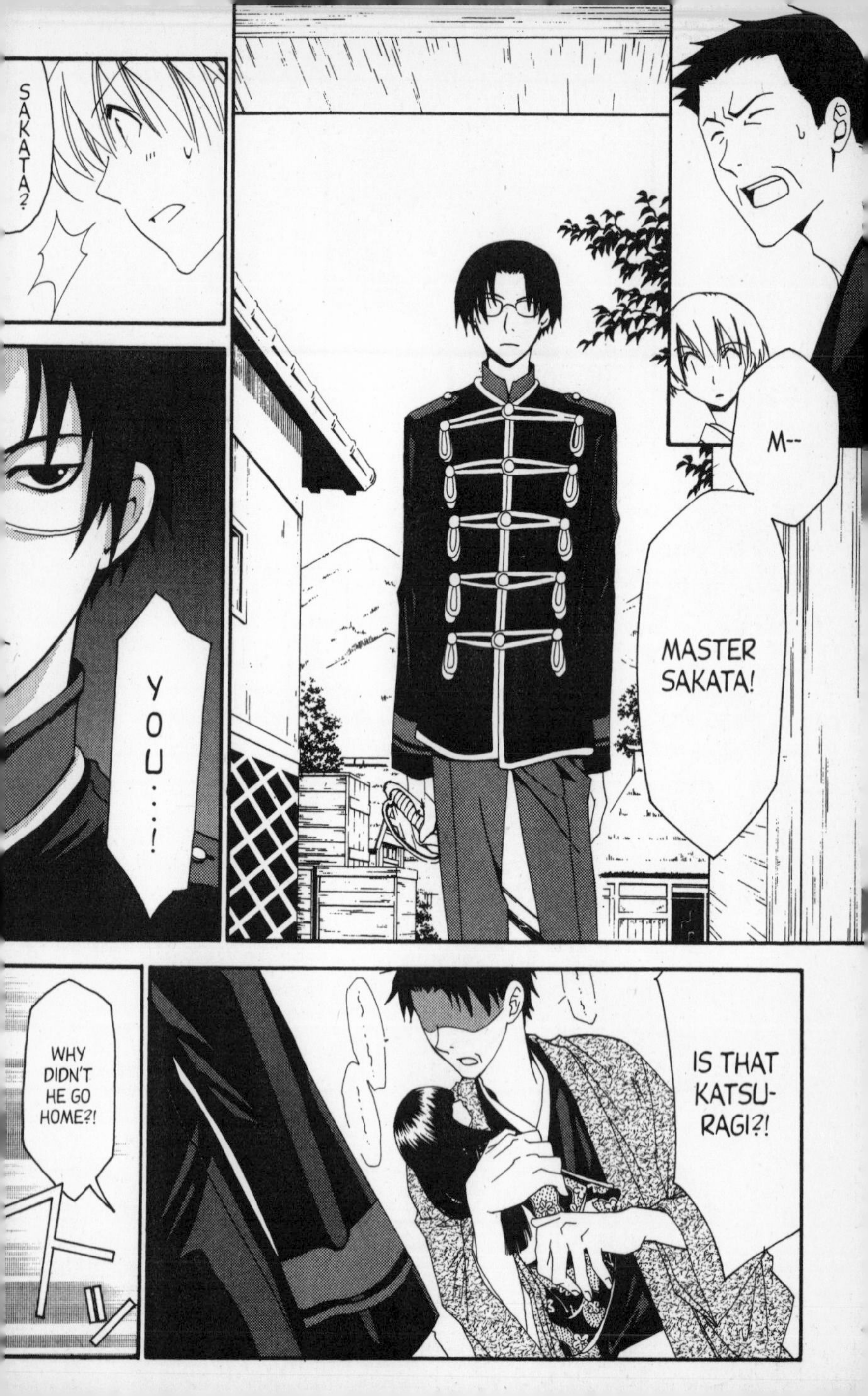
M--
MASTER SAKATA!
SAKATA?
YOU...!
IS THAT KATSU-RAGI?!
WHY DIDN'T HE GO HOME?!

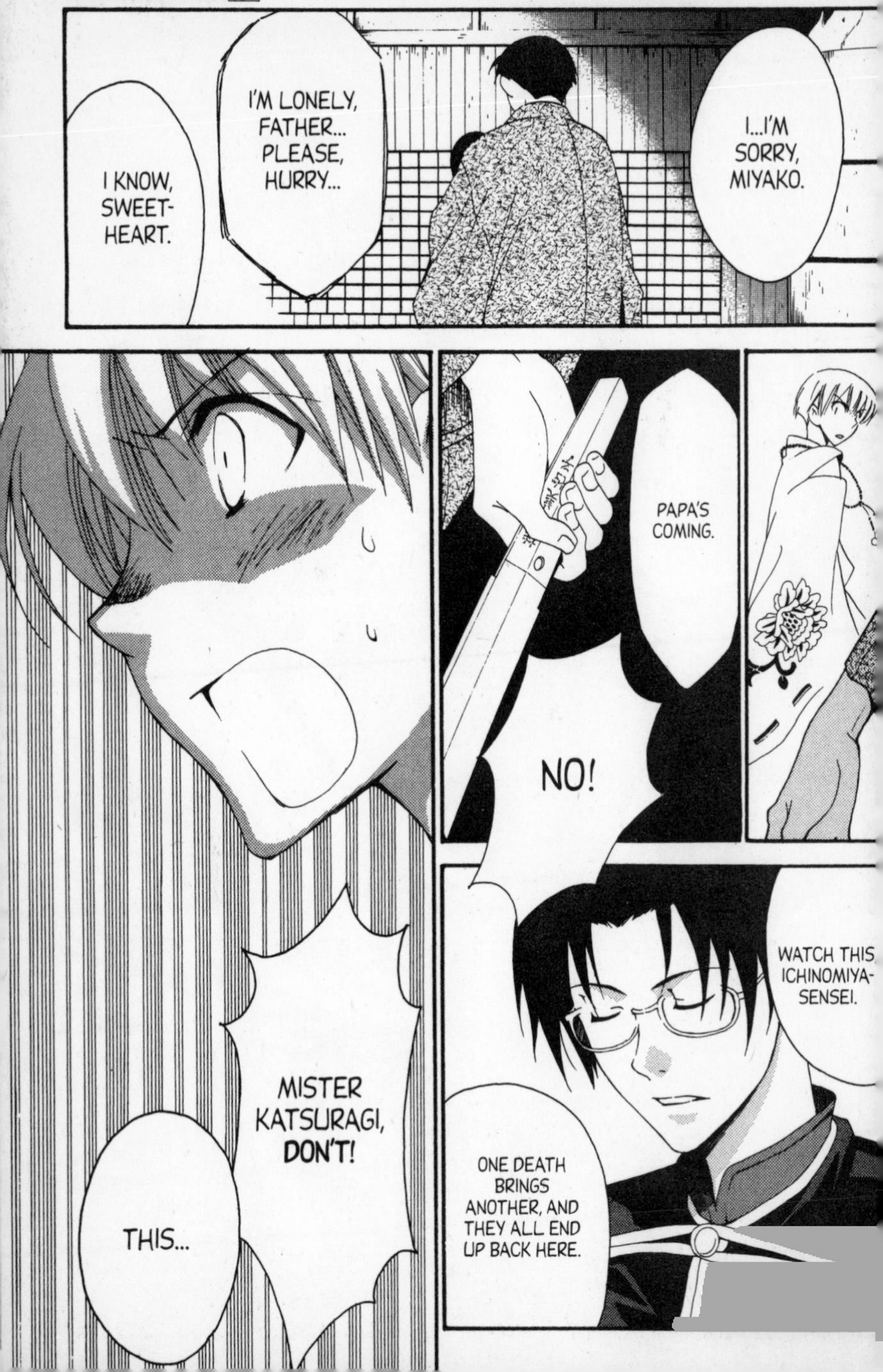
I...I'M SORRY, MIYAKO.
I'M LONELY, FATHER... PLEASE, HURRY...
I KNOW, SWEET-HEART.
PAPA'S COMING.
NO!
WATCH THIS ICHINOMIYA-SENSEI.
ONE DEATH BRINGS ANOTHER, AND THEY ALL END UP BACK HERE.
MISTER KATSURAGI, **DON'T!**
THIS...

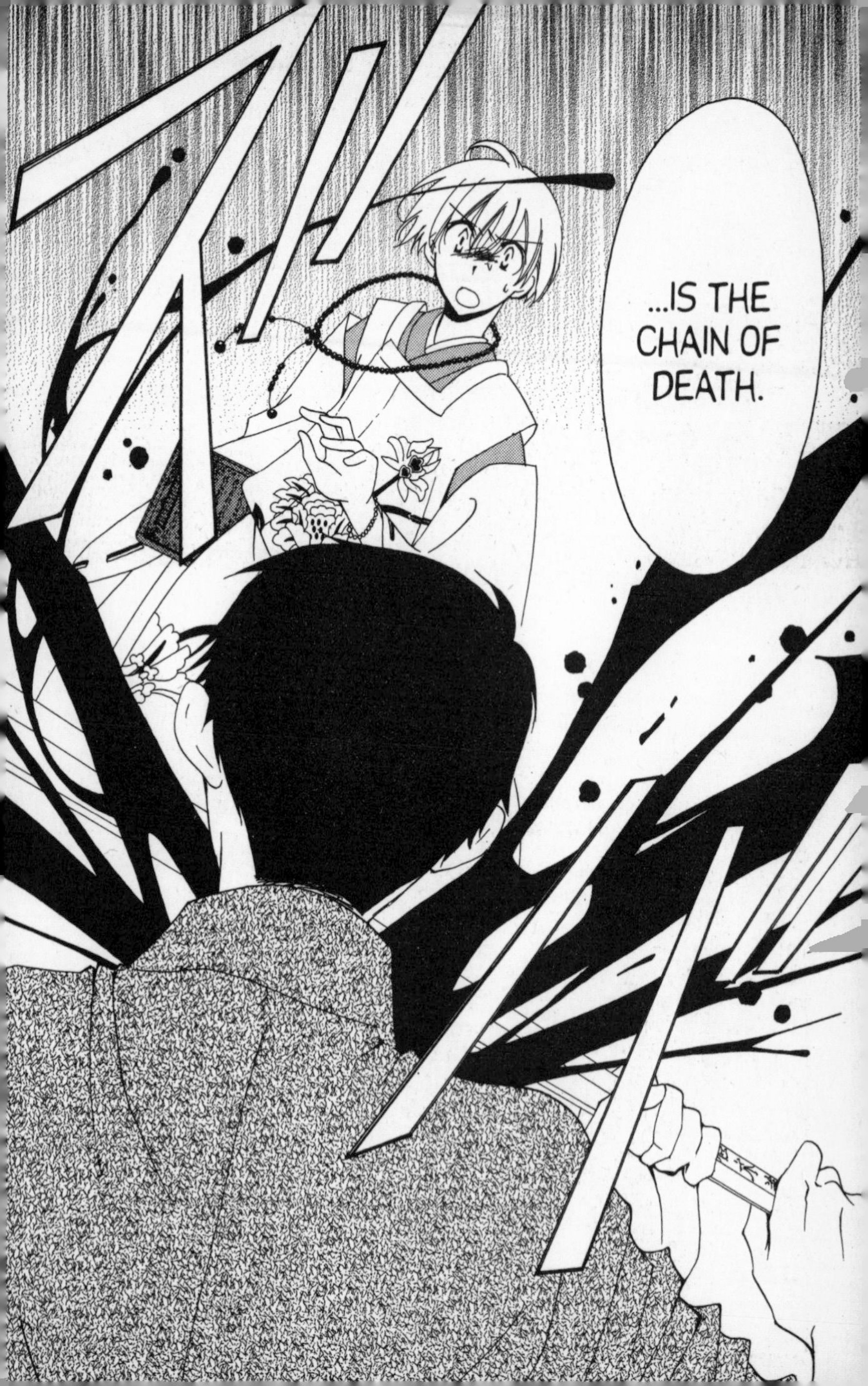
...IS THE CHAIN OF DEATH.

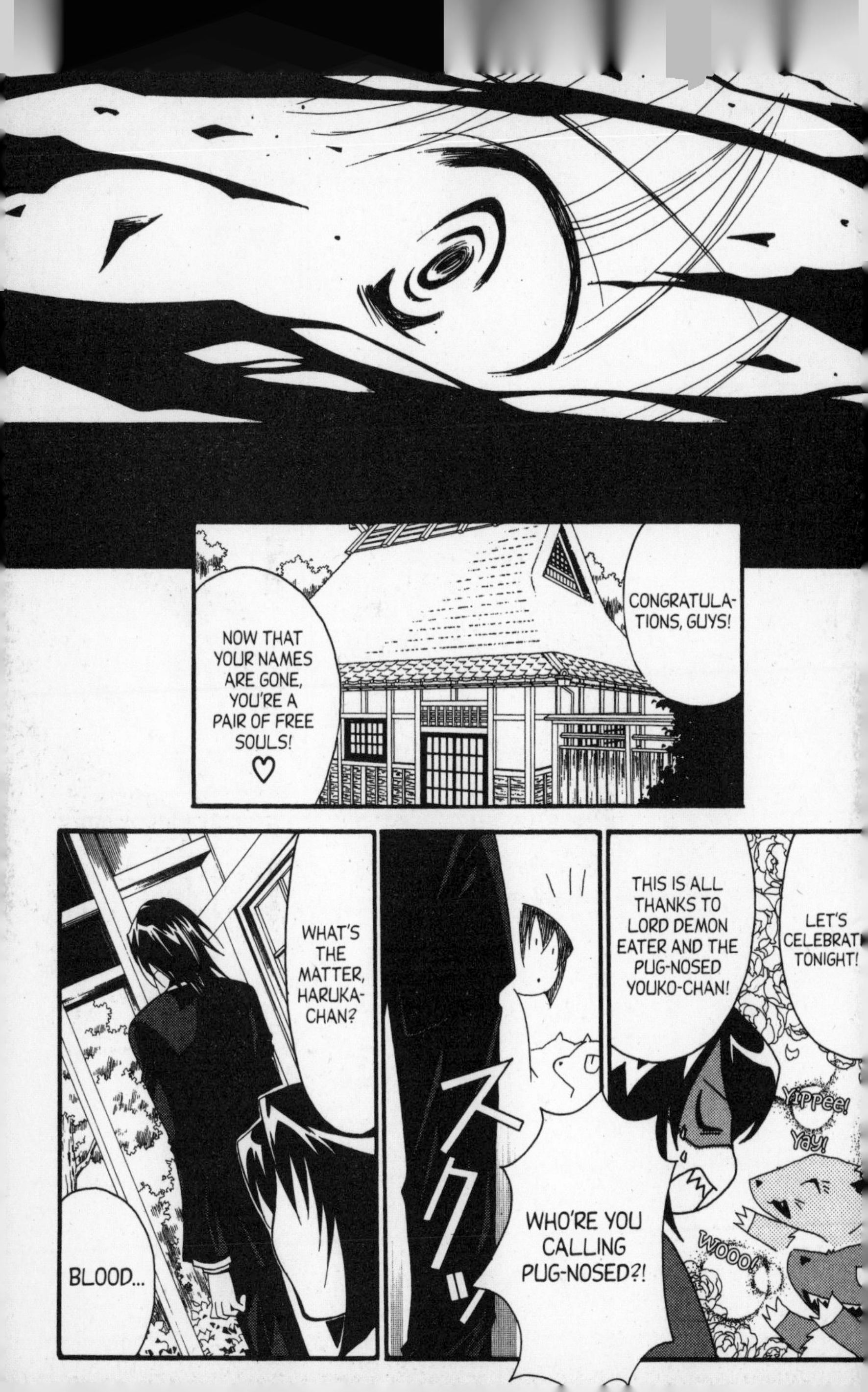
CONGRATULATIONS, GUYS!
NOW THAT YOUR NAMES ARE GONE, YOU'RE A PAIR OF FREE SOULS! ♡
LET'S CELEBRAT TONIGHT!
THIS IS ALL THANKS TO LORD DEMON EATER AND THE PUG-NOSED YOUKO-CHAN!
YIPPEE!
YAY!
WOOO!
WHO'RE YOU CALLING PUG-NOSED?!
WHAT'S THE MATTER, HARUKA-CHAN?
BLOOD...

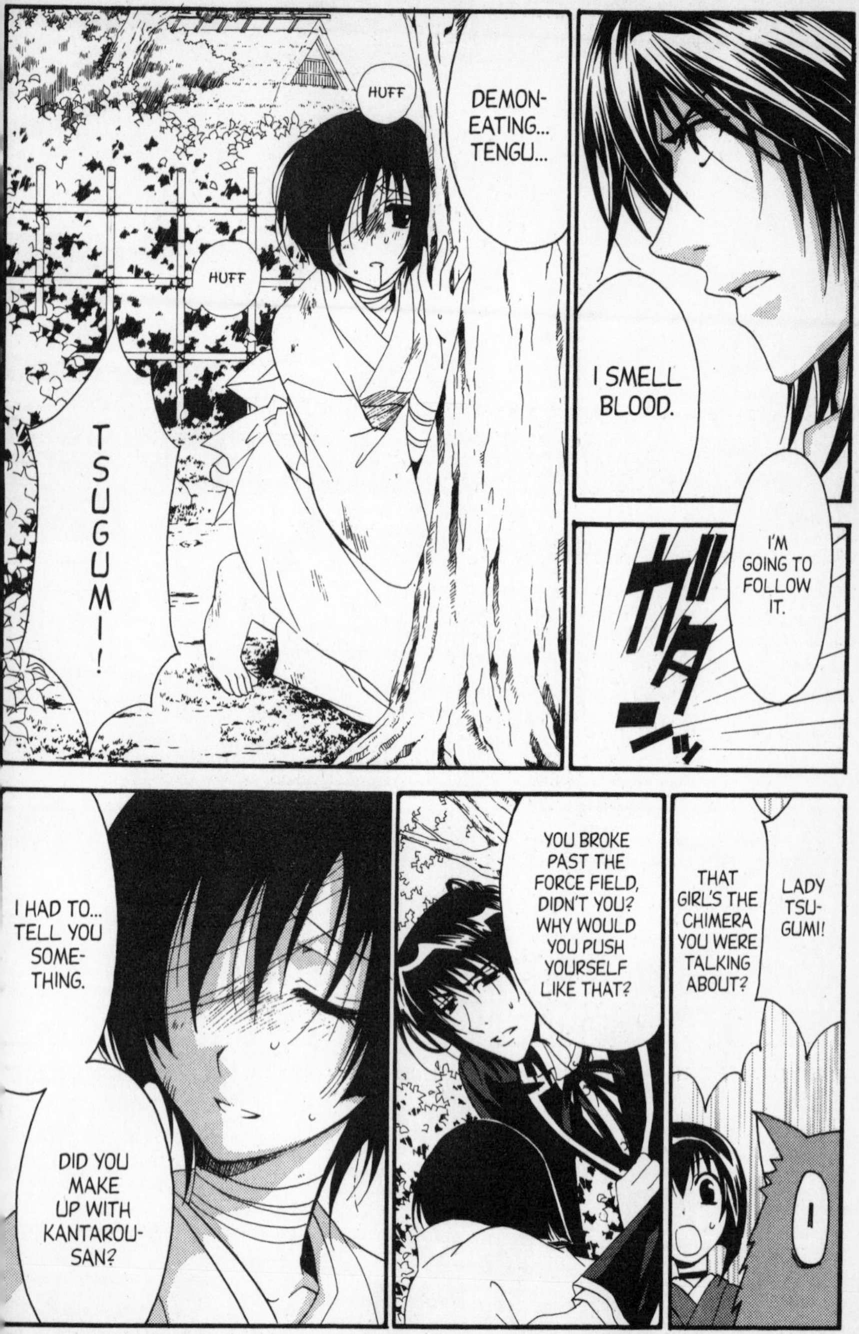
I SMELL BLOOD.
I'M GOING TO FOLLOW IT.
ガタンッ
DEMON-EATING... TENGU...
HUFF
HUFF
TSUGUMI!
LADY TSUGUMI!
THAT GIRL'S THE CHIMERA YOU WERE TALKING ABOUT?
YOU BROKE PAST THE FORCE FIELD, DIDN'T YOU? WHY WOULD YOU PUSH YOURSELF LIKE THAT?
I HAD TO... TELL YOU SOMETHING.
DID YOU MAKE UP WITH KANTAROU-SAN?

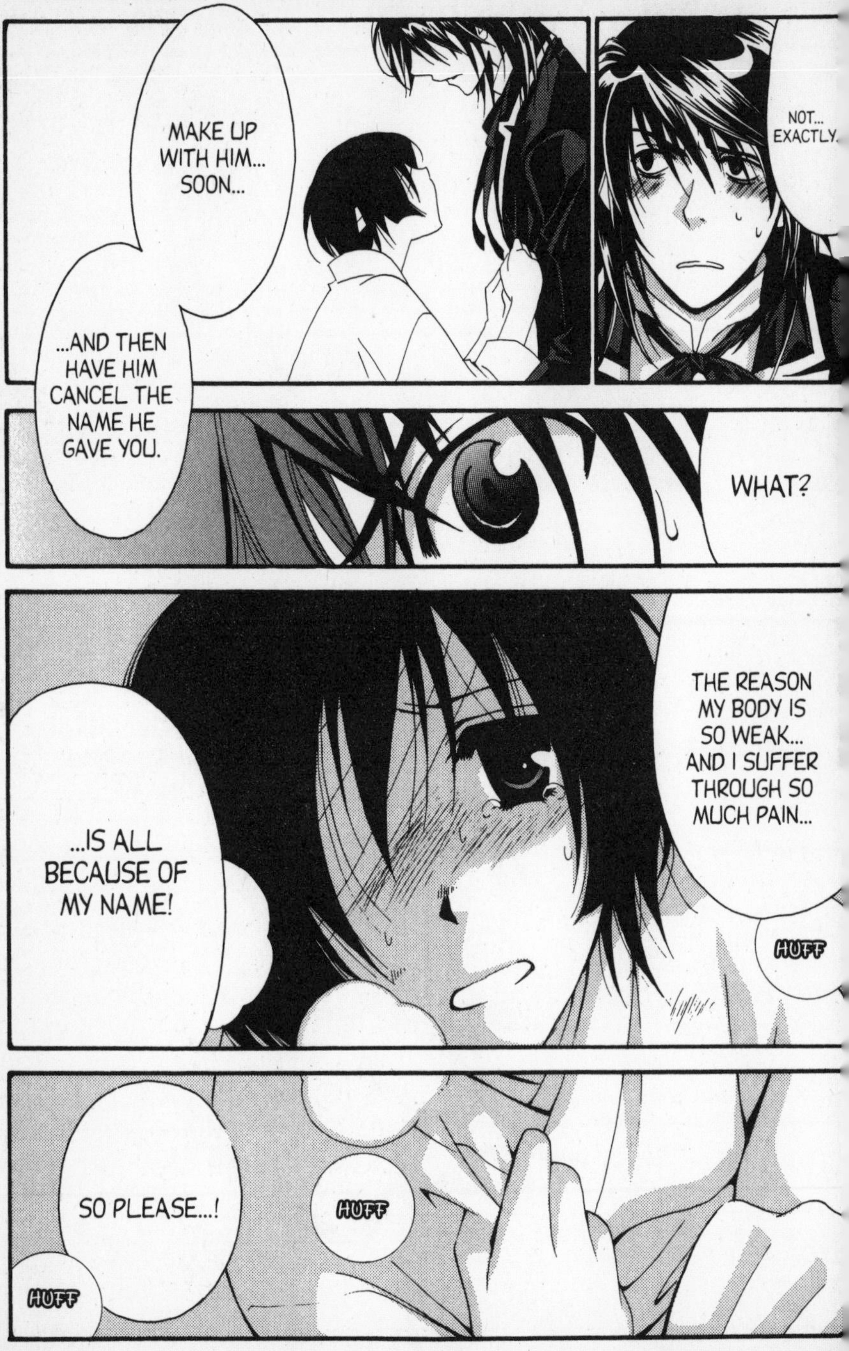
NOT... EXACTLY.
MAKE UP WITH HIM... SOON...
...AND THEN HAVE HIM CANCEL THE NAME HE GAVE YOU.
WHAT?
THE REASON MY BODY IS SO WEAK... AND I SUFFER THROUGH SO MUCH PAIN...
HUFF
...IS ALL BECAUSE OF MY NAME!
HUFF
SO PLEASE...!
HUFF

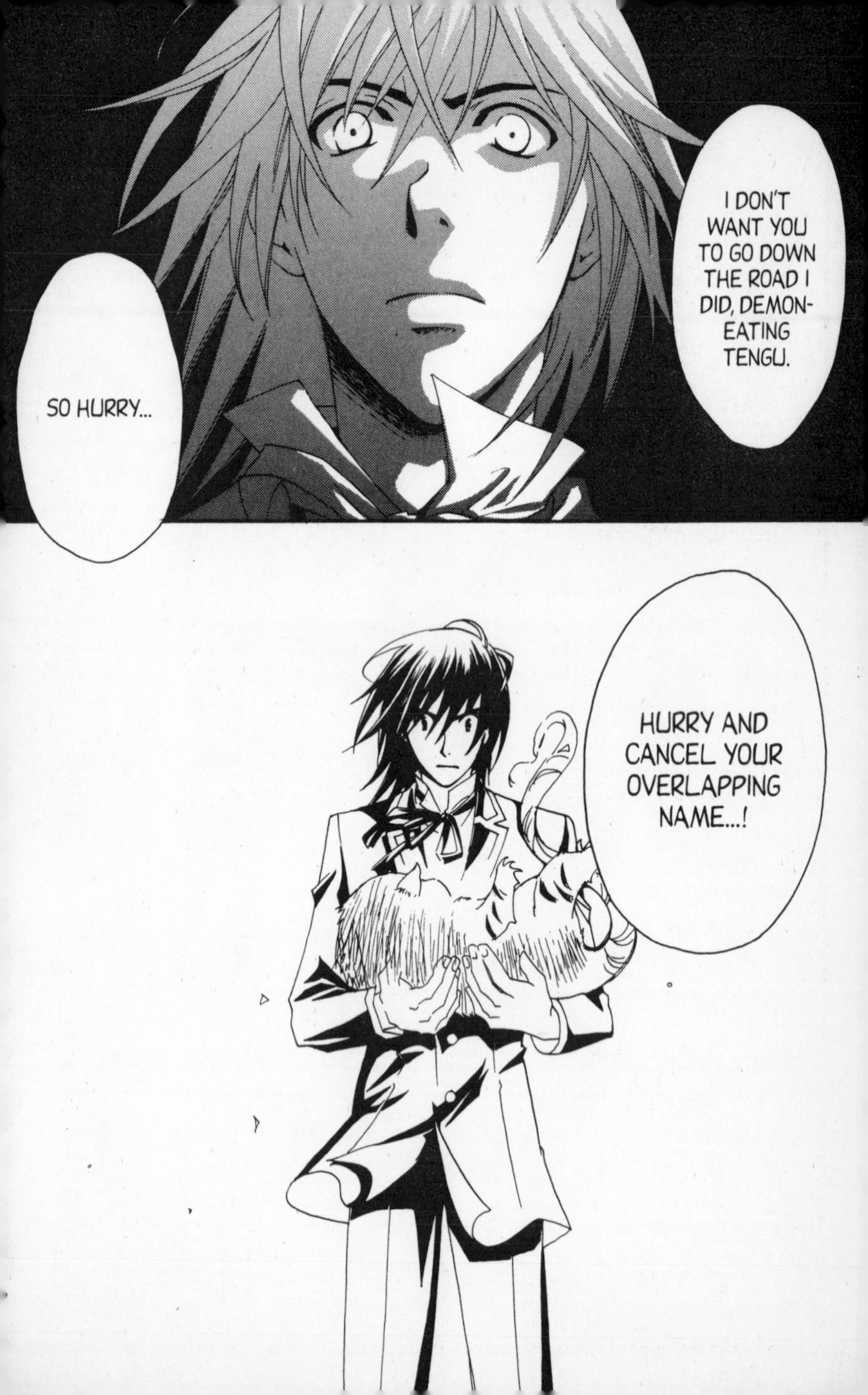
I DON'T WANT YOU TO GO DOWN THE ROAD I DID, DEMON-EATING TENGU.
SO HURRY...
HURRY AND CANCEL YOUR OVERLAPPING NAME...!

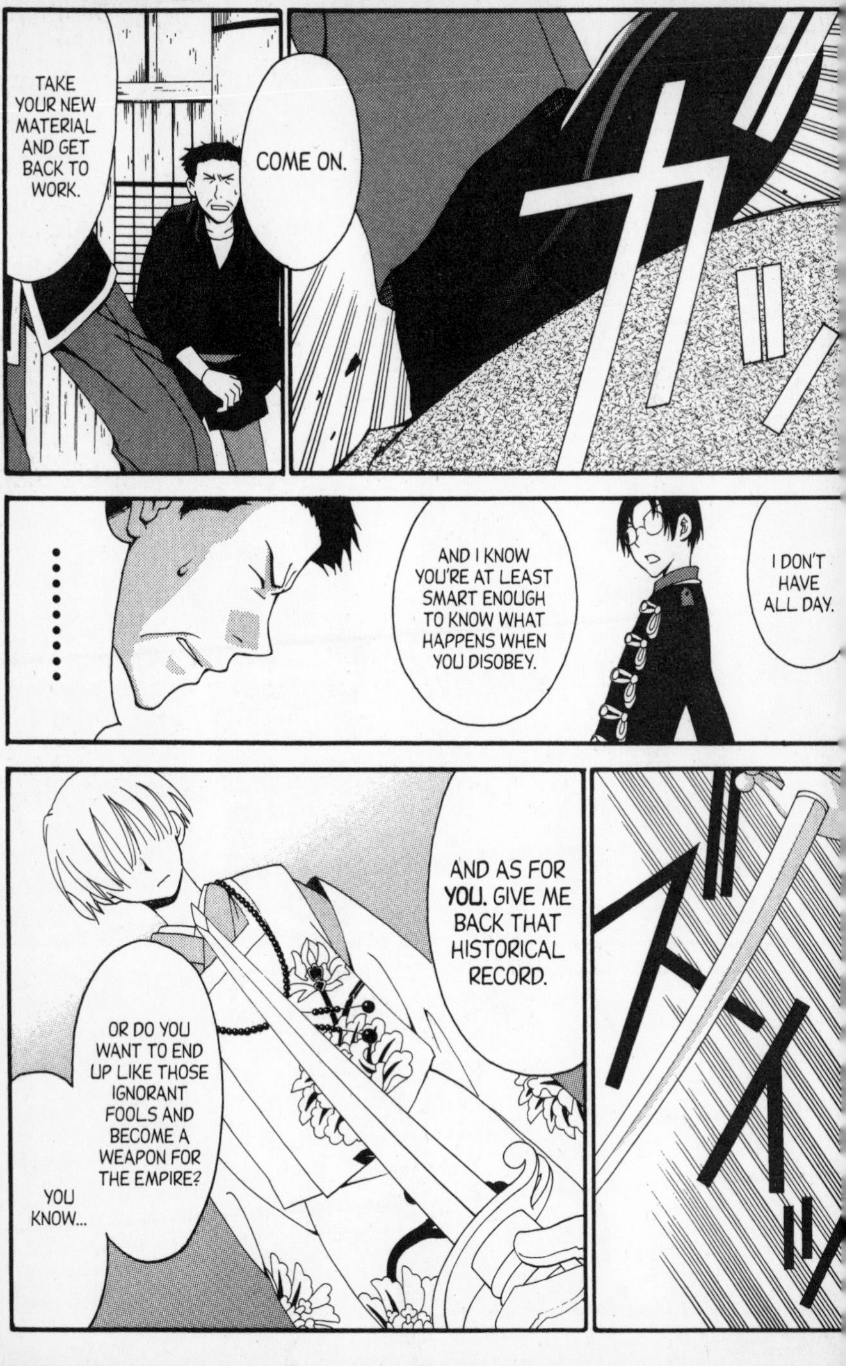
ガッ
COME ON.
TAKE YOUR NEW MATERIAL AND GET BACK TO WORK.
I DON'T HAVE ALL DAY.
AND I KNOW YOU'RE AT LEAST SMART ENOUGH TO KNOW WHAT HAPPENS WHEN YOU DISOBEY.
....
AND AS FOR **YOU.** GIVE ME BACK THAT HISTORICAL RECORD.
OR DO YOU WANT TO END UP LIKE THOSE IGNORANT FOOLS AND BECOME A WEAPON FOR THE EMPIRE?
YOU KNOW...

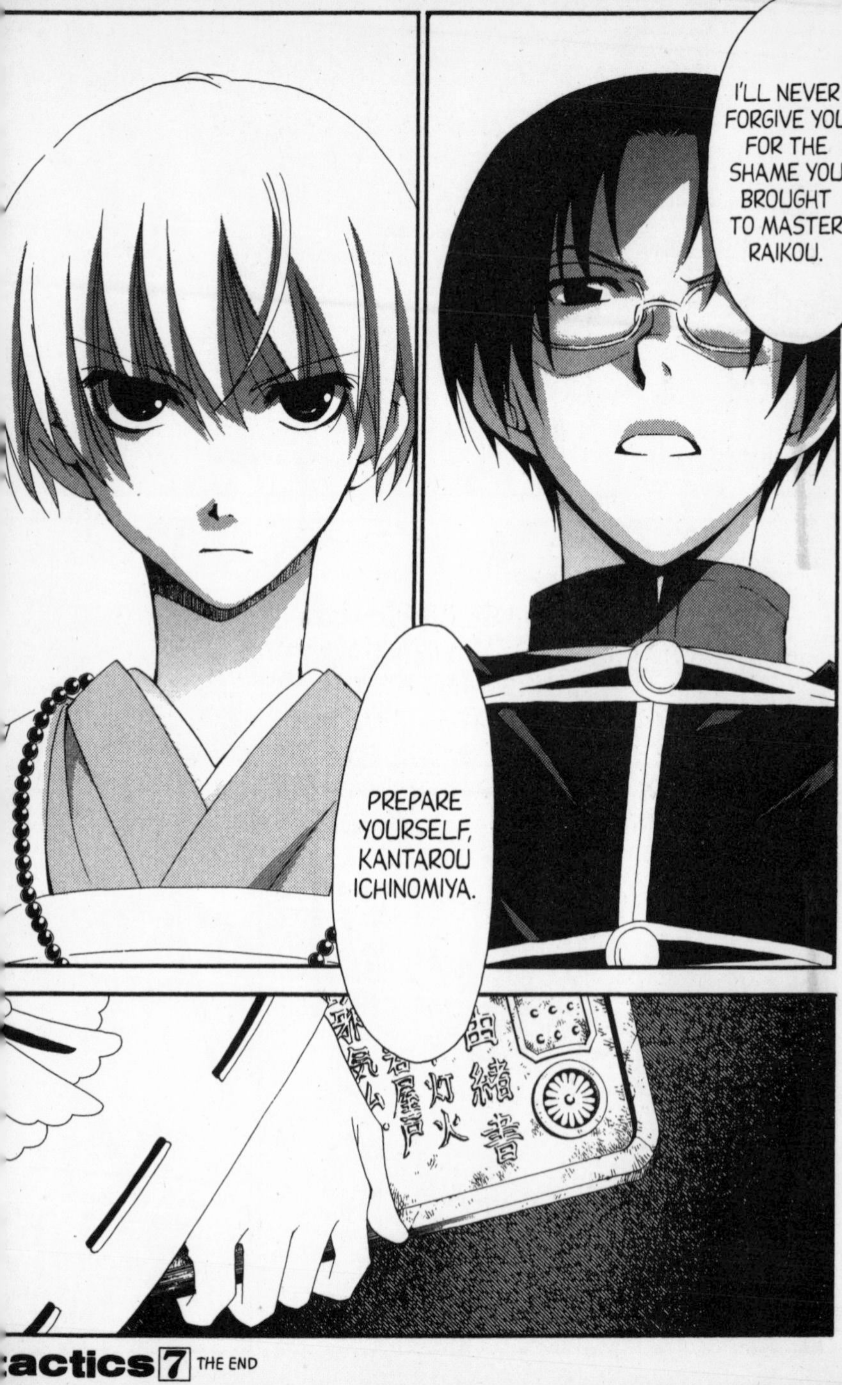

I'LL NEVER FORGIVE YOU FOR THE SHAME YOU BROUGHT TO MASTER RAIKOU.
PREPARE YOURSELF, KANTAROU ICHINOMIYA.

actics 7 THE END

IN THE NEXT VOLUME OF

tactics

The last part of the Chimera arc comes to a close as Kantarou and Haruka battle Minamoto and Sakata. Haruka finally puts Kantarou's worries to rest as he announces his loyalty and friendship to Kantarou, but Minamoto still has one nasty trick up his sleeve. And later, Kantarou comes a little closer to learning the mysterious story of Haruka's former master...

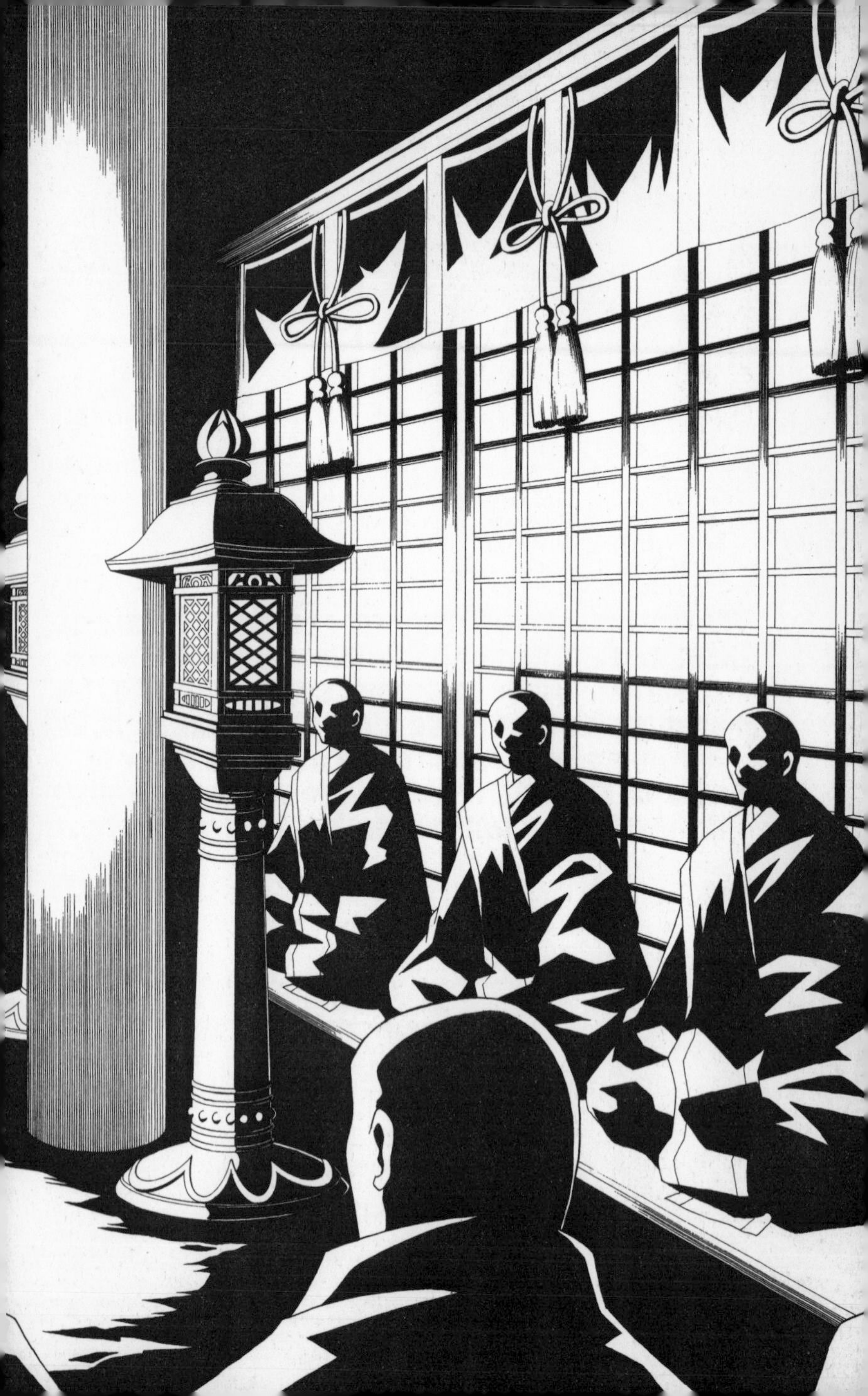

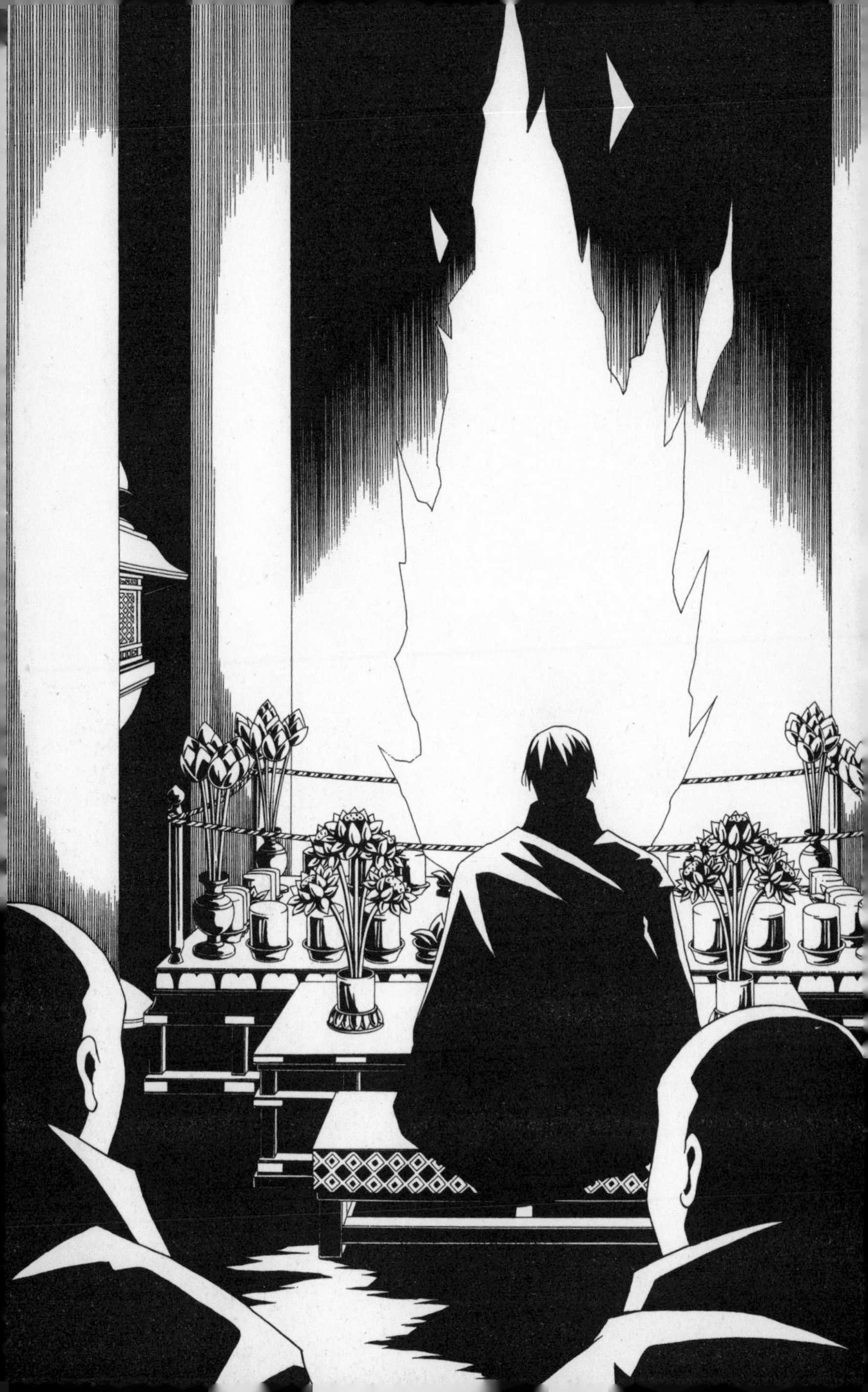

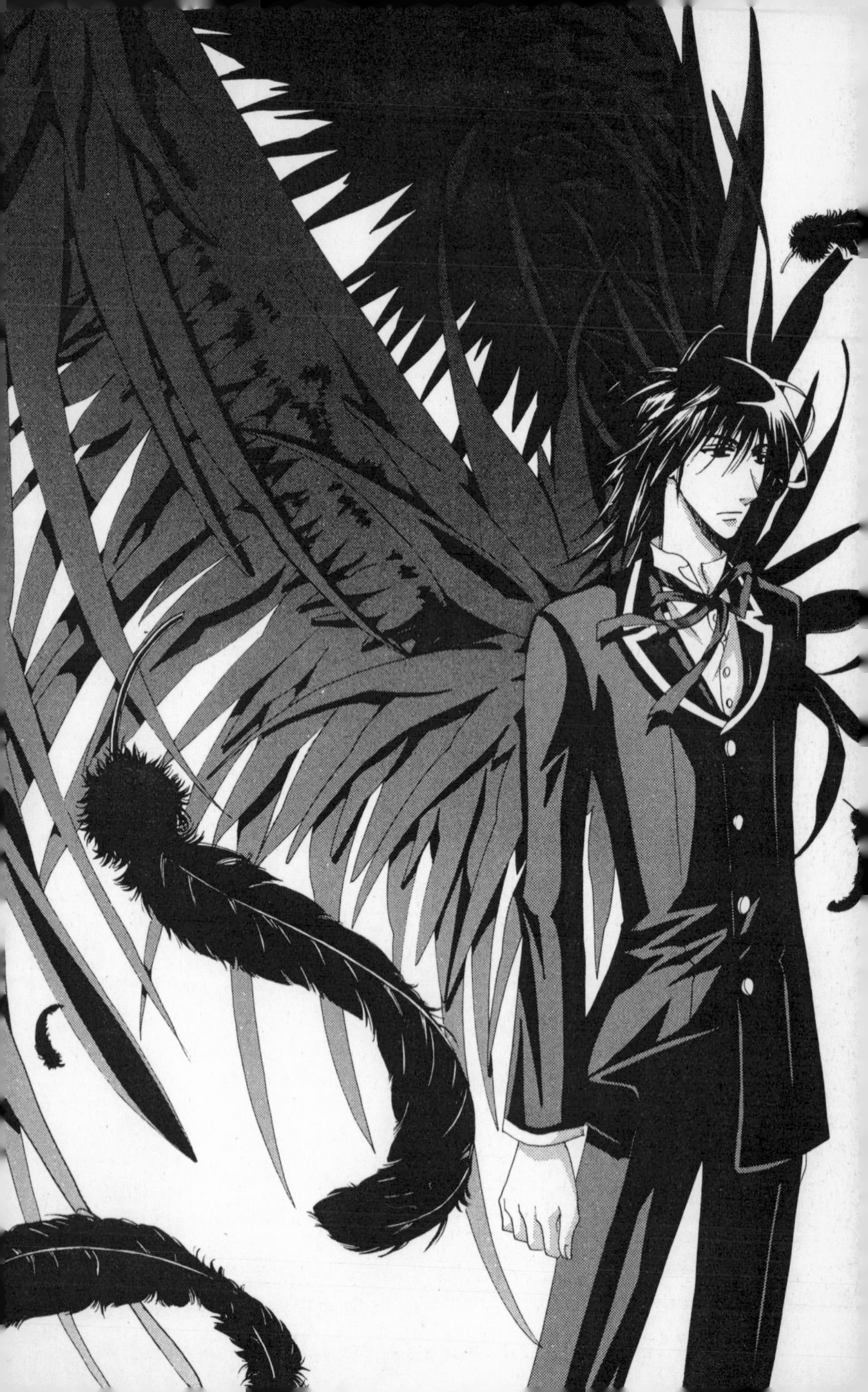

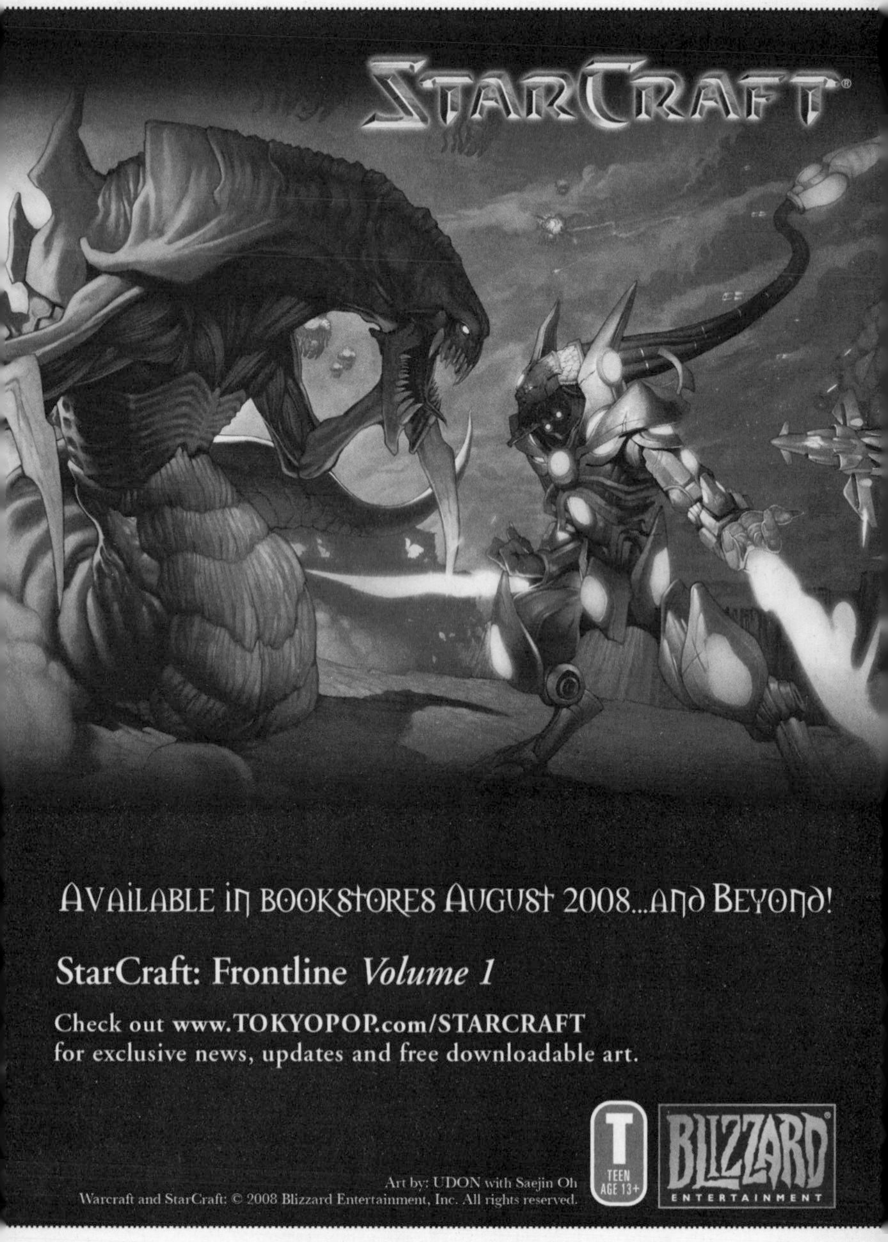
STARCRAFT®
AVAILABLE IN BOOKSTORES AUGUST 2008...AND BEYOND!
StarCraft: Frontline *Volume 1*
Check out www.TOKYOPOP.com/STARCRAFT
for exclusive news, updates and free downloadable art.
Art by: UDON with Saejin Oh
Warcraft and StarCraft: © 2008 Blizzard Entertainment, Inc. All rights reserved.
T TEEN AGE 13+
BLIZZARD ENTERTAINMENT

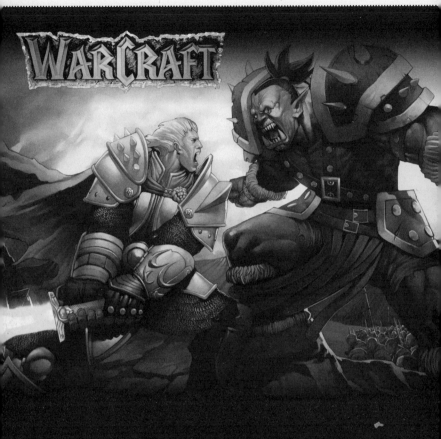

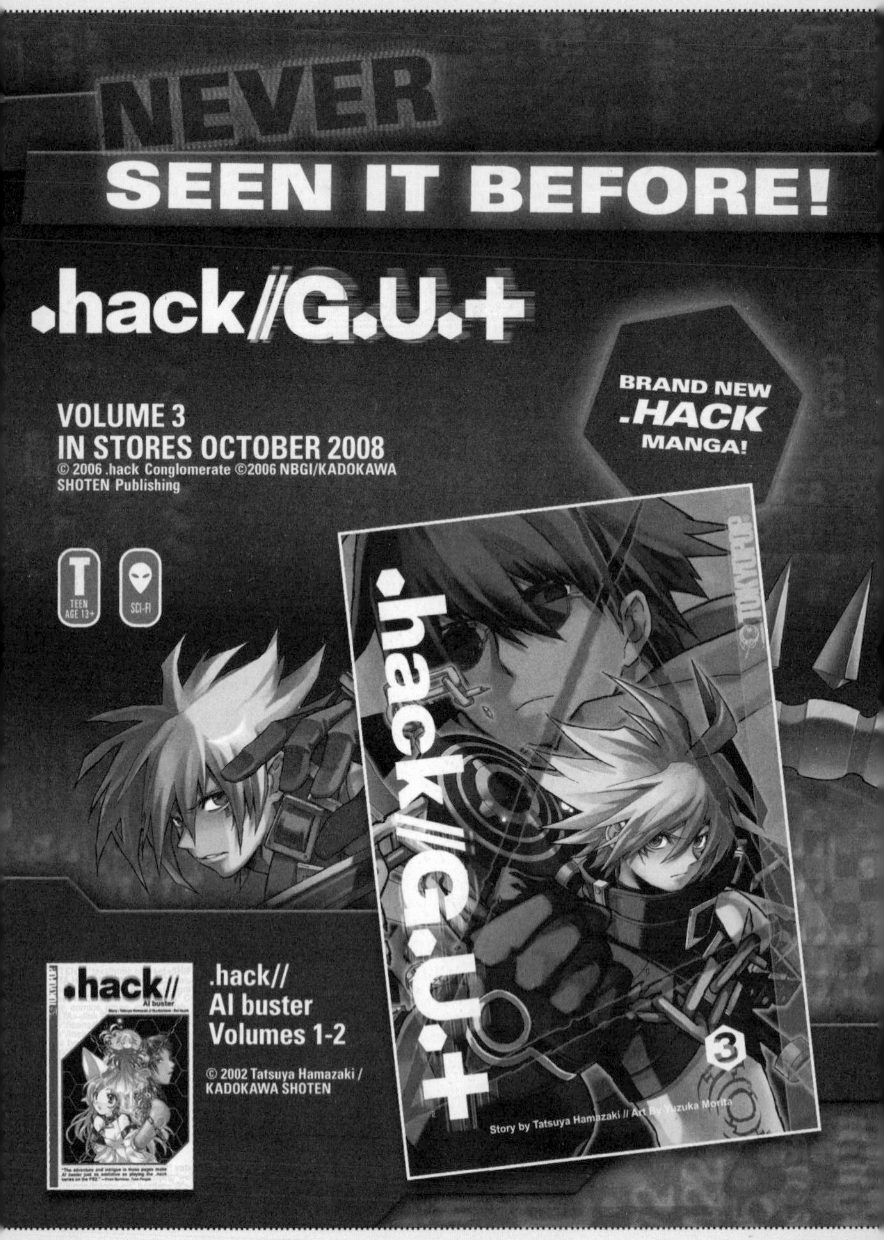
NEVER
SEEN IT BEFORE!
.hack//G.U.+
BRAND NEW
.HACK
MANGA!
VOLUME 3
IN STORES OCTOBER 2008
© 2006 .hack Conglomerate ©2006 NBGI/KADOKAWA SHOTEN Publishing
T
TEEN AGE 13+
SCI-FI
.hack//G.U.+
3
Story by Tatsuya Hamazaki // Art By Yuzuka Morita
TOKYOPOP
.hack//
AI buster
.hack//
AI buster
Volumes 1-2
© 2002 Tatsuya Hamazaki / KADOKAWA SHOTEN

STOP!

This is the back of the book.
You wouldn't want to spoil a great ending!

This book is printed "manga-style," in the authentic Japanese right-to-left format. Since none of the artwork has been flipped or altered, readers get to experience the story just as the creator intended. You've been asking for it, so TOKYOPOP® delivered: authentic, hot-off-the-press, and far more fun!

DIRECTIONS

If this is your first time reading manga-style, here's a quick guide to help you understand how it works.

It's easy... just start in the top right panel and follow the numbers. Have fun, and look for more 100% authentic manga from TOKYOPOP®!